D0457714

FORAGERS,

FARMERS,

AND

FOSSIL

FUELS

FORAGERS,

FARMERS,

AND

FOSSIL

FUELS

How Human Values Evolve

Ian Morris

Richard Seaford • Jonathan D. Spence

Christine M. Korsgaard • Margaret Atwood

Edited and introduced by Stephen Macedo

PRINCETON UNIVERSITY PRESS • PRINCETON AND OXFORD

Requests for permission to reproduce material from this work should
be sent to Permissions, Princeton University Press

Published by Princeton University Press, 41 William Street, Princeton,
New Jersey 08540

In the United Kingdom: Princeton University Press, 6 Oxford Street,
Woodstock, Oxfordshire OX20 1TW

press.princeton.edu

Jacket images © Fedor A. Sidorov, © Kenshi991, © Albert Kam,
© UVAconcept. Images courtesy of Shutterstock.

Library of Congress Cataloging-in-Publication Data
Morris, Ian, 1960-

Foragers, farmers, and fossil fuels : how human values evolve / Ian Morris;
[with responses by] Richard Seaford, Jonathan D. Spence,
Christine M. Korsgaard, Margaret Atwood ;
edited and introduced by Stephen Macedo.

pages cm—(The University Center for Human Values series)

Summary: "This is a successor work to Why the West Rules for Now, in which
Morris once again advances an ambitious account of how certain 'brute material
forces' limit and help determine the 'culture, values, and beliefs,' including
the moral codes, that humans have adopted over the last 20,000 years. The
present volume originated as Ian Morris's Tanner Lectures on Human Values,
delivered at Princeton University in November of 2012"—Introduction.

Includes bibliographical references and index.

ISBN 978-0-691-16039-9 (hardcover : acid-free paper)
1. Social values—History. 2. Social evolution—History. 3. Social change—
History. 4. Power resources—Social aspects—History. 5. Hunting and
gathering societies—History. 6. Agriculture—Social aspects—History. 7. Fossil
fuels—Social aspects—History. 8. Civilization—History. 9. Civilization—
Forecasting. I. Seaford, Richard. II. Spence, Jonathan D. III. Korsgaard, Christine
M. (Christine Marion) IV. Atwood, Margaret, 1939- V. Macedo, Stephen,
1957- VI. Morris, Ian, 1960- Why the West rules—for now. VII. Title.

GN469.M67 2015
303.4—dc23
2014044896

British Library Cataloging-in-Publication Data is available

This book has been composed in Garamond Pro

Printed on acid-free paper. ∞

Printed in the United States of America

1 3 5 7 9 10 8 6 4 2

FOR KATHY AND THE ANIMALS

CONTENTS

FIGURES AND TABLES

ACKNOWLEDGMENTS

No author ever works alone, and this book would never have become a reality without the participation of a lot of people. First came Princeton's University Center for Human Values, whose members kindly invited me to deliver the Tanner Lectures in November 2012. Before I even drafted the presentations, my Stanford colleague (and former member of the Princeton Center) Josh Ober talked me through the issues over several evenings of margaritas in Los Cabos. Once I arrived in Princeton, Erin Graham took wonderful care of me, while the audiences who came to the talks, the members of the Center for Human Values, and above all the respondents—Margaret Atwood, Christine M. Korsgaard, Richard Seaford, and Jonathan D. Spence—challenged me with all kinds of interesting questions. I did most of the work of expanding the two lectures into the first five chapters of this book during the 2013–14 academic year with the kind support of the Hoover Institution (where I held a Campbell National Fellowship) and the School of Humanities and Sciences at Stanford University. As I was writing, Sam Bowles, Giovanna Ceserani, Meiyu Hsieh, Steve LeBlanc, Paolo Malanima, and Rob Tempio guided me to readings that I never would have found for myself, and my arguments were sharpened greatly by conversations with Steve Haber and Richard Wrangham and by presenting a revised version of the arguments to members of al Quds University and the Albright Institute at the École Biblique in Jerusalem. Once the chapters were drafted, Phil Kleinheinz, Josh Ober, Kathy St. John, Walter Scheidel, Paul Seabright, Ken Wardle, two anonymous readers for the Princeton University Press, and my editors Rob Tempio and Steve Macedo read the manuscript and gave me invaluable feedback. Michele Angel drew the marvelous maps, and Sandy Dijkstra, Elise Capron, Andrea Cavallaro, and Thao Le at the Sandra Dijkstra Literary Agency and Rob Tempio, Terri O'Prey, and Jennifer Harris at the Princeton University Press kindly and patiently kept everything moving forward on the many occasions that my attention wandered. I owe a great debt of gratitude to them all, but particularly to Kathy St. John and the animals, who taught me whatever I know about human values.

IAN MORRIS
Boulder Creek, California
October 2014

INTRODUCTION

....

Stephen Macedo

Ian Morris's eleventh book, *Why the West Rules—For Now: The Patterns of History and What They Reveal about the Future*, published in 2010, has been called "brilliant," "ingenious," and "mind-blowing." Its scope and erudition are astonishing. And it is beautifully written. It looks back 15,000 years, considering why Western and Eastern societies have developed differentially, rising and falling relative to one another. And in the end, it asks what the future may hold given the multiple threats to human existence—"climate change, famine, state failure, migration, and disease"—that are the unintended by-product of the tremendous economic and social development from which so many have benefited.

This is a successor work to *Why the West Rules—For Now*, in which Morris once again advances an ambitious account of how certain "brute material forces" limit and help determine the "culture, values, and beliefs," including the moral codes, that humans have adopted over the last 20,000 years. The present volume originated as Ian Morris's Tanner Lectures on Human Values, delivered at Princeton University in November of 2012. Given Morris's thesis, we considered rechristening these the "Tanner Lectures on Brute Material Forces."

Morris's overall argument, in a nutshell, is as follows. Certain basic human values initially arose around 100,000 years ago: "treating people fairly, being just, love and hate, preventing harm, agreeing that some things are sacred." These "core concerns" (chapter 2), which recur in every culture in some form, were enabled by "the biological evolution of our big, fast brains" (chapter 5). Morris also mentions that some of these values are to some extent shared by our "closest kin among the great apes," a point developed in a previous work in this series, by the eminent primatologist, Frans deWaal.[1]

Humans have, however, decisive advantages over the next most intelligent animal species, and our extra sophistication makes possible the invention and reinvention of culture. We develop complex systems of values, norms, expectations, and cultural patterns that sustain forms of cooperation that improve our chances of survival as our environment changes. Like biological evolution, cultural innovations can be understood as part of a "competitive process, played out through millions of tiny experiments"—the cultural equivalents of random mutations in biology. And as these experiments succeed or fail, "traits that work well in a particular environment replace those that don't" (chapter 2).

Morris offers a macro-history of human values that discerns broad similarities within three successive stages of human development. The shape of human culture in these successive stages is defined by progressively more productive modes of energy capture: foraging, farming, and fossil-fuel production. Morris's thesis is that these successive modes of energy capture "determine" or at least "limit" the possible forms of social organization, and therefore the social values that may prevail. Each age eventually settles on the values it needs because of human inventiveness and the tendency of relatively successful social forms to spread and prevail over their competitors. This is a "functionalist" account that views human values as "adaptive traits, which people adjust to maximize their effectiveness as the larger social system around them changes" (chapter 2).

In each successive stage, from foraging, to farming, to fossil-fuel consuming, "modes of energy capture determined population size and density, which in turn largely determined which forms of social organization worked best, which went on to make certain sets of values more successful and attractive than others" (chapter 5). And so, early societies that made a living by foraging, or hunting and gathering, tended to adopt social structures and values that were egalitarian—that involved strong norms of sharing and limited inequality, for reasons Morris explains—while also being quite violent. Farming societies, to function optimally, tended to be hierarchical and less violent. And fossil-fuel societies, which emerged in the eighteenth century, and that include us, tend to be very egalitarian with respect to politics and gender, fairly tolerant of wealth inequalities, and much less violent than their predecessors.

I have greatly simplified Morris's account. He also emphasizes an important role for technological innovations and for geography in determining which societies come to dominate others and how. Readers of *Why the West Rules—For Now* will be familiar with these themes: innovations in ocean transport, for example, made easy access to the sea a great advantage, giving rise to the great European maritime empires.

Morris draws on a wealth of learning in the course of his argument, and he presents it with extraordinary clarity and wit.

Following Morris's five tightly written chapters are the comments of three eminent scholars and of one of the world's most prolific and widely renowned literary figures.

Richard Seaford is Professor of Ancient Greek Literature at the University of Exeter, and the author of many books and scores of scholarly papers on Greek literature, religion, philosophy, and also the New Testament.

Seaford argues that Morris is too much "in the grip of deterministic quantification," which leads him to downplay the diversity of values and cultural forms within his broad stages of human development. Farming, argues Seaford, does not produce the same values everywhere, and he singles out ancient Athens as a challenge to Morris's determinism. He also draws attention, as does Jonathan Spence, to the fact that the historical record generally does not include the judgments of marginalized people, at least so long as they are unorganized. Seaford wonders why what Morris calls the "grumbling resentment" of peasants should not be taken more seriously as evidence of a politically powerless egalitarianism that challenges the idea that farming societies accept inequality or even endorse it as "good" (chapter 6).

Seaford ends with an observation concerning Morris's assertion that "each age gets the thought that it needs." He charges, interestingly, that Morris's own thinking about historical development is closer to the ideas of today's "ruling classes" than to "the thought our age needs." In particular, Seaford suggests that Morris's debt to evolutionary theory and his emphasis on "competition, quantifiability, consensus and efficiency," accepts too uncritically the "central ideas" of our capitalist economic order. If humans are to survive, argues Seaford, our age needs a more critical and enlightened account of the basic human values that Morris himself identifies—"treating people fairly, being just, preventing harm, a sense that some things are sacred" (chapter 6).

As Ian Morris's recent work has concerned the comparative development and future prospects of China and the West, it is fitting that our second commentator is Jonathan D. Spence, formerly the Sterling Professor of History at Yale University, a prolific author and perhaps the world's leading historian of modern China.

Like our other commentators, Spence both applauds Morris's "formidable research skills" and expresses some reservations. In particular, he suggests that while Morris's data is illuminating, the reader would benefit from a richer sense of "what it was like" to live in the "Hilly Flanks" or the "Lucky Latitudes." Spence argues that life was generally far grimmer and harder than these bouncy labels might suggest. In addition, Spence argues, like Seaford, that Morris's broad stages of human development encompass a vast range of different human experiences that we can only begin to understand via description at a much finer level of detail. Spence closes by pointing to the profound developments of just the last few years involving information technology and "cyber warfare."

Our third commentator is Christine M. Korsgaard, the Arthur Kingsley Porter Professor of Philosophy at Harvard University, and perhaps the world's leading Kantian moral philosopher. She has written widely influential works on moral philosophy and its history, practical reason, normativity, the nature of agency and identity, and the ethical relations between humans and other animals.

Korsgaard challenges the adequacy of Morris's treatment of moral values. She distinguishes between the "positive values" that as a descriptive matter actually prevail in particular societies and the "real moral values" that are actually true and that people ought to hold. She argues that "positive values can serve the evolutionary and social functions that Morris identifies for them only if the people who hold them take them to be real moral values." In addition, she notes that people engaged in evaluative practices tend to believe that "valuing is something that can be done well or badly" (chapter 8). As Korsgaard says, "If values were just a way of maintaining the social forms called for by a certain form of energy capture, and people knew that, it is hard to see how they would work. People must believe they are living up to real moral values before values can do that job" (chapter 8). In effect, she is insisting on the primacy, or at least the validity, of the viewpoint of the participants in moral life. Korsgaard goes on to raise the natural next question of whether, "if people came to believe Morris's theory, their values would survive." That is, could participants in farming societies endorse their societies'—indeed, their own—values if they understood them, as Morris does, as functional adaptations to a certain mode of energy capture? No, she insists: we need to understand the activity of valuing from the point of view of those engaged in it, which presupposes that there are "real values" that underwrite our evaluations of others and our own "normative self-conceptions."

Indeed, Korsgaard goes further and suggests that it is not unreasonable to believe that humans' capacity for valuing "has some natural tendency to attach itself to real moral values," so we might tend to see certain forms of moral improvement over the course of history. But she also allows that this tendency is "vulnerable to distortion by sociological forces," including ideology, and by various external pressures including, presumably, material scarcity and insecurity. Social and economic forces of various sorts "put pressure on the shape of our values," she allows, but do not "completely determine" them (chapter 8).

In the end, Korsgaard raises the question of whether Morris believes there are any "real moral values." She acutely points out that Morris's own approach to historical explanation is deeply indebted to the scientific assumptions and methods that he associates with fossil-fuel-consuming societies. However, Morris shows no sign of questioning the genuine superiority of his (and our) scientific methods as compared with the theological worldviews of farming societies, which see "the world as governed by a transcendent god" (chapter 8). When it comes to the practice of history and science, we might say, Morris is not a skeptic, nor does he take the purely "functional" view that each age gets the history or science that it needs. If these modes of human understanding—science and history—can improve (and not merely change), why not ethics?

Our final commentator is a prolific writer whose literary imagination has explored our possible futures. Margaret Atwood is one of the world's great novelists, and also the author of more than 50 volumes of poetry, children's literature, fiction and nonfiction, including *The Handmaid's Tale*, *The Blind Assassin*, *Oryx and Crake*, and many more.

Atwood expresses admiration for Morris's account, but seeks to focus attention on our perilous future, suggesting that to imagine it requires the exercise of our literary imaginations and not only quantifiable data and scholarly observation. She agrees with Morris that our evolved nature contains elements that make us more admirable, or at least more complex, than the "inherently selfish and aggressive nasties that Social Darwinism posited for so long." But what would happen if our fragile biosphere really did break down in a serious way? Because we are so interconnected, she says, "if we fail, we all fail together and we fail big, on a scale unimaginable in the past." And she worries that the "more intricate the technologies" we rely upon, and the larger our society grows, "the smaller the mistake that can break something vital, the quicker the train wreck, and the more catastrophic the results."

Morris, as I mentioned earlier, sets out five possible kinds of shocks that could precipitate civilizational collapse: "uncontrollable migration, state failure, food shortages, epidemic disease, and climate change." Atwood adds two more: the collapse of the oceans and bioengineering. She ends her colorful comments, full of humor that I have not conveyed, with a plea for "megathinking."

Ian Morris gets the last word, in an exhilarating and wide-ranging response. Morris engages his critics deeply, and in so doing clarifies and deepens his argument. He recants nothing, but allows that his critics usefully nudge him to further unpack the account of how energy capture shapes human values.

In response to Spence's call for a finer level of detailed description, Morris clarifies that his foremost aim is to explain why people have had the values they do, rather than to understand those values from within, as it were.

Responding to Seaford's claim that he fails to appreciate the variation within his three broad paradigms of foraging, farming, and fossil-fuel-consuming societies, Morris notes that "farming societies" include "pretty much everyone who lived in the 10,000 years before AD 1800," so naturally, he allows with a touch of understatement, this encompasses "a lot of variety." No doubt, says Morris, commercial city-states like Athens are interesting insofar as they partly prefigure modern values and institutions. This is also true, less dramatically, of "early modern protoindustrial nations," like Britain, who reaped unparalleled amounts of energy from their maritime commercial networks. Nevertheless, Morris insists that Athenian wealth "eased but did not break the constraints of the farming world." Apparent outliers such as ancient Greece and early-modern Britain, qualify but do not "falsify the correlation between energy capture and values" (chapter 10).

In his most extended discussion, Morris sets out to clarify the ways in which successive modes of energy capture shape human values via what he calls "multilevel selection." It is not that individuals are *caused* to adopt values by their society's mode of energy capture. Rather, over the course of long stretches of history, and as a result of innumerable social experiments by inventive humans, the societies that are best organized to exploit available modes of energy capture—by their social structures, economic and political institutions, culture and values—will tend to prevail over and displace other societies that are less well organized. Social forms and the associated values that are ill adapted to human survival and comfort, given available technologies, will give way to more effective institutions and values.

In the course of clarifying his argument, Morris takes up and rejects Korsgaard's distinction between the "positive values" that people actually hold and the "Real Moral Values" that they ought to hold. The only values available to us, observes Morris, are those held by particular people at particular times and places, and so Korsgaard's "distinction between real moral values and positive values is meaningless. . . . It is positive values all the way down." (chapter 10). Recognizing this need not, Morris argues, stop people from being confident about and committed to their own values.

Our Tanner Lecturer also responds to the charge that he is in the grip of capitalist ideology. Morris denies it, and asserts in turn that Seaford and Korsgaard are under the sway of a misplaced "essentialism." This is the conviction that our liberal Enlightenment values, including egalitarian social relations and a preference for nonviolent modes of dispute resolution, represent a better approximation to real moral values, and even constitute "default" positions that humans will move toward when circumstances are favorable and social pressures do not require social hierarchy backed by force.

Morris allows that a certain essentialism is inescapable in explaining how humans evolved to be capable of the complex forms of organization, judgment, and innovation we witness across history. He insists, recall, that "all humans" share a set of core values: "fairness, justice, love, hate, respect, loyalty, preventing harm, and the sense that some things are sacred," and these are reinterpreted across successive ages of human development. Whereas Korsgaard and Seaford defend egalitarianism and nonviolence as better and truer from a moral point of view, Morris insists they are really only particular interpretations of the core human values: well-adapted to the societies made possible by advanced forms of energy capture but unsuited to foraging and farming societies. "For me," says Morris, "wrong behavior is something that violates my strongly held, fossil-fuel interpretations of biologically evolved human values." Morris joins Korsgaard in condemning Taliban efforts to subordinate women and deny them access to education, but insists that the Taliban are wrong because "the farming age is finished." They are "guilty first and foremost of backwardness" (chapter 10).

What, one might ask, makes "backwardness" the main issue here? Is it the assumption that our aim is first and foremost to explain scientifically (or understand historically) rather than to judge morally? But if we are centrally interested in moral assessment, other language will seem more appropriate to describe the Taliban treatment of women: cruel and abhorrent, and not merely "backward," or unsuited to our age. Might we judge that ours is an era of greater justice, and not only different justice, for women?

A further question is this: is there a danger in tying the language of moral assessment to functional standards of institutional and social success? Isn't it possible that particular innovations in political and economic organization might enhance a society's material well-being and power—and its ability to prevail over others—but represent moral decline? Suppose it were true that, as some argue, one-party authoritarianism in China is more conducive to economic growth than liberal democracy (and not just in China's current developmental stage)? We would not want to conclude from that, without more, that it would be a good thing (morally speaking) for the Chinese way to prevail. Or, is that just my circumstances talking?

The point is that there may be good reasons for retaining the idea that moral assessment aspires to a greater independence from particular circumstances than Morris seems prepared to allow. Saying this does not mean that we suppose we can rise above all of the prejudices of our own time, only that we should try to do so as best we can.

What of the charge, mentioned earlier, that our author is in the grip of ideology? Morris defines ideology as "a pack of lies from which someone benefits," but quickly insists, "rarely for long, because common sense is such a powerful tool for revealing what will work best in the material conditions in which we find ourselves" (chapter 10). He also quotes the maxim attributed to Lincoln, "... you can't fool all the people all the time." "Wicked elites" are not powerful or clever enough to bamboozle the mass of people for very long.

This is an interesting expression of confidence in the power of human invention and common sense to eventually overturn social arrangements that deliver benefits to the few at the expense of the many. When modes of energy capture make possible new forms of social organization that deliver greater abundance and/or security for more people than in the past, we can be confident that humans will eventually discover and embrace the new social forms and their attendant values. It suggests further that the case for hierarchy (or centralized authority) needs to be, and will be, "tested" from the point of view of society as a whole.

Does this confidence in humans' capacity to see through and overturn the self-serving lies of ruling elites—when they are lies—help us salvage the idea of real moral progress across the successive phases of human history? Can we make sense of the idea of moral, as distinguished from material, progress? Is Morris operating with his own tacit egalitarianism: that the few ought not, and ultimately will not, prosper at the expense of the many?

I will leave these and other questions to the reader.

Morris closes his wide-ranging discussion by looking once again to the future, and pondering the possibility that our species is creating the conditions for its own extinction. He expresses appreciation for Margaret Atwood's efforts to imagine what life might be like after the next cataclysm, and engages in some educated speculation of his own.

Be assured that what follows is a lively and remarkably stimulating ride, under the guidance of a scholar of remarkable range and erudition, across vast expanses of human experience, posing the most basic questions about where our values come from and what they amount to, and offering some surprising answers.

FORAGERS,

FARMERS,

AND

FOSSIL

FUELS

CHAPTER I

EACH AGE GETS THE
THOUGHT IT NEEDS

Mr. George

In 1982, I went on my first archaeological excavation in Greece. I was thrilled: I had dug a lot in Britain, but this was something else entirely. An ancient Land Rover took me from Birmingham as far as Thessaloniki, where I caught an even more ancient bus to Assiros, the farming village where we would be working (figure 1.1).[1] There I settled into the project's routine. All day long we would count, weigh, and catalogue fragments of prehistoric pottery, and as the sun went down, we would revive ourselves with a glass or two of ouzo in the dig house's dusty front yard.

One evening, an old man came down the dirt road past the house, riding sidesaddle on a donkey, tapping the animal with a stick. Next to him was an old woman, on foot, bent under the weight of a bulging sack. As they passed, one of my fellow students greeted them in broken Greek.

The old man stopped, all smiles. He exchanged a few sentences with our spokesman, and then the little party trudged on.

"That was Mr. George," our interpreter explained.

"What did you ask him?" one of us said.

"How he's doing. And why his wife isn't riding the donkey."

There was a pause. "And?"

"He says she doesn't have one."

It was my first taste of the classic anthropological experience of culture shock. Back in Birmingham, a man who rode a donkey

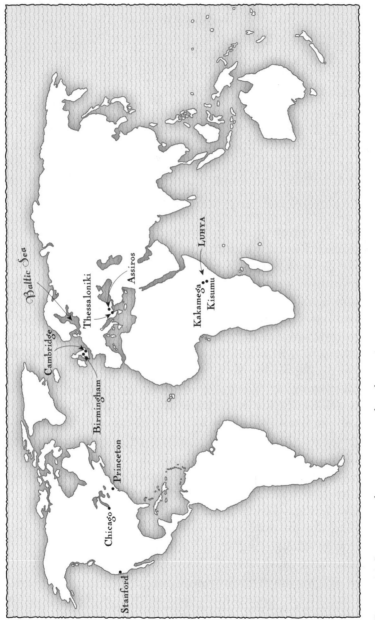

FIGURE 1.1. Locations and groups mentioned in chapter 1.

while his wife[2] struggled with a huge sack would have seemed selfish (or worse). Here in Assiros, however, the arrangement was clearly so natural, and the reasons for it so self-evident, that our question apparently struck Mr. George as simpleminded.

A third of a century later, this book is an attempt to explain what I saw in Assiros. It is based on the two Tanner Lectures in Human Values that I delivered at Princeton University in October 2012.[3] Being asked to give the Tanners is one of the highest honors in academic life, but I was especially delighted by the invitation because I am, frankly, such an unlikely person to receive it. In the thirty years since I met Mr. George, I had never written a single word about moral philosophy. Needless to say, that detail gave me pause, but on reflection, I convinced myself that Princeton's Center for Human Values was actually the perfect setting for me to hold forth on the events in Assiros, because explaining Mr. George's comment and my own reaction to it requires nothing less than a general theory of the cultural evolution of human values across the last twenty thousand years. For that task, a background in history and archaeology rather than in moral philosophy struck me as just the right skillset, and, I told myself, such a general theory of the cultural evolution of human values might be of some interest to moral philosophers too.

Whether I am right or wrong is for you to decide, with some input from the experts. After five chapters in which I set out my theory, in chapters 6 to 9 the four respondents to the original lectures—the classicist Richard Seaford, the Sinologist Jonathan D. Spence, the philosopher Christine M. Korsgaard, and the novelist Margaret Atwood—will have their say. But I get the last word, responding to the responses in chapter 10.

The Argument

In the last forty or fifty years, academics have written hundreds of books and thousands of articles about culture shocks similar to (and often much odder than) my encounter with Mr. George, his donkey, and his wife. What I offer here, though, is rather different from most of these studies. When we look at the entire planet across the last twenty thousand years, I argue, we see three broadly successive systems of human values. Each is associated with a particular way of organizing society, and each form of organization is dictated by a particular way of capturing energy from the world around us. Energy capture ultimately explains not only what Mr. George said but also why it surprised me so much.

Immediately, though, I must make a caveat: because value systems—or cultures, or whatever we want to call them—are such shapeless entities, the only way to present this argument in the space of a hundred or so pages is by focusing on specific subsets of the broader systems. In my comparisons here, I therefore limit myself to ideas about equality and hierarchy (including politics, economics, and gender) and attitudes toward violence. I pick these topics partly because I am interested in them and partly because they seem to be important. However, I also suspect that most subsets of values would reveal similar patterns; and if they do not, comparisons between different subsets of values will be one obvious way that critics might falsify my argument.

I will spend chapters 2 to 4 trying to demonstrate the reality of these three broadly successive systems of human values. I call the first of them "foraging values," because it is associated with societies that support themselves primarily by gathering wild plants and hunting wild animals. Foragers tend to value equality over most kinds of hierarchy and are quite tolerant of violence. The second system I call "farming values," because it is associated with societies that support themselves primarily off domesticated plants and animals. Farmers tend to value hierarchy over equality and are less tolerant of violence. The third system, which I call "fossil-fuel values," is associated with societies that augment the energy of living plants and animals by tapping into the energy of fossilized plants that have turned into coal, gas, and oil. Fossil-fuel users tend to value equality of most kinds over hierarchy and to be very intolerant of violence.[4]

This framework not only explains why Mr. George's comment seemed so odd to me in 1982 (his values were largely those of the farming phase, while mine belonged to the fossil-fuel phase) but also seems to have two broader implications for the study of human values. If I am right that energy capture determines values, it perhaps follows (1) that those moral philosophers who try to identify a one-size-fits-all, perfect system of human values are wasting their time, and (2) that the values that we (whoever "we" happen to be) hold dearest today are very likely to turn out—at some point fairly soon—not to be helpful any more. At that point (again, if I am right), we will abandon these values and will move on to a fourth, post-fossil-fuel, stage. I close, in chapter 5, with some speculations on what such values might look like.

Explaining and Understanding

My study of culture shock differs from most recent studies in trying to *explain* the experience rather than *understand* it. This distinction is usually traced back almost a century, to Max Weber, the founding father of sociology.[5] Weber, however, was not the first scholar to contrast understanding (*verstehen*) and explaining (*erklären*) as ways of thinking about social action. That honor seems to belong to the philosopher and historian Johann Gustav Droysen,[6] who suggested in the 1850s that historians and natural scientists were engaged in fundamentally different activities. Historians, he said, were trying to understand (by which he meant grasping past actors' subjective meanings) their subject matter, while natural scientists were trying to explain (by which he meant identifying causes) theirs.

Weber not only elaborated Droysen's original formulation on a massive scale but also suggested that sociology has a third goal, distinct from both history and science: to synthesize explaining and understanding. "A correct causal interpretation of a concrete course of action is arrived at," he insisted, "when the overt action and the motives have both been correctly apprehended and at the same time their relation has become meaningfully comprehensible. . . . If adequacy in respect to meaning is lacking," he added, "then no matter how high the degree of uniformity and how precisely its probability can be numerically determined, it is still an incomprehensible statistical probability, whether we deal with overt or subjective processes."[7]

In the 1930s, the sociologist Talcott Parsons brought Weber's thought to a broad audience among American social scientists,[8] but the anthropologist Clifford Geertz (who began his career as a student of Parsons) put a very new spin on it in the 1960s–1970s. "Believing, with Max Weber, that man is an animal suspended in webs of significance that he himself has spun," Geertz wrote, "I take culture to be those webs, and the analysis of it to be therefore not an experimental science in search of law but an interpretive one in search of meaning."[9] Building on this interpretation of Weber, Geertz concluded that making sense of social action must be based on "long-term, mainly (though not exclusively) qualitative, highly participatory, and almost obsessively fine-comb field study," producing what he famously labeled "thick description."[10]

Thick description, said Geertz, should normally take the form of "the essay, whether of thirty pages or three hundred, [which is] the natural genre in which to present cultural interpretations and the theories sustaining them." That said, "the claim to attention of an ethnographic account ... does not rest on its author's ability to capture primitive facts in faraway places, but on the degree to which he is able to clarify what goes on in such places, to reduce the puzzlement—what manner of men are these?—to which unfamiliar acts emerging out of unknown backgrounds naturally give rise."[11]

In arguing that social scientists should focus on understanding, rather than the synthesis of understanding and explaining that Weber promoted, Geertz caught a larger mood in American academia. By the mid-1980s, most humanists and many social scientists had followed his lead, transforming culture shock from a problem into an opportunity. We should rejoice, the historian Robert Darnton (at the time, a colleague of Geertz's at Princeton) wrote just a couple of years after my encounter with Mr. George, that "what is proverbial wisdom for our ancestors is completely opaque to us," because "when we cannot get a proverb, or a joke, or a ritual, or a poem, we know we are on to something. By picking at the document where it is most opaque, we may be able to unravel an alien system of meaning. The thread might even lead into a strange and wonderful worldview."[12]

It did cross my mind back in 1982 that Mr. George might be having a little joke at our expense, poking fun at our First World condescension toward his rural ways. And yet the facts remained that it was Mr. George sitting on the donkey and his wife struggling with the bulging sack. I do not doubt that contextualizing his comments within a thick description of Assirote village life would unravel a strange and wonderful worldview,[13] but here I want to do something different. Instead of understanding Mr. and Mrs. George's behavior, I want to explain it.

In doing so, I will draw on a line of inquiry that goes back not just beyond Geertz but also beyond Droysen.[14] If we go back far enough, particularly to the half-century between the 1720s and 1770s, we come to a time when explanation, not understanding, dominated the scholarly study of culture. From Montesquieu to Adam Smith, many of Western Europe's intellectual giants reacted to the flood of information coming in about other continents by positing—as I do here—that humanity had moved through a series of stages of economic development (usually some variation on hunting, pastoralism, farming, and commerce), each of which had its own characteristic system of manners.

Some of these theorists called their work "philosophical history," because they felt that they were using the past to answer some of the central questions of moral philosophy, but others preferred "conjectural history," for the equally good reason that they knew that the schemes rested on conjecture rather than real evidence about the past. From the very beginning, conjectural history attracted a combination of mockery (Walter Bagehot joked that Adam Smith "wanted to show how from being a savage, [man] rose to be a Scotchman") and rage (in the first volume of the *Historisches Journal*, published in 1773, Johann Christoph Gatterer railed against the "pretentious little Humes or Robertsons, the little German Voltaires," and promised "to hunt down these insects without mercy, wherever they may be").[15] By the 1790s, many scholars had concluded that the costs of conjecturing without evidence outweighed the gains of philosophizing, and conjectural/philosophical history went into sharp decline.[16]

But the urge to explain culture shock would not go away. A new approach, which has come to be known as "classical evolutionism," took shape in and after the 1850s, as missionaries and administrators produced a new wave of stories about the weird ways of non-Europeans, and academics developed new explanatory frameworks.[17] By the 1920s, however, the first professional anthropologists had shown that classical evolutionism was almost as conjectural as eighteenth-century philosophical history. Explanation once again went into retreat—only to enjoy another great revival (now in a form called "neo-evolutionism") in the 1950s. By this point, a significant body of archaeological and ethnographic evidence had been gathered, and explainers could ground their claims in statistical analyses of massive datasets, but by the 1980s thick description had routed this third wave of explainers too, albeit this time more on theoretical than empirical grounds.[18]

It might be tempting to interpret this story as just one more piece of evidence that there is no such thing as progress in the humanities and social sciences, but that, I think, would be a mistake. What we really see here is scholarship working the way it is supposed to.[19] Since the eighteenth century, one group of scholars after another has conjectured about the causes of cultural variation, and one group of critics after another has refuted them. In each round of debate, the explainers and understanders forced each other to come up with better theories and data, and in the 2010s, with the understanders in the ascendant, we would-be explainers need to raise our game once again.

Isms

To do this, explainers need to complement the hundreds of thick descriptions of meaning in specific cultures with broad comparisons spanning large areas and long periods of time. These will be thin descriptions, largely (though not exclusively) quantitative, and not very participatory. They will be coarse-grained, because they sweep up into a single story hundreds of societies, thousands of years, and millions of people, and reductionist, because they seek answers by boiling down the teeming variety of lived experience to simpler underlying principles.

The three value systems that I identify—those of foragers, farmers, and fossil-fuel users—are examples of what Weber called ideal types, "achieved," he explained, "by the one-sided *accentuation* of one or more points of view and by the synthesis of many diffuse, discrete, more or less present and occasionally absent *individual* phenomena, which are arranged according to those one-sidedly emphasized viewpoints into a unified mental construct. In its conceptual purity, this mental construct can never be found empirically in reality. It is a *utopia*."[20] Ideal types reduce the real lives of billions of people to a few simple models, and because they subsume such enormous empirical variation, they are necessarily riddled with exceptions. But this is the price we have to pay if we are to identify causes behind the chaos of real life.

This path is bound to strike some readers as leading us into -isms of all the wrong kinds. To begin with, it is reductionist. In most branches of the humanities and some of the social sciences, "reductionist" is a term of abuse, but rather than denying the obvious fact of my reductionism, I want to embrace the charge. My defense is that *all* scholarship is reductionist. Anyone who denies this is not thinking hard enough. To give just one example: I recently had occasion to look up some details in Martin Gilbert's eight-volume biography of Winston Churchill (which was actually published as thirteen separate books, because some of the volumes were too big to be constrained within a single pair of covers).[21] This must be one of the biggest biographies ever written, but it is still reductionist. Reducing any individual's life to words on a page—even five thousand such pages—necessarily involves distorting a more complex reality; reducing the lives of everyone who lived in the last twenty millennia to a few short chapters necessarily does so more. But that is fine. The question we should be asking is not whether a historian, an anthropologist, or a sociologist is being reductionist—the answer is always yes—but what level of reduction is required to resolve the problem being posed. Big questions often need a lot of abstraction, and so that is what I provide.

My argument is also strongly materialist. The labels I use for my three stages give this away: I am convinced, like the eighteenth-century philosophical historians, that the sources of energy available to a society set the limits on what kinds of values can flourish. Foragers living off wild plants and animals find that only a rather narrow range of ways of organizing their societies works out well, and these forms of organization tend to reward particular kinds of values. Living off domesticated plants and animals pushes farmers toward different organizations and values, and people able to tap into the energy locked in fossil fuels find that still another kind of organization and value system works best for them. If I am right, we have to conclude that culture, religion, and moral philosophy play only rather small causal roles in the story of human values. Culture, religion, and moral philosophy certainly do shape the regional versions of each of my three stages—no one would mistake, say, Plato's *Apology* for Confucius's *Analects*—and I devote a lot of space to them in chapters 2 to 4. That said, though, the bottom line is that while cultural traditions generate variations on the central themes, energy capture is the motor driving the big pattern.

Further, my argument is almost—but not quite—universalist. There are some parts of the planet that it does not cover, such as the arid steppe grasslands that stretch from Manchuria to Hungary. This territory cannot support what we normally think of as foraging or farming, because very few plants (other than grass) can grow there, but it has for thousands of years supported distinct kinds of pastoralist societies, whose members eat animals (horses, cows) that can live off grass.[22] However, despite failing the universalism test, my framework does incorporate the overwhelming majority (probably more than 95 percent) of all the people who have ever lived.

I am also guilty of functionalism.[23] Values are adaptive traits, which people adjust to maximize their effectiveness as the larger social system around them changes. This does not mean that what is (let alone what has been) is what ought to be, but it does mean that what is (and what has been) is what was always highly likely to be. Values are functioning parts of larger wholes. Tearing them out of context, weighing them in an imaginary scale, and judging them does not get us any closer to designing a one-size-fits-all, perfect set of values, because values always exist only in the real world, as parts of actual social systems.

Last but not least, my argument is also explicitly evolutionist. Human nature is not a blank slate on which foragers, farmers, and fossil-fuel users just decided to write any moral systems that took their fancy. The three systems I will describe are evolutionary adaptations to changing circumstances.

What I mean by this is that human values have evolved biologically in the seven to eight million years since we split off genetically from the last common ancestor we shared with the other great apes.[24] Because our biology has not changed very much in the ten to fifteen thousand years since farming began, anthropologists, psychologists, and historians find that a few core concerns—treating people fairly, being just, love and hate, preventing harm, agreeing that some things are sacred—recur all over the world, regardless of time or place. To some extent, they recur in our closest kin among the great apes, and perhaps among dolphins and whales too. Up to a point, at least, human values are genetically hardwired, and because of this, the biologist E. O. Wilson observed forty years ago, "Scientists and humanists should consider together the possibility that the time has come for ethics to be removed temporarily from the hands of philosophers and biologicized."[25]

To date, most of the consideration of this possibility has come from scientists, who have made great progress in explaining how these core values of fairness, justice, and so on, descended from those of our apish ancestors, but humanists have been markedly less enthusiastic about biologicizing anything.[26] Perhaps because of this, there has been much less scholarship on how human values have continued to evolve across the last twenty thousand years, and why there are such enormous differences through time and space in what humans have taken fairness, justice, and so on, to mean. Explaining the biological roots of human values is a major achievement, but it is only the first step in the evolutionary explanation of values.

The second step begins from the fact that humans are, with only trivial exceptions, the only animals whose biological evolution has given them the brainpower to invent culture, by which I mean the cumulative body of information that we acquire from other people through teaching, imitation, and other kinds of transmission.[27] Our moral systems are cultural adaptations. As our environments change, we, like other living things, continue to evolve biologically, but humans alone also evolve culturally, changing our behaviors and institutions so that they remain useful (or even become more useful) as the world around us changes.[28]

Evolutionists argue heatedly over every aspect of the workings of cultural selection. Some scholars insist that the main mechanism is something very like natural selection in biological evolution, in which one cultural variant replaces another because it preferentially affects the likelihood that people who adopt it will survive and pass on their genes; others insist that biased transmission (in which one cultural variant replaces another because it affects people's lives in ways that make it more likely to be imitated), which has much less in common with natural selection, is the main force, and that cultural evolution is really very different from the biological version.[29] Units of selection are equally controversial. Here the main argument is between scholars who hypothesize cultural replicators very like the genes of biological evolution (what the biologist Richard Dawkins called "memes"), which are transmitted whole from one mind to another, and those who insist that the units involved would be better labeled "attractors," because attractive ideas are creatively reinterpreted rather than being faithfully transmitted from one mind to another.[30] Finally, the scale (or level) at which cultural selection operates has generated a particularly large literature. This pits those who insist that all selection operates ultimately on the gene (with individuals, kin, and larger groups functioning only as different vehicles for expressing genetic fitness) against those who see selection operating at multiple levels, suggesting that traits that might prove disastrous at the genetic level, such as altruism, are able to flourish because they are highly adaptive at the level of larger groups.[31]

These are all huge and important questions, but—fortunately—we can explain how human values evolve without having to wait until the experts have agreed on the mechanisms, units, and levels of selection. "The evidence suggests that sometimes cultural variants *are* somewhat genelike, while at other times they are decidedly not," observe the evolutionary scientist Peter Richerson and the anthropologist Robert Boyd; "But—and this is a big but—in either case, the Darwinian approach remains useful." The same is true of the kin and multilevel selection debates. After all, Richerson and Boyd observe, no one in the 1850s knew how genetic inheritance worked, but that did not stop Darwin from reasoning his way to the principle of natural selection. "For the same reason," they suggest, "we can black-box the problem of how culture is stored in brains by using plausible models based on observable features that we do understand, and forge ahead."[32] And when we do that, they conclude, we see that "Some moral values [become] more appealing and thus more likely to spread from one individual to another. Those will tend to persist, while less attractive alternatives tend to disappear."[33]

The biggest changes in humanity's environment since the end of the Ice Age have been the explosions in energy capture that we normally call the agricultural and industrial revolutions, which is why the three main systems of values in human history broadly coincide the three main systems of energy capture. In the 1940s, the anthropologist Leslie White suggested that the whole of history can in fact be reduced to the simple equation $C = E \times T$, where C stands for culture, E for energy, and T for technology.[34] "*Culture*," he concluded, "*develops when the amount of energy harnessed by man per capita per year is increased; or as the efficiency of the technological means of putting this energy to work is increased; or as both factors are simultaneously increased.*"[35] White has been unpopular in recent years, but I will argue in this book that he was largely correct. The spiraling amount of energy humans have harvested across the last twenty thousand years has driven a process of cultural evolution, and human values have changed as part of this.

If it is right to think of value systems in these terms, we should probably also conclude—as I argue in this book—that each age gets the thought it needs. According to the psychologist Jonathan Haidt, "We're born to be righteous, but we have to learn what, exactly, people like us should be righteous about,"[36] and long-term history suggests that our choices of what to be righteous about are, to a great extent, forced on us by the ways we extract energy from the world. Methods of energy capture largely dictate what demographic regimes and forms of organization will work best, and these in turn dictate what kind of values will flourish.

Evolution—cultural as well as biological—is a competitive process, played out through millions of tiny experiments. It is path-dependent, meaning that the state of an organism or society today constrains what it might turn into tomorrow, and it is usually messy, noisy, and even violent. But as these competitions between mutations get resolved, traits that work well in a particular environment replace traits that don't. That, I think, is why we see so many similarities in behavior, institutions, and value systems within each of my three broad stages of foraging, farming, and fossil-fuel society—why, for instance, godlike kings and slavery were so common (but not universal) in farming societies and so rare (but not completely absent) in fossil-fuel societies. Peasants tended to opt for hierarchy not because they were all bullies, but because that was what worked; fossil-fuel users tended to opt for democracy not because they were saints, but because a flood of energy had changed the world so much that democracy was now what worked.

Long-term history, then, suggests that the competitive process of cultural evolution shoves us toward whatever values work best at a particular stage of energy capture, regardless of what we may think about it. This has certainly been my own experience of the back-and-forth relationship between values and environment. In 1986, four years after my time in Assiros, I made a brief detour into cultural anthropology. I went to Kenya to visit my wife (then girlfriend), who was studying traditional medicine among the Luhya people.[37] We both took our full-blown fossil-fuel graduate-student values with us, and were particularly keen not to be like the colonialist anthropologists of yesteryear, with staffs of underpaid locals carrying their belongings around. What we discovered, though, was that what sounded good in a pub in Cambridge, UK, didn't translate very well to the hill country between Kakamega and Kisumu. This was largely a pre-fossil-fuel world, even more embedded in the age of farming than Assiros. Consequently, we found ourselves spending several hours each day fetching water from the river and collecting sticks to boil it before we could drink, cook, or wash anything. Kathy needed to teach and do interviews, I needed to finish my first book and write a job talk to give at the University of Chicago, and neither of us had time for hours of waterbearing.

But in a farming economy crippled by underemployment, plenty of local women did have time. For a dollar or so a day, we could buy back several hours. The cash was reasonably small change to us but a huge bonus for a local family. It was a win-win situation, but it was also a classic colonial relationship, and we didn't want to do it. For about a week, we slithered round in the mud, dropping buckets and building fires that wouldn't light. Finally—to everyone's relief, I think—we reassessed our principles. Money changed hands. Interviews got done. I finished my book and got hired, and a couple of family budgets got healthy cash infusions (figure 1.2).

Perhaps we were just weak-willed. Maybe Kant wouldn't have done what we did (although I also have trouble seeing him carrying buckets of water up from the stream). However, I suspect that almost everyone else on earth would have acted like us. There is a story that the economist John Maynard Keynes, when charged with inconsistency, replied "When the facts change, I change my opinion. What do you do, sir?" Whether Keynes actually said this or not,[38] it remains a good description of what has gone on billions of times around the world across the last twenty thousand years. One of the things biological evolution has given us is common sense, and common sense tells us to adapt to the facts.

FIGURE 1.2. The water bearers: Kenyan women collecting water at a stream (from a postcard bought in Kisumu in 1986; author's collection).

On Being Wrong

Ever since the days of the philosophical historians, the greatest challenge for builders of large-scale explanatory models has been how to test them against reality. Because ideal types are so messy, there are inevitably constant exceptions to every generalization; so how do we know when we have reached the point that there are there so many exceptions that the theory must be wrong?

This problem came up the first time I ever attended a Tanner Lecture, when I was invited out from Chicago to respond to Colin Renfrew's lectures on archaeology, language, and identity at Stanford University in 1993.[39] In the seminar following his first talk, Professor Renfrew and the philosopher Alison Wylie had a spirited exchange over falsification. The archaeologists in the room came up with one exception after another to his theory linking population movements and language change, but it was never really clear whether it had been (or could be) falsified.

The biologist-turned-macrohistorian Peter Turchin has suggested that on this, as on many other points, "The history of science is emphatic: a discipline usually matures only after it has developed mathematical theory."[40] If he is right (and I think he is), the obvious solution to the problem of falsification is to reject Geertz's claim that the essay is the natural genre for analyzing culture shock. Rather, I should begin this book by taking a representative sample of societies at different stages of energy capture, reducing their value systems to a numerical code, and comparing the fit between value systems and energy capture. A χ^2 (chi-square) or other significance test could then establish whether we should reject the null hypothesis (that there is no correlation between energy capture and values) at 0.05 or whatever other threshold seems appropriate. I would need to spend several pages explaining my coding system and sampling strategy, but if the test showed a statistically significant correlation between values and energy capture I could move on quickly to my explanation of the causes and implications of the correlation.

For many kinds of large-scale, cross-cultural comparison, this is, in principle, a straightforward business (even if in practice the outcomes of quantitative tests tend to be less straightforward). Big databases (particularly the Human Relations Area Files)[41] already exist, and even better ones are currently under construction.[42] However, if you look for information on values in these databases, you will have little joy. The core problem is that moral values are nominal not interval data—that is, saying that people in one society typically think that wealth inequality is good while those in another think it is bad conveys no information other than that the two societies are different. Their attitudes cannot be ranked or measured: "good" and "bad" are just names (hence "nominal" data), rather than points on a continuous scale that allow us to measure and quantify the distance between them (hence "interval" data).

Because of these (and other) problems, cross-cultural index makers normally avoid values vigorously, and in my own earlier venture into quantitative indices, I happily followed their lead.[43] Of course, it may be that I did not try hard enough, just as I perhaps did not try hard enough to adhere to my fossil-fuel values when I was among the Luhya, and other analysts do, in fact, claim to have found ways to convert human values from nominal to interval data. Since 1981, a large European project called the World Values Survey (WVS)[44] has interviewed more than 400,000 people in 100 countries about their values, ranking the responses along two axes. The first of these runs from "traditional" to "secular-rational" values (measuring attitudes toward religion, family, and authority), and the second from "survival" to "self-expression" (involving concerns with physical and economic security and levels of trust and tolerance). The WVS then bundled the numerical scores together to calculate a single score that could locate each country in the world within a grid of values.[45]

What all this shows, say the political scientists Ronald Inglehart and Christian Welzel, is "that socioeconomic development tends to transform people's basic values and beliefs—and it does so in a roughly predictable fashion."[46] What they mean by socioeconomic development—the transition from predominantly rural societies to

industrial and post-industrial, service-based economies—is similar
to but not exactly the same as what I mean by energy capture, and
so in figures 1.3 and 1.4 I attempt a more direct test, correlating
WVS scores with a crude measure of energy capture. Figure 1.3
is the simplest version, plotting national scores on the WVS's
traditional to secular-rational axis against the proportion of each
nation's wealth generated in the agricultural sector.[47] There is a
clear linear correlation, with values shifting from "traditional" to
"secular-rational" as fossil fuels supplant farming; however, the
correlation is weak, with a score for R^2 (the correlation coefficient) of just 0.24.[48] The relationship between energy capture and
values is real, but figure 1.3 suggests that it is loose. So long as
at least one-quarter of the national wealth comes from farming,
values remain quite traditional, but once nonagricultural sectors
rise above 75 percent, values shift rapidly (but with enormous
variation) toward secular-rational norms. This pattern, as we shall
see in chapter 4, is strongly borne out by the historical evidence.

Statistics being what they are, there are many ways to arrange the
WVS data, but all the comparisons I tried produced roughly the
same results. Figure 1.4, for instance, shows on the vertical axis the
sum of the WVS's traditional-to-secular/rational and survival-to-
self-expression scores for each country. The horizontal axis provides
a composite measure of economic development, dividing output
between the primary sector of farming, the secondary sector of
industry, and the tertiary sector of services, and then assigning
each country one point for each percentage of the work force in
the primary sector, two for each percentage in the secondary sector,
and three for each percentage in the tertiary. This produces a more
respectable correlation ($R^2 = 0.43$), but the overall picture remains
very like figure 1.3. The less developed the economy, the more likely
people are to have traditional values, but as industry and services
become important, people's values generally (albeit with enormous
variation) shift toward rationalism, secularism, and self-expression.

The reason for the messiness of the pattern, the WVS concludes,
is that development is not the only force affecting values. "Although
socioeconomic development tends to bring predictable changes in

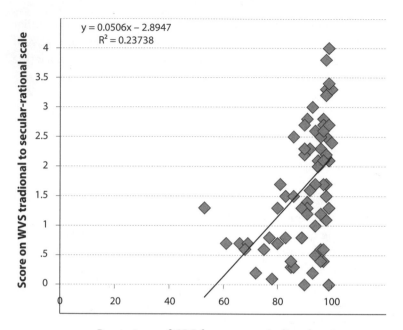

$y = 0.0506x - 2.8947$
$R^2 = 0.23738$

Percentage of GDP from nonagricultural sectors

FIGURE 1.3. Values and energy capture, version I: national scores on the World Values Survey's traditional to secular-rational values scale plotted against the proportion of each nation's wealth generated by nonagricultural work ($y = 0.0506x - 2.8947$; $R^2 = 0.23738$).

people's worldviews," say Inglehart and Welzel, "cultural traditions—such as whether a society has been historically shaped by Protestantism, Confucianism, or communism—continue to show a lasting imprint on a society's worldview. History matters, and a society's prevailing value orientations reflect an interaction between the driving forces of modernization and the retarding influence of tradition."[49]

Inglehart and Welzel's "culture map," based on 2010 data and showing seventy-four of the countries they studied[50] (figure 1.5), illustrates this interaction. The cultural and/or linguistic clusters are striking, and cannot be mere coincidences, but there are also numerous anomalies that need to be explained. Inglehart and Welzel's category of "Catholic Europe," for instance, with its narrow

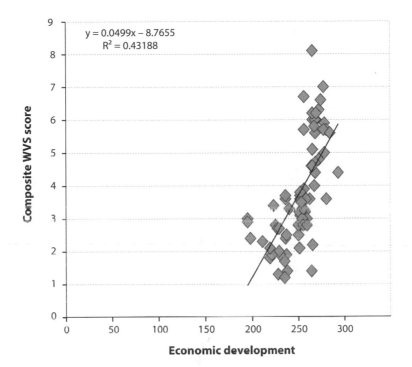

FIGURE 1.4. Values and energy capture, version II: composite scores combining the World Values Survey's traditional to secular-rational and security to self-expression scales plotted against a composite score reflecting the importance of the primary, secondary, and tertiary sectors in the national economy ($y = 0.0499x - 8.7655$; $R^2 = 0.43188$).

corridor connecting Poland to the rest of the cluster, looks alarmingly like a gerrymandered electoral district. According to their positions on the map, most Romanians would like to be Muslims, while Guatemalans want to be Africans, and the Irish (Protestants as well as Catholics) would be most comfortable in Latin America. Neither Greece nor Israel is marked on this edition of the cultural map (although they did appear on earlier versions), but their WVS scores suggest that the home of Orthodox Christianity really lies midway between Slovenia and Belgium, far from its co-religionists, and the Jewish state falls in the very center of Catholic Europe.

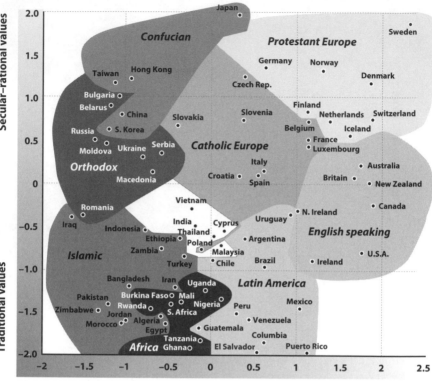

FIGURE 1.5. The "culture map" of World Values Survey data drawn by political scientists Ronald Inglehart and Christian Welzel, demonstrating the correlation between cultural traditions and values.

These quirky outcomes are amusing, but the most instructive anomaly is the cluster of countries in the middle of the diagram. Chile, Cyprus, Ethiopia, India, Malaysia, Poland, Thailand, Turkey, and Vietnam have little in common beyond the fact that they are all going through rapid economic transition—which points, the WVS concludes, to the conclusion that development is the real force driving values, with culture merely inflecting the paths that values take. "Following an increase in standards of living, and a transit from development country via industrialization to post-industrial knowledge society," the WVS website observes, "a country tends to move diagonally in the direction from lower-left corner (poor) to upper-right corner (rich)":[51] development determines the path, and tradition bends it one way or another. The industrialized societies of Latin America and Eastern Europe all score higher in the WVS than the much less industrialized ones of Africa and the Middle East, but thanks to culture, Latin Americans tend to score high on self-expression but low on secular-rational values, while Orthodox Europeans tend to do the opposite.

The WVS data are strongly suggestive. In the end, though, they provide only a very partial test of this book's thesis. The basic problem is that the only way to generate systematic data on values is through opinion polls, and these are available only for very recent times. By 1981, when the WVS began its research, foragers made up just tiny minorities within larger nation-states. Even in Botswana, which probably has a higher percentage of foragers in its population than any other country, the ten thousand hunter-gatherers in the Kalahari Desert are outnumbered more than 200:1 by people who support themselves from farming, factory work, or the service sector. Further, by 1981 almost every farming society—including Mr. George's Macedonia[52]—was moving rapidly along the path toward fossil-fuel dependence. In 2012, there were only seven nations on earth (out of a total of 223) in which farmers generated more than half of the national wealth.[53] By contrast, the whole history of the world from the agricultural revolution up until about AD 1500 had probably produced no more than seven cases in which farmers generated *less* than half of the national wealth.

The only way to carry out rigorous, large-*n* statistical studies of the relationships between human values and energy capture is by restricting ourselves to the last thirty years, which means ignoring almost all of the story. Consequently, I fall back in chapters 2 to 4 on more traditional methods. In fact, this book is an essay along just the lines that Geertz recommended, sketching suggestions rather than demonstrating correlations. Drawing on well-established qualitative generalizations in anthropology, archaeology, and historical sociology, I try to make the case that three broad systems of human values have existed across the last twenty thousand years, and that they roughly correlate with systems of energy capture—in short, that each age gets the thought it needs. My plan is straightforward. In chapters 2, 3, and 4, I look at foragers, farmers, and fossil-fuel users respectively, and in chapter 5, I ask why systems of energy capture changed, whether the changes were inevitable, and what will happen next. In chapters 6 to 9, the experts will explain where I went wrong, and in chapter 10, I will try to salvage whatever remains of my thesis.

....

CHAPTER 2

FORAGERS

....

Who Foragers Are

I begin with foraging societies. "Foraging," one standard reference work helpfully suggests, means the "hunting of wild animals, gathering of wild plants, and fishing, with no domestication of plants, and no domesticated animals except the dog"[1] (hence the common use of the term "hunter-gatherers" as a synonym for "foragers"). The consequence of this strategy of energy capture, another standard work observes, is that foragers "exercise no deliberate alteration of the *gene pool* of exploited resources."[2]

As we will see in this chapter, there are many versions of foraging (some anthropologists therefore prefer to speak of a "foraging spectrum"),[3] and in addition to being very broad, the category of "foragers" is also open-ended. Plenty of societies have combined foraging and farming (anthropologists often call these "horticultural" groups),[4] and in the last few generations some have combined foraging with elements of fossil-fuel life. Despite the variations and transitional cases, though, anthropologists overwhelmingly agree in seeing "foragers" as a fairly coherent analytical category.

We might even call foraging the natural way of life, in that virtually all animals are foragers, and each species has its own distinctive version of foraging. Our own version evolved along the edges of the great central African rainforest as we ourselves evolved out of earlier kinds of *Homo*, somewhere between fifty thousand and two hundred thousand years ago,[5] and we carried it from there as we colonized most of the rest of the planet.[6] Major migrations out of Africa began between 100,000 and 70,000 years ago, and by

10,000 years ago we had settled most habitable parts of the world. For probably the first 90 percent of our history, all humans were foragers; and a few of us, of course, still are.

The Evidence

Scholars of foraging societies[7] have three main sources of information: archaeological evidence for prehistory, a handful of accounts of foragers (going back to Herodotus in fifth-century BC Greece) encountered by literate societies in the past few thousand years, and ethnographic analyses from the last hundred or so years. Each class of data has its own problems, but when brought together, they reveal strong patterns.

Archaeology is the only direct source of evidence for most of the foraging societies that have ever existed, but it has one great drawback—stones and bones are mute on the topic of human values. No matter how sophisticated our fieldwork and theorizing get, interpreting the archaeological finds always depends on drawing analogies between the finds and historical or ethnographic accounts.[8]

Premodern literary accounts of foragers, by contrast, have plenty to say about values, and have the important advantage of being untainted by modern assumptions; but they also have one great disadvantage—that the main reason that educated, agrarian elites wrote about foragers was to use them as echo chambers for their own arguments over values. Consequently, premodern accounts tend to emphasize the exoticness (as members of farming societies saw it) of foragers. Herodotus, for instance, had some solid information about Siberian foragers, but he was still only too ready to believe that some of them were not entirely human. The Arimaspians (figure 2.1), he said, were one-eyed. Beyond them lived the Argippaioi, who had no hair, and the Man Eaters, and still farther north, people who hibernated for six months of the year.[9] Sometimes, Herodotus cast nonfarmers in the role of backward savages who highlighted Greek sophistication; at other times, he made them into noble savages who illustrated Greek decadence.[10] These same themes dominated agriculturalists' writings about foragers for the next two-thousand-plus years.[11]

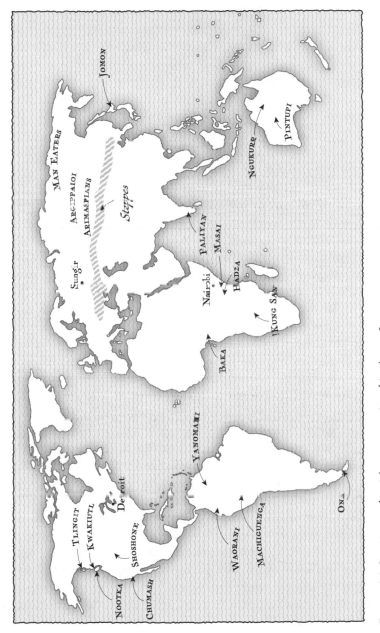

FIGURE 2.1. Locations and social groups mentioned in chapter 2.

Modern ethnographers, writing in the last hundred years, have developed much more sophisticated methods and have built up an impressive body of knowledge about foraging societies. The main difficulty in deploying these data as proxy evidence for prehistoric foragers, though, is that contemporary foraging societies are, in at least some ways, very different from ancient or prehistoric ones. Twenty thousand years ago, everyone on earth was a forager. By five hundred years ago, well under one person in ten still practiced this way of life, and these few had been pushed back into just one-third of the planet, and today, foragers make up much less than 1 percent of the world's population. The few survivors are mostly penned into extreme environments that farmers do not want, such as the Kalahari Desert and Arctic Circle, or have not yet penetrated, such as parts of the Amazon and Congo rainforests. However, even remote refuges can be of economic or political interest to fossil-fuel users, meaning that modern governments, markets, and tastes have had at least some impact on all but the most isolated contemporary foragers. (In Tanzania in 1986, one of the sights that surprised me most was a spear-toting Masai hunter drinking a bottle of Coke while he waited—with his kill slung over one shoulder—for a bus back to his campsite. He was, in fact, anything but unusual; by the 1980s, most hunter-gatherers practiced fossil-fuel-assisted foraging.)

Making comparisons between twentieth-century foragers in very tough environments and prehistoric foragers in kinder, gentler ones obviously presents problems. In the mid-twentieth century, several anthropologists and archaeologists responded by coming up with very useful typologies of foragers,[12] but since the 1980s others have gone much further and suggested that analogies of any kind must be misleading. Far from being relics of an ancient way of life, these anthropologists claim, modern foragers are the products of distinctly modern historical processes, above all European colonialism—which, they conclude, means that contemporary foragers tell us little about prehistory.[13] The very idea of comparing prehistoric and modern foragers, some anthropologists began claiming, is implicitly racist, because it reduces contemporary foragers to the status of "living ancestors" that have been left behind by progress and therefore need to be taken under the wing of fossil-fuel societies.[14]

These claims have generated intense debates, often with strong political overtones.[15] However, not even the nastiness of some of the exchanges can obscure the fact that a century of archaeological and anthropological scholarship has produced effective middle-range theories linking excavated remains via ethnoarchaeological analogies to prehistoric behavior.[16] Some of these methods, to be sure, are little more than refined common sense, and were already obvious to archaeologists a century ago. Despite the ebbs and flows of academic fashion, many of the conclusions that the archaeologist V. Gordon Childe reached in the 1930s, for instance, still seem to be broadly correct (one of my Stanford colleagues likes to press graduate students taking their general exams in anthropology until they admit that our main ideas about prehistoric life have not really changed since 1877, when Lewis Henry Morgan published *Ancient Society*).[17] While many pitfalls confront the incautious analyst, the overall shape of the world of prehistoric foragers does seem fairly clear.

Energy, Demography, and Social Organization

There is enormous variety in the details of how foragers feed and organize themselves,[18] but much of this variation is primarily a function of where different groups live. For foragers, location is everything, determining both energy needs and energy sources. Basically, the nearer foragers live to the equator, the lower their caloric needs. In the tropics, as few as 4,000 kilocalories (kcal) per day often cover a person's basic requirements for food, tools, cooking fuel, a little clothing, and simple shelter. Foragers near the poles, however, may be forced to consume twice as much energy every day for their heating, housing, and thicker clothing.[19] Equatorial foragers tend to obtain most of their energy from plants, which are more abundant (even in deserts) than in polar regions; Arctic and Antarctic foragers get most of their energy from animals (especially fish). There is no reason to suspect that geographical constraints were any weaker in prehistory, and during the Ice Age they must, in fact, have been a great deal stronger.

Contemporary foragers are generally very good at assessing the caloric costs and benefits of different energy sources. Tradition and belief certainly shape their foraging strategies, but a series of ethnographies since the 1970s has confirmed the underlying rationality of foragers' allocations of time and effort.[20] The archaeologist Robert Bettinger in fact suggests that the bewildering variety of ways people hunt and gather can be boiled down to just five basic foraging strategies,[21] and the assumption of economic rationality (often called optimal foraging theory) makes a great deal of sense of prehistoric remains.[22]

The consequences that energy constraints had for foragers (prehistoric as well as contemporary) were already obvious in 1968, when Richard Lee and Irven DeVore published their conference volume *Man the Hunter*, probably the most influential book ever written about foragers. Regardless of where foragers lived, what they ate, and how they found it, Lee and DeVore concluded, pursuing wild food forced foragers to follow two fundamental rules: "(1) they live in small groups, and (2) they move around a lot."[23]

Anthropologists argue over how best to describe forager social organization. In his classic book *Primitive Social Organization*, Elman Service suggested that the fundamental group was the band, made up of a few dozen people linked by kinship. Allen Johnson and Timothy Earle, by contrast, argue that smaller family groups matter more, while Timothy Ingold suggests that forager groups really consist of "two relatively autonomous domains of production and consumption, respectively male and female. What we might recognize as 'families,'" he suspects, "are then constituted at the multiple points of contact between these domains, through relations of exchange involving food and sex."[24]

But despite these disagreements, the central demographic facts are not in dispute. The low density of wild food resources means that most contemporary foragers spend most of their time in very small groups, usually of two to eight closely related people. All, however, need to belong to much larger groups of at least five hundred people, because only these can provide a viable breeding population.[25] It is unusual for so many foragers to congregate physically, but even the smallest groups do regularly assemble in larger bands or camps of perhaps fifty-plus people, and networks of these bands/camps create genetic pools of the required size. In lush environments, people spend more of the year in these larger groups; in harsh environments, less of it. Only in really abundant environments, however, particularly those with rich marine resources, can foragers live permanently in groups several dozens or sometimes hundreds strong. The foraging villages of North America's Pacific Coast, from the Chumash of Southern California to the Tlingit of the Alaska panhandle, are the best-known cases.[26]

Archaeology suggests that prehistoric foragers lived in similar-sized groups. During the cold, dry conditions of the Ice Age, very small groups were probably normal, especially for people living outside the tropics. After about 14,000 BC, as the world warmed up, group sizes seem to have increased, and several post-glacial temperate regions supported semipermanent villages hundreds strong. Some-times—as around the southern shores of the Baltic Sea (ca. 5000 BC) and in southern Japan (ca. 3500 BC)—these were zones of rich maritime resources, but in a few cases—particularly Southwest Asia between 13,000 and 10,000 BC—wild plant and animal food was abundant enough to support permanent villages. With the coming of farming, however, foragers were steadily pushed back into less abundant environments.[27]

Because different wild plants ripen and different species of animals and fish migrate at different times during the year, contemporary foragers have to be very mobile. Even small groups require huge spaces to support themselves, meaning that people are very thinly scattered across landscapes. Densities vary, determined chiefly by the local wild resource base (which is itself determined by geography), but less than one person per square mile is typical, and less than one per 10 square miles is not unusual.[28]

The tiny size of the typical foraging group means that the division of labor is necessarily simple, organized largely at the family level by age and gender. On the whole, women gather plants as well as do most of the food preparation, some handicrafts, and all the childcare; men hunt, do most of the handicrafts, and do some food preparation. Boys and girls help with gender-appropriate jobs.[29] In the last five thousand years, foragers in contact with agricultural or industrial societies have often been eager to buy and apply their more sophisticated technology, but foragers' own tools and weapons are normally very simple (although often ingenious and effective). Throughout history, even after farming societies had learned how to work bronze and iron, almost all foragers carried on living in the Stone Age.[30]

But despite their simple technology and economic organization, foragers can be quite productive. If population density is low and mobility high relative to wild resources, foragers often do not need to work very hard to generate the 1,500 to 2,000 kilocalories of food energy that active adults require each day. Even in an environment as tough as the American Southwest, people put in an average of just two to five hours of foraging per day, which is why the anthropologist Marshall Sahlins famously called foragers the "original affluent society."[31]

The "affluent society" label, though, obscures as much as it reveals. As Sahlins recognized, while foraging tends to provide food with relatively little labor, it does less well at providing other material goods. Sahlins argued that this did not invalidate his affluent society theory, because foragers were not materialists: therefore, he concluded, while "The world's most primitive people have few possessions . . . *they are not poor.*"[32] Some anthropologists, however, take a very different line, accepting that contemporary foragers are in fact very poor indeed, but blaming this on exploitation by farmers and fossil-fuel users rather than on the inefficiency of foraging as a method of energy capture.[33]

The sophistication and wealth of material culture varies from one foraging group to another, with large, mostly sedentary groups such as prehistoric Japan's Jomon culture or the Pacific Northwest's Kwakiutl tending to be the richest,[34] and tiny, very mobile groups in extreme environments the poorest. However, all our sources of evidence—excavations, premodern literary accounts, and ethnographies—point to the same conclusion. Throughout history, even the richest foragers have been poor by the standards of farming societies and very poor by those of fossil-fuel users.[35]

Even more importantly, the affluent society label downplays the fact that even the most leisured foragers go through periods when wild foods are short. Some groups (particularly the larger, more sedentary ones) are able to store foods for bad times,[36] but others are not, and foragers regularly endure periods of food shortage, producing poor health (by modern standards). Life expectancy at birth (e_0) is typically somewhere between the mid-twenties and mid-thirties. While a few people live into their seventies, half of all the children born typically die before reaching fifteen, and most of those who survive into adulthood die before fifty.[37] On the whole, foragers keep their groups small enough to survive on wild resources not by wisely maintaining stable populations below the carrying capacity of their range, but by going through boom-and-bust cycles of rapid population growth and starvation.[38]

Values

Our information on foragers' values comes almost entirely from ethnographies written in the last hundred years. Ancient Greek and Roman writers occasionally comment on the egalitarianism and belligerence of nonfarming groups, but there is really no way to know for sure whether the kind of attitudes we see among contemporary foragers were also normal during the first fifty-plus millennia of human history. Given the multiple parallels mentioned in the previous section between ancient and modern foragers' subsistence, demography, and organization, though, the burden of proof must lie with those who believe that prehistoric and twentieth-century foragers had strongly different values.

Everywhere from the Arctic to Australia, ethnographers have commented on foragers' aversion to political hierarchy.[39] (In the excellent *Cambridge Encyclopedia of Hunter-Gatherers*,[40] for instance, almost all the contributors observe that the people about whom they are writing have no institutionalized leaders.) As usual, there are exceptions, mostly among societies whose food supply permits groups hundreds strong to live together,[41] although some archaeologists claim that even these groups were in reality less hierarchical than they appear.[42] Foragers almost everywhere would probably have understood the answer that the anthropologist Richard Lee received when he asked a !Kung San forager in the Kalahari Desert about the apparent absence of chiefs: "Of course we have headmen! In fact, we're all headmen. . . . Each one of us is headman over himself!"[43] It is, in fact, closely paralleled by what a forager half a world away in Tierra del Fuego told another anthropologist: "Yes, señor, we, the Ona, have many chiefs. The men are all captains and the women are sailors."[44]

Foraging groups sometimes have to make important collective decisions, particularly about where to move next in the endless quest for food, but most groups have developed methods that make it difficult for one person or even one small group to seize control of the decision-making process. The most popular solution is to discuss every decision over and over again in subgroups, until a consensus begins to take shape, and at that point, even the strongest-willed dissenters tend to turn into yes-men and get on board with majority opinion.[45]

Nearly all groups also sometimes engage in activities that call for leaders, such as the famous Shoshone "rabbit bosses" who organize hunts when multiple families convene as bands.[46] These positions, however, normally evaporate as soon as the activity is over or when the band breaks down again into its component families. Men who get too bossy, or extend bossiness into inappropriate contexts, or try to turn their temporary influence into permanent power over others, rarely withstand their companions' disapproval.

Mockery is one of the commonest responses to attempts to create political hierarchy. Richard Lee's meticulous study of the !Kung San again provides the best example. In the Kalahari, the main arena for "upstartism" (anthropologist Christopher Boehm's word for self-promotion) is hunting, and one influential !Kung San told Lee that

When a young man kills much meat, he comes to think of himself as a chief or a big man, and he thinks of the rest of us as his servants or inferiors. We can't accept this. We refuse one who boasts, for someday his pride will make him kill somebody. So we always speak of his meat as worthless. In this way we cool his heart and make him gentle.[47]

!Kung men have been seen to undermine upstarts by sarcastically calling them "Big Chief" and ostentatiously ignoring them, and similar behavior is common all over the world. Among Paliyan foragers in South India, Hadza in Tanzania, and Ngukurr in Australia, for instance, ambitious men are regularly brought down by mockery of their pretensions.[48]

If laughter fails, foragers can escalate their disapproval. Ostracism is a popular technique, and often grows directly out of mockery. A common first step, recorded in several societies, is for people to pretend that they cannot hear or understand what the upstart is saying, howling with laughter as he gets angrier and angrier. If this still does not work, an upstart might be physically expelled from the group for a while, or the other members of the group might themselves decamp, leaving the offending party to scurry after them.

Another strategy is to shift from mockery and ostracism to blunt criticism, telling the offender in no uncertain terms what he or she is doing wrong. The anthropologist Fred Myers, who worked among the Pintupi people of Australia's Western Desert, recorded an episode in which one man began thinking he was better than the other members of his band and took decisions that affected others without consulting them. People mocked him, ignored him, and complained to his face, but nothing seemed to work—until he dropped dead one day in the middle of a ceremony. The Pintupi assumed that the would-be chief must have provoked someone into killing him with sorcery, because (according to Myers's paraphrase of public opinion), "One should assert one's authority only in ways that do not threaten the equality and autonomy of others."[49]

But if neither mockery nor criticism cuts an upstart down to size, unhappy foragers can simply walk away. The Machiguenga of the Amazon Basin, a group that combines foraging with a limited amount of horticulture, call this *ishiganaka*: If a man finds himself becoming angry over another man's pushiness, he is expected to take himself off into the forest. He might come back after a while, or, if he decides that the situation cannot be salvaged, he might take his whole family with him. This, the Machiguenga say, is better than being reduced to using violence to solve the problem.[50]

Nonhierarchical values are just as pronounced in economics as in politics, even if the nineteenth-century notion that foragers practiced "primitive communism," holding all goods in common,[51] was clearly mistaken. Rather, as Johnson and Earle emphasize in their survey of social evolution, foragers "are closely attentive to matters of possession and ownership. As a rule, every item produced has an individual owner who decides how it is to be used."[52]

Yet despite their strong property rights, few foraging societies have much material hierarchy. The standard way for economists to measure income or wealth inequality is on a scale called the Gini coefficient, which expresses the degree of concentration of wealth or income with scores from 0 (complete equality, meaning that everyone in the group has exactly the same amount of wealth or income) to 1 (complete inequality, meaning that one person owns everything, and no one else in the group has any wealth or income at all).[53] Few anthropologists have calculated Gini scores for foragers, but the most successful attempt, looking at five groups of foragers in Africa, South America, Indonesia, and Australia, came up with very low scores that cluster around a mean of 0.25.[54] (I will discuss the Gini scores for farming and fossil fuel societies in the next two chapters.)

There is an obvious reason why wealth inequality is so low among foragers: foraging usually requires people to move around constantly. This can make the accumulation of material wealth not only difficult but also rather pointless. On the one hand, dragging material possessions around the countryside makes hunting and gathering much harder; on the other, the attraction of possessions declines if you have to abandon them every few weeks. Foraging as a system of energy capture puts strict practical limits on the accumulation of wealth.

There are two partial exceptions to this generalization, both of which seem to prove the rule. The first comes from a handful of prehistoric sites that do preserve evidence of wealth inequality—above all, Sungir in eastern Russia. Here, excavators found a group of burials dating around 26,000 BC. Most held few or no grave goods, but two—one containing a fifty-year-old man, the other a boy in his early teens and a slightly younger girl—stood out sharply. More than 13,000 carved mammoth ivory beads had been sewn into their clothes. Around the bodies were dozens of ivory ornaments, including a little carving of a mammoth and several spears, and more than 250 fox teeth adorned the man's hat and boy's belt. The beads represent more than two continuous years of work for a craftsman, and sixty foxes gave up their teeth to decorate the dead.[55] This is an unparalleled concentration of riches, and the fact that the honored dead included children might mean that wealth and even power could be inherited. Why Sungir produced these unique finds remains unclear, although it seems a safe bet that it was a special mammoth-hunting spot; what is clear, though, is that the wealth took the form of tiny, eminently portable objects that could easily be carried from one hunting spot to the next. Sungir perhaps shows that under the right circumstances—where there were rich resources that could be converted to portable forms—economic and perhaps political hierarchies could develop among foragers.

The second set of exceptions comes, once again, from the prosperous foragers of North America's Pacific Coast. For several centuries, abundant wild food (especially fish) allowed these foragers to live in semipermanent villages, sometimes with hundreds of residents. Because they stayed in one place for much of the year, they found it worthwhile not only to build houses but also to accumulate possessions, and some people built and accumulated much more than others.[56] The hunting and gathering were so rich here, it would seem, that the Chumash, Nootka, Kwakiutl, and other groups could even break the Sungir rule, progressing from small, portable riches to large, immovable ones.

One way in which Marx and Engels's vision of primitive communism was correct, however, is that (so far as we know) no subgroup within a foraging society has ever set itself up as a rentier class that owns the means of production.[57] Excluding others from access to wild plants that are scattered over a huge area or wild animals and fish that are constantly on the move is normally impossible, and not even the affluent North American Pacific Coast foragers could find ways to own shoals of tuna, swordfish, and salmon. The closest foragers come to owning the means of production is owning man-made devices that improve access to wild food sources, but knowledge of how to make and use these—baskets for putting plants in, or blinds, bows and arrows, and corrals for hunting—is usually widespread in a foraging group. Most foragers also know how to tend individual trees or bushes to improve their yields, which is often seen as conferring ownership (as, for instance, among the Shoshone, who established family claims to particular pine nut trees).[58] Only in exceptional cases do artifacts give some individuals a great advantage over others, and once again, the Pacific Coast societies stand out. It is probably no coincidence that the years around AD 800, which see the first archaeological evidence for large, oceangoing canoes, also see the first evidence for marked wealth hierarchy.[59]

In almost all foraging societies, these practical constraints on wealth accumulation are reinforced by a strong sense that material hierarchy is morally wrong.[60] In most societies, the value of sharing is drummed into children early on. In one slightly stomach-turning example, an ethnographer watched a Baka boy in Cameroon shoot a large spider with an arrow, and then carefully share the edible parts with his two playmates. One boy got three legs; the others each received two and a half legs, plus half of the spider's cephalothorax to make up the difference.[61]

Refusing to share the good things that come your way is a forager deadly sin, every bit as bad as being an upstart. In fact, greed and upstartism seem to merge in forager thought, as the !Kung informant quoted earlier revealed when he said that a successful young hunter "comes to think of himself as a chief or a big man." Selfish foragers come under intense pressure to give goods away, which some anthropologists call "demand sharing" or even "tolerated scrounging/theft."[62]

For those not used to it, demand sharing can bring on extremes of culture shock. In 1986, a friend of my wife's staying in another part of Kenya made the mistake of announcing that she was going to rent a car to get her luggage back to Nairobi Airport. Everyone she had ever met, it seemed, suddenly materialized outside her hut, demanding that she drive them to visit their cousins, cattle, and friends. The car, people felt, was not really hers; she might be paying the rent for it, but she had not made it herself, so they were perfectly justified in expecting to share it. Realizing that if she refused these requests her last few days in Kenya would be impossible but that if she gave in to them she would never make her plane, she canceled the car reservation, dragged her bags down to the red dirt road, and waited for a *matatu* instead.[63]

My wife's friend's problem was a uniquely modern one, but for most foragers in history there have been good, practical reasons to accede to demand sharing. After all, if there is no way for a hunter who makes a big kill to store the meat for his own or his immediate family's future use, why not share today's abundance, in the hope that someone who benefits from your generosity now will reciprocate in the future?

Forager egalitarianism partially breaks down, though, when it comes to gender hierarchy. All over the world, both sexes tend to take it for granted that men should be in charge in forager societies. I already quoted an Ona informant as saying that "the men are all captains and the women are sailors," and Nisa, a female !Kung San forager made famous by the anthropologist Marjorie Shostak's book named after her, apparently agreed. When an inexperienced teenage girl needed reassurance about her upcoming wedding, Nisa told her that "A man is not something that kills you, he is someone who marries you, who becomes like your father or your older brother."[64]

Social scientists continue to argue over why men normally hold the upper hand in forager societies.[65] After all, evolutionists point out, biology seems to have dealt women better cards. Sperm and eggs are both essential to reproduction, but sperm are abundant (the typical young man produces about one thousand per second) and therefore cheap, while eggs are scarce (the typical young woman makes one per month) and therefore expensive. Women ought to be able to demand all kinds of services from men in return for access to their eggs. To some extent, this does happen, and male foragers contribute substantially more to childrearing than male chimpanzees, bonobos, gorillas, or orangutans (our genetic nearest neighbors). However, some anthropologists speculate, the reason that the price women can demand almost never includes political or economic authority is that semen is not the only thing male foragers are selling. Because men are also the main providers of violence, women need to bargain for protection; because men are the main hunters, women need to bargain for meat; and because hunting together often trains men to cooperate and trust one another, individual women often find themselves negotiating with cartels of men.

Whatever the details, though, the outcome is clear enough: forager bands are male-dominated, but rarely have steep gender hierarchies. Abused wives regularly just walk away from their husbands without much fuss or criticism, and attitudes toward marital fidelity and premarital female virginity tend to be quite relaxed. As Nisa saw it, "When you are a woman, you don't just sit still and do nothing—you have lovers."[66] Promiscuity certainly does cause problems, and can lead to wifebeating and fighting between male rivals for a woman's affections, but people who are seen as overreacting to infidelity will be mocked, and sexual escapades rarely lead to permanent stigma.[67]

The shallowness of gender hierarchies and the weakness of marital ties, like the shallowness and weakness of economic and political hierarchies, seem to be a direct consequence of the nature of foraging as a method of energy extraction. The food that women gather is vitally important, especially near the equator, where plants make up such a large proportion of most foragers' diets, but the ethos of sharing normally means that all members of a group will have access to this. The main reason that male foragers generally care less than male farmers about controlling women—and particularly about controlling women's reproduction—is that foragers have much less to inherit than farmers. For most foraging societies, wild foods are equally available to all, regardless of who their parents are. Consequently, material success depends much more on skill at hunting, gathering, and coalition-building than on physical property that can be passed down between generations, which in turn means that questions about the legitimacy of children matter a lot less than they do when only legitimate offspring will inherit land and capital.

That said, arguments between men over women do seem more likely to end violently among foragers than among farmers (and much more likely than among fossil-fuel users). Some anthropologists do dispute this, arguing that when male foragers fight over women they are "really" arguing about access to food or territory, with women just providing flashpoints and a convenient language for talking about more profound rivalries.[68] No doubt there are cases in which that is true, but on the whole, foragers are so consistent in blaming violence on men's arguments over women that it is hard not to suspect that they know what they are talking about. Among the Yanomami and Waorani (who both live in the Upper Amazon and combine horticulture and foraging), there is even evidence that men who are more violent have more sexual partners and children than men who are less violent.[69]

Arguments over women seem to drive foraging men to violence more often than they drive farmers or fossil-fuel users to that same end because arguments of *all* kinds drive foragers to violence alarmingly often. The data are hotly disputed, but in the last twenty years, more and more anthropologists have recognized that the average forager in the twentieth century faced at least a 10 percent likelihood of dying violently.[70] In some groups (the horticultural Yanomami and Waorani are the best studied), more than one man in four met a grisly end.[71] The archaeological evidence, which is the only way we can know for sure whether such levels of lethal violence were also normal in prehistory, is particularly difficult to interpret, but the frequency of fatal traumas (at least 27 examples are known from Neanderthal skeletons, and 19 from early modern humans) is certainly consistent with the picture of high rates of violent death.[72]

Forager bands vary in their use of violence, as they vary in almost everything, but it took anthropologists a long time to realize how rough hunter-gatherers could be. This was not because the ethnographers all got lucky and visited peculiarly peaceful foraging folk, but because the social scale imposed by foraging is so small that even high rates of murder are difficult for outsiders to detect. If a band with a dozen members has a 10 percent rate of violent death, it will suffer roughly one homicide every twenty-five years; and since anthropologists rarely stay in the field for even twenty-five months, they will witness very few violent deaths. It was this demographic reality that led Elizabeth Marshall Thomas to title her sensitive 1959 ethnography of the !Kung *The Gentle People*[73]—even though their murder rate was much the same as what Detroit would endure at the peak of its crack cocaine epidemic. Anthropologists certainly heard plenty of stories about killing, but they also heard plenty of foragers express fear about violence, and not until the 1990s did they put the clues together to reveal the gruesome reality.

Humans, like most animals, have evolved biologically in ways that make violence one of the tools at their disposal for settling disputes.[74] That said, only a psychopath would try to solve *every* problem confronting him with violence,[75] and would soon find himself isolated and confronted by coalitions that could respond with much greater violence.[76] People are—very sensibly—afraid of violence, and will take steps to make its use unattractive. In complex societies, as Thomas Hobbes recognized in *Leviathan*, the most important of these steps is the creation of a centralized government, with a monopoly over the legitimate use of force, which can punish wrongdoers. Foragers, though, with their shallow political hierarchies, cannot establish such governments; and although mockery, ostracism, criticism, and moving away do work most of the time (Hobbes's vision of life before Leviathan as a "warre of all against all" was purely a thought experiment), they fail often enough that more than one forager in ten dies violently. All too often, when passions run really high—particularly when people are trying to deal with unrepentant upstarts—violence can look like the least bad course of action.

While foragers rarely explicitly condone violence, they do typically recognize multiple situations in which men are expected to use force to solve problems. This might take the form of a sudden outburst of murderous rage, or it can morph into a cycle of tit-for-tat revenge killings, passed down through multiple generations. Sometimes it even turns into a kind of Stone Age *Murder on the Orient Express*,[77] in which an entire community agrees that the only way to put down an upstart is to work together to kill him.[78] None of these situations arises very often in a typical foraging society, but there is nonetheless general agreement that there are times when homicide is legitimate, and that people (nearly always men) who use force in these contexts should not be stigmatized.

Overall, then, most foragers share a very striking set of egalitarian values. They take an extremely negative view of political and economic hierarchy but accept fairly mild forms of gender hierarchy and recognize that there is a time and a place for violence.

The reason these values are so widely shared by foragers is that they are fairly direct consequences of the economic and social constraints created by foraging as a method of capturing energy. In tiny groups of highly mobile hunter-gatherers, creating and maintaining steep political, economic, or gender hierarchies is very difficult, as is managing relationships without occasional resort to violence. Foragers, like everyone else, have free will, and we must assume that over the tens of thousands of years in which all humans were foragers, people tried out pretty much every permutation that can be imagined. Over time, though, most groups evolved toward the ethical equilibrium described earlier, in which values conformed to material realities. The precise balancing point varies from one society to another, with geography explaining much of the variation (and particularly the anomalies we see in the relatively large, rich, and sedentary groups of the Pacific Northwest), but we can certainly identify what Weber would have called an ideal-typical set of forager values. Only in the last ten thousand years, since farming came into the world, have these values gone into decline.

CHAPTER 3

FARMERS

Who Farmers Are

Farmers are people whose most important source of energy is domesticated plants and animals. At the start of chapter 2, I quoted Catherine Panter-Brick's definition of foragers as people who "exercise no deliberate alteration of the *gene pool* of exploited resources" and consequently "live in small groups, and . . . move around a lot";[1] farmers, by contrast, do deliberately alter the gene pool of exploited resources, live in large (often very large) groups, and move around rather little. In foragers' mobile but tiny bands, the places change but the faces stay the same; in farmers' static but big villages, the faces change but the places stay the same.

The key to farming is alteration of the gene pool of exploited resources, which botanists and zoologists normally call "domestication." By this, they mean that humans interfere in other species' reproduction sufficiently to create selective pressures that lead these other species to evolve into entirely new species, which can only go on reproducing themselves with continued human intervention.

Domesticated wheat, which is nowadays humanity's leading source of vegetable protein,[2] is the classic example, although similar genetic processes were involved with other plants and animals in different parts of the world. Wild wheat is an annual plant; when it ripens, its rachis (the little stalks attaching each seed to the plant) weaken and one by one its seeds fall to the ground, where their protective husks shatter and they germinate. Each year, roughly one wild wheat plant per 1 to 2 million produces a random mutation on a single gene that strengthens its rachis, meaning that when its seeds ripen, they do not fall to the ground, and cannot pass on their genes. As a result, these mutant plants disappear from the gene pool (to be replaced by new, random mutants in the next generation). But when human foragers start interfering with the wild wheat's gene pool by harvesting plants and replanting some of their seeds, at least some of these mutant plants *will* pass their genes on, and, very slowly, the proportion of mutants in the gene pool will grow. Computer simulations suggest that in theory, it could take as little as a couple of hundred years for the mutants to replace the original wild plants entirely, although archaeological evidence suggests that in reality it took a couple of thousand. The new—domesticated—wheat can then reproduce only if humans go on harvesting and replanting it, and that is what humans did, because their labor—agriculture—yielded far more calories than foragers could capture by gathering wild wheat. Domesticated plants and animals were the original genetically modified organisms.[3]

The category of "farming" subsumes even more variety than that of "foraging," which is why this chapter is so much longer than chapter 2. The category of "farmers" also has many transitional cases that blur its boundaries. I spent some time in chapter 2 talking about the "foraging spectrum" that runs from very small, mobile, and unstructured groups such as the African !Kung to large, sedentary, and highly structured groups such as the Kwakiutl of the Pacific Northwest. To do justice to farming societies, though, we have to think not of a spectrum but of something more like a three-pointed star (figure 3.1).

At one point are tiny groups such as the South American Machiguenga (whom I mentioned briefly in chapter 2), who, despite having some access to domesticated plants and animals, live much like foragers. Anthropologists typically call such societies "horticultural-ists" or just "food cultivators."[4] The second point is provided by wildly different eighteenth-century AD agrarian states such as Qing dynasty China, Mughal India, Ottoman Turkey, and Enlightenment Western Europe and its overseas settler colonies, some of which were stand-ing at the brink of an industrial revolution; and the third point by small, highly commercial city-states such as classical Athens, medieval Venice, or some of the oases of central Asia, which in certain ways have as much in common with fossil-fuel societies as with farming societies. In the center of the star is the ideal-type peasant society.

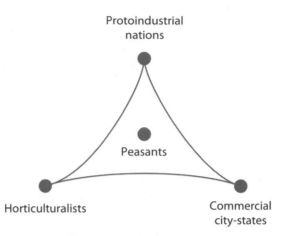

FIGURE 3.1. The farming three-pointed star: each point represents a different kind of extreme case, from horticulturalists to commercial city-states or protoindustrial nations, while the center represents the ideal-type peasant society.

Anthropologists have paid much attention to the distinction between horticulturalists and peasants, usually seeing the rise of a distinct ruling elite as marking the boundary between the two. "It is only when a cultivator is integrated into a society with a state," the anthropologist Eric Wolf suggested in his influential book *Peasants*, "that is, when the cultivator becomes subject to the demands and sanctions of power-holders outside his social stratum . . . that we can appropriately speak of peasantry."[5] Historical sociologists and political scientists have paid at least as much attention to the differences between peasants and the subjects of protoindustrial nations,[6] but the ways in which city-state dwellers differ from peasants have received rather less attention.[7]

As in the case of foragers, though, the exceptions and subcategories should not be allowed to obscure the reality of an ideal type representing in abstract terms the core features of peasant farming society. So strong are the cross-cultural similarities that in 1954, in a lecture comparing three peasant societies (seventh-century BC Greece, nineteenth-century AD southern England,

and 1930s Mexico), the anthropologist Robert Redfield even felt able to suggest that

> if a peasant from any one of these three widely separated communities could have been transported by some convenient genie to any one of the others and equipped with a knowledge of the language in the village to which he had been moved, he would very quickly come to feel at home. And this would be because the fundamental orientations of life would be unchanged. The compass of his career would continue to point to the same moral north.[8]

I will spend most of this chapter describing these "fundamental orientations of life."

Like foraging, farming emerged in a particular place—in this case, what archaeologists call the "Hilly Flanks" (see figure 3.2; basically, an arc curving up through the Jordan Valley to the Turkish border and then back down along the Iraq-Iran frontier)—at a particular time (roughly ten thousand to fifteen thousand years ago), and then spread across the rest of the planet. Where the foraging and farming expansions differed, though, was in their speed, scale, and thoroughness. It took more than fifty thousand years (from roughly 70,000 through 15,000 BC) for modern human foragers to spread from Africa into every suitable and accessible niche on the planet. In the process, global population increased roughly sixty-fold (from about fifty thousand people in 70,000 BC to 3 million in 15,000 BC), and prehumans went extinct everywhere. By contrast, it took farmers just eleven thousand years (from roughly 9500 BC through AD 1500) to colonize all the suitable and accessible niches, during which time the world's population grew ninety-fold, from about 5 million to 450 million. Foragers did not go extinct, but did decline from roughly 99 percent of the world's population around 9500 BC to about 1 percent in AD 1800.[9] By then, farmers had made up the majority of the world's population for at least five thousand years.

FIGURE 3.2. Locations and social groups mentioned in chapter 3.

The Evidence

The evidence for farming societies[10] comes from much the same sources (archaeology, historical texts, anthropology) as that for foragers, but the weighting of the categories is very different. Because all farming societies sooner or later invented or adopted writing, beginning around 3300 BC in what is now southern Iraq, we have enormous numbers of primary sources[11] for farming societies.

However, of the millions of texts that survive, most share a serious problem: their authors belonged to small, educated, and overwhelmingly male elites, and usually wrote for their own peers and purposes. Consequently, the primary historical sources tell us surprisingly little about the lives of the three-quarters or more of the population that actually did the farming. Even in the most literate ancient societies, such as classical Athens (fifth and fourth centuries BC) and late Republican Italy (first century BC), perhaps one male citizen in ten, and far fewer women, had rudimentary literacy skills. Not until the early second millennium AD did rates creep much above 10 percent, and even then probably only in Western Europe and urban China. Genuine mass literacy, with half or more of the population able to read simple sentences, belongs to the age of fossil fuels.[12]

Because of this, historians struggle to find ways to access ordinary farmers' lives. Primary texts provide occasional shafts of light, such as the records of the inquisitor Jacques Fournier (later Pope Benedict XII), who recorded interviews with peasants in the southern French village of Montaillou between AD 1294 and 1324;[13] but most of the time, our evidence for peasant experience comes from archaeology and accounts by twentieth-century anthropologists, rural sociologists, and development economists. Farming societies did produce a lot more material goods (some of them decorated with representational art) than foragers, and so the material record is at least very rich, but, like all archaeological evidence, it is mute and must be interpreted though analogy. Consequently, even though social scientists have provided rich detail on twentieth-century farmers, extrapolating from it to earlier farming societies presents the same problems as in the study of foraging societies.

Energy, Demography, and Social Organization

As was the case among foragers, much of the variety in the ways farmers fed and organized themselves was a function of geography. Initially, at the end of the last ice age the only people who could possibly become farmers were those who lived in places like the Hilly Flanks, where geographical conditions had favored the evolution of potentially domesticable large-grained grasses and big mammals.[14] Again like foragers, the people in these favored locations had to work with the plants and animals that happened to be there, which meant that while the first farmers in the Hilly Flanks domesticated wheat, barley, beans, sheep, goats, and cattle, those in East Asia domesticated millet, rice, pigs, and water buffaloes; those in Meso-america, squash and maize; those in the Andes, squash, peanuts, potatoes, llama, and alpaca; and those in New Guinea, bananas and taro. Each domesticated species yielded different nutrients and demanded different labor patterns.[15]

As population grew in these agricultural cores, people migrated out in search of new farmland, taking domesticated plants and animals from the cores with them. Slow-moving waves of migrants carried the Hilly Flanks' founder crops all the way to what is now France and also to Mehrgarh in modern Afghanistan, while other waves took Chinese crops to Japan and Borneo, and ultimately across Oceania.[16] Taking agriculture into new environments, however, opened new possibilities, and farmers gradually learned that great rivers—particularly the Euphrates, Tigris, Nile, Indus, and Yellow Rivers—could be turned to the purposes of irrigation, transport, and communication. This pushed yields and economic integration higher, and it was along these rivers that farmers built the first true cities, with populations running into the tens or occasionally the hundreds of thousands. Yet if having access to a great river was good for farming, having access to an entire sea was even better. In the late first millennium BC, the Roman Empire brought the whole Mediterranean basin under its control, and the city of Rome grew to a million residents. East Asia had no geographical feature quite like the Mediterranean,[17] but the Grand

Canal, which opened in AD 609, came to function something like a man-made Mediterranean, linking rice-producing South China to the cities and armies of North China. By AD 700, Chang'an also had a million residents.[18]

As each agricultural core grew, it went through a slow-motion explosion in energy capture. By the calculations I describe in my book *The Measure of Civilization*, the typical affluent forager on the eve of the first steps toward domestication (that is, around 10,000 BC in the Hilly Flanks, 8000 BC in East and South Asia, and 7000 BC in Mexico and Peru) captured something like 5,000 kilocalories per day (kcal/cap/day), roughly half of these coming as food and the rest going to fuel, clothing, shelter, industry, transport, and other activities. Roughly two millennia later, when horticultural villages were becoming established (around 8000 BC in the Hilly Flanks, 6000 BC in East and South Asia, and 5000 BC in Mexico and Peru), energy capture had risen to approximately 6,000 kcal/cap/day. Another three millennia took energy capture up to about 8,000 kcal/cap/day, as early farmers learned to exploit domesticated resources more and more effectively (around 5000 BC in the Hilly Flanks, 3500–3000 BC in South and East Asia, and 2000 BC in Mexico and Peru). These farmers found that planting cereals in a garden one year and protein-rich beans the next replenished the soil as well as varying their diet. Crushing cereals on coarse grindstones filled food with grit, which wore people's teeth down to stumps, so farmers learned to sieve out the impurities and to prepare grains in new ways. Herders, meanwhile, realized that instead of killing all their domesticated animals for meat while the animals were still young, they could keep some around for wool and milk and use their manure to fertilize fields. In Southwest Asia, which had more large, domesticated mammals than any other part of the world, people even learned to harness beasts to wheeled carts. Previously, moving anything had meant picking it up and carrying it, but an ox in harness delivered three times as much draft power as a man. By 4000 BC, domesticated animals and plants converged in the ox-drawn plow.[19]

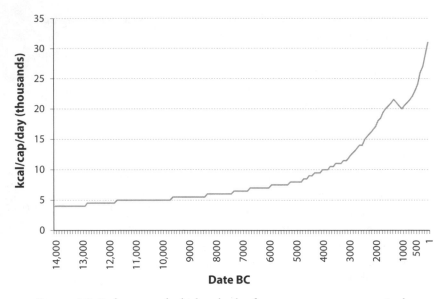

FIGURE 3.3. Peak energy: the highest levels of energy capture per person in the world, 14,000 BC–1 BC (from data in Morris 2013).

And that was just the beginning. By about 4000 BC in Mesopotamia and Egypt, 3000 BC in the Indus Valley, and 2500 BC in the Yellow River Valley, irrigation farmers were capturing something like 10,000 kcal/cap/day, and after another four millennia or so (by the first century AD in parts of the Roman Empire, by AD 1100 in Song dynasty China, and by AD 1700 perhaps in Mughal India too), energy capture had tripled again. The share of energy consumed as food did increase, from 2,000–2,500 kcal/cap/day at the origins of agriculture to something like 6,000–8,000 per day, but most of this increase came from substituting expensive calories (meat, alcohol, cultivated fruits, and so on) for cheap ones.[20] Most farmers remained stunted and poorly nourished across this whole ten-thousand-year history.[21] A sixfold increase in energy capture per person, to about 30,000 kcal/cap/day, appears to represent the outer limits of what could be done in a purely organic economy (figure 3.3).[22]

Because wild plants and animals provided them with so little energy, foragers had moved around constantly to find what they needed, but the steady increase in energy captured per acre of land occupied meant that most farmers did not have to do this. Some members of farming societies, it is true, were very mobile: herders moved flocks between winter and summer pastures, and in maritime, commercial city-states, an unquantifiable but probably quite large minority of people sometimes took to ships for voyages that might be more than a hundred miles long.[23] A few people clearly ranged much more widely than ever before; although foragers were constantly on the move, most stayed within a territory just a few dozen miles across, whereas by the fifth century BC Phoenician sailors had probably circumnavigated Africa. In the first two centuries AD, at least some Egyptian and Indian sailors regularly visited each other's homelands. The mitochondrial DNA of a man buried at Vagnari in Italy in the second century AD suggests that he came from East Asia, and Chinese texts seem to say that in AD 166 Roman ambassadors arrived at the Han capital at Luoyang.[24] By AD 1600, a handful of Europeans had sailed around the whole planet, and over the next two centuries trade turned truly global. On the other hand, while these globetrotters were setting new records, most farmers lived in worlds much smaller than most foragers had done, and never went much more than a day or two's walk from the villages they were born in. To the Hongwu emperor, who ruled China between AD 1368 and 1398, twenty *li* (roughly 7.5 miles) was as far as anyone should be going from home, and it is probably no coincidence that thirteenth-century English laws set just the same limit to "neighboring" (the distance from his village that a reasonable man would travel for a social call).[25]

Even though the primary sources from farming societies are full of tales of vagabonds, wandering minstrels, and young men striking out to make their fortunes, the sixfold increase in energy capture per person unleashed by agriculture in reality made footloose lifestyles increasingly difficult, because it fed an even greater growth in the scale of societies. Foraging landscapes normally supported less than one person per square mile, and in harsh environments, that could fall to one person per 10 square miles.[26] Farming societies, however, usually had densities above ten people per square mile. The thousand square miles of territory belonging to fifth-century BC Athens contained something like 350,000 people,[27] a density two or three orders of magnitude greater than the typical foraging society, and the irrigated farmlands of the Nile Valley and Yangzi and Ganges deltas probably surpassed this.

The size of individual settlements grew even faster. The chances are that no ice-age forager ever saw more than a few hundred people at one time, and even that would only have been when bands gathered together for a few days out of the year. By 7000 BC, however, about a thousand people were living year-round at Çatalhöyük in what is now Turkey; soon after 3500 BC, more than ten thousand had settled at Uruk in southern Iraq; by 700 BC, Nineveh in northern Iraq hosted a hundred thousand residents; and, as mentioned earlier, by AD 100 there were a million people—probably more than had been living in the whole world in 20,000 BC—at Rome, and by AD 700 the same number at Chang'an in China.[28] The Roman Empire and the contemporary Han Empire in China each had at least 60 million subjects; by AD 1600, Ming dynasty China had 160 million.

The steady increase in energy captured per acre of farmland made it possible to feed these millions of mouths, but it came at the price of constant, backbreaking labor.[29] The relatively leisured foragers of Sahlins's primitive affluent society make a striking contrast with the brutally overworked farmers documented by historians, anthropologists, and development economists. "Pile work with work upon more work," advised the ancient Greek poet Hesiod, whose *Works and Days* (composed around 700 BC) is our oldest surviving source purporting to describe life from a peasant's point of view.[30] Twenty-six centuries later, a priest in southern Italy concluded that "the peasant works in order to eat, he eats in order to have the strength to work; and then he sleeps."[31] Excavated skeletons suggest that ancient farmers tended to suffer more than foragers from repetitive stress injuries; their teeth were often terrible, thanks to restricted diets heavy on sugary carbohydrates; and their stature, which is a fairly good proxy for overall nutrition, tended to fall slightly with the onset of agriculture, not increasing noticeably until the twentieth century AD.[32]

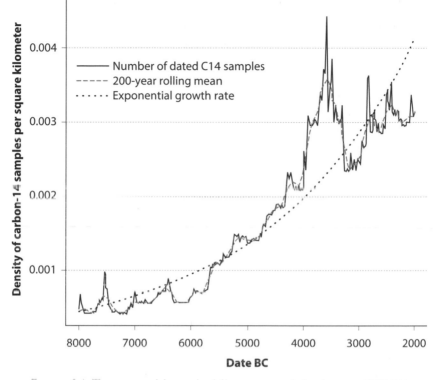

FIGURE 3.4. The exponential growth of European population between 8000 BC and 2000 BC, based on 13,658 published radiocarbon dates (after Shennan et al 2013). Amid a series of crashes and booms, the long-term trend was for population to double roughly every 1,600 years. (All dates in entire study area. Samples $N = 13,658$; bins $N = 6,497$.)

Just how hard a farmer had to work depended not only on where he lived and how rich he was but also on where he stood within the cycles of demographic boom and bust that characterized all agrarian societies. Like foragers, farmers rarely lived in balance with their environments. In Europe, the best-studied region, archaeological data suggest that while population grew exponentially between 8000 and 2000 BC, doubling every sixteen or so centuries, the detailed picture was much more dramatic, with sudden spikes followed by terrible crashes (figure 3.4).[33]

By the second millennium AD, richer evidence allows us to trace the patterns much more precisely. Population grew steadily during the warm, wet era beginning around AD 900 that climatologists call the "Medieval Warm Period." This forced farmers to work harder and harder, sharing the same fields among more hands or taking less fertile lands into cultivation; but between 1346 and 1400, the Black Death—which killed nearly half the continent's population—shifted the land-labor ratio back dramatically in the survivors' favor. Unskilled workers' real wages spiked up to unheard-of levels in the fifteenth century, but as population recovered, farmers once again began having to work harder for lower returns (shown in figure 5.8, later).[34] In eighteenth-century Europe, enlightened intellectuals found that peasants looked back on the fifteenth century as a golden age of leisure, cakes, and ale, in sharp contrast to the misery of their own days. Contemporary peasant villages, John Quincy Adams wrote home in 1800, were "meager composition[s] of mud and thatch . . . in which a ragged and pallid race of beggars reside. . . . The houses are generally full of children, clad in no other garb than a coarse shirt; oftentimes stark naked, and loaded with vermin like the land of Egypt at the last of its plagues."[35]

Even in the happiest phases of the demographic cycle, peasant life would have struck almost any visitor from the fossil-fuel world as nasty, brutish, and poor. Anton Chekhov's grim short story "Peasants," published in 1897, is a case in point. Its antihero, one Nikolay Tchikildyeev, was a poor waiter in Moscow until illness forced him to move back to his ancestral village, but even such a simple man, Chekhov says, was one "who was worn out [on returning to the countryside] by the everlasting hubbub, hunger, stifling fumes, filth, who hated and despised the poverty, who was ashamed for his wife and daughter to see his father and mother."[36] But while there is no reason to doubt Chekhov's grasp of the squalor of peasant life, we should remember that it was at least not as squalid as forager life. The economist Angus Maddison estimated that ancient and medieval peasants typically supported themselves on the equivalent of $1.50 to $2.20 per day—not much, to be sure, but more than the equivalent of $1.10 per day that foragers had to survive on.[37] My own estimates of energy capture suggest that the gap might have been bigger still, with really prosperous farming societies such as the Roman Empire or Song dynasty China enjoying income levels five or six times higher than the most prosperous foragers.[38] Even Chekhov's miserable Tchikildyeevs had a cottage, and inside it a samovar, with tea to put in it and a stove to heat it on.[39]

But while farming societies were more prosperous than those of foragers, they were also *much* more hierarchical. As we saw in chapter 2, under certain conditions (like those prevailing in the eighteenth-century Pacific Northwest, or prehistoric Japan or the Baltic region) wealth can be quite unequally distributed in foraging societies, but this is dwarfed by what happens in farming societies. The earliest case for which we have actual statistics is the Roman Empire, and here some people were astonishingly rich. A certain C. Caecilius Isidorus left at his death in 8 BC 3,600 pairs of oxen, 257,000 other animals, 4,116 slaves, and 60 million sesterces in cash (enough to feed half a million people for a year). Around the same time, a senior military man named L. Tarius Rufus lost 100 million sesterces when a single property deal went wrong,[40] and the historian Chris Wickham suggests that by the fourth century AD, the greatest families—the Anicii, Petronii, and Caeonii—"may have been the richest private landowners of all time."[41]

By the best estimate, the Roman Empire's Gini wealth coefficient in the first century AD was somewhere between 0.42 and 0.44, which, given Rome's level of technology and productivity, means that the Roman elite (comprising something like 10 percent of the population) was extracting wealth from the rest of the Romans at roughly 80 percent of the theoretical maximum possible rate of exploitation.[42] This Gini score is much higher than the foragers' average (mentioned in chapter 2) of 0.25 (figure 3.5), but Roman inequality seems to have been quite typical of that found in farming societies. Another study, comparing thirteen agrarian states, calculated an average Gini score of 0.45,[43] and the same team of anthropologists that calculated the low scores for foraging groups found that the average Gini coefficient among the eight small-scale peasant communities in their sample was 0.48.[44] (The team also studied four horticultural groups and found—not surprisingly—an average score of 0.27, just slightly higher than the foragers' score.)[45]

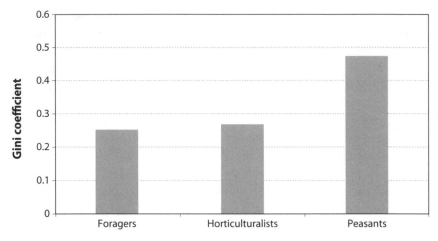

FIGURE 3.5. The measure of inequality: the average Gini coefficients of wealth inequality calculated for foragers (0.25), horticulturalists (0.27), and peasants (0.48) by Smith et al. (2010). The Roman Empire scored roughly 0.42–0.44; around AD 1800, England and France scored 0.59.

Such societies—more crowded and prosperous than those of foragers, but less equal—were only possible because farming simultaneously enabled and required a huge leap in the complexity of the division of labor. The most obvious feature of this was the creation of economic enterprises far bigger than the family, and I will come back to these in a moment; but before looking at such large-scale organizations, I first need to emphasize that the family did remain the basic building block in farming economies, just as it had been in foraging societies. The internal structure of families, however, changed beyond all recognition.

Two main forces were at work. The first was the nature of labor itself. In foraging societies, women usually did most of the plant gathering and men most of the hunting. This sexual division of labor did not usually change very much in horticultural societies, where hunting and gathering remained important and farmwork was fairly light. Land that could be used for gardens was in many places quite abundant while labor was relatively scarce, and horticulturalists would work large areas lightly, with men and women hoeing and weeding together. But as population grew, making land scarcer relative to labor, people worked it more intensively, squeezing more output from each acre through the heavy labor of plowing, manuring, and even irrigating. The further that a society went in this direction, the more men's upper body strength became a plus in farmwork, and the more people began to define outdoor activities as men's work.[46]

This long-term shift must have been important in pushing women out of the fields, but a second force, demography, was probably even more important in pulling women into the home. Before the invention of farming, population had on average doubled every ten thousand years, but after agriculture began, the doubling time fell to less than two thousand years. Farmwives had a lot more babies than female foragers—so many more that some prehistorians speak of a "Neolithic demographic transition."[47] The typical woman in a farming society carried seven babies to term, spending most of her adult life pregnant or minding small children,[48] and since these activities would be very difficult for women who were pushing plows, demography and the patterns of labor conspired to separate male/outdoor and female/indoor spheres.

Because (1) the foods produced by farmers often required more processing (threshing, sifting, grinding, baking, and so on) than those brought home by foragers; (2) the increasingly permanent homes that farmers built required a lot more upkeep and cleaning than foragers' temporary shelters; and (3) these activities could be done in the home by women supervising small children, the logic of farming pointed toward a new sexual division of labor and space. The conclusion that farmers all over the world apparently reached was that men should go out to work in the fields while women stayed home to work in the house. So obvious did this decision seem, in fact, that no farming society that moved beyond horticulture ever seems to have decided anything else.[49]

A study of 162 skeletons from Abu Hureyra in Syria suggests that the gendered restructuring of labor was already well under way in the Hilly Flanks by 7000 BC. Both men and women had enlarged vertebrae in their upper backs, probably from carrying heavy loads on their heads, but only women had a distinctive arthritic condition caused by spending long periods kneeling and using their toes as a base to apply force, probably while grinding grain.[50]

Abu Hureyra was a very simple farming society, but even in the Roman Empire, arguably the most sophisticated of all preindustrial economies,[51] surprisingly little changed. As late as the 160s BC, said the geographer Pliny the Elder, there had been no commercial bakeries in the city of Rome, because women had baked all the bread at home.[52] First- and second-century AD inscriptions suggest that just one in seven paid workers outside the home was female,[53] and only 35 occupations are listed for women, as opposed to 225 for men. The classicist Susan Treggiari concluded that "Women appear to be concentrated in 'service' jobs (catering, prostitution); dealing, particularly in foodstuffs; serving in shops; in certain crafts, particularly the production of cloth and clothes; 'fiddly' jobs such as working in gold-leaf or hairdressing; certain luxury trades such as perfumery."[54]

In twentieth-century preindustrial farming societies, anthropologists and sociologists typically found strong correlations between the intensity of agricultural practices, the importance of inheritance, and male obsession with female sexual purity.[55] This too seems to be a consequence of the logic of agriculture. Foragers share their knowledge with the young, teaching them how to find ripe plants, wild game, and safe campsites, but farmers have something much more concrete to pass on: property. To flourish in a farming world, people need a house, fields, and flocks, not to mention wells, walls, and tools, and improvements such as weeding, watering, terracing, and removing stones. Inheriting property from older generations literally becomes a matter of life and death, and with so much at stake, peasant men want to be sure that they are the fathers of the children who will inherit their property. Foragers' rather casual attitudes about sex yield to ferocious policing of daughters' premarital virginity (the "symbol of symbols," one anthropologist of southern Italy called it in the 1950s)[56] and wives' extramarital activities. Peasant men tended to marry around the age of thirty, after they had come into their inheritance, while women generally married around fifteen, before they had had much time to stray.

We cannot be certain that these patterns go back to the dawn of agriculture, but there are several hints that they do. Many early farming societies seem to have been obsessed with ancestors, and even to have worshipped them as supernatural beings. Several sites in the Hilly Flanks have apparent ancestor cults (strange semisubterranean rooms containing jawless human skulls) going back to 10,000 BC, just as domestication was beginning. By 7000 BC, people at Jericho, Çatalhöyük, and numerous other sites were burying their ancestors under their house floors while cutting off and keeping their heads, often coating the skulls with painted plaster and passing them around for generations.[57] By this time, girls in the Hilly Flanks probably no longer lived like the !Kung forager Nisa. Instead, they grew up under the authority of their fathers and then, as teenagers, exchanged that for the authority of husbands old enough to be their fathers.[58]

Twentieth-century ethnographies and historical sources as well as archaeological traces of weaving, metalworking, pottery production, and other activities all seem to suggest that most material goods, in most farming societies, were produced within the household.[59] The ancient Greek farmer-poet Hesiod assumed that farmers would make everything they possibly could at home, rather than buying, bartering, or borrowing outside the household.[60] His *Works and Days* describes a strongly gendered craft system, with women responsible above all for weaving cloth while men made tools in the agricultural off-season (he provides quite detailed advice on how to build carts and plows) [61]

Despite his commitment to self-sufficiency, however, Hesiod recognized that no farm family could do everything for itself, and the intensification of the gendered division of labor within households went hand-in-hand with increasing specialization between households. Hesiod took it for granted that there would be a village blacksmith (a hub for malicious gossip, to be avoided as far as possible) and that households would specialize in particular crafts, exchanging goods in marketplaces and competing with each other.[62] "Potter is angry at potter, craftsman at craftsman," he famously sang; even "beggar envies beggar and minstrel minstrel."[63] Archaeology suggests that specialists (particularly in the manufacture of high-quality stone tools and weapons) became important very early in the history of farming society.[64]

Some families specialized in providing services. Religious experts probably go back to the earliest days of farming; excavators have plausibly suggested that an elderly, crippled woman buried at Hilazon Tachtit in Israel around 10,000 BC along with fifty tortoise shells, and parts of the bodies of a wild boar, an eagle, a cow, a leopard, two martens, and—disturbingly—someone else's foot was a shaman, believed to be able to travel between this world and a supernatural sphere.[65] Priestly families were a commonplace in agricultural societies, but houses specializing in a wide range of other services are also well documented. Nineteenth-century BC clay tablets from Kanesh in modern-day Turkey reveal Assyrian family firms running long-distance trade networks, and in sixth- and fifth-century BC Babylon, families such as the Murashûs and Egibis ran impressive commercial operations, leaving behind substantial archives.[66] A millennium and a half later, very similar family firms were running even more sophisticated financial and trading operations out of Cairo, Genoa, and Hangzhou in China.[67]

Specialization by household, though, was just the beginning of the ways that the sheer scale of farming societies both required and made possible a more complex division of labor. Many of the tasks that have to be performed in large farming societies are beyond the capacity of household-level organization. Obviously, Egyptians could not have built their pyramids or Romans their roads if only the architects' brothers and cousins had showed up for work. Tasks of this magnitude called for bigger, suprafamilial organizations, going far beyond Shoshone rabbit hunts in their structure and permanence.[68]

Farming societies found many ways to organize work above the household level.[69] Some farming societies organize kin groups larger than the family to provide big workforces to meet ritual obligations,[70] and some of prehistory's most impressive monuments, including Stonehenge, may have been built in this way.[71] As a system for staffing permanent, large-scale organizations, though, kinship seems to have had strict limits, and those farming societies that have left written records seem to have relied more heavily on two other institutions.

The first was the market, through which workers sold their labor for wages, whether in coin or in kind. Hesiod seems to speak of hired hands on his farm,[72] but wage labor goes back much further. The Third Dynasty of Ur, which ruled much of Mesopotamia between about 2200 and 2000 BC, paid salaries (often translated as "rations") to laborers in state-owned workshops and bakeries. One of these facilities, a textile operation in the city of Lagash, had six thousand employees.[73] Two thousand years later, the tens of thousands of men who built Rome's gleaming marble monuments and unloaded the grain ships that kept the city's million residents fed (not to mention the 350,000 soldiers serving in Rome's armies) were mostly wage laborers,[74] and in medieval and early modern times, the market may have been the commonest mechanism for mobilizing labor above the household level everywhere from England to Japan.[75]

That said, entrepreneurs in farming societies (whether based in the countryside or in the city) complained constantly about the difficulty of drawing reliable labor into the market solely through wages. On the whole, they found, anyone who had enough land to support a family preferred to make a living by working it rather than by selling labor. What the economic historian Gavin Wright says of one of the most developed of these agrarian economics—the early nineteenth-century American South—probably applies even more strongly to earlier farming societies:

> The family farm provided a substantial measure of security—against starvation, unemployment, or old-age destitution. In an era of undeveloped and risky financial institutions, the family farm provided a means of accumulating wealth in a reasonably safe form—the wealth being largely the product of the family's own labor in land clearing, fencing, drainage, etc.—and self-cultivation helped ensure that the earnings from this wealth were continuous and fell into the proper hands.[76]

The basic problem was that the low output per premodern farm-hand meant that the marginal product of labor—that is, the gain to an employer from hiring an extra worker—was often too small to make wages attractive to people who had any alternative means of support-ing themselves.[77] Hence the appeal of the second great alternative to kinship as a method to mobilize more workers than the family could supply: forced labor. Using violence to depress the costs of labor to the point that its marginal product became positive for employers made slavery and serfdom the obvious answers to the labor market's failures.[78]

Forced labor was almost unknown within foraging societies. Hor-ticulturalists often took slaves in raids and wars, but these captives (especially the women) were normally incorporated fairly rapidly into their captors' kinship structures—unlike the slaves in many of the more developed farming societies, who remained permanent, subjugated outsiders.[79] Farming societies seem to have shifted toward forced labor because they had to: neither kinship nor the market could generate the labor needed to build the ships, harbors, roads, temples, and monuments without which their (relatively) huge popu-lations could not have fed themselves or maintained their societies. In a classic paper published in 1959, the ancient historian Moses Finley asked "Was Greek civilization based on slave labor?"[80] The answer, he concluded, was yes, and, if we broaden the question to include forced labor of all kinds, Finley's answer applies (to varying degrees) to all farming societies. In extreme cases, of which classical Athens was one, as many as one person in three was a chattel slave, and few if any farming societies did without slavery or serfdom altogether.[81] Forced labor, like patriarchy, was functionally necessary to farming societies that generated more than 10,000 kcal/cap/day.

A sunnier side of the increasing division of labor, though, was the professionalization of intellectual life, which massively expanded the stock of knowledge. One of the greatest achievements of twentieth-century anthropology was to show just how sophisticated intellectual life could be among preliterate foragers, but what the cultural elites of farming societies accomplished was on a different plane altogether. The key to their success was literacy, itself largely a side effect of the increasing professionalization of management. At the eastern and western ends of Eurasia, which have the fullest archaeological records, a few people seem to have begun using symbols to keep household accounts in the very earliest stages of domestication (around 9000

BC in Mesopotamia and 6250 BC in China),[82] but another five to six millennia would pass before more specialized bureaucrats turned these into systems that we can really call writing.

In Mesoamerica, no proto-writing associated with domestication has yet been found, but the first proper writing systems go back to the first millennium BC, roughly the same length of time after farming was established as the oldest full systems from Mesopotamia and China.[83] However, the development of a literate elite culture in the New World then lagged behind that in the Old, where the third millennium BC saw the rise of highly sophisticated scholarship in Egypt, the Levant, and Mesopotamia, and the first millennium BC saw similar developments in India and China. Anthropologists continue to argue over whether writing enabled people to think in entirely new ways,[84] but the specialized educational systems and huge investments in human capital behind the extraordinary academic advances that the Old World made in the age of farming would have been impossible without it.

The increasingly elaborate division of labor in farming societies ultimately depended on one more kind of specialist: the masters of violence, who converted a comparative advantage in killing to control over politics. In each of the areas where agriculture was invented, people seem to have got by for a good three or four millennia without the help of governments that monopolized legitimate violence, but in every case, by the time that energy capture rose above about 10,000 kcal/cap/day and towns grew past about 10,000 souls, a few people had taken charge. This happened somewhere around 3500 BC in Mesopotamia, 2500 BC in the Indus Valley, 1900 BC in northern China, and 100 BC in Mesoamerica and the Andes.[85]

Almost always, one member of the new elite made himself king over all the others, but to hang on to his throne, he invariably had to form broader coalitions, turning would-be rivals into supporters. To coopt these near-peers, the ruler normally confirmed them as aristocrats with legal title to huge estates, and to make themselves indispensable to the ruler, his noblemen normally repackaged themselves as useful specialists in religion, law, letters, or war. Working together, these different kinds of elites could coordinate the larger society's activities by raising taxes, enforcing laws, performing rituals, fighting neighbors, suppressing uprisings, and all of the other government activities that fill the annals of ancient and medieval history.[86]

Figure 3.6, drawn by the anthropologist-cum-philosopher Ernest Gellner, is a highly abstract but very helpful summary of the general outcome. Gellner called this ideal-type farming society "Agraria,"[87] and suggested that in this mythical but typical community, "the ruling class forms a small minority of the population, rigidly separate from the great majority of direct agricultural producers, or peasants." A double line in the diagram marks this rigid mass-elite division, while single lines mark the ruling class's internal divisions, between specialists in military, administrative, clerical, and other tasks, with their own hierarchical ranking and legally defined boundaries.

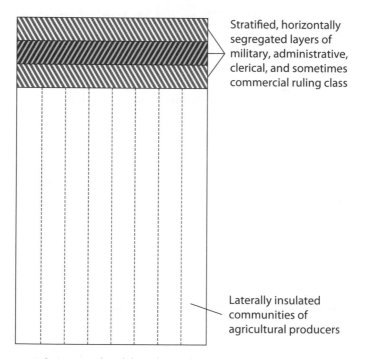

FIGURE 3.6. Agraria: the philosopher-anthropologist Ernest Gellner's ideal-type model of agrarian states (after Gellner 1983).

"Below the horizontally stratified minority at the top," Gellner explained, "there is another world, that of the laterally insulated petty communities of the lay members of society"—that is, peasant villages. Gellner described these as "laterally insulated" because peasants do not get out much; through most of history, most farmers probably stayed within walking distance of their birthplace. In Agraria, peasants in each district tend to have their own dialects, rituals, and traditions—living, says Gellner, "inward-turned lives." The broken vertical lines in the diagram symbolize the fragmentation of the peasant world, in sharp contrast to the bigger world in which its rulers live. In the Roman version of Agraria, for instance, an emperor, a senator, or a well-paid professor could travel from Britain to Syria, eating larks' tongues, drinking Falernian wine, making small talk in Greek and Latin, and dropping the same witty allusions to Homer and Virgil in every villa he stopped at. The peasants on his hosts' estates, however, could not have gone more than twenty or thirty miles without finding themselves in effect in a foreign country. "The state," Gellner observes, "is interested in extracting taxes, maintaining the peace, and not much else, and has no interest in promoting lateral communication between its subject communities."[88] One agrarian aristocrat after another confirmed this: "We knew as much about the Tula countryside," said the Russian Prince Lvov (who spent the 1890s in Tula), "as we knew about Central Africa."[89]

The sociologist John Hall showed in his book *Powers and Liberties* that imperial Chinese, Mughal Indian, and medieval Muslim and Christian societies can all be made to fit rather easily into variants on Gellner's box,[90] but, as Gellner recognized, there are also cases for which figure 3.6 is a much less comfortable match. "The Agrarian Age," he suggested, "was basically a period of stagnation, oppression, and superstition," and yet, he added, "Exceptions do occur, but we are all inclined, as in the case of classical Greece, to call them 'miracles.'"[91]

The miraculous exceptions, as Gellner observed, were mostly city-states.[92] In the farming societies of later prehistory, networks of such city-states were probably common: in Egypt, Mesopotamia, the

Indus and Ganges Valleys, the Yellow River Valley, Peru, Yucatan, and the Valley of Mexico, city-state networks seem to have flourished until one city-state outgrew the others, conquered them, and swallowed them up into a larger Agraria. In some cases, though, particularly in Europe and the Mediterranean (ancient Phoenicia, Greece, and Italy; medieval Italy, Flanders, and the Baltic) and the oases of central Asia and the Sahara, city-state systems survived and even flourished into historically documented periods around the edges of the great empires.[93]

Nearly all these textually documented city-states shared one important feature: a commercial, and usually maritime, orientation. This eased some of the constraints imposed on other societies by the limits of agricultural energy capture. Athens, for instance, imported most of its food in the fourth century BC, using its position at the center of extensive trade networks to increase dramatically the energy available per person. This not only made possible the high population densities mentioned earlier in this chapter but also sustained economic growth (per capita consumption may have doubled between 800 and 300 BC), leading to real wages that would rarely be matched until the age of fossil fuels. Literacy rates were also extraordinarily high, and Athens enjoyed a cultural explosion that earned it the label "classical."[94]

In many ways, classical Athens, medieval Venice, and several other city-states can seem more modern than agrarian.[95] The contrast between figure 3.7 (my own attempt to squeeze—or fail to squeeze—classical Athens into Gellner's format)[96] and figure 3.6 is strong. Athens, like most other prosperous, commercial, maritime city-states, lacked Agraria's small, highly distinct stratified elite, rigidly separated from a great mass of peasants. Instead, it had only a weakly stratified upper class, marked off by wealth but not by legal distinctions from equally weakly laterally insulated groups of fellow-citizens.[97] In Athens and dozens of other Greek examples, stratification was so weak that the state was run not by a king or even by a commercial oligarchy, but by what Greeks called a *dēmokratia*, a democracy of the entire male citizen body.[98]

Not surprisingly, wealth hierarchies were relatively low. By my calculations, the Gini score for landholding in fourth-century BC Athens was just 0.38–0.39, and the ancient historian Josiah Ober estimates that overall Athenian income inequality (for the whole resident population, including slaves) in the late fourth century BC stood at 0.40–0.45[99]—comfortably below the average of 0.48 that Smith et al. calculated for income inequality in agrarian societies. Wealth was generally seen as good in a way that it was not in foraging societies. Some Athenians were very rich indeed by Greek standards, but the average real wage was also unusually high, and the remains of excavated houses suggest that classical Greeks lived much better than most people in farming societies.[100]

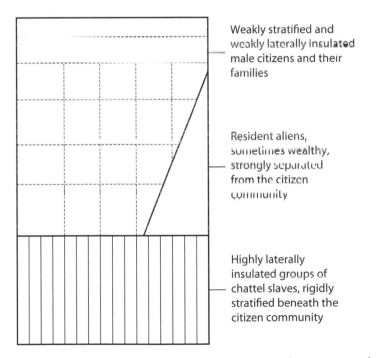

FIGURE 3.7. The Greek miracle: one version of how commercial city-states remade Agraria (after Morris 1997).

Even so, Athens still had much in common with Agraria. Athenian citizens were the top group in a profoundly hierarchical system, and below the weakly stratified and weakly laterally insulated citizenry was another world, that of the highly laterally insulated chattel slaves, who, as mentioned earlier, probably made up one-third of the population in the fourth century BC. In spite of the energy bonanza unleashed by Mediterranean trade, forced labor remained functionally necessary to Athens and all other Greek city-states. Athens in fact had one of the strictest slave systems on record, with very low rates of manumission and a requirement that the state's top decision-making body (the citizen assembly) must vote on every single attempt to confer citizenship on a freed slave. It also had one of the steepest systems of gender inequality in the ancient world. No woman ever held citizenship in a classical Greek city.[101]

Rather than abolishing the boundaries within Agraria, the city-state miracle consisted of broadening the elite. In classical Athens, which was probably the extreme case, roughly one-third of the resident population (the free adult male citizens plus their sons) belonged to this ruling elite. Depending on the precise questions they are asking, historians can choose to focus on this extraordinary achievement (the "cup half full" view of Athens, as Josiah Ober calls it) or on the dispossession and oppression of non-elite Athenians (the "cup half empty" view).[102]

For the question being asked here, we should perhaps see Athens and other city-states as a historically important exception to the larger agrarian pattern, qualifying but not falsifying the model in figure 3.6—much as the sedentary, affluent, and complex hunter-gatherer societies found in the Pacific Northwest and prehistoric Baltic and Sea of Japan qualify without falsifying the model of forager society presented in chapter 2. On the one hand, the Kwakiutl and the Athenians both found ways to raise energy capture well above the norm and moved toward unusual social systems that capitalized on this. But on the other hand, sedentary foragers and commercial city-states could flourish only in very specific ecological zones—for the former, coastal zones rich in marine food sources, such as the prehistoric Baltic and Sea of Japan or the historic west coast of North America; for the latter, positions astride trade routes (usually maritime, sometimes riverine, and occasionally overland) supplying bigger empires.

In the final analysis, sedentary foragers could not escape the constraints imposed by hunting and gathering, and commercial city-states were equally confined by those imposed by tilling the earth. Although the size and density of sedentary foraging populations went well beyond what was normal in more mobile foraging groups, none ever broke through to the kind of levels normal in farming societies, and although commercial city-states also supported populations that were large and dense by the standards of farming societies, none ever broke through to the kind of levels common in fossil-fuel societies. In the case of Athens, we can even see that scaling up made the city look more and more like Agraria. As Athens brought other Greek cities under its control in the fifth century BC, the Athenian citizen body started functioning like the stratified elite in figure 3.6, and as the subject cities that had previously looked much like figure 3.7 in their own right were brought under Athenian rule, they began looking like the laterally insulated communities in figure 3.6.[103] As we shall see in chapter 4, the only way to escape Agraria was by having an industrial revolution.

Values

For a few years in the 1760s, a Swiss peasant named Jakob Gujer (usually known by his nickname Kleinjogg, "Little Jake") briefly became the most famous farmer in the world. J. K. Hirtzel, the physician and social reformer who discovered this articulate and ambitious agriculturalist, promoted him as "the rural Socrates." Rousseau sang his praises, and Goethe made a pilgrimage to the backcountry of Zurich, where Kleinjogg dispensed rustic wisdom guaranteed to warm the heart of any enlightened aristocrat. "We are both of us good if each does what he should," Kleinjogg told Prince Ludwig Eugen of Württemberg in 1765. "You lords and princes must order us peasants what to do, for you have the time to decide what is best for the state, and it is for us peasants to obey you and work with diligence and loyalty."[104]

We might call the relationship that Kleinjogg championed the "Old Deal," a social contract that dominated the agrarian world before the coming of the various New Deals of the industrial age. It was a simple idea: that nature and the gods required that some people should give commands while others obeyed them, and so long as everyone played their parts properly, all would be for the best in the best of all possible worlds.

The clearest statement of the Old Deal was written down two thousand years before Kleinjogg talked to Prince Eugen and five thousand miles to the East, in China. "When the Great Way prevails," the fourth-century BC *Classic of Rites* pronounced,

> public-mindedness rules all under Heaven. The worthy and the able are selected to office; their words are honest, and they cultivate harmony. Therefore, people don't just take care of their own parents, nor do they favor their own children. The aged are cared for until the end of their lives, the able-bodied are properly employed, and the young are nurtured. Widows, widowers, orphans, the elderly, and the disabled are all cared for. Men have their proper work, while women have their homes.[105]

Things were equally clear to Hesiod: "When [lords] give straight judgments," he explained, "and do not depart from what is just, their city flourishes and the people in it prosper. Peace, the nurse of children, is in their land, and all-seeing Zeus never sends cruel war to them. . . . The earth bears food for them in plenty. On the mountains, oak trees bristle with acorns on top and honeybees in the middle. Their woolly sheep are heavy with fleece. Their women bear children who are like their parents." Such lords, Hesiod tells us in another poem, are Zeus's gift to mankind. "Whichever of the divinely favored lords the daughters of great Zeus honor when he is born, they pour sweet dew on his tongue, and gracious words flow from his lips. All the people look to him when he settles quarrels with true judgments," and when ordinary folk see such a lord, "they greet him with reverence as they would a god, and he is conspicuous among the assembly. Such is the holy gift of the Muses to men."[106]

The Old Deal goes all the way back to one of the world's earliest political documents, the laws of King Uru'inimgina of Lagash, written in what is now southern Iraq in the 2360s BC. Uru'inimgina announced that he had "freed the inhabitants of Lagash from usury, burdensome controls, hunger, theft, murder, and seizure. He established freedom. The widow and the orphan were no longer at the mercy of the powerful: it was for them that Uru'inimgina made his covenant with [the god] Ningirsu."[107] This image of the king as his people's shepherd, dealing directly with the divine sphere on their behalf and protecting them from predators, became a staple of political philosophy in most agrarian societies. All over the world, political hierarchy tended to rest on the idea that the men (or, very occasionally, women) at the top were to some degree godlike, and in extreme cases, such as pharaonic Egypt, the rulers actually *were* gods.[108]

The Old Deal was at heart a circular argument, tying political and economic inequality together and justifying both. Virtue and power followed each other: because the gods loved the rulers, the rulers were rich, and the fact that the rulers were rich showed that the gods loved them. Hesiod, as usual, was explicit. "Virtue and reputation attend upon wealth . . . shame accompanies poverty and confidence comes with riches."[109] In the fifth century AD, more than a millennium after Hesiod, St. Augustine took it for granted that the poor in what is now Tunisia did not want to abolish inequality; they just wanted to join the ranks of the rich. "When the poor catch sight" of the upper classes, he said, "they murmur, they groan, they praise, and they envy, wanting to be their equals, grieving that they cannot make it. In between the praises of the rich, they say: 'These are the only ones who matter; these are the only ones who know how to live.'"[110]

In Kleinjogg's day, economic inequality still seems to have struck most people as natural. When French peasants were given the opportunity to send *cahiers de doléance* outlining their grievances to the crown in 1789, remarkably few complained about wealth inequality; nor, when reformers went into peasant villages, did they hear many demands for the redistribution of property. Rather, to their evident surprise, they found that most peasants felt that the masses had to be poor while the few were rich.[111]

Agraria, Gellner suggested, "exaggerates rather than underplays the inequality of classes and the degree of separation of the ruling stratum."[112] Farming societies often seem obsessed with the symbolism of rank, subdividing themselves into legally defined orders and marking each with its own insignia. "Among the nobles, the mere gentlemen have their coats of arms surrounded by helmets, [and] the knights have their spurs and gilded armor," noted a seventeenth-century French lawyer, while "among the commoners, the doctors, licentiates, and bachelors have their different kinds of hood." And while early-modern France was perhaps an extreme case, it was hardly unique. At the other end of Eurasia, a nineteenth-century Englishman observed that in Burma, "Almost every article of use, as well as ornaments, particularly in their dress, indicated the rank of the owner."[113]

Examples could easily be multiplied, and much of the time, the very language that people spoke reinforced the Old Deal. The rich and powerful were aristocrats, noblemen, and gentlemen; the poor and weak were base, vulgar, and villeins. In the twentieth century, when anthropologists were able to talk to members of farming societies, they regularly found that having a healthy respect for authority—knowing your place—was a key part of their informants' sense of themselves as good people. The anthropologist Donald Brown, for instance, tells how, one day in Brunei in the 1970s, he was sitting on a bench with a group of young Malays. Growing stiff, he decided that he might be more comfortable on the ground, but to his surprise, his companions immediately leapt off the bench so that they would not be sitting higher than the respected foreigner. Brown urged them to stay on the bench: no one else was around, and he himself, a good citizen of Industria, didn't care about hierarchy. Their answer, though, brooked no rebuttal: "They said it wouldn't look nice."[114]

Anthropologists have found that while modern peasants often do complain about their lot, their complaints have a certain ambivalence.

Villagers tend to resent urban elites while also respecting them, mixing fear and admiration in equal parts. To function at all, the laterally insulated peasants below the double horizontal line in Gellner's diagram have to engage with members of the statewide elites. Peasants need cash to buy goods they cannot make for themselves and to pay taxes, which means selling their produce in markets, even though they are often aware that well-connected merchants are exploiting them. "We know they are laughing at us," a peasant in the North Indian village of Karimpur told anthropologists in the 1920s. "But we want cloth, and the next shopkeeper will cheat us as badly as the last." The speaker's anger was obvious, but so too was his grudging respect for education and elite knowledge. "You cannot know unless you are a villager, how everyone threatens us and takes from us. When you [the anthropologists] go anywhere, or when a sophisticated town man goes anywhere, he demands service and gets it. We stand dumb and show our fear, and they trample on us."[115]

So deep is the interdependence of mass and elite that Alfred Kroeber, one of the first anthropologists to have much to say about peasants, concluded that "Peasants . . . constitute part-societies with part-cultures."[116] Robert Redfield went further, seeing peasants as "rural people in old civilizations . . . who look to and are influenced by gentry or townspeople whose way of life is like theirs but in a more civilized form. . . . The intellectual and often the moral life of the peasant village is perpetually incomplete," he concluded, because the "little tradition of the largely unreflective many" depends on leadership from the "great tradition of the reflective few . . . [the] remote teachers, priests, or philosophers, whose thinking affects and perhaps is affected by the peasantry."[117]

The Old Deal at the heart of the relationship between the great and little traditions ran both ways, imposing duties as well as rights on all parties, and not surprisingly, people on either side of the divide tended to have complicated opinions about those on the other. In medieval Europe, for instance, aristocrats created what the historian Paul Freedman calls "a variegated discourse, a grammar, by which peasants could be regarded *both* as degraded and as exemplary, as justly subordinated yet as close to God."[118] Similarly, the anthropologist James Scott suggests that the "hidden transcripts" of peasant values (Scott calls them "hidden" because they are difficult to decipher behind the elite "official transcript") build on rather than rejecting outright elite views of the world. "Whether he believes the rules or not," Scott concludes, "only a fool would fail to appreciate the possible benefits of deploying such readily available ideological resources."[119]

Just like the foragers who used mockery, ostracism, and finally violence to punish upstarts who ignored their obligations to share and take turns, farmers reserved the right to resist and even overthrow the elites if their supposed betters seemed to be ignoring the Old Deal and turning into tyrants. The most remarkable thing about the waves of leveling rage that periodically swept through farming societies, though, is how rarely the target of the protests was inequality as such: most of the time, it was limited to specific individuals among those who currently held power, whose wicked actions violated the Old Deal.

When protests and threats failed to change elite behavior, farmers sometimes took direct action, but when they did do this, they regularly insisted that they were attacking only the local authorities rather than the ultimate authority, be he king, emperor, or pope. The distant ruler, they asserted, remained virtuous, but his underlings were betraying him ("The tsar is good, but the boyars are bad," went a Russian saying).[120] By attacking these wicked minions, the logic of peasant resistance said, rebels were actually helping the king maintain the Old Deal.[121]

So it was, for instance, that in AD 1380 an Englishman named Richard de Leycestre "went through the whole town of Ely, commanding that all men, of whatsoever estate, should make insurrection and go with him to destroy divers traitors whom he would name to them on behalf of the lord King Richard and the faithful commons." De Leycestre and his followers then assaulted, robbed, tried, and decapitated a local judge, putting his head on the town pillory. When captured, de Leycestre refused to answer the charges brought against him, insisting that he held "a protection of the lord the King granted to him for the security of his person and his possession." The magistrates were unimpressed. "Because it is clear and plain enough to the aforesaid justices that the same Richard [de Leycestre] is guilty of all the felonies and seditions aforesaid," they recorded, "by the discretion of the said judges he was drawn and hanged the same day and year."[122]

A pattern emerged of general acceptance of glaring wealth inequalities, combined with grumbling resentment against them and occasional outbursts of leveling rage. If things got to the point that rebels concluded that the ruler himself had broken the Old Deal, however, the regime had little to fall back on but force, and its prospects would then be poor. Asked in 1907 how the slaughter of peaceful protestors two years earlier had changed his view of the state, one Russian peasant replied that "Five years ago there was a belief [in the tsar] as well as fear. Now the belief is all gone and only the fear remains."[123] A decade later, the tsar was all gone too.

Three thousand years before Tsar Nicholas II's disastrous reign, the chiefs of the Zhou people in China's Yellow River Valley had started calling this idea the Mandate of Heaven. Once upon a time, they suggested, the high gods had given a mandate to the kings of the Shang dynasty, but the current kings' violent, drunken behavior showed that they had forfeited it. The Zhou were therefore justified in resisting the Shang, and by overthrowing the Shang in 1046 BC, the Zhou proved that the Mandate of Heaven had now passed to them.[124]

Other farming societies developed somewhat similar ideas. Just a couple of generations after the Mandate of Heaven passed from the Shang to the Zhou, some Israelites—alarmed at the erratic behavior of their own King Saul—concluded that their God had also transferred his affections. As the Hebrew Bible describes it, "The LORD said to [the prophet] Samuel, 'How long will you grieve over Saul? I have rejected him from being king over Israel. Fill your horn with oil and set out; I will send you to Jesse the Bethlehemite; for I have provided for myself a king among his sons.'" Samuel promptly anoints David, who, after a tough civil war, overthrows Saul.[125]

Claims that a ruler had lost the Mandate of Heaven could be broadened to include the entire elite, as when the prophet Micah concluded in the eighth century BC that Israel's lawcourts "judge for a bribe, her priests teach for pay, and her prophets divine for money." But God sees all, Micah warned them; if they persisted in their corruption, "because of you Zion shall be plowed *like* a field, Jerusalem shall become heaps of ruins, and the mountain of the temple like the bare hills of the forest."[126] Hesiod took a similar line. Outraged that "lords who eat up gifts" had cheated him out of his inheritance, he warned them that unless they changed their ways, "a whole city pays for the deeds of one bad man who sins . . . [and Zeus] lays great trouble on the people, famine and plague together; and the men perish. Their women bear no children, their houses become few . . . [and Zeus] destroys their wide army, or their walls, or puts an end to their ships on the sea."[127]

Rebellion in farming societies often takes a good-old-days form, insisting that its goal is simply to restore the Old Deal to the standards observed by the ancestors. The standard biblical criticism of an unpopular king was that "he did not do *what was* right in the sight of the LORD his God, as his father David *had done*,"[128] and in many cases, educated elites would pinpoint a specific moment at which they thought morality had broken down. For the aristocratic Roman politician Sallust (who was himself expelled from the Senate in 50 BC for immorality), the good old days had ended when Rome destroyed Carthage in 146 BC. "It was then that fortune turned unkind and confounded all Rome's enterprises," he wrote. "Growing love of money, and the lust for power that followed it, engendered every kind of evil. Avarice destroyed honor, integrity, and every other virtue, and instead taught men to be proud and cruel, to neglect religion, and to hold nothing too sacred to sell."[129]

Anthropological accounts suggest that poorer peasants at least sometimes felt the same way. An anthropologist working in Sri Lanka in the 1970s, for example, found that "Older inhabitants of contemporary Rangama/Devideniya assert that despite the pervasiveness of inequality and discrimination in the past [as well as in the present], the relationship between rich and poor, the powerful and the powerless, the high castes and the low castes, was not characterized by bitterness, rancour and antagonism, as is the case today."[130] Even in the miserable world of Chekhov's "Peasants," Father Osip could assert that "Things were better in the old days under the gentry. . . . You worked and ate and slept, everything in its turn. . . . And there was more strictness."[131]

A shared theme runs through all these challenges to authority: that the real problem is not political or economic hierarchy, but their abuse by wicked men who do not adhere to the Old Deal. As Augustine saw it, "Get rid of pride, and riches will do no harm."[132]

In the earliest farming societies for which we have written evidence—third-millennium BC Mesopotamia and Egypt, late second-millennium BC China, and early first-millennium AD Mesoamerica—the chief anchor of the Old Deal seems to have been the king's divinity, and even in early complex societies for which we have no useful texts, such as the third-millennium BC Indus Valley or first-millennium BC Andes, the artistic and architectural evidence seems consistent with the same principles.[133] A great chain of being linked the humblest peasant to the supreme beings, via the intercession of priests, nobles, and godlike kings, guaranteeing the fundamental justice of the political and economic hierarchy. There was probably constant conflict between kings and priests to define and control this idea, and on occasions—particularly following the collapse of the Akkadian Empire in Mesopotamia and the Old Kingdom in Egypt around 2200 BC—it seems to have broken down altogether.[134] Not until the first millennium BC, however, and even then only in Eurasia, did new ideas seriously challenge divine kingship as the basis of moral order.

I will come back in chapter 5 to why these first-millennium BC challenges arose when and where they did, but right now I want to take a page or two to look at what the new ideas meant for the Old Deal. Since the 1950s, intellectual historians have often described them as an "Axial Age," following the German philosopher Karl Jaspers's portentous claim that the "axis of history is to be found in the period around 500 BC . . . [when] Man, as we know him today, came into being."[135] In these years, Jaspers argued, Confucians and Daoists in China, Buddhists and Jainists in India, Zoroastrians in Iran, Jews in Israel, and pre-Socratic philosophers in Greece all began asking new questions about the human condition, which would be reformulated over the next millennium as the basis of Christianity and Islam.[136]

Defining exactly what united these new schools of thought has proved difficult, but the classicist Arnaldo Momigliano's formulation—that "Everywhere one notices attempts to introduce greater purity, greater justice, greater perfection and a more universal explanation of things"[137]—has been influential. From China to the Mediterranean, the writings of the Axial Age became "the classics," timeless moral masterpieces that defined the meaning of life for billions of people across the next two millennia.

The fact that many key Axial thinkers (including Socrates, the Buddha, Zoroaster, and Jesus) wrote little or nothing down makes it difficult to know exactly what they thought they were doing, but they do seem to have agreed on the general point of the exercise: that people needed to transcend the squalor, corruption, and impermanence of our own sullied world to attain a state of purity and goodness that lies beyond it. One key factor behind this claim seems to have been a general loss of confidence in older visions in which the great chain of being, culminating in a godlike king, was enough to anchor the moral order.[138]

From China to Greece, Axial theorists generally felt that the transcendent realm beyond this world—the Buddhist nirvana (literally "blowing out," a state of mind in which the passions of this world are snuffed out like a candle), the Confucian *ren* (often translated "humaneness"), the Platonic *to kalon* ("the good"), the Christian Kingdom of Heaven, and the Daoist "Way"—was ultimately indefinable, but despite their vagueness about where they were going, they showed remarkable agreement on how to get there. Neither godlike kings nor the priests who worked for them, the new critics argued, could anchor the moral order by providing transcendence. That depended on *self*-fashioning, an internal, personal reorientation toward goodness. Each Axial tradition had its own recommended way to achieve this (meditation for Buddhists, conversation for Socratics, study for Jews, a combination of study and punctilious observation of ritual for Confucians), but all these techniques—and others—worked to guide followers toward the same ends: living ethically, renouncing desire, turning the other cheek, and generally doing unto others as you would have them do unto you.

Much in Axial thought was radical and countercultural, threatening Agraria's status quo. Axial thinkers (and their first-millennium AD heirs) tended to be men from the lower reaches of the elite (Socrates, Confucius, Muhammad, and most of the Hebrew Prophets fit this bill), or even from outside it (such as Jesus). They also hailed from the geographical margins of the great empires—places like Confucius's home state of Lu, the Buddha's of Sakya, or peripheries such as Israel, Greece, and Arabia—rather than from great, powerful states such as Wei and Zhao in China, Magadha in India, or Assyria, Persia, and Egypt. At least some of them cast doubt on the need for the poor to defer to the rich, the humble to the wellborn, and even women to men. Daoists and Buddhists tended to ignore political hierarchy; Confucius, Socrates, and Jesus upbraided rulers for their ethical shortcomings; and the Hebrew Prophets positively abused their kings. Agrarian elites regularly returned the compliment, persecuting, exiling, or executing Axial thinkers, but overall, all the great ancient empires eventually coopted the critics, taming the wilder fringes of Axial thought and bringing its bright young men into the establishment.

In India, the warrior king Ashoka proved himself a master of this game, announcing after destroying the rival state of Kalinga in the 250s BC that he would henceforth follow *dhamma* (apparently, his own idiosyncratic version of Buddhism). On the one hand, this required him to renounce war, but on the other, it gave him a sturdy new prop to support the Old Deal. He set up "officers of *dhamma*" throughout the Mauryan Empire, charging them with implementing a battery of new laws. The result, Ashoka concluded, was that "evil among men has diminished in the world. Among those who have suffered it has disappeared, and there is joy and peace in the whole world."[139]

The Han dynasty that united China in 206 BC did even better at turning Axial critiques into a state ideology, rewarding with wealth and influence those Confucians who emphasized texts that stressed duty and submission to authority rather than those that pointed toward independence and critique. The cozy relationship between the throne and the Confucian bureaucracy periodically broke down in coups and purges, but by and large, it survived until the Qing dynasty fell in AD 1911.[140]

The greatest success story of all, though, was surely the Roman Empire. Greek philosophy caused constant conflict within the Roman ruling class in the second century BC, but over the next hundred years or so the state turned Stoicism into the same kind of ideology of public service as Confucianism. No sooner was this accomplished, though, than Christianity emerged as a much more powerful critique—only for Rome to tame it too.[141] "It is easier for a camel to go through the eye of a needle than for a rich man to enter the kingdom of God,"[142] Jesus famously told his disciples, but by AD 400, the super-rich of the Roman Empire had colonized the upper reaches of the church hierarchy so completely that the historian Peter Brown admits "I am tempted to call this period the Age of the Camel."[143]

The Old Deal proved to be remarkably resilient. Despite constant criticism of inequality in Buddhist, Confucian, and Christian texts, post-Axial political and economic hierarchy was just as robust as the pre-Axial version (in the fourteenth century AD, one pope even tried to ban Christians from saying that Jesus had been poor). In the early second millennium AD, some of the greatest minds of the agrarian age—al-Ghazali (1058–1111) in the Middle East, Zhu Xi (1130–1200) in China, Thomas Aquinas (1225–74) in Europe— perfected sophisticated syntheses between the idea of the equality of all humans in the face of the divine order and the hierarchical needs of this life. Only a few intellectuals actually read their books, but the principles that informed them went all the way down the ladder.

I mentioned earlier that when European reformers began venturing outside their urban enclaves into the countryside in the eighteenth century, they were often astonished that instead of complaining about inequality and demanding the redistribution of property, peasants largely took it as right and proper that most people were poor and weak while a few were rich and strong.

Some of the reformers concluded that the peasants they met must have been so completely ground down by their poverty that they could not imagine any other way of living. Their "circumstances are so miserable," a Danish reformer wrote in 1763, "that it is easy to believe that a certain degree of stupidity and insensitiveness alone can render their condition supportable and that the happiness of the peasant, if he still enjoys any, would cease as soon as he should begin to think and as soon as he should be deprived of those two principal consolations, ignorance and brandy." Half a century later, a British observer in Moldova came to similarly condescending conclusions: "Accustomed to the state of servitude which to others might appear intolerable, [the peasants] are unable to form hopes for a better condition; the habitual depression of their minds has become a sort of natural stupor and apathy."[144] And in a striking extension of the argument, the social historian Stanley Elkins set off an academic firestorm in the 1950s by arguing that slaves in the nineteenth-century American South became so accustomed to servitude that they bought into their masters' stereotypes of them as feckless, lazy, and childlike "sambos."[145]

The problem with the apathy argument, though, is that it does not fit well with figure 3.3, earlier. Foragers rarely captured much more than about 5,000 kilocalories of energy per person per day, and for several millennia after the last phase of the Ice Age ended in 9600 BC, no horticulturalists captured more than 10,000 kilocalories. But despite being poorer than anyone in eighteenth-century Denmark or Moldova, foragers and horticulturalists generally rejected inequality and servitude. Between about 4000 BC and 1 BC, on the other hand, energy capture tripled but political and economic inequality became deeply entrenched.

The explanation is, once again, that each age gets the thought it needs. In the absence of fossil fuels, the only way to push energy capture far above 10,000 kilocalories per person per day is by moving toward Agraria, where economic and political inequality are structurally necessary, and in the face of necessity, we adjust our values. Moral systems conform to the requirements of energy capture, and for societies capturing between 10,000 and 30,000 kilocalories per person per day, one of the most important requirements is acceptance of political and economic inequality.

Only as these requirements changed, with the rise of large-scale maritime trading systems that pushed some farming societies away from the Agrarian center toward either the city-state or the early-modern point in figure 3.1, did attitudes begin to shift. In sixth- and fifth-century BC Greece, for instance, anger against incompetent and corrupt rulers was increasingly redirected from replacing them with better rulers toward a generalized critique of political inequality. Extraordinarily strong ideas about male equality took shape, and more and more cities began making the key decisions in one-man-one-vote assemblies of all free male citizens. Small groups of talented and motivated men continued to make most of the speeches and design most of the policies, but even such outstanding leaders as Pericles and Demosthenes had to appear to accept the idea that they were the same as any other citizen. For much of the fifth century, wealthy Greeks avoided building lavish houses or tombs that would attract charges of upstartism, and the richest of the rich insisted that they were in fact perfectly average. Athenians began to speak of finance and trade as an immoral "invisible economy," where the rich hid their ill-gotten gains from public scrutiny.[146]

I will have more to say in chapter 4 about the rise of large-scale maritime commerce in early-modern Western Europe. For the moment, though, I will just observe that by the seventeenth century, as energy capture climbed well beyond 30,000 kilocalories per person per day, both the Eastern and Western ends of the Old World began seeing highly unusual demands to do away with political and economic hierarchy altogether, rather than just rearranging people's positions within the system. The most famous of these levelers were in England, where one Richard Rumbold, for instance, insisted in 1685 that "None comes into the world with a saddle upon his back, neither any booted and spurred to ride him." In 1649—the very year that his fellow countrymen beheaded their king, and decided that they did not need a new one—Abiezer Cooper called God himself "that mighty Leveller."[147] However, these English radicals were not the only levelers of the 1640s; in China, according to an official report submitted in 1644, angry peasants

> sharpened their hoes into swords, and took to themselves the title of "Leveling Kings," declaring that they were leveling the distinction between masters and serfs, titled and mean, rich and poor. The tenants seized hold of their masters' best clothes . . . they would order the master to kneel and pour wine for them. They would slap them across the cheeks and say: "We are all of us equally men. What right had you to call us serfs?"[148]

This leveling rage went beyond anything seen in mainstream Agraria, but it still had distinct limits. So far as we can tell from the surviving sources, almost no one ever seriously entertained the possibility of leveling the sexes.[149] Admittedly, until social scientists began talking to peasant women in the twentieth century, hardly anyone wrote down what women thought about patriarchy, but male authors certainly had plenty to say about what women *ought* to think. "The husband is heaven," a now-nameless Chinese author announced in the ninth-century AD *Classic of Filial Piety for Girls*. "How could one not serve him?"[150]

To most male writers, this question would apparently have seemed purely rhetorical. If "wives will have the same freedom as husbands," the Roman orator and politician Cicero joked in 51 BC, "amid such freedom dogs, horses, and donkeys will run around so freely that men have to yield the road to them,"[151] and classical Athenians, so opposed to hierarchy within the male citizen community, found Aristophanes' comedies about women with political authority side-splittingly funny.[152]

The scarcity of evidence for women challenging patriarchal values is not necessarily evidence for the scarcity of such ideas, and we certainly do get occasional glimpses of different ways of thinking in our sources. Around 550 BC, for instance, an Egyptian woman named Tsenhor not only engaged in business in her own right but also insisted in her will that her son and daughter would have equal inheritances.[153] But that said, the near-total absence of challenges to patriarchy in the historical sources, which span four continents and five millennia, is resounding. In Europe, well over a millennium and a half passed between Plato's discussion of the equality of the sexes in the *Republic* (ca. 380 BC) and Boccaccio's *On Famous Women* (ca. AD 1360). Even Christine de Pizan's *Treasury of the City of Ladies* (1405), with its explicit criticism of medieval misogyny, only goes as far as proposing that elite women ought to be given the same education as men. The closest thing to a premodern critique of patriarchy appears to be the so-called *Querelle des femmes*, a battle of the books that produced at least fifty published volumes in Italy's cities between 1524 and 1632 as well as bestsellers in France and contributions in England, and yet the most striking thing about this literature, the modern editor of one of its most important works points out, is "the distance that separates the Renaissance and early-modern tradition of defenses of women from the nineteenth- and twentieth-century tradition of political feminism."[154] Some scholars even suspect that the *Querelle des femmes* was more a literary game than a serious challenge to patriarchy.[155]

So far as I know, no one has bothered to count them up, but I suspect that for every agrarian text objecting (no matter how mildly) to patriarchy, dozens stress women's fundamental inferiority.[156] Nearly all were written by men, but when ethnographers started asking women about it in the early twentieth century, they found that many accepted the basic rightness of gender inequality. The attitudes identified by the sociologists William Thomas and Florian Znaniecki in Polish villages of the 1910s—that "The norm of respect from wife to husband includes obedience, fidelity, care for the husband's comfort and health; from husband to wife, good treatment, fidelity, not letting the wife do hired work if it is not indispensable"—could safely be generalized to most of Agraria.[157]

Patriarchal values made sense in societies that captured energy through farming. Male power over women increased after the agricultural revolution not because male farmers were more brutish than male hunters, but because this was the most efficient way to organize labor in peasant societies. In a world of constant competition over scarce resources, over the course of several thousand years the most efficient societies replaced less efficient ones, and because patriarchy proved so successful, men and women alike accepted patriarchal values as just. If either of these conditions had not applied, the historical and anthropological records would contain at least some examples of farming societies organized along different lines and expressing different values.

Criticism of gender hierarchy, like criticism of political and economic hierarchy, tended to focus less on rejecting inequality than on settling scores with men or women who broke the terms of the patriarchal contract. "In general," Thomas and Znaniecki observed in Poland, "neither husband nor wife ought to do anything which could lower the social standing of the other, since this would lead to a lowering of the social status of the other's family."[158] This made the preservation of farming values a group activity. "Most of what she learned she was taught by her mother," the historians Michael Mitterauer and Reinhard Sieder say of the typical European peasant girl. "From her [mother] she also learned, at an early age, to adopt an attitude of subordination and dependence that would befit her future role as a wife and mother in the patriarchal family."[159] Just as forager bands acted collectively to mock upstarts, so too entire villages cooperated to mock husbands who gave their wives too much leeway, or to punish wives who were too assertive.[160]

Like all the best value systems, patriarchy was very flexible, and in every age, women of strong character found ways to operate within its confines. Some are famous, such as Margaret of Anjou, who fiercely defended the rights of her mentally unstable husband King Henry VI and their infant son in fifteenth-century England. "O tiger's heart wrapt in a woman's hide!" Shakespeare had her archenemy, the Duke of York, rage at her. "Women are soft, mild, pitiful, and flexible;/Thou stern, obdurate, flinty, rough, remorseless." A contemporary called her "a manly woman, using to rule and not be ruled," and yet she consistently deployed her flintiness to advance the cause of the men around her.[161]

At the other end of Eurasia, and nearly four hundred years earlier, the wealthy widow Li Qingzhao achieved somewhat similar ends through very different means, not only making a name for herself in China's exclusively male literary circles with poems honoring her dead first husband but also winning a tough battle to divorce her abusive, gold-digging second husband. Li found ways to protect her family without being forced into opposition to the fundamental values of farming society.[162]

The most moving example, however, might be Turia, a rich Roman woman who died around 5 BC. Turia left no writings behind her, but her grieving husband Quintus had the long oration he delivered at her funeral engraved on stone, and roughly three-quarters of it survives.[163] By the austere standards of Roman epigraphy, this text stands out for its intensity. Quintus loved Turia fiercely. "I wish that our long union had come to its final end through something that had befallen me instead of you; it would have been more just," he said. "Along with you I have lost the tranquility of my existence. . . . Natural sorrow wrests away my power of self-control and I am overwhelmed by sorrow."

Turia had been a strong woman, not the kind of doormat evoked by the *Classic of Filial Piety for Girls* or the normative writing of Greek and Roman philosophers.[164] "Why," Quintus asked, "should I mention your domestic virtues: your loyalty, obedience, affability, reasonableness, industry in working wool, religion without superstition, sobriety of attire, modesty of appearance?" The answer: because "very few women have encountered comparable circumstances to make them endure such sufferings." Turia stood up for her values, no matter what the cost. As a teenager, she took on her own relatives when they challenged her father's will; as an adult, she confronted one of the most powerful men in Rome to demand that her husband be allowed to return from exile; and when she and Quintus did not produce a child, she offered to let him divorce her so he could find another wife who would give him heirs. He refused, and they spent forty childless but happy years together.

There were no feminists in Agraria, and precious few communists or anarchists either. Rather, most people recognized that hierarchy, and its endless degrees of rank, was the moral foundation of the good life. No one put the point better than Shakespeare's Ulysses in *Troilus and Cressida*, written some sixteen centuries after Quintus mourned Turia. "O, when degree is shaked," he observed,

> The enterprise is sick! How could communities ...
> But by degree, stand in authentic place?
> Take but degree away, untune that string,
> And, hark, what discord follows! ...
> Force should be right; or rather, right and wrong,
> Between whose endless jar justice resides,
> Should lose their names, and so should justice too.
> Then every thing includes itself in power,
> Power into will, will into appetite;
> And appetite, an universal wolf,
> So doubly seconded with will and power,
> Must make perforce an universal prey,
> And last eat up himself.[165]

Less than fifty years after Shakespeare wrote these lines, Thomas Hobbes turned Ulysses' point into one of the most important arguments ever made in political philosophy: that the only way to prevent the war of all against all is to enshrine degree so firmly that it brings forth a Leviathan, a government powerful enough to intimidate its unruly subjects into living peacefully.[166] Hobbes had rather little interest in evidence, but we now know that he was largely right. As noted in chapter 2, foragers, who largely lacked degree, had rates of violent death above 10 percent, while—by my calculations—rates among farmers were closer to 5 percent, and sometimes much lower still.[167]

Farming could only work if rates of violent death fell. Foragers, who lived off wild foods and moved around a lot, had simple divisions of labor and few capital investments in the landscape. They did not enjoy rates of killing above 10 percent, but could function in the midst of such bloodshed. Farmers, however, could not. Because they depended on domesticated energy sources, they

needed complex divisions of labor and massive capital investments in the landscape, which could not survive in a world as
violent as the foragers'. "In such a [violent] condition," Hobbes
famously said, "there is no place for industry; because the fruit
thereof is uncertain: and consequently no culture of the earth;
no navigation, nor use of the commodities that may be imported
by sea; no commodious building; no instruments of moving, and
removing, such things as require much force; no knowledge of
the face of the earth; no account of time; no arts; no letters; no
society; and which is worst of all, continual fear, and danger of
violent death; and the life of man, solitary, poor, nasty, brutish,
and short."[168]

But if farming turned high rates of violence into a problem, it
also provided the solution. Foragers living in a relatively empty
landscape always had the option of running away from aggression
and hunting and gathering in a new place, but farmers, trapped
in increasingly crowded landscapes, did not. As a result, farmers who won wars against their neighbors sometimes ended up
incorporating the losers into a larger society. This was a brutal
process, usually involving rape, pillage, and enslavement, but over
time, it created bigger societies, whose rulers—as Gellner said of
Agraria—"are interested in extracting taxes, maintaining the peace,
and not much else."[169] Rulers had strong incentives to pacify their
subjects, persuading them to work hard, render unto Caesar what
was Caesar's, and not to kill one another or destroy each other's
productive assets. Rulers who succeeded in pacification tended to
flourish at the expense of those who did not, and, over the course
of ten thousand years, the net effect was that rulers gradually drove
down rates of violent death.[170]

To accomplish these goals, rulers needed to convince their subjects that government alone had the right to use violence—that, as
Weber put it, "only certain political communities, viz, the 'states,'
are considered to be capable of 'legitimizing,' by virtue of mandate
or permission, the exercise of physical coercion by any other community." The main tool available to a government trying to persuade
its subjects that it is the only group permitted to act violently is law,

but the legitimacy of law itself ultimately rests on the government's comparative advantage in force:

> For the purpose of threatening and exercising such coercion, the fully matured political community has developed a system of casuistic rules to which that particular "legitimacy" is imputed. This system of rules constitutes the "legal order," and the political community is regarded as its sole normal creator, since that community has, in modern times, normally usurped the power to compel by physical coercion respect for those rules.[171]

Premodern states did less well than modern ones at monopolizing the legitimate use of force, but the further they went in this direction, the less their subjects felt that it was right to use violence to solve their own problems. The injunction to turn the other cheek, shared by most Axial Age belief systems, surely helped in this process, and in the Roman Empire and again in early-modern Europe we can trace in some detail how elite males gradually surrendered the right to pursue vendettas. In the process, the idea of the "man of honor" shifted from describing someone ready to use violence to describing a man who restrained himself.[172]

The scope for legitimate violence remained wider in farming societies than it is in smoothly functioning fossil-fuel societies, if only because forced labor—so fundamental to Agraria—depended on the ability of masters to coerce dependents. An unpleasant story preserved by the second-century AD Roman grammarian Aulus Gellius illustrates the tension between increasingly negative valuations of violence and Agraria's requirements. One day, Gellius says, Plutarch—a learned Greek gentleman who, among many other works, had written a treatise called *On Freedom from Anger*—decided to have one of his slaves flogged. The slave in question complained that Plutarch was giving in to the very fault he had criticized in his booklet; whereupon Plutarch invited the slave to engage in a philosophical debate while the whip tore the flesh off his back.[173] Such were the moral complexities of farming life.

Assiros Revisited

"Farming society" is a huge category, embracing almost the whole of recorded history, but we can nevertheless identify a broadly shared set of moral values within it. At their heart is the idea that hierarchy is good. Hierarchy reflects the natural/divine order, in which some were put on this earth to command, and most to obey. Violence is valued according to the same principle: when legitimate rulers demand it, it is a force for good; otherwise, it is not.

Farmers' values were very different from foragers' because farmers and foragers lived in different worlds. Capturing energy from domesticated sources imposed different constraints and created different opportunities than capturing energy from wild resources. Farmers could survive only in a hierarchical, somewhat pacified world, and they therefore came to value hierarchy and peace. That is why, in 1982, Mr. George and his wife—who, despite the partial electrification of the Greek countryside and somewhat erratic bus service from Assiros to Thessaloniki, still lived largely in the farming world—thought it right and proper that he should ride a donkey while she walked. So far as I heard, he was not a brute and she was not a doormat; rather, among farmers as among foragers, values evolved to conform to material realities.

CHAPTER 4

FOSSIL FUELS

Who Fossil-Fuel Folk Are

Humanity has always depended on solar energy. Sunlight hits the earth, where plants photosynthesize it into chemical energy; animals eat the plants, converting their chemical energy to kinetic energy; and humans eat both plants and other animals. In the last two centuries, however, humans have vastly increased the amount of energy they capture by learning to tap into fossilized sunlight. This comes chiefly in the form of vast deposits of coal, gas, and oil buried under the earth's surface since the Carboniferous Era, roughly 300 to 360 million years ago. Exploiting fossil fuels has set off an energy bonanza, transforming human societies and values.[1]

Fossil fuel society is the product of two innovations. The first, which some northwest Europeans had already made two thousand years ago, was the discovery that coal could be burned to release heat. Only around AD 1000 (in China) and 1600 (in England), however, did coal begin to rival wood as an energy source. The second breakthrough, initially made in the third century BC by engineers in Egypt, was that heat could be converted to motion by burning wood to boil water and then using the steam to power pistons. Egyptians did little with this idea, however, beyond providing their gods with steam-powered temple doors that appeared to open magically by themselves.[2]

Not until the seventeenth century were fossil fuels and steam power put together in a productive way, by northwest European coalminers who realized that they could burn the coal they dug up to power engines that would pump water out of their mineshafts, allowing them to dig deeper to find more coal. The earliest steam engines burned so much coal that they were economical only if used right next to the mines that fed them, but in 1776, James Watt and Matthew Boulton managed to build an engine with separate heating and condensing chambers, dramatically cutting its coal consumption. Industrialists quickly figured out how to augment human and animal muscles with steam power in all walks of life. Productivity soared and prices collapsed, but despite this, sales increased so much that profits rose much higher than ever before.[3] Energy capture per capita in the most industrialized Western economies grew sevenfold, from roughly 38,000 kilocalories per person per day around 1800 to 230,000 by the 1970s (figure 4.1).[4] The age of energy abundance had begun.

People of course still needed to eat, which meant that domesticated plants and animals remained vital sources of energy, but fossil fuels quickly transformed farming too. By the late nineteenth century, trains and steamships had made it much easier and cheaper to move food to people, and in the twentieth, chemical fertilizers, gasoline for tractors, and electricity to pump water to fields directly increased output. By 2000, each acre of American farmland absorbed, on average, eighty times as much energy as it had done in 1900, and yielded four times as much food.

Like foraging and farming, serious fossil-fuel use began in a specific place (Northwest Europe) at a specific time (roughly two hundred years ago). The great difference between the industrial revolution and the two earlier transformations in energy capture, though, was that industrialization changed the world much more abruptly. It made so much energy available so suddenly that Britain, where (for reasons I will return to in chapter 5) the initial breakthrough came, was able to project its power across the entire globe in the nineteenth century. Consequently, once Britain began its industrial revolution, there was no time for anyone else to invent fossil-fuel industry independently. By 1914, most of the people on earth were part of a Western-dominated fossil-fuel economy and tied to global markets,[5] and Europeans and their overseas colonists had exploited

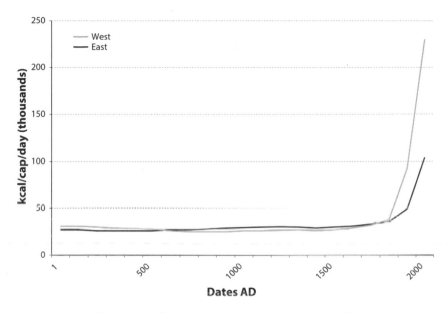

FIGURE 4.1. The energy explosion: per-capita energy consumption in the core regions of the West and East, AD 1–AD 2000 (after Morris 2013).

the advantages of being early adopters to take control of 84 percent of the planet's landmass and 100 percent of its oceans. The Industrial revolution is the biggest discontinuity in human history—so far.

The Evidence

The explosion in energy capture has driven an even more spectacular explosion in information technology,[6] with the result that there is far more evidence available for the last two hundred years than for all previous history put together. The material is unevenly distributed, with richer countries and people leaving many more traces than poorer ones, but as we move through the twentieth century, the problem increasingly becomes one of filtering the masses of data rather than of struggling to find information.

Energy, Demography, and Social Organization

Fossil-fuel users constantly revolutionized energy capture. After the initial breakthroughs with coal, they quickly discovered new sources of hydrocarbons (oil and natural gas), invented new methods of extraction (such as deep sea drilling and hydraulic fracturing), and learned to transmit power in new forms (above all, electricity). They also created new business, legal, and financial institutions to organize the energy boom. The speed with which all this happened bewildered contemporaries. "All fixed, fast-frozen relations, with their train of ancient and venerable prejudices and opinions, are swept away, all new-formed ones become antiquated before they can ossify," said Marx and Engels in 1848, when the changes had barely begun. "All that is solid melts into air."[7]

As with the earlier energy revolutions, the most obvious result was a leap in scale, although the fossil-fuel version was far bigger and faster than the foraging or farming versions. Initially, the explosion in scale was concentrated in Northwest Europe (figure 4.2). Europe's population doubled in the nineteenth century, becoming what the historian Niall Ferguson evocatively calls a "white plague," leaping like an infection to other continents, borne on steamships and trains.[8] Between 1800 and 1900, the proportion of the world's population living in Europe and North America (the main target of European migration) surged from 15.8 to 23.6 percent. Particularly after 1945, however, as more and more of the world embraced the fossil-fuel revolution, the growth in scale was globalized. By 2000, Europe and North America's share of world population had shrunk to just 13.7 percent.[9]

The world's population grew from just under 1 billion people in 1800 to 1.6 billion in 1900 and 6 billion in 2000. Averaged across the whole planet, there are now 45 people per square kilometer of land, which means about $100/km^2$ in the habitable parts of the world. Farming societies typically had population densities above $30/km^2$, with a few city-states (such as classical Athens) running to $100/km^2$, but in the fossil-fuel world, entire nations regularly have

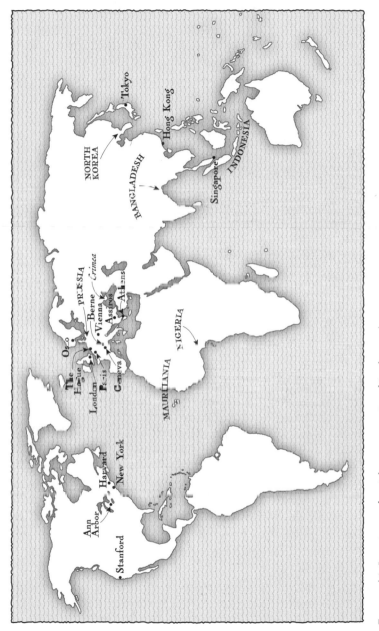

FIGURE 4.2. Locations and social groups mentioned in chapter 4.

densities over 200/km². Bangladesh, which covers about 150,000 km², averages over 1,000/km², and some city-states (notably Hong Kong and Singapore) have densities above 6,000/km². The biggest cities in farming societies had about 1 million people, but by 1900 London had ballooned to 6.6 million, and as I write (in late 2014), Tokyo has 38.2 million residents (more than the entire world's population in 5000 BC).[10]

It is one of the great ironies of intellectual history that in the late eighteenth century, just at the moment that fossil fuels were shattering the energy constraints on farming society, Northwest European thinkers finally laid bare the principles underlying agricultural life. In 1798, Thomas Malthus recognized that while population can grow exponentially, potentially doubling and redoubling every twenty years, the food supply normally grows arithmetically. This means that while good fortune (agricultural innovations, better weather, and so on) can temporarily raise productivity, in the long run hungry mouths will always multiply faster than the food available, forcing the masses back into poverty.[11] By 1850, however, it had become clear that fossil fuels were changing this. Steam-powered transport made it much easier to move food from where it was grown to where people were, increasing supply so much that prices fell even though demand rose as populations boomed. By 1900, Westerners were not just twice as numerous as they had been in 1800, they were also (on average) taller, better fed, in better health, and lived longer. Since 1900, applying fossil-fuel energy directly to fields (in the forms, mentioned earlier, of chemical fertilizers, gasoline-powered tractors, and electric motors) has massively increased output, and since 1950, the globalization of fossil-fuel society and the green revolution have spread these gains around the world. In 2000, the average human was ten centimeters taller than his or her great grandparents had been in 1900, lived thirty years longer, and earned six times as much in real terms.[12]

Just a couple of decades before Malthus explained the logic tying demography to production, the Scottish philosopher Adam Smith had done much the same for the logic of distribution.

The wealth of nations, Smith saw, came not from plunder or monopolies, but from the size of markets and the division of labor that they promoted. This division of labor, Smith speculated, was itself the "consequence of a certain propensity in human nature . . . to truck, barter, and exchange one thing for another." In pursuing profit, people specialize on the jobs that they do particularly well or inexpensively, and exchange the fruits of their labors for goods and services that other people produce particularly well or inexpensively. By creating markets for these goods and services, they simultaneously lower costs and raise quality, making everyone better off. "It is not from the benevolence of the butcher, the brewer or the baker that we expect our dinner," Smith observed, "but from their regard to their own interest."[13]

"By directing [his] industry in such a manner as its produce may be of the greatest value," Smith explained, a man "intends only his own gain; [but] he is in this, as in many other cases, led by an invisible hand to promote an end which was no part of his intention. . . . By pursuing his own interest, he frequently promotes that of the society more effectually than when he really intends to promote it."[14] The implication was obvious: the larger the number of people who got on with trucking, bartering, and exchanging, the better off everyone would be.

The great problem in Smith's day was that although farmers were richer than foragers, productivity was still very low (according to the calculations by the economist Angus Maddison that I mentioned in chapter 3, the typical peasant earned $1.50 to $2.20 per day and the typical forager just $1.10). Because peasants had little purchasing power, they could support only small, fragmented, and inefficient markets, and because markets could not bring enough people together to do everything that farming societies needed, state intervention and forced labor were often the most effective ways of mobilizing workers and goods.

Fossil fuels changed the structure of markets, setting off feedback loops that swept away the old barriers to scale and integration. There was not much point in using steam power to produce vast quantities of manufactured goods if there were no markets to absorb them. Fortunately, steam power simultaneously solved this problem by generating profits that made it possible to pay higher wages, which gave workers more disposable income to buy the goods that factories turned out. It was a virtuous cycle: steam-powered transport drove the cost of traded goods down and down, making it possible for even more people to buy them, and high wages tempted more and more people to take factory jobs rather than staying home on the farm, producing an ever more complex division of labor and churning out even more goods.

Fossil fuels joined Malthus's and Smith's problems together and solved both. With population booming (Britain's roughly doubled, to 14 million, between 1780 and 1830), poverty and the threat of starvation were staring many late eighteenth-century farmers in the face. Nineteenth-century sources make it very clear that entering the wage-labor market could be a traumatic experience, requiring workers to submit to strict time discipline and factory conditions unlike anything they had known in the countryside;[15] and yet millions chose to do so, because the alternative—hunger—was worse.[16]

So eager were poor farmers for dirty, dangerous factory jobs that British employers only needed to increase wages by 5 percent (in real terms) between 1780 and 1830, although output per worker grew by 25 percent. Wage increases accelerated only in the 1830s, and even then only for urban workers. The great motor was productivity, which was now rising so high that employers began finding it cheaper to share some of their profits with their workers than to try to break strikes.[17] (In another great irony, by the time that Dickens, Marx, and Engels were writing, wages were rising faster than ever before in history.) For the next fifty years, wages rose as fast as productivity; after 1880, they rose even faster. By then, incomes were beginning to rise in the countryside too.[18]

In 1955, the economist Simon Kuznets hypothesized that income inequality in industrializing economies should follow an inverted-U pattern, rising in the early stages and then declining, and Gini scores calculated from nineteenth-century documents suggest that

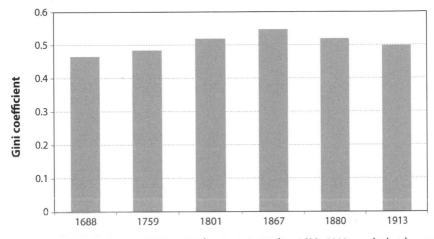

F<small>IGURE</small> 4.3. The Kuznets Curve: British income inequality, 1688–1913, as calculated by Lindert and Williamson (1983).

he was broadly right.[19] In the seventeenth century, British income inequality (figure 4.3) had been fairly typical for an advanced farming society, but it rose sharply across the eighteenth century as workers' wages stagnated while capitalists' profits increased. Although urban workers' wages began increasing around 1830, the returns to capital rose faster still, and in 1867 the Gini score reached 0.55, almost as high as the most unequal farming societies on record. By 1913, however, the Gini score—while still extremely high by twenty-first-century standards—had fallen back close to its eighteenth-century level.[20] In France, where industrialization only really got going in the 1830s, income inequality followed a similar curve, peaking around 0.60 in the 1860s but returning to 0.48 by 1901; in the United States, the post-tax Gini score shot up from 0.44 in 1774 to 0.51 in 1860.[21]

Despite the increasing inequality of early fossil-fuel societies, the rising tide of fossil-fuel energy lifted all the boats, and higher wages changed everything. By making wage labor attractive enough to draw in millions of free workers, higher wages made forced labor less necessary, and because impoverished serfs and slaves—unlike the increasingly prosperous wage laborers—could rarely buy the manufactured goods being churned out by factories, forced labor increasingly struck business interests as an obstacle to growth (especially when it was competitors who were using it). The more a society moved toward fossil fuels, the more political support swung behind abolition and emancipation. Between the 1780s and 1848, most of continental Europe abolished serfdom, with even Russia following suit in 1861. Britain banned slave trading in its empire in 1807 and banned slaveholding altogether in 1833.

Serf- and slaveholders pushed back, naturally caring more about their own sunk costs than the logical requirements of fossil-fuel economies. Sometimes they could be bought off, with generous compensation for the loss of their human capital, but sometimes overthrowing forced labor required violence. By 1865, a civil war had freed 4 million slaves in the United States and the Royal Navy's West Africa Squadron had intercepted and freed a further 150,000 Africans as they were being shipped across the Atlantic for sale. The biggest slave society, Brazil, abolished human bondage in 1888, and although forced labor survived in the least developed parts of Africa and the Middle East[22] (Mauritania banned slavery only in 1981), in the twenty-first century slavery and serfdom are illegal everywhere, surviving only in disguised forms or in lawless backwaters.

Forced labor had been indispensable to farming societies for thousands of years, but fossil fuels swept it away in less than a century; and no sooner had free wage labor triumphed than fossil fuels also began dissolving another ancient and indispensable blockage in farming societies' labor markets, the gendered division of labor. As in the case of forced labor, both supply and demand contributed to the changes. On the demand side, machines powered by fossil fuels steadily reduced the economy's need for muscle power as the nineteenth century went on, but increased its need for organization; and since women could provide brainpower and services just as well as men, female workers potentially offered a way to double the size of the labor market. White collars turned pink.

On the supply side, the most important factor was babies. Because infant mortality was so high, peasant societies had needed women to carry an average of six or seven pregnancies to term if they were even to maintain a stable population. The energy released by fossil fuels, however, produced bigger, healthier, better-fed women, whose bigger, healthier, better-fed babies fared much better. In the 1850s, about one-quarter of all children born in the United States died before their first birthdays, but by 1970 this had fallen to one in 50 babies, and by 2014 to just one in 163. The worldwide spread of fossil-fuel-powered transport since World War II played a big part in driving global infant mortality down by two-thirds, and in 2014 no fewer than 55 countries had rates even lower than America's (in Japan, the safest big country for babies, just one infant per 400 dies in its first year).[23]

Before the coming of fossil fuels, the average woman had to spend most of her adult life bearing and rearing children, but once that necessity was removed, parents increasingly preferred investing more heavily in feeding and educating smaller families to breeding as much as possible.[24] Before the nineteenth century was out, the low wage–high mortality–high fertility regime of farming societies was yielding to a high wage–low mortality–low fertility regime (demographers call this "the demographic transition"),[25] and in the twentieth century, markets responded to parents' demand for sex without procreation by bringing forth the latex condom in 1920 and the oral contraceptive in 1960.[26] By 2002, the average number of live births per woman in the European Union had plunged to 1.46, well below the replacement rate, and as fossil fuels spread around the world after 1950, total fertility rates more than halved (figure 4.4).[27] In the fossil-fuel age, the average woman spends only a few years childbearing and childrearing, leaving her free to spend several decades adding to household income by taking paid employment.

In the farming world, one of the advantages of having women stay home to tend their numerous offspring was that they could also attend to the tremendous amount of housework that had to be done. This meant that if families were to exploit falling

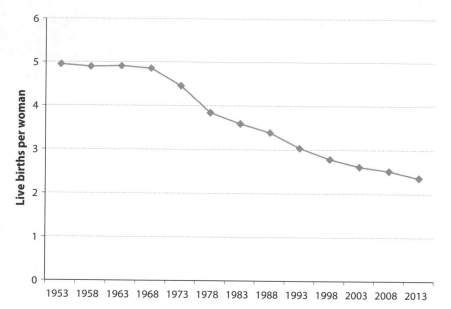

FIGURE 4.4. Global birthrates: the halving of the average number of live births per woman between the 1950s and 2010s.

fertility by having women work for pay outside the home, they would need to find some way to do the unpaid work that had formerly filled women's days. The answer came from machines— "engines of liberation," as the economists Jeremy Greenwood, Ananth Seshadri, and Mehmet Yorukoglu call them.[28] Because women's potential earnings now made it worthwhile for families to spend money on labor-saving devices, markets moved quickly to supply their demand. Commercial laundry services boomed in the late nineteenth century, but it was electricity that really broke the back of domestic drudgery. In 1928, almost a million electric washing machines were sold. In 1937, the first fully automatic home vacuum cleaner was advertised, and in 1938 the Steam-O-Matic iron, priced at just $10, became a runaway commercial success (figure 4.5).

Women's participation in work outside the home crept up across the late nineteenth and early twentieth centuries, but as late

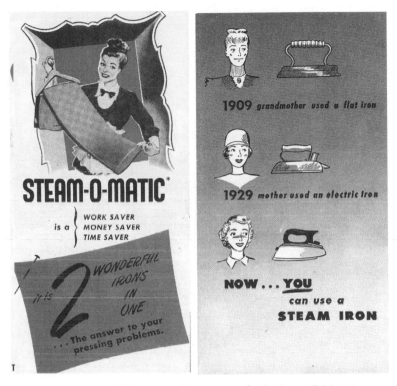

FIGURE 4.5. Engines of liberation: advertisements for the Steam-O-Matic iron, ca. 1950 (author's collection).

as 1940, the vast majority of women in the paid labor force (even in Western Europe and North America) were still young and single, working chiefly in poorly paid and effectively female-only domestic, secretarial, nursing, and teaching jobs. That, however, changed rapidly after World War II. In the United States, the proportion of women in paid work doubled between 1940 and 1990 (figure 4.6). Already in 1950, fully half of American workingwomen were married, and by the end of the century hardly any jobs were closed to women (although women were underrepresented at the top ends of most professions and, on average, earned only 77 percent of male incomes).[29]

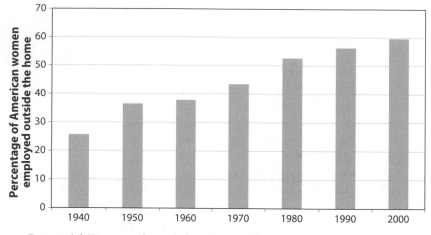

FIGURE 4.6. Women in the workplace: the proportion of American women in paid employment, 1940–2000 (data from J. Patterson 1996, pp. 32–34; 2005, pp. 54–55).

Agraria had worked by drawing lines, not just between elite and mass or men and women, but also between believers and nonbelievers, pure and defiled, free and slave, and countless other categories. Each group was assigned its place in a complex hierarchy of mutual obligations and privileges, tied together by the Old Deal and guaranteed by the gods and the threat of violence. Fossil-fuel societies, however, work best by erasing lines. The more a group replaces the rigid structure of figure 3.6 with the anti-structure of figure 4.7—a completely empty box, made up of interchangeable citizens—the bigger and more efficient its markets will be and the better it will function in the fossil-fuel world. Industria, as we might call this diagram, is as much an ideal type as Agraria, and no actually existing society has ever come very close to it[30]—but it is nonetheless the direction in which the world has been moving since AD 1800.

Fossil-fuel societies found two main ways to get from Agraria to Industria, one liberal and the other illiberal.[31] Both paths proceeded by sweeping away the lines in figure 3.6, but they did so in very different ways. The liberal approach involved declaring Agraria's boundaries irrelevant and giving everyone, no matter what category

FIGURE 4.7. Industria: the ideal-type fossil-fuel society, completely free of internal divisions and made up of interchangeable citizens.

they would have belonged to in a farming society, equal freedom and equal rights before the law. If traditional rules about how people should worship, whom they could marry, and what jobs they might do interfered with the growth of the markets that were needed to absorb and exploit the energy released by fossil fuels, then those traditions had to go. The illiberal path, by contrast, aimed not at ignoring difference but at eliminating it, by force if necessary. Consequently, illiberal methods tended to be much more backwardlooking than liberal versions and regularly relied on violence, forced labor, and even updated versions of godlike kingship. The two paths were mutually exclusive, and attempts to combine them were disastrous, as the Habsburg Empire demonstrated after splitting into Austrian and Hungarian halves in

1867. The historian Geoffrey Wawro observes that while the Austrians viewed their state power "as license merely to patronize ... Slavs by requiring them to interact with Habsburg officialdom in the German language, the Hungarians viewed theirs as license to *abolish* ... other nationalities."[32] The dysfunctional compromise between liberal and illiberal paths proved a disaster. "Austria is the loser—the Schlemiel—of Europe," Vienna's *Die Zeit* newspaper conceded in 1913; "No one likes us and every disaster befalls us."[33]

The first indications of the liberal path appeared around the shores of the North Atlantic in the late seventeenth century, as the intercontinental expansion of markets began pushing up the amount of energy in the system (I return to this theme in chapter 5). It was only around 1800, though, as the industrial revolution began in England, that the liberal path really became established. For nearly two thousand years, Christians had been persecuting Jews and anyone who followed Jesus incorrectly, but all of a sudden, other people's faiths seemed to be their own business, and certainly no reason to stop them from owning property, voting, or (eventually) even marrying into the Christian mainstream. In fact, for growing numbers of people in the nineteenth century, faith seemed less of an issue altogether, and new, secular ideologies—socialism, evolutionism, nationalism—spread rapidly. Secularization—defined by the sociologist Steve Bruce as "the displacement of religion from the centre of human life"[34]—marks the fossil-fuel world off sharply from that of farmers.[35]

Some atheists pursued anticlericalism with a zeal that it is tempting to call religious. In 1871, for instance, the violently left-wing Commune that briefly ruled Paris started rounding up priests, and Raoul Rigault—State Prosecutor on the Commune's Revolutionary Tribunal—opened his interrogation of a Jesuit with the following notorious line of questioning:

RIGAULT: What is your profession?
PRIEST: Servant of God.
RIGAULT: Where does your master live?

PRIEST: Everywhere.

RIGAULT (to a clerk): Take this down: *X*, describing himself servant of one called God, a vagrant.[36]

It would be funny, had Rigault not gone on to shoot quite so many priests over the next few weeks. Most atheists, however, were less aggressive, and contented themselves with voting against God with their feet. In Britain, church attendance fell from roughly 60 percent in 1851 to 12 percent in 1979, 10 percent in 1989, and 7.5 percent in 1998. Even in the United States, where religion has remained more popular, church attendance probably halved between 1939 and the 1990s.[37]

Not surprisingly, the retreat of religion went hand-in-hand with the erasure of one of Agraria's strongest distinctions, the rigid line between a god-given elite and a politically impotent mass. As I mentioned in chapter 3, the energy-rich city-states of classical Greece had partially erased this boundary by allowing all free men to vote on important group decisions, and when energy capture soared in seventeenth- and eighteenth-century Western Europe, the idea regained its appeal. "I do not find anything in the law of God," the English Leveller Thomas Rainsborough insisted in 1647, "that a lord shall choose twenty burgesses, and a gentleman but two, or a poor man shall choose none. . . . The poorest man in England is not at all bound in a strict sense to that government that he hath not had a voice to put himself under."[38] The Levellers were soon defeated, but after 1688 English monarchs nevertheless increasingly submitted to the will of a commercial oligarchy. A century later, as the industrial revolution was taking off in Britain, American and French revolutions opened political power to mass participation.[39]

By twenty-first-century standards, neither of these systems was very democratic: both barred women from voting, the American version tolerated mass slavery, and the French version degenerated first into a bloodbath and then into an autocracy. But as fossil fuels restructured markets across the nineteenth century, freeing people to truck and barter as they saw fit, old-style ruling elites found it harder and harder to defend their political privileges against newly rich capitalists or increasingly prosperous workers.

The details varied from country to country. The British landed elite fought a skilled rearguard action, fudging, compromising, and making piecemeal concessions. English-speaking emigrants overseas tended to be more decisive, embracing democracy in one fell swoop. In continental Europe, however, the story was more violent and uneven. A wave of revolutions in 1848 largely failed; a Russian revolution in 1905 succeeded but was rapidly undermined. But despite the noisy variations, by 1914 Western governments were all moving toward representative democracy, broad male franchises, and regular elections. Barriers to political participation based on property, race, religion, education, and even sex came under attack, crumbling almost everywhere in the West by the 1960s (strangely, Switzerland did not grant women the vote until 1971). By almost any measure, societies that moved toward democracy outperformed those that did not.[40]

Outside Europe and its settler colonies, democratization proceeded more slowly. Japan, the first non-Western country to industrialize, moved toward democracy too in the 1880s, but retained emperors that were at least to some extent considered divine. Only when fossil-fuel economies and open markets penetrated Asia and Latin America, in the later twentieth century, did democracies start to thrive. In much of Africa, the Middle East, and Central Asia, where fossil-fuel economies remain weak and tentative even in the 2010s, so too do democracies.[41]

While there was, as always, great variation, nineteenth-century liberals (or "classical liberals," as they are often called, to distinguish them from their twentieth-century namesakes) tended to see small government as the best path toward Industria. The basic principle—mocked by the German socialist Ferdinand Lassalle as the "night-watchman state"—was that governments should do as little as possible, enforcing property rights and protecting the nation against attack, but leaving the promotion of the general welfare to free markets. The sheer complexity of fossil-fuel society, however, made it difficult to stick to this principle rigidly. As early as the 1830s, Britain's government felt compelled to legislate on workplace conditions,[42] and by the 1870s most liberal regimes had legalized trade unions and introduced free compulsory primary education. Some governments even offered saving plans for retirement, public health programs, and unemployment insurance. By the end of the nineteenth century, many Europeans spoke of a "new liberalism," very different from the "classical" version, and relying as much on the invisible fist of the state as on the invisible hand of the market to promote the greater good.[43]

Government intervention to level Industria's playing field rested on the state's ability to use force to overcome resistance, and on some occasions—most famously, to desegregate the southern United States in the early 1960s—democratically elected leaders did use troops to coerce their own citizens.[44] On the whole, though, the liberal path toward Industria led away from state violence—in sharp contrast to the illiberal path. In the nineteenth and early twentieth centuries, even the most liberal regimes had treated some groups within their populations as so undesirable that they should be quarantined, protecting the homogeneous community of interchangeable citizens from contagion. Britain, for instance, herded paupers into workhouses, while the United States first drove many Native Americans beyond its advancing borders and then confined them on reservations, on the principle—as President Andrew Jackson put it in 1832—that "independent farmers are everywhere the basis of society, and the true friends of liberty."[45] Less-liberal regimes, such as Tsarist Russia, interned much larger numbers as they went through their own industrial revolutions. In the twentieth century, however, a much sharper split developed, as Britain, the United States, and many other countries became much more liberal and abandoned such policies, while Russia and a number of other states veered off toward increasingly illiberal solutions, augmenting internment with expulsion and extermination.

Twentieth-century communists defined the desirable in-group through class, while fascists did the same thing through race, but both tried to purify their in-group by applying massive violence to those they defined as not belonging.[46] The ideal type of this policy is perhaps the Soviet collectivization of peasant farms in the 1930s, summed up by the historian Orlando Figes as "a social holocaust—a war against the peasants—uprooting millions of hardworking families from their homes and dispersing them across the Soviet Union. This nomadic workforce became the labour force of the Soviet industrial revolution, filling the great cities, the building-sites and labour camps of the Gulag."[47]

The communist and fascist paths toward Agraria were deeply paradoxical, subjecting their citizens to harsh discipline in the name of creating homogeneous classless societies, deploying huge slave-labor forces in the name of economic progress, and even swinging back toward godlike rulers in the name of the people. Despite these contradictions, though, there were several points in the twentieth century—especially the 1930s and 1970s—when the illiberal path toward Industria seemed to be faster than the liberal one, and since the 1980s, China's post-Maoist reinvention of illiberal development has also produced faster economic growth than the liberal versions (albeit from a lower starting point, and also generating the negative externalities of environmental disaster, massive corruption, and violent protests).[48]

In the end, the liberal path decisively did outperform its major twentieth-century illiberal rivals, Nazi Germany and Soviet Russia; and since the Soviet Empire collapsed in 1989–91, representative democracy, rule of law, and free speech have spread rapidly. Figure 4.8 shows the shift since 1972, using the categories of political and civic freedom developed by the think tank Freedom House. In 1972, Freedom House ranked just 29 percent of the world's societies as free, as compared to 46 percent unfree. By 1998, it had reversed these proportions, calling 46 percent of societies free and 26 percent unfree, and since then, the figures have remained very stable.[49]

The liberal path's success depended on defeating the illiberal version not just at generating wealth and freedom but also at projecting violence, and this took the liberal path into contradictions of

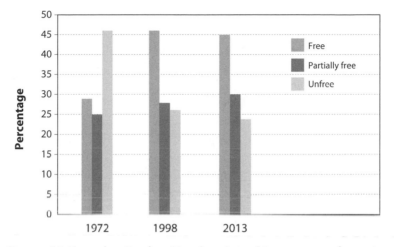

FIGURE 4.8. Free at last: Freedom House's analysis of the percentage of countries with political and civil freedom, 1972–2013.

its own. The liberal democracies probably could not have defeated fascist Germany, Japan, and Italy in the 1940s without making common cause with the illiberal Soviet Union, and in the 1980s, the liberals outlasted the Soviets only by amassing greater means of destruction as well as greater wealth while simultaneously entering into an implicit agreement with them *not* to use violence.[50]

One consequence of the half century of struggle between liberal and illiberal regimes was a massive expansion of state power in both kinds of societies, as governments tried to mobilize national will and resources. This trend ran directly against the nineteenth-century night-watchman tradition, but did mesh with the "new liberal" tendency to use activist big government to dissolve the distinctions left behind by Agraria. The outcome was the forging of liberal New Deals that replaced the last vestiges of Agraria's Old Deal in the mid-twentieth century.

For five thousand years, governments had managed defense, law and order, property rights, and worship, but in the mid- and late twentieth century most New Deal regimes also took responsibility (to greater or lesser degrees) for education, health, employment, and the environment. Some instituted wage and price policies, replacing markets with civil servants; others nationalized vital industries, from coalmining to banking. Bureaucracies and tax rolls ballooned, and steeply progressive income taxes drove income inequality back into a range not seen since the age of foragers. By the 1970s, pre-tax Gini coefficients in countries belonging to the Organisation for Economic Cooperation and Development (OECD: basically, a club for rich fossil-fuel nations) averaged 0.40, but government-imposed net transfers from rich to poor drove these down to an average of just 0.26 (figure 4.9). Even Americans, who show less enthusiasm for redistribution than many OECD members, saw their post-tax and post-transfer Gini score fall from somewhere close to 0.50 in the late 1920s to 0.36 in 1970. Almost everywhere, the sharpest falls in post-tax Gini scores began during World War II, and economists often call the period between the 1940s and 1970s the "Great Compression."[51]

Since the late 1970s, however—for reasons that remain controversial[52]—many fossil-fuel national income distributions have decompressed. The average post-tax OECD Gini score had moved back up to 0.31 by 2012, while the U.S. score had climbed to 0.38. Rising income inequality within fossil-fuel nations has fueled mass protests against the top 1 percent, and the economist Thomas Piketty foresees dire consequences: "When the rate of return on capital exceeds the rate of growth of output and income, as it did in the nineteenth century and seems quite likely to do again in the twenty-first, capitalism automatically generates arbitrary and unsustainable inequalities that radically undermine the meritocratic values on which democratic societies are based."[53]

The bigger picture, however, is more complicated. Most obviously, even though the 2012 post-transfer Gini scores are higher in many countries than the equivalent scores in 1970, the 2012 scores nevertheless remain lower—usually much lower—than the typical Gini score (around 0.48) for wealth inequality in farming societies, and because output per person has risen so much since the farming age (according to the economist Angus Maddison, from a global average of $615 per year in AD 1700 to $7,614 in 2008),[54] the decompression of national incomes since the 1970s has not even

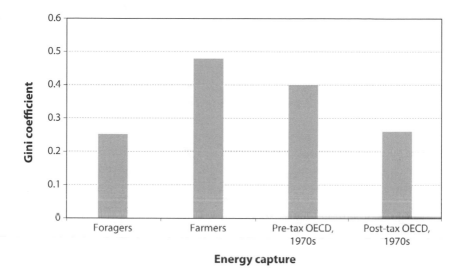

FIGURE 4.9. Foragers, farmers, and fossil fuels: by the 1970s, government transfers had driven income inequality in rich countries down to levels not seen since the age of foragers (data from Smith et al. 2010; Chu et al. 2000).

begun to dent the most important legacy of the industrial revolution—its creation of an enormous middle class able to buy the goods and services that fossil-fuel economies produce. Finally, and arguably even more importantly, when Kuznets identified his curve in 1955, the Great Compression was largely confined to the Western nations that had begun industrializing in the nineteenth century. As a result, even though Gini coefficients fell *within* Western nations across the first half of the twentieth century, when measured across the planet as a whole they increased, because the gap between the fossil-fuel West and the farming rest was growing. By the economist Branko Milanovic's estimate, the worldwide Gini coefficient nearly quadrupled between 1820 and 1950. Between 1955 and 2002, however, the fossil-fuel age went global—with the result that although within-nation Gini scores are now rising, the increase in global inequality has either slowed sharply or gone into reverse, depending on how exactly the 2002 score is calculated (figure 4.10). Since 2002, the whole-earth Gini score has fallen by almost any measure.[55]

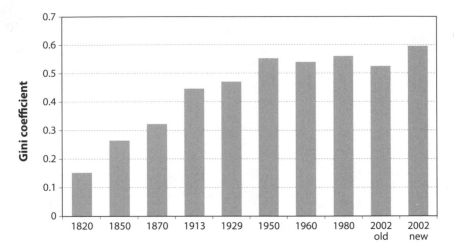

FIGURE 4.10. The great convergence follows the great divergence: the West's industrial revolution almost quadrupled global income equality between 1820 and 1950, but the East's industrial revolution has slowed or even reversed the trend since 1950 (after Milanovic 2011, 2012).

The spread of fossil-fuel economies around much of the planet has taken liberalization with it, to the extent that many activists now speak of a worldwide human rights revolution since the 1950s.[56] The erasure of Agraria's internal boundaries that began in the nineteenth century in Europe and its overseas colonies has been globalized, and in the most advanced fossil-fuel economies, rights have been pushed into areas undreamed of just a generation ago. In the 1990s, the issue of gays in the American military was still controversial enough that even liberal politicians agreed to evade it by adopting the notorious "don't ask, don't tell" policy. In 2011, however, all prohibitions were lifted, and a 2013 report concluded that the changes had had no impact on the military's readiness.[57] By that point, more than half of all Americans approved of same-sex marriage, and sixteen nations had legalized it.[58]

Nor is the rights revolution nowadays restricted just to humans. In 1789, Jeremy Bentham had felt the need to remind Englishmen that in dealing with animals, "The question is not Can they *reason*?

nor Can they *talk*? but Can they *suffer*?" Two hundred years on, the revolution has gone so far that Swiss citizens are required by law to attend a four-hour seminar on the principles of animal companionship before they can adopt a dog.[59] When I met Mr. George in 1982, it was not uncommon to see acts of unspeakable cruelty toward animals in Greece, but in 2009, returning after an absence of nearly ten years, I was astonished to find Athenians putting bowls of water on the sidewalk for strays. And yet like so much in the fossil-fuel world, humans' treatment of other animals is riddled with contradictions. While the Swiss run their seminars, hundreds of millions of animals are suffering and being killed in factory farms. "In their behavior toward creatures, all men were Nazis," the Nobel Prize winner Isaac Bashevis Singer wrote in 1968. "For the animals, it is an eternal Treblinka."[60]

Within our own species, however, the patterns are simpler. "I want a kinder, gentler nation," George H. W. Bush told the Republican party when he accepted their presidential nomination in 1988,[61] and in the quarter-century since he spoke, that is precisely what he got. Even before 1988, fossil-fuel societies (especially liberal ones) had pacified themselves to an extraordinary degree. By 1900, the murder rate in Western Europe had already fallen below one in 1,600, and even the United States, where the rate was eight times higher, was safe by the standards of any earlier age.[62] The World Wars that fossil-fuel societies fought were the bloodiest in history, and the twentieth century's illiberal dictators the most murderous, but when we add up all the casualties in wars, genocides, state-induced famines, and murders, the 100 to 200 million people who died violently between 1900 and 2000 nevertheless represent just 1 to 2 percent of the 10 billion people who lived. The fossil-fuel twentieth century was ten times safer than the world of foragers, and two or three times safer than that of farmers.[63]

But that, it turned out, was just the beginning. Since 1989, the number of wars (interstate and civil) has plummeted, 95 percent of the world's nuclear warheads have been scrapped, violent crime has tumbled, and, according to the World Health Organization, the global rate of violent death has sunk to just 0.7 percent.[64] Things got so peaceful that on Monday, November 26, 2012, the unthinkable happened: an entire day (in fact, almost thirty-six hours) passed without a single person being shot, stabbed, or otherwise done to death anywhere in New York City.[65] Violence has not gone away, but the world has never been so safe.

The more that fossil-fuel societies have moved toward peace, democracy, open markets, gender equality, and equal treatment before the law, the more they have prospered. Consequently, over the astonishingly short period of two centuries, large parts of the world have moved far from Agraria toward Industria. There is still, of course, a long way to go to reach the truly open social space of figure 4.7; economic elites and organized business groups continue to have much more influence on social policies than ordinary citizens, and a recent study of the prevalence of family names in high-status occupations suggests that Industria still has clearly definable elites of birth.[66] But even so, never before in the course of human history has so much changed so quickly for so many.

Values

The last quarter-millennium has seen a correspondingly enormous transformation of moral systems. As the industrial revolution unleashed vast quantities of energy, rewarding societies that moved from Agraria toward Industria, billions of people recalibrated their values. In less than ten generations, political, economic, and gender hierarchy have gone from seeming entirely natural and just to being—to varying degrees—bad. This transformation began around the shores of the North Atlantic and has proceeded fastest and furthest there, but as fossil-fuel energy and organization spread in the twentieth century, it has impacted almost every part of the planet.

Three hundred years ago, this outcome did not look very likely. From China to the Mediterranean, the forces of reaction seemed to have defeated the seventeenth-century "Levellers" whom I mentioned in chapter 3, restoring Agraria's traditional social and religious order. Only Northwest Europe provided an exception to this rule,[67] and even there, the exception initially looked rather limited.

The first signs of Europe's intellectual oddness had come in the sixteenth century, and in my book *Why the West Rules—For Now* I suggested that the new ideas were largely a response to the rise of a novel kind of economy around the shores of the North Atlantic.[68] This economy worked like a supersized version of the trade routes that had made some city-states so prosperous in earlier times, pushing Northwest Europeans away from Agraria. Growing numbers of intellectuals turned from explicating classical or biblical texts toward trying to explain how the winds and tides really worked and why the stars moved as they did, rapidly converging on mechanical models of the universe.[69]

Men like Copernicus, Galileo, and Descartes, who went around saying that the growth of trees was no more mysterious than the workings of a clock, or that the sun, not the earth, was the center of the universe, struck powerholders everywhere as suspicious characters. As the seventeenth century wore on, though, elites in those Agrarias that were profiting most from the Atlantic economy—and who therefore had most to gain from explaining how the world worked—gave the new natural scientists more and more scope to follow the evidence wherever it led. While Italy's papal court felt compelled to bully Galileo into silence in 1633, England's rulers were sufficiently secure to tolerate Newton's *Principia Mathematica* in 1687.

Northwest European intellectuals quickly moved on to extending the mechanical model from the natural to the social order, looking at politics as a mechanism and asking which kinds of machines would work best. As late as 1700, though, the new thinking's challenge to the Old Deal remained very limited. Not even John Locke's famous claim in his *Second Treatise of Government*—that because man is "by nature all free, equal and independent, no one can be put out of this estate, and subjected to the political power of another, without his own consent"[70]—necessarily required rejection of kingship, aristocracy, or the established church, and in 1688 the English elite brought half a century of conflict to a close not by abandoning the Old Deal but by compromises that enmeshed monarchy in a constitutional web.[71]

The most sustained challenge to Agraria began in France. "One must examine and stir up everything, without exception and without caution," Denis Diderot wrote in the *Encyclopédie* in 1751. "We must trample underfoot all that old foolishness, overturn barriers not put there by reason."[72] Voltaire, in exile in Switzerland, did just this, explicitly denouncing the privileges of church and crown, which he labeled "the infamous thing," and yet not even he went so far as to reject Agraria's royal and clerical basis altogether. The way to end the infamy, he insisted, was not by making France a republic, but by modeling it on China. There, he claimed, Europeans would find in the Qianlong emperor a truly wise despot, ruling in consultation with a Confucian civil service that preferred reason to superstition.[73]

At first, eighteenth-century European monarchs coopted Enlightenment critiques as smoothly as ancient emperors had tamed the most alarming implications of Axial Age thought. In 1740, Frederick the Great of Prussia conceded to Christian Wolff that "Philosophers should be teachers of the world and teachers of princes," but, he added, "they must think logically and we must act logically."[74] By self-identifying as enlightened despots, eighteenth-century kings brought the new ideas within a vision of the Old Deal very like that being offered by the enlightened peasant Kleinjogg, mentioned in chapter 3.

Not until the second half of the eighteenth century did the Old Deal itself come under real pressure. In 1762, when Rousseau announced in *The Social Contract* that the only source of political legitimacy was the "general will" of the people, he was still very much an eccentric (albeit a literary celebrity), in exile not only from his native Geneva but also from France and the city-state of Berne. Just a quarter of a century later, however, the Founding Fathers of the United States—men deeply enmeshed in the new Atlantic economy—had moved far enough away from the values of Agraria to feel that they could write their new constitution in the name of "We the People," rather than in the name of God or a king. Just two years after that, the bourgeois gentlemen who gave France a *Declaration of the Rights of Man and the Citizen* baldly stated that "Law is the expression of the general will."[75]

By the 1780s, French and American revolutionaries had become every bit as radical as the men who created democracies in classical Greece,[76] but when fossil fuels began flooding the North Atlantic world with energy, the challenges to the Old Deal really took off. By the mid-nineteenth century, societies that had reorganized themselves to look like figure 4.7 were reaping huge rewards, and values that fitted with this boundary-free structure flourished. By the 1860s, a century after *The Social Contract*, political values had shifted in most industrializing societies. Elites had come to recognize that grounding political power on the general will rather than tradition or claims to divinity would not bring on anarchy. In fact, they saw, in a community of interchangeable citizens the general will really was the only secure basis for legitimate political authority.[77]

In the 2010s, two-and-a-half centuries after *The Social Contract*, the general will has defeated almost all rival sources of political authority. "Democracy," the philosopher and economist Amartya Sen suggests, is now "a universal value,"[78] and across most of the world, respondents tell pollsters that they prefer democracy to any other political system.[79] Polls conducted in 2007 pointed to 80 percent support for democracy worldwide, with remarkably little variation by geography, gender, religion, or age (figure 4.11).[80] Plenty of scope remains for arguments over just what "democracy" means, but in much (probably most) of the world, it rests heavily on the belief that steep political hierarchies are bad.

The most extreme version of the critique of political hierarchy, shared by a number of anarchists, libertarians, and communists, holds that a proper Industria will not need rulers at all. As early as 1794, American libertarianism was sufficiently strong that Alexander Hamilton felt that he had to defend his fledgling country against the idea that "government itself will become useless, and Society will subsist and flourish free from its shackles,"[81] and nearly a century later, Engels was insisting that after the communist revolution, "State interference in social relations becomes, in one domain after another, superfluous. . . . The state is not 'abolished.' It *withers away*."[82] In practice, however, neither American political elites nor communists abolished government. In fact, communists enthusiastically embraced it. As early as Lenin's funeral in 1924, Soviet propagandists were promoting a cult of personality, hoping to solve the problem posed by the refusal of political hierarchy to wither away by suggesting that

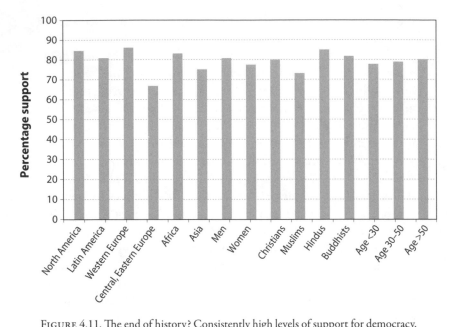

FIGURE 4.11. The end of history? Consistently high levels of support for democracy, ranging from 66 through 86 percent, regardless of geography, gender, religion, or age (2007 poll data).

the communist party had leaders so wise that they singlehandedly embodied the general will.[83] Mao Zedong and North Korea's Kims went further, and fascists further still, taking the cult of personality into territory that George Orwell famously labeled "doublethink."[84] By creating the steepest possible political hierarchy and concentrating power in one person, illiberals claimed, they were really eradicating political hierarchy.

None of these creative interpretations of the general will proved viable in the long run. In 1956, just three years after Stalin's death, Nikita Khrushchev denounced the cult of personality. Five years later, he tried out a new sleight of hand, suggesting that the Soviet Union had in fact evolved into a "state of the whole people," with the party embodying the general will. China also backed away from leader-worship after Mao's death in 1976, and while the Kims have hung on for more than sixty years in North Korea, they have brought disaster on their subjects, and their prospects do not look good in the 2010s.[85]

Radical anarchism has also lost ground, this time to more pragmatic libertarian views. In his influential 1974 book *Anarchy, State, and Utopia*, for instance, the philosopher Robert Nozick suggested that for libertarians, "a minimal state, limited to enforcing contracts and protecting people against force, theft, and fraud, is justified. Any more extensive state," he argued, "violates persons' rights not to be forced to do certain things, and is unjustified";[86] but having no state at all is simply not an option.

And yet although the state shows no signs of withering away, fossil-fuel attitudes toward steep political hierarchies and upstarts nevertheless have more in common with foragers' views than with farmers'. Political scientists have long suggested that even democracies necessarily spawn powerful elites that constitute themselves as permanent political castes,[87] but democrats have consistently preferred visions of government by everyman to the idea of a natural ruling class.

The struggle between these ideas goes back to the earliest days of modern democracy.[88] That the Federalist Alexander Hamilton would be appalled in the 1780s at having to share power with the kind of "man whose ignorance and perverseness are only surpassed by his pertinacity and conceit" should not surprise us, but even the arch-egalitarian Thomas Jefferson admitted to believing that only a tiny elite, "whom nature has endowed with genius and virtue," could "be rendered by liberal education worthy to receive, and able to guard the sacred rights and liberties of their fellow citizens."[89] The United States had remarkable luck, however, in the person of its first president. On the one hand, George Washington struck many observers as being the absolute embodiment of a natural ruling class, but on the other, he made it abundantly clear that he had no interest whatsoever in actually ruling.[90] The moment he won military victory in 1783, Washington surrendered his sword to Congress, vowing not to have "any share in public business hereafter." He had to be dragged reluctantly out of retirement to take up the presidency in 1789, served out of a sense of duty, and then—as one admirer put it, likening Washington to the haughty Roman hero Cincinnatus—returned as soon as he decently could "with contentment and with pleasure [to] the peaceful labours of a rural and independent life."[91]

Since Washington's day, many American politicians have claimed to be following his example in not wanting power, but others have taken a subtly different line, insisting that despite very obviously belonging to privileged elites, they are really the same as everyone else.[92] Neither immense wealth (for example, Ross Perot in 1992), nor membership in a political dynasty (for example, George W. Bush in 2000), nor even both at once (for example, John Kennedy in 1960), need stop a would-be president from claiming to be middle class.

One side effect (surely unintended) of the maneuvers forced onto would-be rulers by the popular mistrust of steep hierarchies has been a collapse of deference. In 1998, Bill Clinton, the most powerful man on earth, was almost hounded out of office over an extramarital sexual affair; in 2011, just a year after being named by the *Jerusalem Post* as the sixth-most powerful Jew in the world,[93] Dominique Strauss-Kahn actually was hounded out of the director-generalship of the International Monetary Fund over accusations of raping a hotel maid. This did not happen to Roman emperors.

The kinds of compromises between steep and shallow hierarchies that characterize fossil-fuel politics are even more apparent in economics. Industria seems to call for a wealth hierarchy that is low (by the standards of Agraria, anyway) but not *too* low. On the one hand, Industria can flourish only if it has affluent middle and working classes that create effective demand for all the goods and services that fossil-fuel economies generate, but on the other, it also needs a dynamic entrepreneurial class that expects material rewards for providing leadership and management. In response, fossil-fuel values have evolved across the last two hundred years to favor government intervention to reduce wealth equality—but not too much.

According to opinion polls carried out since 1990, most Americans—the numbers have varied between a high of 67 percent in

1990 and a low of 58 percent in 2008, with the most recent score (for 2011) being 66 percent—want to see wealth distributed more evenly, and in polls in 2013, majorities in China (52 percent), the European Union (60 percent), and India (a whopping 82 percent) said that they considered income inequality "a very big problem." However, none of these groups thought that economic inequality was the *biggest* problem facing their country. Europeans and Chinese ranked it third, Indians fifth, and Americans twelfth. When asked whether the best way to reduce the wealth gradient was through heavier taxes on the rich, Americans were quite evenly split, with 52 percent saying yes and 45 percent saying no. These attitudes have changed little since at least 1999, when 45 percent said yes and 51 percent no. However, the split on this issue often reflects deeper regional or party divides. The 2013 polls found that within the European Union, 84 percent of Greeks but only 50 percent of Britons thought that wealth inequality was a very big problem, and in the United States, 75 percent of Democrats said that they wanted to increase taxes on the rich as against just 26 percent of Republicans—although by 2014 several leading Republicans were ready to support raising the minimum wage.[94]

One way to make sense of the intellectual and cultural ferment over economic hierarchy across the last two centuries is to see it as an argument over what "equality" actually means when it comes to wealth. Some people emphasize equality of opportunity, making everyone equally free to truck and barter in the marketplace without too much concern over the resulting distribution of spoils, while others emphasize equality of outcome, favoring regulation of market behavior so that no one can pull too far ahead of the rest.[95] Broadly speaking, classical liberals and libertarians champion equality of opportunity and worry that regulation stifles liberty (and with it economic growth); new liberals and socialists generally champion equality of outcome and worry more that malefactors of great wealth will undermine liberty (and with it economic growth).[96]

Thanks to the abundant evidence available for the last two hundred years, we can trace in detail how the liberal and illiberal paths toward Industria worked as two great experiments in the interpretation of fossil-fuel values. The most important twentieth-century illiberal regimes—Nazi Germany, the Soviet Union, the People's Republic of China—all claimed to seek equality of economic outcomes, but in practice none could escape the tension between the two different senses of economic equality. In their first months in government, the Nazis—who, after all, officially called themselves the National Socialist German Workers' Party—strongly championed equality of outcome. Activists in their Labor Front imposed paid vacations, wage agreements, and equal pay on employers, threatening to send those who argued to concentration camps. This did not last, however; even before 1933 was over, party leaders began siding with the bosses, whose support they needed for Hitler's ambitious rearmament program. "We are all soldiers of labor," the new head of the Labor Front told workers in the Siemens factory in Berlin that November, but "some command and the others obey. Obedience and responsibility have to count." Wages stagnated in 1934, and wealth inequality soared over the next decade.[97]

Communist regimes were caught in the same trap. Confronting mass starvation in 1921, Lenin backed away from his revolutionary principles and liberalized the Soviet economy to encourage production. Opinions differed over how serious he was about this; Grigorii Zinoviev, Lenin's colleague on the Politburo, insisted that "The [New Economic Policy] is only a temporary deviation, a tactical retreat, a clearing of the land for a new and decisive attack of labor against the front of international capitalism," but Lenin himself suspected that "building communism with bourgeois hands" was in fact the only viable path.[98] The consequences of the New Economic Policy, however, were clear to all. "Shops and stores sprang up overnight, mysteriously stacked with delicacies Russia had not seen for years," the American anarchist Emma Goldman noted in 1924. "Men, women and children with pinched faces and hungry eyes stood about gazing into the windows and discussing the great miracle."[99] When Stalin reversed Lenin's New Economic Policy a few years later in the name of true socialism, the results were catastrophic. Millions starved to death in the 1930s as farm output fell, and yet wage and housing differentials kept widening as party officials created a black economy. The Soviet Union increasingly got the worst of all worlds, with the wealth hierarchy becoming steeper even though growth was sluggish, and when Gorbachev tried to reintroduce equality of economic opportunity in the 1980s, the entire system came apart.[100]

Under Mao, China had experiences that were arguably even worse as it lurched back and forth between radical attempts to suppress equality of opportunity and periods of relative liberalization and modest growth. By the time the Great Helmsman died in 1976, the risk of yet another famine was very real. Deng Xiaoping reacted by embracing equality of opportunity for at least some sectors of the economy. "To get rich is no sin," he famously announced, unleashing both productivity growth and income inequality. China's post-tax and post-transfer Gini coefficient, which stood at 0.31 when Mao died in 1976, hit 0.51 in 2003, before falling back to 0.47 in 2009.[101]

Liberal regimes also found the quest for the perfect balance between steep and shallow wealth hierarchies challenging, but their experiments have been less traumatic. In the classic statement of nineteenth-century liberalism, John Stuart Mill argued that "The sole end for which mankind are warranted, individually or collectively, in interfering with the liberty of action of any of their number is self-protection. Over himself, over his own body and mind, the individual is sovereign."[102] If pushed to its logical extreme, however, this means that state redistribution of wealth is always wrong. In fact, the libertarian philosopher Robert Nozick points out, "Taxation of earnings from labor is on a par with forced labor," the antithesis of liberal Industria. "Seizing the results of someone's labor," Nozick explains, "is equivalent to seizing hours from him and directing him to carry on various activities. If people force you to do certain work, or unrewarded work, for a certain period of time, they decide what you are to do and what purposes your work is to serve apart from your decisions. This . . . makes them a part-owner of you; it gives them a property right in you.[103] Rousseau put it even more bluntly: "I hold enforced labor," he wrote in *The Social Contract*, "to be less opposed to liberty than taxes."[104]

Refusing to extract forced labor (in the form of taxes) from the rich, however, often seemed to mean extracting a different kind of forced labor (in the form of long working hours to earn a living wage) from the poor, and across the nineteenth century, socialist alternatives emphasizing equality of outcome gained ground in Europe. By the century's end, many governments had warmed to the new liberalism and were betting that using state power to redistribute wealth would generate larger aggregate growth. This trend accelerated after World War I, picked up more speed still in the Great Depression, and was enshrined after 1945 in a variety of liberal New Deals. The job of postwar government, the British politician William Beveridge predicted in 1942, would be to make a world "free, as free as is humanly possible, of the five giant evils, of Want, of Disease, of Ignorance, of Squalor and of Idleness." To do this, "we ought to be prepared to use the powers of the State so far as may be necessary without any limit whatever, in order to abolish those five giant evils"—while also remembering, Beveridge added, "that the individual is more than the State, and is the object for which the State exists."[105]

This program called for complicated economic and social juggling, and the postwar liberal experience suggests that there is no perfect, one-size-fits-all solution to the contradictions between equalities of opportunity and outcome. Fossil-fuel values have evolved to reflect this, approving of wealth hierarchies that are low but not too low. What "low" and "too low" actually mean seems to depend heavily on the rate of economic growth, with people in poor, rapidly growing economies being more tolerant of steep wealth hierarchies than those in rich, slowly growing ones. Judging from voters' enthusiasm for fiscal conservatism in many OECD countries in the Reagan-Thatcher years, post-tax Gini scores around 0.25 may be too low for developed economies, but judging from the widespread rage against the 1 percent in many of the same countries in the 2010s, Gini scores above 0.35 may be too high. In fast-growing India and China, by contrast, people grumble but have so far put up with stratospheric scores (0.50 and 0.47 respectively in 2009).[106]

In comparison with these complicated attitudes toward economic hierarchy, fossil-fuel ideas about gender inequality seem much more straightforward.[107] As recently as 1869, John Stuart Mill was being self-consciously radical when he wrote that "The principle which regulates the existing social relations between the two sexes—the legal subordination of one sex to another—is wrong in itself and now one of the chief hindrances to human improvement. . . . No slave is a slave to the same lengths, and in so full a sense of the word, as a wife,"[108] but since then, Agrarian attitudes have collapsed completely. In a 2009 poll in sixteen countries, 86 percent of respondents said that gender equality was important, with national responses ranging from 60 percent in India to 98 percent in Britain and Mexico. Islamic nations lay toward the top end of this distribution. Even though legal protections for women are often weak in the Muslim world (Egypt, for instance, passed a law defining sexual harassment only in 2014),[109] 78 percent of Iranians, 91 percent of Indonesians and Turks, and 93 percent of people in the Palestinian Territories agreed that gender equality is important. Globally, 81 percent of respondents favored government intervention to promote gender equality, and 53 percent of interviewees thought that their governments were currently not doing enough.[110]

Illiberal societies fostered more extreme attitudes about gender hierarchy than liberal ones, with communists normally promoting women's equality energetically. "Petty housework crushes, strangles, stultifies, and degrades" women, Lenin announced in 1920,[111] and in 1959 Khrushchev was confident that communism had already buried capitalism when it came to women's rights. "You want to keep your women in the kitchen," he told Richard Nixon in the famous "Kitchen Debate," but "we don't think of women in those terms. We think better of them."[112] The reality, needless to say, was messier. After major legislation on women's rights in the 1920s, Stalin retreated to pro-natalist policies in the 1930s, and although more Soviet wives did work outside the home than Americans when Khrushchev and Nixon squared off, Soviet wives also generally spent longer doing housework than American wives (and much longer than Soviet husbands).[113] Nazi Germany, however, went in the opposite direction, aggressively separating male and female spheres and insisting on reproduction as a woman's first duty.[114]

Initially, liberal societies were more cautious about gender equality. As mentioned earlier, few women had the right to vote before 1918, and female participation in paid labor only really took off after 1940. When pollsters asked Americans in 1937 whether they would consider voting for a female presidential candidate, just one-third said yes, while 64 percent said no. By 1949, the responses were evenly split, but in 2012, 95 percent answered yes and just 5 percent no. Other attitudes took longer to change: in 1977, respondents split evenly when asked whether it was best for men to be the breadwinners and women the homemakers, and in 2012, 19 percent still answered yes, as against 75 percent no.[115]

Overall, the speed of postwar change has been extraordinary. In the 1970s, when I was a teenager, comedians regularly cracked jokes about "women's libbers" and "bra burners" on primetime television. By 2005, however, values had shifted so far that it was no longer acceptable for Harvard University's president Larry Summers even to ask in an academic seminar whether biology might have anything to do with men's dominance of the highest levels of science and engineering. Summers observed that some tests seemed to suggest that male cognitive abilities were more widely distributed around the mean than female, which, if correct, would mean that men were more common than women at the extreme ends of the distribution. "My best guess, to provoke you," he mused, is

> that in the special case of science and engineering, there are issues of intrinsic aptitude, and particularly the variability of aptitude, and that those considerations are reinforced by what are in fact lesser factors involving socialization and continuing discrimination. I would like nothing better than to be proved wrong, because I would like nothing better than for these problems to be addressable simply by everybody understanding what they are, and working very hard to address them.[116]

The resulting uproar certainly played a part in the Harvard faculty's vote, two months after Summers's remarks, of no confidence in his leadership; probably contributed to Summers's decision, less than a year later, to resign the Harvard presidency; and possibly influenced his withdrawal from consideration for the chairmanship of the Federal Reserve Bank in 2013.[117]

Mainstream liberal values do not deny all differences between men and women in the name of erasing gender hierarchy. However, the number of spheres in which it is considered legitimate to make biological distinctions has certainly narrowed sharply since 1945, and the last of my categories of analysis—violence—is one of the few remaining realms of behavior where it is politically correct to recognize huge differences between men and women. Police statistics from around the world show that regardless of religion, culture, or any other factor, men are nearly ten times as likely as women to commit violent crimes.[118] The explanation is debated, but it seems likely that an innate predisposition[119] to use force is an evolved adaptation, common among human males but much less common among females.[120] Consequently, it should not surprise us that the abrupt collapse of Agraria's generally positive valuation of male dominance has been accompanied by an equally abrupt collapse of its limited tolerance of force.[121]

Just as the complex division of labor and long-distance trade that made Agraria possible could not have functioned if farmers had been as violent as foragers, so too Industria's open space of interchangeable citizens could not function if people still settled their disputes as violently as they did in the farming age. Fossil-fuel society depends on extreme pacification, enforced by Leviathans vastly stronger than anything Hobbes ever imagined (it is no coincidence that the first modern police force was created in early-industrial London in 1828). As so often in the past, people adjusted their values to reflect the new reality they lived in. Farming societies reduced the scope for legitimate use of violence to settle disputes, and fossil-fuel groups have reduced it much further.

The historian Martin Ceadel suggests that "fatalism" is a good description of worldwide attitudes toward violence before the eighteenth century AD. Many people (especially Axial Age religious leaders) preached against violence, and most civilizations developed subtle and often self-serving distinctions between just and unjust wars, but there was broad agreement that the use of force by legitimate authorities was necessary, and could even be admirable.[122] Not until the eighteenth century, and even then only in Europe and its North American colonies, do we see a real break with this pattern of values. New ideas—that war is unnatural, that man in his natural state was peaceful—bubbled up just as the broader critiques of political, economic, and gender hierarchies were beginning,[123] and in the 1790s, a Peace Society in industrializing Britain publicly and noisily opposed war against France on principle.[124]

Peace movements—like attacks on political, economic, and gender hierarchy—began flourishing in the nineteenth century, as the notion of Industria as an open space of interchangeable citizens gained ground. By 1854, when the Crimean War broke out, significant numbers of educated European liberals took it for granted that war was an abnormal and immoral state; in 1899, twenty-six countries sent delegates to an international peace conference at the Hague; and in 1919, hope flared briefly that a League of Nations would abolish war. The next twenty-five years were tough times for pacifism, but nevertheless by the 1950s, Western European and North American academics had established think tanks (the Center for Research on Conflict Resolution, founded at Ann Arbor, Michigan, in 1952, and the International Peace Research Institute, at Oslo in 1959) and journals (the *Journal of Conflict Resolution* began publishing in 1957, and the *Journal of Peace Research* in 1964) that enshrined the assumption that force was almost always wrong.[125]

Scholars of the peace movement often distinguish between people whom they call "pacifists," who "do not rule out all armed force: they allow its defensive use to protect the values they hold," and more doctrinaire advocates whom they call "absolute pacifists," who "reject war unconditionally, and advocate non-resistance in all circumstances."[126] In the twentieth century, absolute pacifists were rather rare, but recent poll data suggest that in the twenty-first, that is changing (or at least that large numbers of people now want to tell pollsters that they reject violence completely).

Between 2008 and 2010, Gallup interviewed people in Africa, America, Asia, and Europe about their attitudes toward individual and state violence. Sixty-nine percent of the respondents claimed to be absolute pacifists in matters of interpersonal violence, saying that force is never justified, while just 13 percent said that using force is sometimes right (the other 18 percent either didn't have an opinion or said "it depends"). Attitudes toward state violence, however, were more complicated. When asked whether it was acceptable for governments to kill civilians in wartime, 60 percent said never and 21 percent said sometimes.[127] A Pew poll in 2011 asked Westerners the broader question of whether governments sometimes need to use military force to maintain order in the world, and found rather more readiness to accept state violence, with yes votes ranging from 50 percent in Germany to 75 percent in the United States. Even then, though, the pollsters found that Westerners harbored reservations: most Europeans (ranging from 66 percent in France through 76 percent in Germany) and 45 percent of Americans said that governments needed United Nations approval before using force.[128]

Some strategists conclude that the West has now entered a "postheroic" era,[129] in which citizens no longer recognize any national goals important enough to justify casualties (whether inflicted or suffered). However, fossil-fuel postheroism may have as much to do with the kinds of conflicts Western nations have engaged in since 1989 as with a complete aversion to killing. When considering existential threats, respondents take tougher positions. No nuclear-armed democracy has ever voted into office a party promising unilateral disarmament, and a 2007 poll found at least some willingness to contemplate nuclear war. Asked whether there were any circumstances in which it would be right for their government (or, in non-nuclear countries, their alliance) to use nuclear weapons, 70 percent of Italian and 77 percent of German respondents said no, but only 49 percent of Britons, 43 percent of French, 40 percent of Americans, and 22 percent of Israelis felt the same way.[130] Humanity has never been as peaceful as it is today, or as opposed to settling problems with force; but we do not yet live in a world of absolute pacifists.

After Assiros

The argument advanced in chapters 2 to 4, I believe, largely explains my culture shock in 1982. Assiros still had at least one foot in Agraria; the English Midlands, where I had grown up and where Industria had been born two hundred years earlier, did not.

Table 4.1 sums up the arguments in chapters 2 to 4. I readily concede that table 4.1 is reductionist, and that it simplifies and necessarily distorts a much more complex reality, but I think it does make an important point: that foraging, farming, and fossil-fuel moral systems are very different. It is a rare thing for people in two different energy capture categories to agree on moral questions.

TABLE 4.1. **How values evolved: the differences between ideal-type moral values among foragers, farmers, and fossil-fuel users**

	Foragers	*Farmers*	*Fossil-Fuel Users*
Political Inequality	Bad	Good	Bad
Wealth Inequality	Bad	Good	Middling
Gender Inequality	Middling	Good	Bad
Violence	Middling	Middling/bad	Bad

Figure 4.12 is even more reductionist, simplifying and doubtless distorting the complicated world of culture even further,[131] but in doing so, I think it adds a second important point to table 4.1. In the graph, we see not only that all value systems are different but also that some value systems are more different than others. The gap separating farming values from those of the foraging and fossil-fuel ages is much bigger than the gaps separating foraging and fossil fuel values from each other.

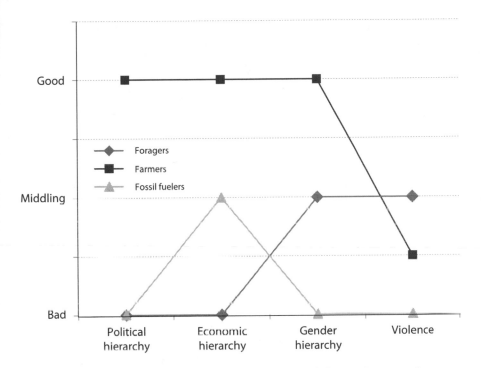

FIGURE 4.12. A picture worth a thousand words? The differences between value systems expressed graphically.

When professors of psychology want to test their theories about how the brain works, they regularly round up and question volunteers from among their own students—even though, as the psychologists themselves regularly admit, their students are WEIRD.[132] WEIRD, in psychology-speak, stands for Western, Educated, Industrialized, Rich, and Democratic; it means, in a nutshell, people who are perfectly groomed to fit into Industria.[133] (Cynics might even say that the whole point of college is to make sure that students are properly WEIRD by the time they graduate.)

One of the main things I have learned in nearly thirty years of teaching premodern history is that students tend to find Agraria and its values hard to understand and even harder to love. Foragers and their values, by contrast, often seem very attractive to the WEIRD young. There are exceptions, of course; foragers sometimes act like savages, while commercial city-states such as classical Athens can strike a chord, at least until we start talking about slavery and the oppression of women. But on the whole, the foragers we meet in *Nisa* (the anthropologist Marjorie Shostak's biography of a !Kung woman, mentioned in chapter 2) seem very like the kind of people we might meet on the quad, while those in the eleventh-century epic *The Song of Roland* seem to come from another planet.

I had a particularly interesting experience with this in 1996, at the end of my first year of teaching at Stanford University, when I offered an undergraduate seminar on ancient and modern slavery. In one of our meetings, it came out that several students had ancestors—great-great or great-great-great grandparents—who had been slaveholders in the southern states before the Civil War. Without exception, my students agreed that slavery was bad. When I asked whether they thought their relatives had been morally retarded,[134] however, most of them seemed uncomfortable and avoided giving a straightforward answer. As the discussion widened, other students in the class offered other possible explanations. Perhaps, some suggested, the slaveholding relatives had known that slavery was wrong, and had therefore been hypocrites. Or perhaps slavery wasn't really wrong at all, and everything was relative. Both of these ideas generated even deeper discomfort.

This classroom debate was, by definition, academic, and no great consequences hung on its outcome. Sometimes, though, the failure of farmers and fossil-fuelers to understand each other's values has very serious results. On October 9, 2012, one week before I delivered the lectures this book is based on, a man climbed onto a school bus in northwest Pakistan, asked if Malala Yousafzai was on board, and then pulled out a Colt 45 and shot the sixteen-year-old girl in the face. Her crime: "She was pro-west, she was speaking against Taliban and she was calling President Obama her ideal leader," according to a Taliban spokesman. When Yousafzai did not die, the Taliban vowed to try again (and to kill her father too).[135]

The shooting came up several times in discussions after my lectures at Princeton. To the WEIRD denizens of Industria (and I suspect that there is no WEIRDer place on earth than Princeton), the only explanation for the attempted assassination seemed to be that the Taliban were guilty of profound moral failures. Women have a right to be educated, and the world needs educated women. Yousafzai's blogging and protests about the Taliban's ban on girls going to school had made her a heroine even before the attack. Bishop Desmond Tutu had nominated her for the International Children's Peace Prize, and Pakistan's modernizing prime minister had given her the country's National Peace Award for Youth.[136] Since the attack, Yousafzai has become the youngest-ever recipient of the Nobel Peace Prize.[137] In trying to kill her, the Taliban had surely trampled on the highest moral virtues.

To the Taliban, however, things evidently look very different. Their hardline version of Agrarian values emphasizes female subordination, respect for divinely sanctioned political authority, and the righteous use of violence; in such a world, Yousafzai must seem to be the one trampling on the highest values.[138] Nor are the Taliban alone in feeling this way: between April and June 2014, as I was finishing the written version of this chapter, the Islamist group Boko Haram (a Hausa name that roughly means "Western Education is Evil") kidnapped more than 250 schoolgirls in Nigeria.[139] In a 2009 interview, the group's founder had described its mission as rejecting democracy and modern education (particularly the theory of evolution and the idea of a spherical earth), instituting religious law, and returning to traditional gender roles.[140] The kidnapped girls, a spokesman said, should have been married instead of being in school, adding that one appropriate response to their failings might be to sell them into slavery.[141]

In the Agrarian world we saw in chapter 3, the Taliban and Boko Haram might well have seemed extreme or even misguided, but not wicked. For ten thousand years, farming societies regularly used violence to deter or punish much more modest affronts to the divine order than the one offered by Yousafzai. Even the enlightened Athenians had executed Socrates in 399 BC for corrupting the young and believing in gods that the city did not believe in.[142] Boko Haram and the Taliban are playing by the rules of Agraria, and interpret the biologically evolved human values of justice, respect, and decency accordingly. They are not guilty of moral failings for thinking that girls who want to go to school should be punished violently, but they are guilty of backwardness—as, in a much, much milder way, was Mr. George.

Each age gets the thought it needs, and the age that needed Taliban-type values is now passing from this world. For the last two hundred years, societies that remained true to Agrarian values have been going extinct, and as industrialization continues its inexorable expansion, the remaining holdouts will perish too. The WEIRD shall inherit the Earth.

I hope to have shown in chapters 2 to 4 that what explains my culture shock in Assiros in 1982 is the dramatic evolution of human values since the Ice Age, driven not by biological changes (the actual human animal seems to have changed rather little in the last fifteen thousand years) but by the evolution of our systems of energy capture and the kinds of social organization they require. I have not, though, tried to explain *why* this dramatic coevolution of energy, organization, and values occurred, or to ask the obvious question of how human values are likely to change as our systems of energy capture and organization continue to evolve. It is to these questions that I now turn.

CHAPTER 5

THE EVOLUTION

OF VALUES: BIOLOGY,

CULTURE, AND

THE SHAPE OF

THINGS TO COME

Biologicizing Ethics

In chapters 2 to 4, I attempted to tell the story of human values across the twenty thousand years since the coldest point of the last ice age. I suggested that modern human values initially emerged somewhere around 100,000 years ago (± 50,000 years) as a consequence of the biological evolution of our big, fast brains, and that once we had our big, fast brains, cultural evolution became a possibility too. Because of cultural evolution, human values have mutated rapidly in the last twenty thousand years, and the pace of change has accelerated in the last two hundred years.

I identified three major stages in human values, which I linked to foraging, farming, and fossil-fuel societies. My main point was that in each case, modes of energy capture determined population size and density, which in turn largely determined which forms of social organization worked best, which went on to make certain sets of values more successful and attractive than others.

Foragers, I observed, overwhelmingly lived in small, low-density groups, and generally saw political and wealth hierarchies as bad things. They were more tolerant of gender hierarchy, and (by modern lights) surprisingly tolerant of violence. Farmers lived in bigger, denser communities, and generally saw steep political, wealth, and gender hierarchies as fine. They had much less patience than foragers, though, for interpersonal violence, and restricted its range of legitimate uses more narrowly. Fossil-fuel folk live in bigger, denser communities still. They tend to see political and gender hierarchy as bad things, and violence as particularly evil, but they are generally more tolerant of wealth hierarchies than foragers, although not so tolerant as farmers.

In this, the final chapter before I hand the book over to the respondents, I want to ask why values changed in this way. I already gave a proximate explanation, linking each value system to a system of energy capture, but now I want to go further by posing three more questions. First, I ask why systems of energy capture change; second, whether these shifts are inevitable; and finally, what the answers mean for the future of human values.

In chapter 1, I quoted the naturalist E. O. Wilson's suggestion that "the time has come for ethics to be removed temporarily from the hands of the philosophers and biologicized,"[1] and I now want to suggest that it is to Wilsonian biologicization that we should look to answer my three questions. In the final chapter of his monumental book *Sociobiology*, Wilson urges readers to imagine themselves as "zoologists from another planet completing a catalog of social species on Earth." From this perspective, he says, "the humanities and social sciences shrink to specialized branches of biology; history, biography, and fiction are the research protocols of human ethology; and anthropology and sociology together constitute the sociobiology of a single primate species."[2] History and moral philosophy become subfields of biology.[3]

Darwin famously defined biological evolution as "descent with modification,"[4] and a century and a half on, biologists are able to peer inside our cells to explain the mechanisms that drive this. The process of transmitting huge amounts of genetic information across generations always produces a tiny number of random mutations. Most of these make little difference; some are positively harmful, and make their recipient less likely to pass his or her genes on to the next generation; but a few are helpful, making the organisms that inherit them more likely to pass their genes on to the next generation. Over time (usually, a lot of time) competition between organisms for energy and mates will mean that adaptively positive mutations will spread through the gene pool. This is what Darwin called natural selection: those organisms best adapted to the environment tend to flourish, gradually replacing those that are less well adapted. At the same time, however, a feedback process operates, so that species that evolve to fit better with their environment simultaneously transform that environment, sometimes in ways that make their evolution counterproductive.[5]

Some biologists call this the Red Queen Effect,[6] after a much-loved scene in Lewis Carroll's *Through the Looking-Glass* in which the Red Queen takes Alice on a madcap race through the countryside. They run and they run, "so fast that at last they seemed to skim through the air," says Carroll, but then Alice discovers that they're still under the same tree that they started from. "In our country," Alice tells the queen, "you'd generally get to somewhere else—if you ran very fast for a long time." Astonished, the queen explains things to Alice: "*here*, you see, it takes all the running you can do, to keep in the same place."[7]

Biologists sometimes elevate this Red Queen Effect into an evolutionary principle. If foxes evolve to run faster so they can catch more rabbits, the biologists observe, then only the fastest rabbits will live long enough to reproduce, breeding a new generation of bunnies that run faster still—in which case, of course, only the fastest foxes will catch enough rabbits to thrive and pass on their genes. Run as they might, the two species just stay in place.

The Red Queen effect certainly does exist, but in the real world its effects are rather different. Foxes and rabbits do not just interact with each other; they also interact with their total environments. While they may still be under the tree they started from, the tree is no longer the same tree: the race between the foxes and rabbits has changed it into something else.[8] To escape from this now rather tortured metaphor to a more philosophical one, we might say that species running the Red Queen's race never step into the same stream twice—and, to add even more messiness, the evolutionary race can be massively affected by exogenous inputs.

My premise throughout this book has been that our values change in similar ways to our genes, through back-and-forth interactions between moral systems and the environment (social and intellectual as well as physical), combined with external shocks. Just as the race between foxes and rabbits is played out in millions of little biological competitions of sex, chasing, and eating, with small statistical shifts in the odds producing massive changes in the animals themselves across thousands of generations, so too the race between values and environments is played out in billions of little cultural competitions, as individuals decide what is the right thing to do. Once again, small statistical shifts in the odds produce massive changes in the cultures, but this time with consequences that sometimes need mere decades, rather than millennia, to make themselves felt.

In the rest of this chapter, I will try to answer my three questions (why systems of energy capture change, whether these shifts are inevitable, and what it all means for the future of human values) by looking at the evolution from foraging to farming values and from farming to fossil-fuel varieties, and then extrapolating the results forward.

From Foraging to Farming

In chapter 3, I suggested that the most important consequences of the domestication of plants and animals were that it increased the energy available to humans (albeit at the cost of requiring humans to work much harder) and that humans then turned a lot of this extra energy into more humans. Mounting population pressure increasingly rewarded more stratified organizations, leading stratified societies to outcompete and replace less stratified ones, and in these new kinds of societies, people who interpreted fairness, justice, and so on to mean that political, economic, and gender hierarchies were good and that settling disputes by violence was bad (unless a god-like ruler said otherwise) flourished more than those who did not.

The obvious question, posed by Marshall Sahlins in his classic essay "The Original Affluent Society," is why people chose to exchange the freedom and leisure of foraging for the bondage and drudgery of farming—a choice that the biologist and geographer Jared Diamond once labeled "The worst mistake in the history of the human race." The historian Yuval Noah Harari has recently gone further still, calling the agricultural revolution "history's biggest fraud."[9] The evolutionists Peter Boyd, Robert Richerson, and Robert Bettinger, however, suggest that we might do better to frame the question in an entirely different way. What we should be asking, they suggest, is "Was agriculture impossible during the Pleistocene but mandatory during the Holocene?"[10] This, I suspect, is the most instructive way to pose the question: the shift from foraging to farming was not inevitable—nothing involving humans ever is—but the probabilities were stacked so heavily in farming's favor that the likelihood of it *not* happening was vanishingly small.[11]

One of the main reasons that people began farming was a massive exogenous shock, in the shape of climate change.[12] The earth's path around the sun is constantly shifting, and after 14,000 BC temperatures began rising, albeit inconsistently, as small tilts and wobbles in the planet's orbit produced abrupt bursts of warming or cooling (figure 5.1). By 12,700 BC, temperatures were close to modern levels, and by some calculations, the mercury rose by 5°F in the space of a single thirty-year generation. Glaciers melted, and great low-lying plains—including what we now call the Persian Gulf and the Black Sea—were submerged. Every few centuries of warm, wet weather, however, were followed by several more of cold and ice, and around 10,800 BC, a genuine mini–ice age (known to specialists as the Younger Dryas) set in, plunging the world back into glaciation for twelve centuries.[13] When it ended, though, the world quickly (by geological standards—the process took another two thousand years) became even hotter than we are used to today. As figure 5.1 shows, there have been plenty of climate fluctuations since 9600 BC, but none has been even remotely like the Younger Dryas. For nearly twelve thousand years, we have been living in what the archaeologist Brian Fagan calls a "long summer."[14]

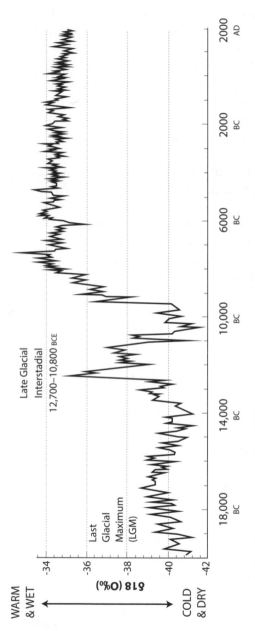

FIGURE 5.1. Global warming: temperature shifts across the last 20,000 years, as reconstructed from oxygen isotopes recovered from the polar ice sheets.

The long summer was a necessary condition for the invention of farming, but it was not a sufficient condition. For sufficiency, a second condition was needed: us. There had been warm, wet interruptions of the Ice Age (what geologists call interstadials) around 135,000 years ago, 240,000 years ago, and 320,000 years ago, long before fully modern *Homo sapiens* came on the scene, but none had led to farming.[15] Rather, each had set off much the same boom-and-bust pattern. As the world warmed up, plants reacted to the increase in solar energy by multiplying madly; animals then reacted to the abundance of plants by eating them, and multiplying too; and premodern species of humans reacted to being surrounded by so many plants and other animals by eating everything, with predictable results. But when—as always happened—the soaring numbers of each species of plant or animal outran the resources they fed off, population crashed.

In the long summer, that did not happen. At the coldest point in the last ice age, twenty thousand years ago, there were only about half a million people on earth; ten thousand years later (that is, in 8000 BC), there were six million;[16] and now, another ten thousand years on, there are seven billion. What broke the boom-and-bust demographic cycle was the combination of the long summer and modern humans, which made farming as close to inevitable as anything can be in history.

The way this worked was that then as now, while global warming affected every part of the planet, it affected some parts more than others. In a zone running from China to the Mediterranean in the Old World and from Peru to Mexico in the New—which, in an earlier book, I labeled the "Lucky Latitudes" (figure 5.2)[17]—climate and ecology had conspired to favor the evolution of large-grained grasses (such as wild wheat, barley, and rice) and big, meaty mammals (such as wild sheep, cows, and pigs). The hunting and gathering were better here than anywhere else on earth, and population boomed.

In some parts of the Lucky Latitudes (particularly the Jordan Valley), the pickings were so good that foraging bands were able to settle in semipermanent villages, feeding almost (or sometimes completely) year-round from the wild foods that lay within reach of

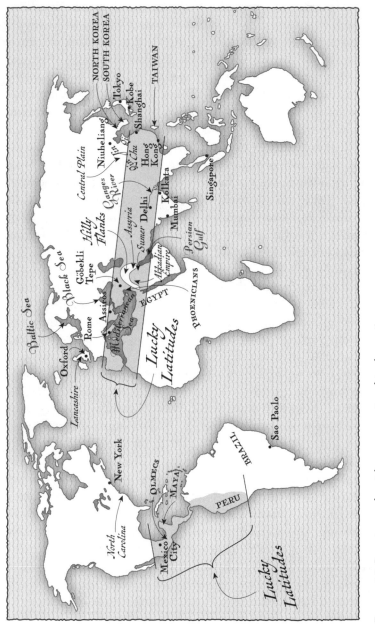

FIGURE 5.2. Locations and social groups mentioned in chapter 5.

a single favored spot. Modern humans are not unique in being able to change their mobility patterns in response to the abundance or scarcity of food, but what happened next could have come about only once animals as brainy as us had evolved. As people increasingly stayed put, exploiting the plants and animals around their villages more intensively and cultivating and tending them selectively, humans unconsciously (and very slowly) exerted selective pressures that modified their food sources' genetic structures.[18]

This process of domestication happened first in the Lucky Latitudes, not because people there were cleverer or more energetic than people in (say) Siberia or the Sahara, but because the Lucky Latitudes had by far the densest concentrations of potentially domesticable plants and animals on earth. Human beings were much the same everywhere on the planet, and so, as we might expect, domestication happened first in the places where it was easiest.

Jared Diamond makes the point powerfully in his outstanding book *Guns, Germs, and Steel*.[19] The world, Diamond observes, contains roughly 200,000 species of plants, but humans can eat only about two thousand of these, and only about two hundred have much genetic potential for domestication. Of the fifty-six domesticable plants with seeds weighing at least 10 milligrams, the wild ancestors of fifty originally grew in the Lucky Latitudes, and just six in the whole of the rest of the planet. Of the fourteen species of mammals weighing over a hundred pounds that humans domesticated before twentieth-century science kicked in, nine were natives of the Lucky Latitudes.

No surprise, then, that domestication began in the Lucky Latitudes, nor that within the Lucky Latitudes, it appeared first in the region of Southwest Asia that archaeologists call the Hilly Flanks (mentioned earlier in chapter 3), which had the densest concentrations of potential domesticates of all (figures 5.3 and 5.4). The wild ancestors of cattle, sheep, goats, wheat, barley, and rye all evolved here. The first signs of this process (the evolution of unnaturally large seeds and animals, which archaeologists usually call cultivation)[20] show up in the Hilly Flanks between 9500 and 9000 BC, and full-blown domestication is evident by 7500 BC.[21]

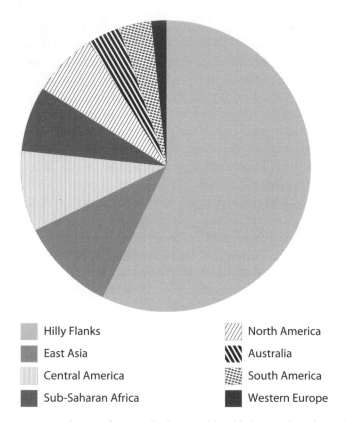

Hilly Flanks

East Asia

Central America

Sub-Saharan Africa

North America

Australia

South America

Western Europe

FIGURE 5.3. Distribution of potentially domesticable wild plants with seeds weighing at least 10 milligrams.

What we now call China had high concentrations of domesticable plants and animals too, but not as high as those in the Hilly Flanks. Between the Yellow and Yangzi Rivers, rice was being cultivated by 7500 BC and domesticated by 5500 BC. Millet and pigs followed over the next millennium. In Pakistan, barley, wheat, sheep, and goats were cultivated and then domesticated on roughly the same schedule. Squash, peanuts, and teosinte were being cultivated in Mexico by 6500 and had been domesticated by 3250, and quinoa, llamas, and alpacas in Peru by 6500 and 2750. The fit between the density of potential domesticates and the date at which domestication began is almost perfect.

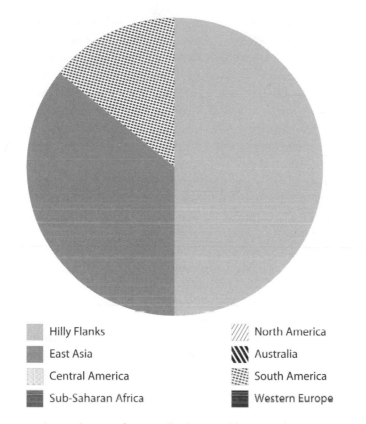

	Hilly Flanks		North America
	East Asia		Australia
	Central America		South America
	Sub-Saharan Africa		Western Europe

FIGURE 5.4. Distribution of potentially domesticable mammals weighing over a hundred pounds.

It is this fit that makes it so likely that Sahlins's question—of why people chose the bondage and drudgery of farming over the freedom and leisure of foraging—misses the point, while Boyd et al.'s rephrasing—asking whether farming was impossible before 9600 BC but mandatory after—hits it squarely. The first farmers had free will, just like us. As their families grew, their landscapes filled up. As their primitive affluent societies got hungrier and hungrier, they could have looked their children in the eye and told them that it was better to starve than to work harder at cultivating plants and animals. For all we know, some foragers in the Jordan Valley ten thousand years ago did just this. The problem, though, was that they were not making a one-time choice. Tens of thousands of other people were asking the same question, and each family had to revisit the decision of whether to intensify or go hungry multiple times every year. Most important of all, each time one family chose to work harder and intensify its management of plants and animals, the payoffs from sticking with the old ways declined a little further for everyone else. Every time cultivators started thinking of the plants and animals on which they lavished care and attention as *their* personal gardens and flocks, not part of a common stock, hunting and gathering would become that much more difficult for those who stuck to it. Foragers who clung stubbornly and/or heroically to the old ways were doomed because the odds kept tilting against them.

In reality, people would rarely, if ever, have confronted the choices quite so starkly as Sahlins imagined. A farmer who left his plow in the Jordan Valley around 6000 BC and started walking would not cross a sharp line into foragers' territory. Rather, he would start to encounter people who farmed a little less intensively than he did (maybe hoeing their fields instead of plowing and manuring), and then people who farmed less intensively still (maybe burning patches of forest, cultivating them till the weeds grew back, then moving on), and eventually people who relied entirely on hunting and gathering. Ideas and people drifted back and forth across broad contact zones.

When people realized that neighbors with more intensive practices were killing the wild plants and chasing off the animals that their own foraging lifestyles depended on, they could fight these vandals, run away, or join the crowd and intensify their own cultivation. Instead of picking farming over foraging, people really only decided to spend a little less time gathering and hunting and a little more time gardening and herding. Later they might have to decide whether to start weeding, then plowing, and then manuring, but this was a series of baby steps rather than a once-and-for-all great leap from the original affluent society to backbreaking toil and chronic illness.

On the whole, across hundreds of years and thousands of miles, those who intensified also multiplied; those who clung to their old ways dwindled. In the process, the agricultural "frontier" crawled forward. No one chose hierarchy and working longer hours; these things crept up on them.

The great prehistoric exceptions to this pattern—the affluent foragers of Jomon Japan and the Baltic shores, mentioned in chapter 2—seem to prove the rule. Farming advanced swiftly across the plains of Central Europe and Northeast Asia until its frontier came within fifty miles of the Baltic coast (around 4200 BC) and to the shores of Japan (around 2600 BC); but at both these points, it stopped in its tracks for more than a thousand years. Japan and the Baltic boasted wild resources of such richness that foragers had little to gain from working harder and cultivating plants and animals, and if horticulturalists tried to force their way into these hunter-gatherer paradises, disrupting the abundance with farms and fences, they found themselves outnumbered by natives who knew how to fight. Even in these extraordinary locations, however, the wave of agricultural advance did eventually resume, until farmers had taken over every place on earth where agriculture could be made profitable.[22] Hence my conclusion: the shift from capturing energy by foraging to capturing it by farming was not inevitable, but once the world had warmed up and modern humans had evolved, it was as close to inevitable as anything in history can be.

From Farming to Fossil Fuels

The same evolutionary, competitive forces that made the transition to farming so likely also made it overwhelmingly probable that farmers would keep finding ways to capture more energy, until they ran up against the limits of what was possible within an agrarian regime. Agriculture therefore continued evolving, unfolding through millions of cultural competitions spread across hundreds of generations. It typically took about two thousand years, once cultivation had begun in a region, for domesticated crops to replace wild plants altogether and for scary wild animals to finish mutating into cuddly farm versions. Farmers then needed at least a couple more millennia to work out all the refinements that made for proper agricultural life, such as alternating pulses with cereals to replenish the soil, processing grains to get rid of the impurities, and harnessing cattle or buffalo to plows and carts.

Figure 5.5 shows the pattern in eight major regions. After farming was fully established in one of these areas, about four thousand years was normally required for farmers to move to Agraria by inventing cities, governments, and writing. Other things being equal, after a further thousand years these early states evolved into full-blown empires (here defined simply as territories of much more than one million square kilometers), with another two thousand years taking them from empires to industrialization.

The details of course vary from one region to another, but the basic narrative was always much the same. Most farmers ended up in Agraria because with every passing year, a little bit more of the wild would be planted and a few more of the fields weeded, hoed, plowed, watered, and fertilized. The food supply grew and grew, and humans carried on doing what all animals do in the face of plenty: they turned the extra calories into more of themselves. But then they did what no other animals do: they restructured their communities to create the centralized authority that could hold together groups hundreds-, thousands-, or millions-strong. All across the Lucky Latitudes, people moved to Agraria, not necessarily out of choice but because the alternative was to be steamrollered by neighboring Agrarias.

One of the most striking things about the early Agrarias is that pretty much everywhere that we have evidence, the glue that held them together was religion. From the Younger Dryas onward, the most impressive monuments always seem to have had religious connotations, and symbols of secular and religious authority regularly occur together. We see it in the extraordinary sanctuary at Göbekli Tepe in Turkey around 9500 BC, the "Goddess Temples" at Niuheliang in Manchuria around 3500 BC, and the Olmec colossal stone heads in Mexico around 1000 BC; in the pyramidal monuments of Egypt, Mesopotamia, Mesoamerica, and Southeast Asia; and in the earliest writings from Sumer, Shang China, and the Maya city-states, where religious, economic, military, and political power always seem to go together. We should probably assume that people tried lots of different ways to solve the collective action problem of how to create larger, more integrated societies with more complex

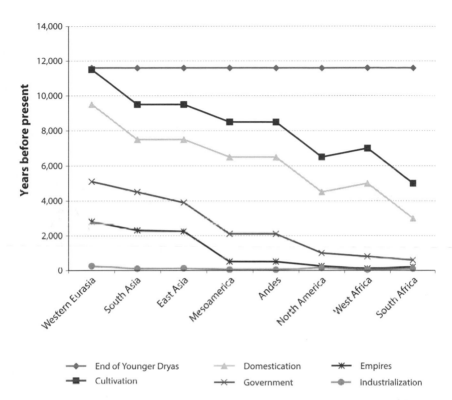

FIGURE 5.5. The timetable: the date at which cultivation began in each part of the world was determined largely by the density of potentially domesticable wild plants and animals, but once cultivation began, changes unfolded up until AD 1500 on roughly the same schedule everywhere. Other things being equal, it typically took about 2,000 years to move from cultivation to domestication; 3,500 to 4,500 more to move from domestication to the rise of cities and states (that is, full-blown Agraria); a further 1,000 to move from cities and states to empires (here, defined simply as territories of much more than 1 million square kilometers); and another 2,500 years to go from empires to industrialization. The lines converge toward the bottom of the graph because after AD 1500 Western Europeans exported empire by conquering the New World, and then after AD 1800 Western Europeans also exported fossil fuels. Note that the vertical scale represents years BP—before present—not BC, and that the lines connecting regions serve only as a visual aid, not necessarily to imply diffusion of practices from one region to another.

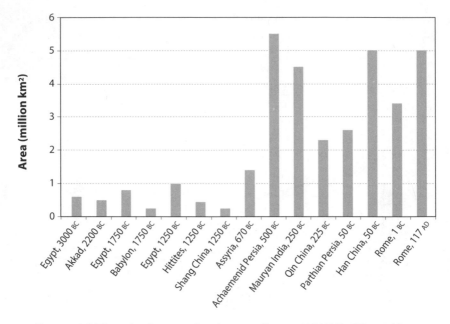

FIGURE 5.6. The scale of major political units in Eurasia, 3000 BC–AD 117 (data from Taagepera 1978, 1979, with some minor corrections).

divisions of labor as they moved from foraging to farming, but almost everywhere, it seems that the solution that worked best was the idea of the godlike king.[23]

Over time, this changed. Once again, we seem to be looking at a process in which more efficient societies increased energy capture, which drove up scale, which in turn forced people to rearrange their societies to remain effective in competition with neighbors going through the same process. Between the third and first millennium BC, the scale of political units leapt by an order of magnitude (figure 5.6), and by the end of this period, we can see two big changes all across Eurasia's Lucky Latitudes.[24]

The first was organizational. Over and over again, we see competition between growing societies driving a shift away from religious sources of power toward more bureaucratic and military ones (beginning with the Assyrians in Southwest Asia, the Nandas and

Mauryans in South Asia, and the Qin and Han in East Asia). In the interstices between these empires, smaller and more commercial city-states (Greeks and Phoenicians in the East Mediterranean, the Vrijji clan-states in the Ganges Valley, the Spring and Autumn period city-states in China's Central Plain) could flourish, often (as we saw in chapter 3) in ways that flouted some of the basic rules of Agraria. All these interstitial cultures were eventually swallowed by empires, but while they lasted, they tended to be hotbeds of innovation and creativity. In particular, they were largely responsible for the second big change of the first millennium BC: the rise of Axial thought, discussed briefly in chapter 3.

In the increasingly crowded and competitive landscapes of the first millennium BC, people tried desperately to find new ways to succeed. We first see bureaucratic, centralized states being tried in Assyria by Tiglath-Pileser III (reigned 744–727 BC), and the textual record is good enough that we can observe other rulers who were trying to resist Assyria adopting and adapting its institutions for their own ends. Rulers, soldiers, and bureaucrats tinkered with the model, until in the third century BC Rome hit on a particularly successful version. In East Asia, the states of Chu, Qi, and Jin independently went down the same path in the sixth century BC, until Qin came up with a winning version, again in the third century, and in India the same process went on in the same years, until the Mauryans—another third-century dynasty—won out. The *Mahabharata* called it "the law of the fishes": in times of drought, the big fish eat the little ones.[25]

In my book *The Measure of Civilization*, I argued that the new, high-end, bureaucratic states invented in first-millennium BC Eurasia provided institutional and legal frameworks that allowed people to push energy use as high as was possible in pre-fossil-fuel societies. By my calculations, energy capture peaked at a little over 30,000 kilocalories per person per day in the Roman Empire two thousand years ago, then fell back. It hit the same level in Song dynasty China one thousand years ago, and again fell back; and hit it again in Qing China, Western Europe, and probably Mughal India about three hundred years ago.[26]

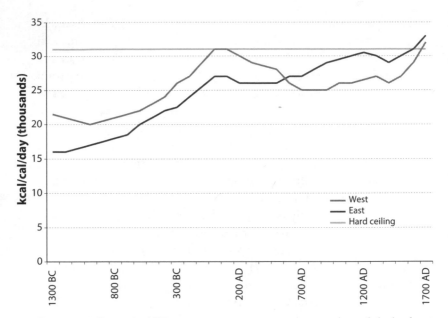

FIGURE 5.7. Eastern and Western energy capture per person per day and the hard ceiling limiting agrarian development, 1300 BC–AD 1700 (data from Morris 2013).

This level was a hard ceiling that limited what it was possible to do in a farming society (figure 5.7). Romans, Song, Qing, Mughals, and early-modern Europeans found themselves in situations that had a lot in common with those of the affluent foragers of the Lucky Latitudes thousands of years earlier, whose development had also pressed against a hard ceiling. People in these societies thought of pretty much everything that could be thought of by way of reorganizing organic economies to make them more efficient, but the only way to break through the hard ceiling was by revolutionizing energy capture—for foragers, by adding farming, and for farmers, by adding fossil fuels.

Scholars who are perfectly comfortable with evolutionary explanations for prehistoric social change often balk at applying the same principles to the search for ultimate causes in more recent periods, in which we know the names of real people. It seems to me, however, that the explanation for the industrial revolution and the replacement of farming by fossil-fuel values is much the same as the explanation for the agricultural revolution and the replacement of foraging by farming values. In each case, pressures were mounting on traditional ways of doing things, and people were trying to find new ways. Most of the time they failed in this. Thousands of foraging societies did not domesticate plants and animals; only a few did. Similarly, when farming societies pressed against the hard ceiling in Roman, Song, Mughal, Qing, and early-modern European times, most of the societies that had pushed energy capture up to 30,000 kilocalories per person per day failed to break through.

Like farming, fossil-fuel societies emerged from a single breakthrough, in a particular place (northwest Europe) and at a particular time (around AD 1800). Why it began then and there, though, is one of the most hotly debated questions among historians. Northwest Europe's technology was not strikingly superior to Asia's around 1700, and although European science and mathematics had pulled ahead, many of the advances were available to Asians who wished to take them up. China's Kangxi emperor (reigned 1661–1722), for instance, studied with Jesuit mathematicians and even learned to play the harpsichord.[27] Some scholars think that European institutions were decisive, while others focus on religion, culture more broadly, climate, or resources, and others still argue that instead of asking what happened to propel Europe forward into the fossil-fuel age, we should be asking what happened to hold other parts of the world—especially China—back.[28]

In my earlier book *Why the West Rules—For Now*, I argued that the reason that fossil-fuel society began when and where it did was the same as the reason that foraging and farming societies began when and where they did: geography.[29] From antiquity until about AD 1400, northwest Europe had labored under serious geographical disadvantages. It was a long way from the real centers of action (in the Mediterranean, Middle East, and South and East Asia) and was cut off from the rest of the world by the huge Atlantic Ocean, which acted as a barrier to trade.

That began to change, though, with the invention of ships that could be relied upon to cross entire oceans. Chinese vessels probably had this capability by AD 1200, although the Pacific Ocean was so enormous that many centuries would pass before crossing it became commercially attractive. By 1400, however, Western Europeans had developed their own versions of oceangoing ships, and these transformed the much narrower Atlantic Ocean from a barrier into a superhighway. By 1500, Europeans had used this superhighway to round the bottom of Africa and enter the Indian Ocean, and, because Western Europe is so much closer to the Americas than East Asia is, it was Europeans rather than Asians who discovered, plundered, and colonized the Americas after 1492, drawing the New World into an economy focused on Europe and not one focused on Asia. In the seventeenth century, the North Atlantic became a kind of Goldilocks Ocean, neither too big nor too small—big enough that very varied societies and ecologies flourished along its African, European, and American shores, but small enough that European ships could rush around it, making profits at every point. Historians call this the "triangular trade" network, and by 1700 the Atlantic economy had become the most powerful wealth-creation machine in history.

Tapping into energy sources all around the Atlantic drove Northwest European energy capture up by 10 percent during the seventeenth century,[30] and, just as had happened when maritime city-states such as Athens and Venice had mastered the Mediterranean centuries earlier, the energy bonus loosened at least some of Agraria's constraints. I commented in chapter 3 on the genuine "leveling" movements that sprang up after 1600 and in chapter 4 on the eighteenth-century political revolutions. There was, however, one big difference between Northwest Europe after 1700 and the earlier city-states: only eighteenth-century Europe learned to exploit fossil fuel.

All over Europe, ordinary people's incomes had risen sharply after the 1340s, when the Black Death shifted the land-labor ratio in favor of workers by killing one-third to one-half of the population, but by 1500, population growth had begun driving wages back down (figure 5.8).[31] By the eighteenth century, as we saw in chapter 3, peasants in Southern and Eastern Europe were often desperately poor. In Northwest Europe, however, the Atlantic economy was growing faster than the population, not just holding wages steady but actually driving them upward in England and the Netherlands.

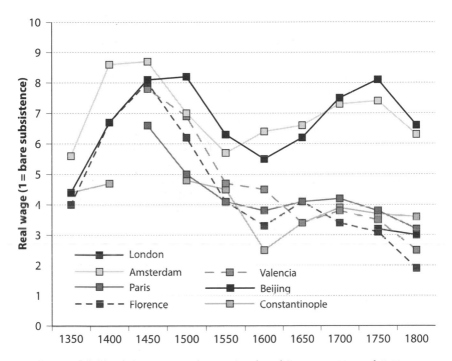

FIGURE 5.8. Trends in average real wages in selected European cities and Beijing, AD 1350–1800 (data from Pamuk 2007 and Allen et al. 2011).

The growth of global markets gave all Eurasian entrepreneurs incentives to augment expensive human labor with cheap machine power in the seventeenth and eighteenth centuries, and the basic technologies that would launch the fossil-fuel revolution were well known everywhere from Lancashire to the Yangzi Delta. However, the incentives to experiment with machines were stronger in Northwest Europe (where wages were so high) than anywhere else, and strongest of all in England, where wages reached such levels by 1750 that English goods were beginning to be priced out of some continental markets. Not surprisingly, it was England where the breakthrough came first. But much as it pains someone who grew up in the English Midlands to say it, the entrepreneurs who ushered in Britain's industrial revolution—Boulton, Watt, Trevithick,

Stevenson—were no smarter, bolder, or more imaginative than their contemporaries in China, India, or the Middle East. It was just that geography had stacked the odds in Britain's favor.[32]

After Southwest Asians invented agriculture nearly twelve millennia ago, it was independently reinvented a couple of thousand years later in East Asia, another thousand years after that in Central and South America, and multiple more times over the millennia that followed. After Northwest Europeans invented fossil-fuel industry, though, no one else independently invented it, because fossil fuels suddenly allowed Northwest Europeans and their colonists in North America to project power globally. Fossil-fuel societies overwhelmed resistance from societies that still lived in the Agrarian age. By 1850, Britain bestrode the world like a colossus.

It was not inevitable that there would be a fossil-fuel breakthrough around AD 1800, nor that it would happen in Northwest Europe, just as it had not been inevitable that there would be an agricultural breakthrough after 9600 BC or that it would come in Southwest Asia. But the constant rerunning of experiments in cultural evolution did make it highly likely that both breakthroughs in energy capture would eventually come, and geography meant that the most likely places for them to happen were the ones where they did in fact happen.[33] Similarly, once farming and fossil fuels had been discovered, while it was not certain that people would drift toward the kind of values that worked best in Agraria and Industria, that was always the most likely outcome—not inevitable, but highly probable.

Quo Vadis?

I opened this chapter by saying that I wanted to answer three questions. The first was what caused the shifts from foraging to farming to fossil fuels that produced the big revolutions in value systems that I described in chapters 2 to 4, and my answer was cultural evolution. The second question was whether these changes were inevitable, and while my answer was no, I did suggest that they came as close to being inevitable as things ever get in history. My final question is what these first two answers might mean for human values over the next century or so.

If I had been thinking about such matters back in the 1970s, when I was a teenager, my schoolbooks might have pointed me toward the answer. All our British history textbooks stopped around 1870. Nothing in this struck me (or, apparently, anyone else) as peculiar, but on reflection, 1870—when my great-great-grandparents' generation[34] had been busy bestriding the world like colossuses—was a very convenient place for British history to come to a full stop. Modern Britain's great problem, though, has been that history did not stop in 1870. The same forces that had propelled Britain to a position of global dominance in the eighteenth and nineteenth centuries—rising energy capture, competition, open markets, and above all the relentless shrinking of distance—just kept working.

Seventeenth- and eighteenth-century sailing ships had put Britain at the center of an Atlantic economy, drawing North America, West Africa, and continental Europe in as peripheries. In the later nineteenth century, steamboats, trains, and the telegraph shrank the world even more, and Britain's former colonies in North America had their own industrial revolutions. In 1903, the U.S. gross domestic product (GDP) overtook Britain's; in 1913, so did its industrial output per capita. By the middle of the twentieth century, the old Atlantic economy had grown into a properly global economy, and the United States, with its enormous resources, huge internal market, and direct access to both the Atlantic and the Pacific Oceans, was its core.

I did not study history in an American high school in the 1970s, but friends who did do so assure me that their textbooks stopped around 1970. This too was a fine place to stop, with the United States now busy bestriding the world, but America's great problem was—and is—that history showed no more inclination to stop around 1970 than it had done around 1870. Container ships, jet aircraft, and the Internet shrank the Pacific just as ruthlessly as steamboats, trains, and the telegraph had previously shrunk the Atlantic, and East Asian countries went from being peripheries to an American core to being cores in their own right and having their own industrial revolutions. Many analysts now expect China's GDP to overtake American in the late 2010s or early 2020s (although GDP per capita will take decades longer).[35]

What will this mean for human values? One popular theory (popular in Western intellectual circles, at least) holds that economic development will inevitably lead to adoption of the same views of freedom and democracy that swept Europe and America in the nineteenth and twentieth centuries.[36] The journalist James Mann calls this the "Soothing Scenario":[37] the richer the East gets, the more its values will look like the West's.[38] To some extent, this has clearly happened in Japan, South Korea, Taiwan, Hong Kong, and Singapore since 1945.[39]

Many observers (Mann included), however, remain skeptical. Some critics think that the Westernization of the Asian Tigers has more to do with their position in an American-led alliance than with the logic of industrialization itself.[40] History seems to suggest that when one region of the world gains in military and economic hard power, it normally gains in cultural soft power too, which might mean that what we currently call Westernization will actually wax and wane with the U.S. military and financial fortunes. After all, as American power grew in the twentieth century very few Americans worried about the United States being Europeanized, but plenty of Europeans complained that their homelands were becoming Americanized. As the twenty-first century goes on, perhaps we will hear more and more Americans grumbling about Chinese-ification.[41]

Alternatively, some suggest, the twenty-first century might bring not a shift from Western to Eastern global dominance but the evolution of a network with no single core. "Instead of the anticipated convergence toward a common set of values," says the political economist Hilton Root, "the growing economic interconnectedness is establishing new norms of optimal governance based on growing diversity."[42] Such a world might see a thousand value systems blooming, or perhaps the rise of hybrid values. The Chinese philosopher Jiang Qing suggests that a new interpretation of Confucianism, coupled with a tricameral parliament, might be the perfect arrangement for everyone, while the Korean thinkers Young-oak Kim and

Jung-kyu Kim argue that a different reinterpretation of Confucianism could revive the hollowed-out moral systems of both China and the West.[43]

The argument of chapters 2 to 4, however, implies that the liberal, individualist values that the contributors to this debate normally call "Western" would be better labeled "fossil-fuel." These values initially took off around the shores of the North Atlantic because that was where the industrial revolution began, but essentializing them as specifically Euro-American makes no more sense than thinking of farming values as essentially Southwest Asian or foraging values as essentially African. Liberalism and democracy have spread around the world because the industrial revolution has spread around the world; and because liberal, individualist values are the ones that work best in Industria, people all over the world have, to greater or lesser degrees, embraced them. Japan's failure to liberalize its political institutions adequately had much to do with the economic stagnation that set in there in the 1990s; the broader East Asian failure to liberalize financial institutions had much to do with the great meltdown of 1997–98; and the greatest challenge for China in maintaining its economic growth in the 2010s will probably be how it handles its own liberalization. It may well be that India's more liberal society will turn out to be its great advantage over China in the next few decades.

The rise of Japan and China as economic heavyweights has been among the most important developments of the last fifty years, and the rise of India, Brazil, and parts of sub-Saharan Africa is likely to be among the most important in the next fifty. All of these changes, though, are just the most recent chapters in the larger story of the playing-out of the fossil-fuel revolution that began in Northwest Europe in the late eighteenth century. It took modern human foragers about sixty thousand years to spread out of Africa across all the usable niches in the world, generalizing hunter-gatherer societies and values. It took farmers less than ten thousand years to expand from the original agricultural core in Southwest Asia (and later centers of independent invention) into every usable niche, generalizing Agraria and its values. It will probably take industry less than three hundred

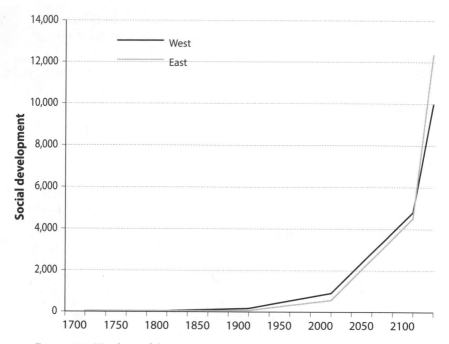

FIGURE 5.9. The shape of things to come? A conservative projection of rising social development in the twenty-first century (after Morris 2010, figure 3.9)

years to do the same, generalizing fossil-fuel societies and values across the whole planet. When I met Mr. George in 1982, farming values were already under siege in the Greek countryside; by 2082, they will probably be extinct everywhere on Earth.

By then, however, an entirely new revolution in energy capture may be under way. Figure 5.9 is a graph that I first published in my book *Why the West Rules—For Now*. In that book, I calculated general social development scores for East and West since the end of the Ice Age, and this graph shows what will happen to those scores if we make the very conservative assumption that social development will carry on rising in each region in the twenty-first century at the same speed that it rose in the twentieth. It shows Eastern development catching up with Western, and overtaking it in the year 2103.

Though I say it myself, this is a fine graph. Apart from any other merits it might have, it fulfills the two essential requirements of any good prediction: first, it is very precise, so it will be easy to tell if I got things right; and second, by the time anyone finds that out, I'll be long dead. It is overwhelmingly likely, of course, that my projection will be wrong; every prediction that anyone has ever made has been wrong, and there is no reason to think mine is any different. That, though, is probably neither here nor there, because the most interesting thing about this graph is not where the lines cross on the horizontal axis, but where they meet on the vertical axis. Even on my implausibly conservative assumption that twentieth-century rates of growth will simply continue across the twenty-first century, by 2103 the Eastern and Western development scores will both be above five thousand points.

To get from the cave paintings at Lascaux to you reading this book required social development to rise from about four points on my scale to about nine hundred points, but to get from 2015 to 2103 will take the score up by another four thousand points—more than four times as much as it has risen since the Ice Age. This is literally mindboggling.

It implies energy capture leaping from 230,000 kilocalories per person per day (kcal/cap/day) to more than a million,[44] cities of 140 million people (imagine Tokyo, Mexico City, Mumbai, New York, São Paulo, Delhi, Shanghai, and half of Kolkata all rolled into one), weapons that will make hydrogen bombs look like matchlock muskets, and, most likely, a revolution in what it means to be a human being. The implication of the graph is that the next hundred years will see more change in human nature, and human values, than the previous hundred thousand.

If this sounds hyperbolic, bear in mind that the last hundred years have arguably already seen more change in our bodies than the previous hundred thousand. Globally, humans are now typically four inches taller than ever before, live thirty years longer, and are 50 percent heavier. Our world would seem like a magical kingdom to a Roman or Song Chinese. Humans of all kinds routinely use technology to augment their bodies. Almost everyone on the planet can get access to eyeglasses—more magic—and in rich countries, laser surgery can give us better-than-perfect vision and genetic surgery can give us the kinds of children we choose. Three million people are walking around with pacemakers, and a man with no legs ran in the 2012 Olympics. Within the next few decades, we can expect technological fixes for some kinds of blindness, life expectancy at birth of a hundred years in rich countries, and functional telepathy.[45] Technology is feeding back into biology.

Where this process will take us, and how fast, is anybody's guess. Some technological futurists, most notably Google's director of engineering Ray Kurzweil, expect the coming century to see an evolutionary leap on a par with the shift from single- to multicelled organisms 600 million years ago. The mid-twenty-first century, he predicts, will bring not only scanning technology powerful enough to produce neuron-by-neuron maps of individual brains but also supercomputers so powerful that bioengineers will be able to upload scans of every one of the eight or nine billion people on earth and run them in real time. This, Kurzweil argues, will effectively merge the whole of humanity into a single superorganism.[46]

Kurzweil expects something like this to become a reality as soon as 2045, but others are even more bullish. Neuroscientist Henry Markram, who directs the Human Brain Project, predicts that with the aid of his €1.2 billion grant from the European Union he will merge humanity with its machines around 2020.[47] On the other hand, plenty of critics remain unconvinced. One unnamed neuroscientist, asked about Markram's claims at a Swiss Academy of Sciences meeting in 2012, bluntly told *Nature* magazine "It's crap."[48]

The soundest course is probably to hedge our bets. Miguel Nicolelis, a neuroscientist who in 2012 used the Internet to link the brain of a rat in Brazil and that of a second rat in North Carolina, allowing the South American rodent to move the North American's paws, calls Kurzweil's prophecy "a bunch of hot air." Scanning brains and merging them on computer platforms, Nicolelis argues, is impossible. However, he adds, augmenting brains by inserting microcomputers and Internet connections into them is not, and we will get to at least some of the same places that Kurzweil anticipates (sharing thoughts, memories, and personalities) by this different route.[49] "There's a long way to go before you get to proper mind-reading," Jan Schnupp (who sits in Oxford University's chair in neuroscience) told a British newspaper in 2012, but "it's a question of when rather than if. . . . It is conceivable that in the next ten years this could happen."[50]

As if to underline the point, in January 2014 scientists announced that the Fujitsu K supercomputer at Kobe in Japan had successfully simulated human brain activity—although the experiment had been limited to modeling just 1 percent of the brain's entire neural network, and required 40 minutes to do the calculations that a brain does in a single second. As Schnupp says, there's a long way to go, and yet, one of project's researchers points out, "If peta-scale computers like the K computer are capable of representing 1 percent of the network of a human brain today, then we know that simulating the whole brain at the level of the individual nerve cell and its synapses will be possible with exa-scale computers hopefully available within the next decade."[51]

Judging from the dismal record of crystal-ball gazers in the past, all these predictions will turn out to be comically wide of the mark, but predicting that human beings will be recognizably the same kind of animals in 2112 as the people in the room when I delivered these Tanner Lectures in 2012 seems likely to be even wider of it. If energy capture continues soaring up toward a million kilocalories per person per day, the posthumans of 2112—and their values—could well be as different from us as we are from Neanderthals (and their values).[52]

All this will come to pass . . . unless, of course, it doesn't.

I have suggested in this chapter that the big transitions since the Ice Age—from foraging to farming to fossil fuels—happened when successful societies pressed against the hard ceiling of what was possible given their stage of energy capture and found themselves taking part in a natural experiment. This happened thousands of times in the case of foragers turning to farmers and at least five times (Romans, Song, Mughals, Qing, early-modern Europeans) in the case of farmers discovering fossil fuels. More often than not, people failed to revolutionize their energy capture and suffered Malthusian collapses.

The obvious question to ask is whether fossil fuels, like foraging and farming, have a built-in hard ceiling. This has been a politically controversial question in recent years, but the answer does seem to be yes. By burning fossil fuels, humanity has pumped 100 billion tons of carbon into the air since 1750, with a full quarter of that quantity being belched out between 2000 and 2010. On May 10, 2013, the carbon content of the atmosphere briefly peaked above four hundred parts per million, its highest level in 800,000 years. Average temperatures rose 1.5°F between 1910 and 1980; the ten hottest years on record have all been since 1998; and 2014 has been the hottest year of all. Just what we should expect if seven billion of us carry on burning fossil fuels with abandon is disputed (in a rare piece of good climate news, the global average temperature actually stopped rising between 2002 and 2012), but climate scientists overwhelmingly agree that the consequences will be somewhere between terrible and catastrophic.[53]

Every great collapse in the past (and our record goes back more than four thousand years, to the breakdown of the Akkadian Empire and Egyptian Old Kingdom around 2200 BC) has involved the same five forces: uncontrollable migration, state failure, food shortages, epidemic disease, and—always in the mix, though contributing in unpredictable ways—climate change. Even a quick look at the weekly news magazines suggests that these five horsemen of the apocalypse all seem to be threatening to ride again in the twenty-first century. Past collapses have typically been horrific for the people involved, producing millions of excess deaths, falling living standards, and dark ages.[54] After Roman energy capture peaked in the first few centuries AD, a millennium would pass before Song China equaled its performance; and after the Song peak, another six centuries would go by before the Qing, Mughals, and Europeans returned to the same levels.

This is a grim story, but any twenty-first-century collapse promises to be far, far grimmer. For one thing, the increase in the scale of societies across the last twenty thousand years has hugely whittled down the number of natural experiments being run, meaning that we now basically have just one global experiment, and just one chance to get it right; and for another thing, we now have ways to fail that no society has ever had before. Most obviously, we have nuclear weapons, and the Romans did not. The good news is that for every twenty warheads in the world in 1986, there is now only one,[55] but the bad news is that proliferation threatens to spiral out of control, and is running fastest in what intelligence analysts often call an "arc of instability" curving from Central Africa through East Asia. This arc takes in most of the world's poorest and worst governed states, and is likely to be more severely impacted by climate change than any other part of the planet. It takes a lot of optimism to think that no government in this region will ever conclude that nuclear war is its least bad option, and so long as the great powers depend so heavily on this region for their energy, it takes at least as much optimism to think they could stay out of a nuclear confrontation between—say—Israel and Iran, India and Pakistan, or North Korea and anyone within range.[56]

Of course, no one knows how these possibilities will play out. For now, though, the only point I need to make is that whether we soar toward five thousand points or collapse into nuclear winter, the twenty-first century shows every sign of producing shifts in energy capture and social organization that dwarf anything seen since the evolution of modern humans. If this is in fact what the twenty-first century brings, the lesson of the last twenty thousand years is that we should expect values to evolve just as dramatically. Perhaps the liberalization of everything will accelerate even more; perhaps it will be thrown into reverse. But whatever happens, well before 2103 we might need to add a fourth column to table 4.1, for the values of post-fossil-fuelers.

Einstein once joked that "I do not know how the Third World War will be fought, but I can tell what they will use in the Fourth—rocks,"[57] and one possibility, much beloved in science-fiction circles, is that war will plunge humanity back to the foraging stage, reinstating its values. Alternatively, if the technofuturists are closer to the mark, all kinds of possibilities open up. At one extreme, the merging of minds and transformation of energy capture might perfect Industria, producing a world in which there truly are no internal barriers, and hierarchy and violence lose all meaning. At the other, uneven technological enhancement of humans might produce a world in which a handful of posthumans outperform unenhanced *Homo sapiens* even more completely than our ancestors once outperformed Neanderthals. Our version of humanity might then follow all the protohumans into extinction, in which case our discussions of the future of human values will be beside the point.

As I mentioned in chapter 1, I will leave it to the experts to have their say in chapters 6 to 9 on whether this sweeping, broad-brushstroke attempt to explain the culture shock I experienced in Assiros in 1982 and to draw out its implications is helpful for thinking about human values or not, but some brief summing up may be in order at this point. Because we are like other animals, all humans share a core set of evolved values; justice, fairness, love, loyalty, self-respect, decency, and a host of other issues matter to everyone. But because we are not like other animals, we have evolved culturally across the last twenty thousand years, and in the process have interpreted these biologically evolved adaptations in wildly different ways. I have argued that rising energy capture—itself an almost-inevitable cultural adaptation to changing environments and the growing stock of knowledge—has exerted selective pressures favoring different kinds of social organizations. Consequently, as people shifted from foraging to farming, they found that Agraria was a better survival machine[58] than a tiny band, and as they shifted from farming to fossil fuels, they found that Industria was a better survival machine than Agraria. And just as rising energy capture exerted selective pressures on the evolution of social organization, so too did the evolution of social organization exert selective pressures on the interpretation of the core, biologically evolved human values. Good and bad moral behavior are simply different things for the !Kung forager Nisa in the Kalahari Desert, Hesiod and Mr. George in the Greek countryside, and me in fossil-fuel California.[59]

This empirical observation does not necessarily mean that there is no such thing as a single, all-best set of human values, whether it be calculated in terms of a telos toward which our values inevitably move, or utility, or the categorical imperative, or a difference principle.[60] My argument does, though, seem to me to give attempts to identify "the" rules of morality a certain scholastic, angels-on-pinheads quality. Appealing to our biologically evolved values is no different from any other state-of-nature argument; if we really wanted to be natural, we would all be illiterate and most of us would be dead at thirty, which hardly seems a good basis for life in the twenty-first century. The reality is that values cannot be separated from the concrete world in which they are held. Throughout history, all the way from the elders in foraging bands through Plato and Mencius to Kant and Rawls, what moral philosophers have really done is to argue about what kinds of values work (or what kind of values they wish worked) best at their own stage of energy capture, without much interest in or awareness of what works at other stages.

That, of course, is a sweeping criticism, dismissing the claims to universality of an entire scholarly discipline. But let me close on what I hope is a balanced note. Even if I am right, and if the last quarter-millennium of moral philosophizing has in fact accomplished nothing more than clarifying the thought our own age needs by setting out competing visions of the model citizen of Industria, that is still a lot more than most academic disciplines can claim.

CHAPTER 6

ON THE IDEOLOGY

OF IMAGINING THAT

"EACH AGE GETS THE

THOUGHT IT NEEDS"

Richard Seaford

I too, as Ian did, would in Kenya have paid a local family to fetch and boil the water. He drew the lesson that biological evolution has given us *common sense*, which tells us to adapt to our circumstances. But "common sense" is—paradoxically—usually *ideological*. Ian was in Kenya as a temporary individual observer. For the villagers, it would be better *not* to adapt to the circumstances but to *transform* them, by working for the improvement of the water supply. Ian's lectures were learned, stimulating, persuasive, and misleading in a way that I consider politically disastrous.

According to Ian—and I agree—

human values have evolved biologically in the seven to eight million years since we split off genetically from the last common ancestor we shared with the other great apes. Because our biology has not changed very much in the ten to fifteen thousand years since farming began, anthropologists, psychologists, and historians find that a few core concerns—treating people fairly, being just, love and hate, preventing harm, agreeing that some things are sacred—recur all over the world, regardless of time or place. To some extent, they also recur in our closest kin among the great apes, and perhaps among dolphins and whales too. Up to a point, at least, human values are genetically hardwired (chapter 1).

Foraging groups are egalitarian. Why? Because, as Ian emphasises, there is far less material wealth to be distributed. But also, I emphasize, because of their small *scale*. Even in our society, small, active autonomous groups are likely to be more egalitarian than larger ones, and certainly more egalitarian than society as a whole. Consider a camping expedition: the group is on its own in the wild, and there is much for everyone to do—hierarchy of command and control may be acceptable, but inequality in the distribution of food or of canvas chairs will create tensions. That is to say, our hardwired sense of justice is on the camping expedition generally allowed to prevail, just as it was in the foraging band.

Now consider an ancient farming society, a rural village of the same size as a large foraging band, of say fifty people, in what Ian calls Agraria. The villagers may well maintain egalitarian values within the village, and have vertical lines of connection in the form of patrons in the nearest town. But none of this threatens the horizontally interconnected elite, who—though the military, administrative, and ideological control provided by the state—may *impose* what others resent as unjust, *transform* values by persuading them that it is just, or *deter* them from egalitarianism. But crucially any egalitarian resentment will *in itself* (without large-scale organization) have no political effect, and may well leave no mark on the archaeological and historical records.

So far, Ian may agree with me. He referred in his lectures to the fact that "a pattern emerged of general acceptance of glaring wealth inequalities combined with grumbling resentment against it and occasional outbursts of leveling rage" (chapter 3). This is not surprising, given that—according to Ian—we are hardwired with justice and fairness.

But Ian in his table 4.1 labels wealth inequality in such a society as "good." How does this accord with the resentment and the occasional leveling rage that belong to what Ian regards a "pattern" that emerges with agrarian society? It seems that his solution is to privilege the "general acceptance" of the wealth inequalities. But why privilege the "general acceptance" rather than the "grumbling resentment"—or rather than the internal conflict between the two that is widespread today? Acceptance (because there seems to be no practical choice) is not endorsement.

Politically powerless egalitarianism may find expression in religious belief. When Paul wrote in *Galatians* (3.28) that "there is neither Jew nor Greek, neither slave nor free, neither male nor female, for you are all one in Christ Jesus," that was not a political program, which is why he could elsewhere write "Slaves, obey your earthly masters" (*Ephesians* 6.5; *Colossians* 3.22). Paul in *Galatians* was rather merely projecting equality onto the transcendent sphere, just as the accessibility of early Buddhism to everybody was not a call to overthrow the caste system. But this does not of course mean that religious, transcendent egalitarianism, even if politically unmotivated, cannot eventually inspire political action. Both the Christian and the Buddhist versions, for instance, have clearly done so.

On the matter of gender inequality, on the other hand, I do agree with Ian that male (and even female) attitudes to it may have been changed from "middling" to "good" by the inheritance of material wealth. As for violence, the main reason why there is more of it in foraging than in farming societies is again largely a matter of scale. Large-scale societies have had to develop forms of nonviolent deterrence and punishment, such as imprisonment. They may also have more need to control violence, for *uncontrollable* reciprocal violence is perhaps less likely in a smaller group, in which people know each other, than in a large group, in which moreover uncontrollable violence has more scope. In ancient Greece, the danger presented by reciprocal violence to the large group was an important motive for the creation of the polis: to prevent reciprocal violence engulfing the politicized community there is needed a neutral third party, in the form of the law court.

This brings us to what Ian calls "a historically important exception to the larger agrarian pattern," the Greek city-states.

He tries hard to limit the exceptionality by noting that "Athenian citizens were the top group in a profoundly hierarchical system." In doing so, he has to downplay both the disjunction between economic and political equality (many of the politically excluded could be wealthy: women, resident foreigners, freed slaves) and the profound difference between a state ruled by the democratic assembly of all its numerous male citizens and a state ruled by a king who is (or has a special relationship with) the supreme god.

Further, it is not just that democratic Athens was economically far more equal than the United States and Britain today. Solon and Aristotle among others were more hostile than we are to the unlimited accumulation of individual wealth,[1] and the Athenian state forced the wealthy to pay for communal projects.[2] It is true that we hear much more of the importance of *political* equality than we do of *economic* equality, in part perhaps because ancient texts tend to be written by the relatively wealthy. But we do hear of the popular demand for economic equality (*isomoiria*). We are told that the ordinary people of Athens arrange things "so that they get more and the rich become poorer."[3] And a democratic leader in Syracuse accuses oligarchs of greed to the point of wanting everything.[4]

Finally, there is another reason why Athens cannot be marginalized as merely "qualifying" rather than challenging the model of agrarian values. The exceptionality of Athens is strikingly inseparable from an even more exceptional cultural preeminence, which included potent expressions of pride in precisely what distinguished Athens from more hierarchical societies, especially from the Persian Empire (for instance in Aeschylus's *Persians*). This suggests the potential vigor of values present but generally suppressed in the agrarian model.

And so farming does not produce the same values everywhere. It is rather an important factor in producing different values—along with other factors, one of which is geography: the Greek city-states were small-scale because isolated by mountains and by sea. A third factor is the tenacity of attitudes from the foraging past. The Greek practice of sacrificing animals, which has been shown to preserve practices from hunting,[5] is described in detail in Homeric epic. Homeric epic is aristocratic in its values, but insists on the egalitarianism of the animal sacrifice: everybody has an equal portion of meat. This egalitarianism of their most important ritual act then became an important factor in the development of two uniquely Greek institutions, citizenship and coined money (to say nothing of the Christian eucharist). I cannot here discuss how that happened.[6] Instead I emphasize first that this is another example of the political significance of religious egalitarianism, and second that in this way animal sacrifice has been a channel for foraging values to survive into fossil-fuel societies. For however marginal and exceptional Ian considers the Greek polis to be, it is an exception that has in the long term—along with that other marginal "exception" Israel—had vastly more influence than the mainstream god-kings of Egypt and Mesopotamia. But in his lectures, Ian, in the grip of deterministic quantification, dismissed cultural traditions as "just variations on the central theme."

What Ian calls "exceptions" are more damaging to his overall theory than he is prepared to acknowledge, especially as he presents his theory as perhaps useful for us now. In his second lecture, he described the "changes" (in energy capture *and* in the resulting values) as "pretty much inevitable." But his link between energy capture and values is neither universal nor necessary. Farming is perfectly consistent with egalitarian values. True, farming has frequently *allowed* large-scale societies, in which typically the control both of wealth distribution and of violence is lost by the majority to a small group at the center who also exercise some ideological control. But farming societies may also be small-scale, in which case the values that Ian has identified as those of the foraging band may be less constrained.

Now Ian may want to respond as follows: "yes, I agree with much of what you say: but I am dealing with 20,000 years, and so have to confine myself to the *fundamentals* (primarily energy capture)." To this I would reply that my disagreement is precisely about what is fundamental to human values. Forms of energy capture are not necessarily more fundamental in determining human values than are the millions of years in which, as Ian himself points out, we acquired biologically a set of values that is currently universal and is shared to some extent even by animals.

This criticism matters, because Ian presents his account of the past as potentially a guide for the future.

He does not claim that human choices are entirely irrelevant. But he does believe that the changes in values were "as close to inevitable as anything can be in history." And he has, crucially, dismissed the idea of appealing to our biologically based universal values:

> Appealing to our biologically evolved values is no different from any other state-of-nature argument; if we really wanted to be natural, we would all be illiterate and mostly dead at fifty (chapter 5).

He claims instead that

> the competitive process of cultural evolution shoves us toward whatever values work best at a particular stage of energy capture (chapter 1).

And so

> each age gets the thought it needs.

There is, first, an obvious problem with Ian's analogy. Whereas modifying nature (if that is what it is) by teaching literacy and extending life expectancy is easily justified and generally accepted, it is much harder to find a value (gross domestic product?) that is so much more valuable than the moral values with which we are hardwired that it would be generally agreed to justify the extremely complex task of deactivating that hardwiring (however successful may have been the constant unacknowledged attempts to manipulate or neutralize those values).

Second, it is implied by Ian's argument that—despite the massive dangers we face—we will be shoved toward the values that work. But does "each age get the thought it needs"? Others have claimed that the ruling ideas of each age have always been the ideas of its ruling class. Do we now have the thought we need? Of course not.

Are our ruling ideas the ideas of our ruling class—no longer god-kings, just masters of the universe (and their adherents)? Yes and no. But I want to end by making the counterintuitive claim that Ian's thought is itself much closer to the ideas of our ruling class than to the thought that our age needs.

My point is about unconscious preconceptions in the selection of what seems fundamental. Ian selects competition, quantifiability, consensus, and efficiency, all of them central ideas for a capitalist enterprise and a capitalist society. His privileging of inevitable *competition* and *quantifiability* (as opposed to culture or values) is obvious. The word "consensus" he does not mention. But the idea was implicit throughout both lectures, in which he failed to mention the possible relevance of social conflict (and indeed of internal, psychological conflict): this is—in a broad discussion of historical change and its causes—a telling omission. As for "efficiency," he claims that from foraging to early-modern societies "people . . . thought of pretty much everything that could be thought of by way of reorganizing organic economies to make them more efficient" (chapter 5). But the constant search for efficiency, familiar to us from capitalist economies, is simply not a feature of ancient economies.

All four ideas are implicit in Ian's remark that

> the competitive process of cultural evolution shoves us toward
> whatever values work best at a particular stage of energy cap-
> ture (chapter 1).

"Work" for whom? And how do we decide whether something "works"? By reference to the GDP?

Given Ian's entirely justified concern with energy, let us take as an example the ever-expanding use of fossil fuels producing climate change. Will the need for changes in energy use shove us toward values that work? Of course not—unless we ourselves apply two internal resources. One of them is a kind of understanding, which Ian in his lectures did not mention. The other is a kind of emotion, which Ian dismissed.

Ian claimed that all human values are successive ways of accomplishing the same thing, which is keeping human beings going. It is fundamental to the capitalist outlook, unconsciously internalized by Ian, to imagine itself to be "common sense." Accordingly, in his lectures delivered at Princeton, Ian did not once even mention capitalism, and in the expanded chapters in this volume it is still not given the prominence it deserves. But capitalism's dynamic of necessary self-expansion, and the values it produces, are different in kind from what precedes it. Understanding this dynamic is crucial for our attempt to prevent climate change, but it had no place in Ian's lectures. It should moreover be obvious that people will never accept the limitations needed to save our environment in a society of glaring inequalities. Why should I cut down on flights when the sky is full of private jets? I am not at all reassured by Ian's positive remarks, in *Why the West Rules—For Now*, about a future of robots and enhanced artificial intelligence.

Robots and enhanced artificial intelligence, and even enhanced human understanding, are far from sufficient to prevent climate change (among other disasters). We also need values sustained by emotion. But Ian propounds a politically disastrous dismissal of our set of what he himself describes as universal values that evolved biologically: treating people fairly, being just, preventing harm, a sense that some things are sacred. These values have often been, and still are, sacrificed to the supposed inevitability of quantifiable competition. In the past, they were merely desirable, but now they are also—if we are to survive—necessary.

CHAPTER 7

BUT WHAT WAS IT

REALLY LIKE? THE

LIMITATIONS

OF MEASURING

HISTORICAL VALUES

Jonathan D. Spence

In my response to the Tanner Lecture presentation made by Ian Morris, I emphasized the great distance that separated the our two scholarly approaches to history. Morris worked on a complex global scale, moving back and forth across vast spans of time and space, whereas I stayed with specific individuals in all their intricacies at the local level, in the fleeting integrations that constituted human life in the past. To Morris, the past and the distant historical times and spaces could be calculated with precision, and were subject to order and quantification; that made sense, since Morris's ultimate goal was the creation of an index of human social development, which would leave no structures and spaces unexplored. Each segment would link in linear fashion to other phenomena of growth and change, which were also subject to rigorous examination, with the goal of attaining a virtually total coverage of time and space. It is in these subshoots of the index that one can get down to the figures that are subject to precise measurement. These in turn help us chart the index with increasing precision.

Though categories inevitably overlap to some extent, Morris seems to find four sets of data as being especially pertinent to his index and its scope. One was (and is) the amount of "energy capture per person," which enables us to see how the extraction and usage of energy has changed over time in different societies, and affected their declines, rises, and falls. Feeding into this dominant concept, Morris sees a trio of concepts as being especially salient. To these three, Morris helpfully assigns an alliterative listing: foraging, farming, and fossil fuel. To bring balance and a measure of standardization to his calculations, Morris displays formidable research skills, drawing on evidence from astronomy, geology, oceanography, botany, archaeology, forestry, to name just a few. In different sections of his researches, this eclecticism can be called upon by a wide spectrum of general and specialist readers, and deepens the directions of the argument: "urban density," for example, emerges as a major factor in the index, as does "the ability to wage war," and skills in "information technology." Cumulatively, these various zones of information add greatly to the composite index, and also suggest possible additions or refinements.

If I have a criticism about Morris's work, it springs from what I see as a certain blandness in his picture of the world. He has chosen to take on the most colossal task, and the reader therefore is emotionally primed to probe the history of the world under Morris's guidance. Thus Morris needs the clarity and boldness to match his ambitions, and to ensure his claims to our attention. It is here, I feel, that despite all his ingenuity a gap remains between the tables and the descriptions, a reduction in scope that could perhaps be called a "gentrification of data." Morris tells the reader everything he has learned during his explorations, "everything" that is except for giving us some deeper feeling of "what it was like," whether in the "Hilly Flanks" or the euphemistically named "Lucky Latitudes." Perhaps the fates were as benign as Morris suggests, whether for the farmers or the foragers, but even so I suspect there were many who succumbed to the savagery or greed that were an equally potent part of the mix. My own reading of Morris tugs me back to a more conventional view that the demands and perils of warfare, property accumulation, childrearing and sickness remained as they had usually been—a grim reality for hundreds of thousands, perhaps millions, of humans, scattered in countless pockets around the warmer reaches of the globe.

That is my speculation, of course, not historical fact, even though the moods of the past can be so insistent that they take on a reality of their own. So perhaps it is more constructive to close these thoughts with some reflections on the nature of the data itself. When we are seeking to fit past modes into modern frames, we encounter a different set of challenges, which are linked to the descriptive use of terms. Briefly put, the problem is one of detailing, of calculating whether one set of terms for the realities of everyday life do in fact fit with another. One can, for example, use an apparently simple word such as "farming" or "working" without taking account of the countless varieties of experience that might be involved in a particular relationship or situation. Those differences, in turn, might seem deceptively similar to current practices in a given locality, and yet be utterly alien to them in intent or practice. Morris is of course aware of intersecting definitions of labor across long spans of time, and yet he knows it is easy to get caught in a morass of overlapping terminology. Just to suggest a few examples, let us take rural China. (This happens to be the main area of my own historical interest, but any other example, though different, would probably serve equally well.) Rural Chinese villages, at a certain moment in time, would perhaps need little glossing, if we were simply establishing a statistical base of some kind. But for comparing qualities of life, and moving beyond a basic farmer/forager separation, we have to pose our questions with more details and shading. Was work a constant, across space or across gender? Did women work longer? Did they work when child-raising? How large was a dwelling space in terms of family? What was an adequate plot of land to support a family? What were the patterns of child labor on the land? Was commerce integrated with farmwork? Was weaving a customary occupation, and were looms adjusted in size to suit girls or boys or the elderly? Who had the right to bear arms? Who did corvee labor, and for how long each year? Who had access to the state, at any level? How many families borrowed money seasonally to see the family through bleak months? How many anxious farmers hired even poorer farmers to watch over their crops and prevent theft? How many farmers had boats to get food to market? Who paid for paths, bridges, and walls? That is just a short and random list of factors that might affect the meaning of the larger concepts like foraging or farming, or help us calculate some of the parameters of rural living at a certain time or place.

One last thought about Morris's index of human social development: how constant are his categories? Can even the largest of his categories stand alone? Or are things changing even faster than he envisioned them? Take the example of the ability to wage war being listed as one of his key categories. Take the global spread of information technology as another. Take fossil fuels as a third. Add cyber warfare as another factor. Surely the events and disclosures of the last two years alone have alerted us to the shape of new alliances and factors that are already transforming our once permanent certainties. Is a new patterning of global concentrations already under way? Ian Morris has constructed a formidable edifice; but no thinking in the world can stop that edifice from being modified, or perhaps changed beyond recognition.

CHAPTER 8

ETERNAL VALUES,

EVOLVING VALUES,

AND THE VALUE

OF THE SELF

Christine M. Korsgaard

Forager: "Of course we have headmen! In fact we're all headmen.
. . . Each one of us is headman over himself."
–*A !Kung San forager*[1]

Farmer: "For when the Gentiles, which have not the law,
do by nature the things contained in the law, these,
having not the law, are a law unto themselves."
–*Romans 2:14*[2]

Early Fossil-Fueler: "The human being . . . is subject only
to laws given by himself. . . . Autonomy is . . . the ground of
the dignity of human nature."
–*Immanuel Kant*[3]

Ian Morris assures us that he does not think his view implies "that
what is (let alone what has been) is what ought to be."[4] Nevertheless,
Morris's speculations raise questions about the relationship between
the values that people actually do hold, or have held, and the values
that we ought to hold, if indeed there are any such values.

In order to make it less cumbersome to talk about this, I want to mark the distinction terminologically, but it turns out that that is rather hard to do. I could call the values that we ought to hold "real values," but I am afraid that some readers might take that to mean, "the values that people really hold," as opposed to, say, "ideal values." I could call the values we ought to hold "ideal" values, but of course the values of a culture always represent its ideals, whether they are the values it ought to hold or not. Another option is to call the values that we ought to hold "moral values," but that might also be confusing, since it might be taken to refer to the kind or the content or the function of the values in question. We think of things this way when we identify "moral" values as the ones that govern human relationships, as opposed to say, the aesthetic values that govern our assessment of works of art and beauty. The values that Morris focuses on, embodied in our attitudes toward violence and various forms of equality and hierarchy, are all "moral values" in that sense, whether they are the ones that are actually embodied in some society or culture's attitudes, or the ones that ought to be enshrined there. My solution will be to compound the available adjectives, and call the values that we ought to hold "real moral values."

For the other side of the contrast, I am going to borrow a word from legal theory. In legal theory, the statutes that are actually written down and enforced by a society are called "positive laws," while the laws, if any, that ought to be enforced—the ones we can endorse from a moral point of view—are, at least in some traditions, called "natural laws." This distinction has its roots in Stoic ethics and the natural law theories of morality that are derived from Stoic ethics. But it goes all the way back to Aristotle, who distinguished "legal" from "natural" justice, asserting that natural justice is the same everywhere and, as he says, "does not exist by people's thinking this or that."[5] So I will call the values that people actually hold "positive values," and ask you to hear that on an analogy with positive law. Positive values vary from age to age, society to society, culture to culture, and era to era. Real moral values, I will suppose, do not vary, at least not at bottom, because if there are genuine differences between the values that, say, foragers ought to endorse, and the values that farmers ought to endorse, we will be able to explain those differences in terms of yet more fundamental real moral values that farmers and foragers both ought to endorse. Aristotle emphasized that natural justice is everywhere the same. Early-modern moral philosophers liked to make the same point even more emphatically by saying that values are eternal and immutable. Philosophers do not go in for that way of talking much any more, but if we did, then we might see the difference between real moral values and positive values as the difference between eternal values and values that are in fact endorsed only in certain times and places.

One reason why Morris's ideas raise questions about the relation between positive values and real moral values is that he suggests that positive values are shaped in part by biological evolution, and that raises questions about whether real moral values are shaped that way as well. Morris cites Frans de Waal's Tanner Lectures, also given at Princeton, in support of the claim that "our values have evolved biologically in the seven to eight million years since we split off genetically from the last common ancestor we shared with the other great apes."[6] I was also a commentator for Professor De Waal's lectures, and I would like to repeat a point I made then, though in a slightly different way.[7] If we are going to talk about the evolution of values, it is important that we attend to the fact that it is not only the content of our values, but the very form of valuing, that must have evolved. What I mean by that is that valuing is a different kind of mental attitude than say, liking something, or wanting something, or being instinctively drawn to do something, or feeling compelled to do something. I will say how it is different later. Whatever explains our values must also explain the origin of that distinctive mental attitude or activity. Evolution's contribution must involve giving us the capacity for valuing things, not, or at least not just, the content of our values.

There are three reasons why this is important. First, Morris follows De Waal in suggesting that some of the other animals also have moral values.[8] I do not find this plausible, not because I think that the other animals act badly, or something like that, but because I think they are incapable of the distinctive mental attitude that I call "valuing."[9] Again, I will explain why later. Second, I think that once we remind ourselves that valuing is something that people *do*, we may see a route to identifying real moral values. They would be the ones that would be held by people who were doing their valuing correctly. That is to say, it is possible that once evolution has put the capacity for valuing things into place, it is the correct exercise of that capacity that determines the content of real moral values, rather than evolution itself.

Of course, a skeptic might doubt that anything counts as "doing your valuing correctly." But the bare fact that a capacity evolved does not prove that it has no correct exercise: after all, reason itself must have evolved. And—and this is my third point—Morris's story, or at least the part of his story that I think works, works better if there is something that counts as doing your valuing correctly—that is to say, more simply, it works better if there are real moral values. Or rather, to put the point more carefully, it works better if the people that Morris is theorizing about *think* that this is so. The reason for this is simple. Positive values can serve the evolutionary and social functions that Morris identifies for them only if the people who hold them take them to be real moral values. For positive values to sustain forms of social organization made necessary by different methods of energy capture, people must suppose their positive values are real moral values, and that means that people must have the concept of real moral values—they must believe that some forms of human interaction are genuinely valuable.

This point is worth emphasizing. Morris's story raises issues about what philosophers sometimes call "transparency." That is to say, it raises the question whether, if people came to believe Morris's theory, their values would survive. Suppose people understood that their values functioned to support forms of social organization required by different modes of energy capture. Would female farmers still accept male hegemony? It seems unlikely that you could continue to believe that your king is a god if you knew that belief could be traced to the fact that it supported a certain form of social organization. Would you still be willing to treat your king *as if* he were someone with a godlike authority over you, a right to determine whether you lived or died? I rather doubt it, but if you would, it would at least have to be because you yourself valued that form of social organization, and thought that you were right to do so. Values can function to sustain forms of social organization only if people believe they are genuine. So people must have the concept of real moral values, or anyway of some kind of real values. And the most natural way to explain why people have the concept of real values—perhaps not the only way, but the most natural—appeals to the fact that such values exist.

The argument that I just made has a long legacy. Gilbert Harman famously argued that we do not need to appeal to real moral values to explain people's moral reactions: we need to appeal only to their beliefs about moral values.[10] The argument I just made makes a counterpoint, which is that we still have to explain how it is possible for people to have such beliefs. Where did people get the concepts in terms of which their beliefs about moral values are framed—the concepts of right and wrong and obligation?

David Hume and Frances Hutcheson made a similar point against Bernard Mandeville's idea that virtue is an invention created by politicians who reward people with praise when they behave in desirable ways.[11] Morris's view has a rather Mandevillian air about it, since he sees values as socially useful, so their argument seems relevant here. Hume and Hutcheson pointed out that if the only concept of "good" people operate with is the concept of "furthering someone's self-interest," no one would be flattered or rewarded by praise. When someone said you are "good," you would just take him to be saying that you are useful to him in some respect, and you would have no reason to be especially pleased by this unless it was useful to *you* to be that way. Even then, it would not affect your self-conception. We can only persuade people that certain attributes are virtues if they operate with the concept of virtue, and we need an explanation of how people came to do that.[12] So the concept of virtue—the idea that the self itself can be valuable or disvaluable in a certain way—cannot be created in any straightforward way from the concept of self-interest. In the same way, a story about how people come to have values with a certain content has to be preceded with a story about how people come to have such a concept as "value" at all. That story has to explain why people believe that some things really are valuable or ought to be valued.

Now let me return to the question what sort of activity valuing is. One philosophical issue about valuing concerns the order of priority between values and valuing. Some philosophers believe that values simply exist—that some things simply have the property of being valuable, by virtue of their intrinsic nature—and that valuing is a response to that property. Correctness in valuing would then just be a matter of valuing those things that actually have value—in the case at hand, it would be a matter of somehow apprehending the real moral values that exist independently of that capacity. Others believe that valuing is prior to value, and that the things that have value are just the things that are correctly valued. We would then need a different account of what the correct exercise of the capacity for valuing comes to. I do not think I need to settle this issue in order to make the point I want to make here, although it seemed worth mentioning, since the second possibility—that valuing is prior to values, and values do not exist independently of it—may seem friendlier to the scientific conception of the world. If we can find a different account of what the correct exercise of the power of valuing comes to, something other than simply apprehending independently existing values, then we will have shown that the idea that there are real moral values is not in any tension with a scientific view of things.[13]

Leaving that aside, many philosophers, representing a variety of different moral theories, have made a link between valuing and our evaluative or normative conceptions of people, of ourselves and others. So for instance, philosophers in the "expressivist" tradition have pointed out that valuing something involves not merely wanting it, but being disposed to think badly of people who do not want it, and of ourselves should we cease to want it.[14] I can want chocolate ice cream without thinking that I would be a deplorable human being if I ceased to want it; indeed, I can want it while strongly wishing that my appetite for it would go away. But I cannot value truthfulness without thinking that I would be a deplorable human being if I became an unscrupulous liar, and without hoping very much that I will go on both valuing truthfulness and actually being a person who tells the truth. Harry Frankfurt, in his own Tanner Lectures, makes a similar point about the attitude he calls "caring," which I take to be a species of valuing. Frankfurt says:

> When we ...care about something, we go beyond wanting it. We want to go on wanting it, at least until the goal has been reached. ...[W]e feel it as a lapse on our part if we neglect the desire, and we are disposed to take steps to refresh the desire if it should tend to fade. The caring entails, in other words, a commitment to the desire.[15]

The common thought here is that our values are essentially connected to our capacity for evaluative or normative self-conception. The way in which they guide us is not merely by prodding us to satisfy them, like a desire, but by prodding us to live up to them: they determine not only what states of affairs we want to realize, but who we want ourselves to *be*. If something along these lines is true, then only a creature with the capacity for an evaluative or a normative self-conception is capable of valuing things. To get back, for just a moment, to the other animals, I do not believe that the other animals *are* capable of normative self-conception. Normative self-conception depends on the fact that human beings are reflective in a particular way: we have evaluative attitudes not only about things in the world, but also about our own inner states and attitudes themselves. We endorse or reject our own likes and dislikes, attractions and aversions, pleasures and pains, declaring them to be good or bad. And we think of ourselves as worthy or unworthy, lovable or unlovely, good or bad, accordingly. All of this, I believe, is a feature of human life that makes it very different from the lives of the other animals.[16] Some of the other animals may seem to have moments of pride, but they do not seem in general to think of themselves as worthy or unworthy beings. Some of them certainly want to be loved, but they do not seem to worry about being lovable. My own view is that our capacity for normative or evaluative self-conception, or rather the source from which it springs, also involves us in the construction of our own identities. You can do your valuing well or badly, because the construction of your own identity is an activity that can be done well or badly, depending on whether it renders you a well-integrated agent or not.[17]

Earlier I proposed that an insight into the nature of valuing might give us the key to real moral values. Real moral values might be the ones that are held by people who are exercising their capacity for valuing correctly. Obviously, nothing short of a full moral theory could vindicate this proposal. Equally obviously, I cannot give you such a theory on this occasion. But I would like to point out that the connection between valuing and normative self-conception at least suggests an account of what correct valuing might amount to. Although the connection is admittedly a little vague, it seems plausible to suppose that people who have a positive normative self-conception would be prepared to make certain claims for themselves.[18] They would, for instance, treat their own interests seriously and demand that others do so as well. They would resist violence exercised toward them if they could, and demand that others aid them in this resistance. They would be unwilling to allow themselves to be sacrificed merely to serve the interests of others, or to be ruled by the judgment of others in preference to their own. They would treat themselves, and demand that others treat them, as what Immanuel Kant called "ends in themselves" or John Rawls called "self-authenticating sources of valid claims."[19]

In saying this, I am not disagreeing with Ian Morris when he traces apparently universality of some values—his list is "treating people fairly, being just, love and hate, preventing harm, agreeing that some things are sacred"[20]—to the fact that the hardware of human brains has not changed much since we were ice-age hunters. I am only making a suggestion about what it is about our brains that dictates these values. But it actually does not matter for the point I want to make now whether you accept my suggestion or not. All I need for the point I want to make now is that you grant that if there are any real moral values, and we sometimes know what they are, then you should also think that the connection between them and our capacity for valuing is not accidental.[21] Whether the connection between the capacity for valuing and real moral values is made by right reasoning or correct apprehension or in some other way does not matter for present purposes, as long as you suppose that there is such a connection. If you think that, you will think that when the capacity for valuing does manage to attach itself to real moral values, it is not an accident. After all, why we would ever even suspect that there are such things as real moral values, if we had no reason to suppose that valuing is something that can be done well or badly? This is where I begin to take issue with Morris.

After conceding that there are apparently universal values, Morris goes on to say that "there are . . . enormous differences through time and space in what humans have taken fairness, justice, and so on to mean" and to connect these differences to the different social forms required for different forms of energy capture.

Now of course I do not mean to deny the banal truth that human beings have had different ideas about what justice, fairness, and other values require of us. It is obvious to everyone that this is true about issues of hierarchy and domination, part of Morris's focus. But here are three different things we might say about these differences. I will give them names.

1. The first view we might call "sociological positivism," although I hasten to say it is only loosely connected to the other things that have called themselves that. According to this view, human beings have a capacity for valuing, but what people actually value can be wholly explained by sociological forces, which may in turn be driven by evolutionary forces.

2. The second view we might call the "enlightenment view." According to the enlightenment view, human beings have a capacity for valuing, and that capacity has some natural tendency to attach itself to real moral values. But like our capacity for scientific knowledge, it develops slowly through history, and manages to bring its proper object, real moral values, only slowly into view.

3. The third view we might call the "distortion view."[22] According to the distortion view, human beings have a capacity for valuing, and that capacity has some natural tendency to attach itself to real moral values, but its tendency to do that is vulnerable to distortion by sociological forces. Traditionally, this view has been associated with the claim that our values are subject to distortion by what is called, in the pejorative sense, "ideology."

I think there is something to be said for the enlightenment view, but even more to be said for the distortion view. After all, I have already suggested that the capacity for valuing is essentially connected to our capacity for normative or evaluative self-conception, and that is a capacity that is notoriously susceptible to all sort of disorders, some of which we may well wish to call distortions. Normative self-conception may be the source of our capacity for valuing, but it is also the source of our liability to a whole set of unique human maladies and delusions. People suffer profoundly from the idea that they are worthless or unlovely specimens of humanity, and can even be driven to suicide to escape from these thoughts. Freud and Nietzsche, seeing the connection between our capacity for valuing and our normative self-conceptions, occasionally went so far as to characterize morality itself as a kind of disease.[23] Our sense of self-worth makes us vulnerable to all kinds of influences, and those influences work by distorting our values. After all, in one of the cases that Morris focuses on—gender inequality—that is plainly at least part of how it works. Male hierarchy is maintained by the propagation of gender ideals, especially ideals of femininity, which make women believe that they are worthless and unlovely women if they are not pretty, vulnerable, obedient, nurturing creatures. Gender ideals, as we all know, can cause a woman to value looking a certain way over her own health, having a manner soothing to men over the assertion of her own autonomy, and exercising a capacity for wifely and motherly self-sacrifice over pursuing her own rights and happiness. I, for one, am prepared to say that such gender ideals lead to distortions of value, rather than merely saying they explain the specific form that certain values take. Perhaps I am just hopelessly locked into the fossil-fuel mentality.

But I do not think so. I have already made one criticism of the view I have just called sociological positivism. If values were just a way of maintaining the social forms called for by a certain form of energy capture, and people knew that, it is hard to see how they would work. People must believe they are living up to real moral values before values can do that job. Now let me admit that if I try to spell out this thought in a certain way, I will be liable to a valid objection. If I said in this context, as I did earlier, that subjects would not obey sovereigns unless they actually believed that sovereigns had authority over them, or that women would not stay home if they didn't think that was really their place, you might protest that I am assuming that I know what people would do or would want if their values did not tell them otherwise, or perhaps even that I am assuming that I know what their values would be if they were undistorted. And of course I do think something like that. But it would not be quite fair for me to appeal to those claims in assessing the three possible explanations of differences in value, since these claims presuppose that there are real moral values and that our capacity for valuing would attach itself to them if no distorting influences were at work.

So I am happy to see one small piece of evidence for my view, in the person of the !Kung San forager whom Morris quotes in his lectures. If we take him to be a representative of our foraging ancestors, then the basic principle of Kantian moral autonomy finds expression almost as far back in the history of values as we can go—I mean, of course, the principle that we are all headmen, because each one of us is headman over himself. This glorious idea was doomed to be quashed by the forces of state and church control, eventually convincing ordinary people that they must obey what British people a hundred years ago quaintly called their "betters." And perhaps, as Morris speculates, the needs of energy capture are somehow working in the background of this quashing.

But I am not going to try to convince you of my view about that; instead I am going to explain why Morris does not convince me of his. Part of the problem is that if each age got exactly the values it needs, then each of the values Morris offers to explain would have to make some positive contribution to upholding the social forms needed for its mode of energy capture. But Morris does not always show that. Sometimes, all he shows, or all he obviously shows, is that the *opposite* value is *not* especially needed to uphold the social forms in question. For instance, to carry on with the theme of self-rule, Morris tells us that in foraging societies, "men who get too bossy, or extend bossiness into inappropriate contexts, or try to turn their temporary influence into permanent power over others, rarely survive their companions' disapproval."[24] Now we might accept that authoritative structures are necessary for farming societies in a way that they are not for foraging societies, if only because of the larger populations. But that does not show why egalitarian structures are necessary or even good for foraging societies: perhaps, for whatever reason, equality is just the default when hierarchy is not necessary. Now I can imagine an answer in this particular case—if foragers go out and forage alone, perhaps they need to learn the kind of independence that egalitarian structures tend to foster. But I am a little more puzzled to see how promiscuity and marital infidelity might be a good thing for foraging societies. Morris points out that foraging societies do not encourage wealth inequalities, without those there is not much to inherit, and so issues about the legitimacy of children matter less.[25] But that only shows that there is no special reason, based in its method of energy capture, for foraging societies to enforce marital fidelity. It does not show why marriages in such societies do take the loose form that they do.

Another explanation that does not convince me is the one about why farmers go in for gender hierarchy. Morris's explanation is primarily that the farming way of life requires a strict gender-based division of labor. But even if that is right, it does not explain male hegemony. One can imagine a world in which women dominate men from a basis in the home, ordering them out to work in order to earn money since that is the only thing they are good for, and taking control of the money as soon as the men bring it home. I am ready to agree that it is no accident that it never happens this way at the level of whole cultures, but the explanation of that cannot rest in the division of labor alone.

But the most obvious problem of this kind concerns the tolerance for violence. According to Morris, foragers tolerate an astonishing amount of it, and farmers think it is permissible in cases in which we would not, while we fossil-fuelers are supposedly dead set against it. Perhaps violence poses a bigger problem for societies organized for farming than for ones organized for foraging, and a bigger problem still for industrial societies. But that does not explain why it is tolerated in foraging societies.

Now let me be fair. I have suggested, as an alternative to the idea that our values are shaped by our method of energy capture, that the capacity for valuing has some tendency to attach itself to real moral values, but that this tendency is extremely fragile and subject to distortion. Of course if you agree with this, and you also agree that the forager's easy tolerance for violence is wrong, then you must also think that that easy tolerance calls for an explanation. So my alternative style of explanation fares no better than Morris's so far as this example goes. What was the distorting force that caused foragers to fail to notice that people should not go around killing each other, while we ourselves can see that plainly? I think a lot depends on what the usual motives for violence are in forager societies.

So here is some very raw speculation. First of all, it is sometimes observed that at least some people in the past have had a more social, public, conception of their identities than we have now. We now readily say that it does not matter what people think of you if you know inside that you are a good person, but it was not always so. People used to speak of their "characters" as if the term at once meant both what we mean by "reputation" and their inner identities. And they seemed to feel that their inner identities could be damaged or destroyed by what people thought about them. The defense of honor was a defense of one's very identity in this public sense. So we might speculate that, say, killing someone in defense of your honor may once have seemed much more like the one form of violence that many of us even now find perfectly acceptable— namely, self-defense. If this is the motive for forager violence, then the source of distortion—or anyway of difference from us—was the way that people thought of themselves.[26] I do not know enough about hunter-gatherer societies to know how plausible this is. The two sources I consulted—Lee's book on the !Kung and Marlowe's book on the Hadza—do not make it clear whether something like the sense of honor is involved.[27] What they do make clear is that sex is very often involved—infidelity and jealously are the causes of a lot of the violence.[28] And of course sex is a subject on which even modern people do tend to have very sensitive evaluative self-conceptions.

My other thought is that there are now, among us, people who design designer drugs, people who spend their time devising advertisements aimed at luring young people into smoking, people who try to save themselves a little money by using risky inferior ingredients in products on which people's lives depend, and many other people who lure others to their deaths, or put them at grave risk of death, from motives of profit, without ever wrapping their own hands around a gun or a knife. My guess is that when social scientists tally up the number of people who die by violence, the victims of these people are not included. Yet the people who kill these victims are surely just as much killers as those who take the gun or the knife in hand. This makes me wonder just how useful "violence" is as a morally significant category. In the modern world, we do a lot of things less directly by hand, including injuring and killing.

Actually, there is another problem with what Morris says about violence, which I can best bring out by reference to table 4.1.[29] In the original lectures on which his text is based, Morris used the term "OK" where he now uses "middling." "OK" suggests "permissible," while "middling" has no evident normative implications, and it is not clear what it means. He explains his reason for using it in chapter 1, when he discusses the possibility of assigning a score to each group's attitude toward a certain action by arbitrarily assigning +1 to actions regarded as good and −1 to actions regarded as bad. Here, however, it does matter what philosophical conception of morality you have in mind. Philosophers sometimes argue that on a consequentialist conception of morality, where the concern is simply with how much good you do, it makes better sense to rank actions simply as better and worse than as forbidden, permissible, and obligatory. On a consequentialist conception, the use of "middling" might make sense, for it is possible to think of good and bad as two ends of a scale. But it is not possible to think of forbidden and obligatory that way—the permissible does not in any sense rest "between" them. So Morris now seems to be presuming some sort of consequentialist view. However that may be, I do not think the idea that more violence is tolerated in foraging societies is adequately captured either by the thought that it is "middling" or by the thought that it is "OK." No society thinks that violence is permissible in the sense that, say, spending your afternoon off at the movies if you want to is permissible. Violence always requires a justification or an excuse—to say it is tolerated is just to say that it is more often regarded as justifiable or excusable. It is clear from Morris's own descriptions, and others, of the attitudes of foragers, that they regard violence in that way.

But leaving that aside, my main point has simply been that there are various ways to explain changes in value systems over time, and some of them allow us to admit that social forms, and whatever in turn causes them, put pressure on the shape of our values without concluding that social forms completely determine the shape of our values. Morris has not shown us that his own explanation is better than some others that seem possible—in particular, what I have called the distortion view. In fact if we look at Morris's table 4.1, we are just as likely to be struck with the broad similarity of the values of foragers to our own—a reaction that, by Morris's report, his own students share.[30] Instead of thinking that values are determined by modes of energy capture, perhaps we should think that as human beings began to be in a position to amass power and property in the agricultural age, forms of ideology set in that distorted real moral values, distortions that we are only now, in the age of science and extensive literacy, beginning to overcome.

It is unclear whether Morris believes there are any real moral values. Perhaps a story of the sort he tells does not necessarily have skeptical implications. Indeed, it is easy enough to imagine telling a story, parallel to Morris's story about changing values, about changing conceptions of how the world works. Foragers, we will say, have an animistic view, seeing the world as inhabited by immanent spirits who make things happen. Farmers have a theological view, seeing the world as governed by a transcendent god. And fossil-fuelers have a scientific view, seeing events as determined by efficient causes. Perhaps each age gets the thought it needs! But even if such a case could be made, I do not suppose any of us, including Morris, would be eager to give up on the idea that events really are determined by efficient causes.

However that may be, the closest Morris comes to conceding that there may be values people ought to hold is a remark in chapter 5 that there might be "a single, all-best set of human values, whether it be calculated in terms of a telos, utility, the categorical imperative, or a difference principle."[31] The remark surprised me, because we might suppose that Morris's view of values as socially useful devices commits him to a specific way of "calculating" the best set of values. If we finally arrived at a stable and sustainable mode of energy capture—say, economically feasible solar power—at that point the best set of values would be the ones that supported whatever social forms were required for that.

But in any case I am not sure what exactly Morris means to concede when he says that there might be a "best" set of values. As Morris reports, in the discussion following his lectures, we brought up the then-recent shooting of Malala Yousafzai, to try to see whether we could elicit any moral views from Morris himself. Here was a chance to make a practical test of what I earlier called "transparency." What effect does believing Morris's theory have on Morris's own values? Morris reports that we thought that "the only explanation for the attempted assassination was that the Taliban were guilty of profound moral failures." Actually this is not true. The question whether an action is wrong and the question why someone nevertheless thinks it's right are two different questions, and we were not taking a position on why the Taliban did what they did or thought it was right. Our point was just that this action was obviously wrong. On the occasion, as in the discussion of the text, Morris tried to sidestep making any moral claims of his own. In the text, Morris talks instead about how things "would seem" to agrarians and industrialists. Oddly enough, this is preceded by a discussion in which Morris accuses his own students of trying to sidestep the other question of what explains someone's doing something morally wrong—in this case, holding slaves. The students had no trouble saying that slavery is wrong, but were reluctant to attribute this to moral "retardation" (Morris's word). I think the students were right to resist that simplified explanation of the slaveholders' wrongdoing, just as I think an explanation of the attitudes of the Taliban toward women might well involve a complex mixture of some morally faulty attitudes, some genuine religious conviction, and the usual murkiness of human attitudes about sex. That thought need not interfere with our conviction that slavery and shooting girls who want to go to school are wrong.

Morris's text sometimes reads as if he is not one of the human beings he is theorizing about, as if he has no personal stake in the answers to these questions. I think we all do. But Morris does seem to be speaking in his own voice when he says that the Taliban who shot Malala Yousafzai and the Boko Harum who kidnapped the Nigerian schoolgirls "are not guilty of moral failings for thinking that girls who want to go to school should be punished violently."[32] If Morris means only that their holding the views that they do does not spring from *any* defects in their moral characters, I doubt that it is true, but I suppose it is possible. But if he means that shooting girls in order to punish them for wanting to learn about the world they live in is not wrong, or that it has not always been wrong, I can only conclude that he is a moral skeptic, who does not believe that anything has any real moral value at all.

Bibliography

Aristotle. *Nicomachean Ethics*. In *The Complete Works of Aristotle*. Translation by W. D. Ross; revised by J. O. Urmson. Princeton, NJ: Princeton University Press, 1984, vol. 2, pp. 1729–1867.

Blackburn, Simon. *Ruling Passions: A Theory of Practical Reason*. Oxford, UK: Clarendon Press, 1998.

De Waal, Frans. *Primates and Philosophers: How Morality Evolved*. Edited by Stephen Macedo and Josiah Ober. Princeton, NJ: Princeton University Press, 2006.

Frankfurt, Harry. *Taking Ourselves Seriously and Getting It Right*. Edited by Debra Satz. Stanford, CA: Stanford University Press, 2006.

Freud, Sigmund. *Civilization and Its Discontents*. Translated by James Strachey. New York: W. W. Norton & Company, 1961.

Harman, Gilbert. *The Nature of Morality: An Introduction to Ethics*. New York: Oxford University Press, 1977.

Hobbes. *Leviathan*. Edited by Edwin Curley. Indianapolis: Hackett Publishing Company, 1994.

Hume, David. *A Treatise of Human Nature*, 2nd ed. Edited by L. A. Selby-Bigge and P. H. Nidditch. Oxford, UK: Clarendon Press, 1975.

———. *Enquiry Concerning the Principles of Morals*. In David Hume, *Enquiries Concerning Human Understanding and Concerning the Principles of Morals*, 3rd ed. Edited by L. A. Selby-Bigge and P. H. Nidditch. Oxford, UK: Clarendon Press 1975.

Hutcheson, Francis. *Inquiry Concerning the Original of Our Ideas of Beauty and Virtue*. In D. D. Raphael, *British Moralists 1650–1800*. Indianapolis: Hackett Publishing Company, 1991, vol. 1, pp. 261–99.

Kant, Immanuel. "Conjectures on the Beginning of Human History." In *Kant: Political Writings*, 2nd ed. Translated by H. B. Nisbet; edited by Hans Reiss. Cambridge, UK: Cambridge University Press, 1991, pp. 221–34.

———. *The Groundwork of the Metaphysics of Morals*. Translated by Mary Gregor. Cambridge, UK: Cambridge University Press, 1998.

Korsgaard, Christine M. "Morality and the Distinctiveness of Human Action." In Frans De Waal, *Primates and Philosophers: How Morality Evolved*. Edited by Stephen Macedo and Josiah Ober. Princeton, NJ: Princeton University Press, 2006, pp. 98–119.

———. "Reflections on the Evolution of Morality." At http://www.amherstlecture.org/korsgaard2010/index.html.

———. *Self-Constitution: Agency, Identity, and Integrity*. Oxford, UK: Oxford University Press, 2009.

Lee, Richard. *The !Kung San: Men, Women, and Work in a Foraging Society*. Cambridge, UK: Cambridge University Press, 1979.

Mandeville, Bernard. *The Fable of the Bees: or, Private Vices, Public Benefits*. Edited by F. B. Kaye. Indianapolis: Liberty Classics, 1988.

Marlowe, Frank. *The Hadza: Hunter-Gatherers of Tanzania*. Berkeley and Los Angeles: University of California Press, 2010.

Nietzsche, Friedrich. *On the Genealogy of Morals*. In *On the Genealogy of Morals and Ecce Homo*. Translated by Walter Kaufmann and R. J. Hollingdale. New York: Random House, 1967, pp. 15–163.

Rawls, John. *Political Liberalism*. New York: Columbia University Press, 1993.

Rousseau, Jean-Jacques. *Discourse on the Origin of Inequality*. In *The Basic Political Writings of Jean-Jacques Rousseau*. Translated by D. A. Cress. Indianapolis: Hackett Publishing Company, 1987, pp. 25–110.

Smith, Adam. *Theory of the Moral Sentiments*. Edited by D. D. Raphael and A. L. Macfie. Indianapolis: Liberty Classics, 1982.

Street, Sharon. "A Darwinian Dilemma for Realist Theories of Value." *Philosophical Studies* 127, no. 1 (January 2006): 109–66.

CHAPTER 9

....

WHEN THE LIGHTS GO

....

OUT: HUMAN VALUES

....

AFTER THE COLLAPSE

....

OF CIVILIZATION

....

Margaret Atwood

I would like to thank Professor Morris for his stimulating, bracing, synthesizing, and heart-stoppingly terrifying lecture, which I predict will soon become a video game, like Snakes and Ladders but with a lot more snakes.

Let me briefly place myself. I'm a writer of fiction—I say this without shame, especially since the brain gurus have revealed that the narrative skills that we evolved in the Pleistocene were a prime driver of evolution. Without them, we'd have the language aptitudes of the Walking Dead, and would thus be unable to discuss human values in the way that we are doing today. So, scientists and philosophers, don't sneer at tale-tellers, please. My discipline is more foundational than yours.

But before taking to fiction-writing, I grew up among the biologists, and almost became one of those myself. I keep up with biogeekery as best I may, and am ever on the alert for cyborg insect spies, man-made sausage meat, headless chickens, and more, which impelled me to write, for instance, *Oryx and Crake*, a novel that plays with our latest toy: genetic engineering. We can now create new life forms, and are bent on transforming the human race from the inside out. (Hint: geeky-looking biologists will design beautiful females with an inborn lust for geeky-looking biologists. Watch out for this trend.)

We are living in a time in which our complacencies about our innate virtues and capabilities are being strenuously challenged, at the same time as our view of the boundlessness of the biosphere on which we depend is also being challenged. Where Do We Come From? What Are We? Where Are We Going? (To quote the painter Paul Gauguin.) Those have been the essential human questions for a very long time, but the answers are changing rapidly.

And that is important, because the answer to the third question—*Where are we going?*—will depend quite a lot on how we parse the first two: *What are we?* and *Where do we come from?* The neuron guys, the DNA historians, and a whole boatload of affiliated researchers are busily at work on these questions. As are the wider-picture biologists such as Franz deWaal, most recently in *The Age of Empathy*—it seems we are not merely the inherently selfish and aggressive nasties that social Darwinism posited for so long—and E. O. Wilson, recently in *The Social Conquest of Earth*—it seems that some of our core value-linked characteristics have survived as we moved from foraging to farming to latte-drinking in airports. (Not incidentally, Professor Wilson's most recent book, *The Meaning of Human Existence*, places at the center of the ongoing human endeavor not the sciences, but the humanities. Which will surprise a lot of people.)

We used to hear quite a lot about "the human spirit," and I'm not giving up on that, though Professor Morris's hook-and-eye model of our ethical values causes serious quavering. Our ethical values are, it seems, joined at the hip to whatever it is that causes the lights to go on and the wheels to roll round, which in turn has a profound effect on what's for dinner, if any: raw seal, heaps of glistening meat as in *The Odyssey*, a mess of pottage as in the saga of Jacob and Esau in the Bible, vegan stew as in my corner raw-foods bistro. And those values are also joined to who will be cooking that dinner, if there is any dinner, and if there is any cooking: Mom, slave, Parisian chef, Momslave, KFC deepfat fryer—and serving it, if it is not self-serve: Mom; procession of seminaked slaves; waitress;

Automat; Hi, I'm Bob, Your Server for Today; Dad in BBQ apron; Mildred the Robot; and so forth. And who will get the best bits, if any: Mighty Hunter; Mighty Warrior; Aristocratic Landowner; Dad the Patriarchal Businessman; Mom, the modern entrepreneuress; the spoiled kids; Rover the Dog; Mildred the Robot; and so forth.

It's all very fascinating, especially to a person such as myself, in the habit of writing fun-filled, joke-packed romps in which most of the human race has been obliterated—but some have survived, because otherwise there wouldn't be any plot, would there?

But suppose there really is a collapse such as the ones in my fictions, and also the one hinted at by Professor Morris. You might think that under such conditions those of us who are left would go back one step—from fossil-fuel values to agricultural ones—but in conditions of widespread societal breakdown, we'd more likely switch to early foraging values almost immediately, with the accompanying interpersonal violence. Short form: when the lights go off and the police network fails, the looters will be out looting within twenty-four hours. Agriculturalists have land to defend and therefore borders to protect, but urban dwellers minus their usual occupations are nomads, dependent not on what they can grow—that's a long seed-to-harvest cycle anyway—but on what they can scrounge, filch, or kill.

These scenarios are of value to fiction writers as plots; indeed, they are popular plots at the moment, as witness the Zombie Apocalypse. But like everyone else, I'd also like to have a realistic take on our chances of survival, not only as a species, but as a society. As Professor Morris has pointed out, globalization means that, due to our network of supply and distribution, it's increasingly one society—one social experiment—that's going on now, thanks to our fossil-fuel-driven electrical interconnection. What we're building looks—from space—very much like a great big brain, with an imponderable number of light-up neural connectors, or else like a huge anthill, with a network of electrochemical pathways. So if we fail, we all fail together and we fail big, on a scale unimaginable in the past.

The more intricate the technologies of a society and the larger such a society grows, the smaller the mistake that can break something vital, the quicker the train wreck, and the more catastrophic the results. And the harder it is to rebuild functionality, since nobody knows how to fix stuff any more. Your car, your computer, your outboard motor: it's all digital. If our society crashes, it's unlikely to be reconstructed, because the specialized expertise needed to work the machinery of resource extraction and manufacturing will be gone with the cloud.

However, suppose there is no crash. In that case, says Morris, there will be a steady upward climb—"upward" being a term applied here only to graphs. The scale-out will be unimaginable: we'll be living in megalopolises that will be very vulnerable to any supply cutoff. So even nonfailure means we'll be changing past our own recognition of what it is to be a five-star human, says Morris, and we'll be doing it very quickly. What we think is kind and right and just today may be seen as stupid and antisocial tomorrow.

As Professor Morris has indicated, there are exogenous shocks that may also influence events, as they have in the past. He cites five forces that have either precipitated or accompanied the collapse of larger civilizations: five horsemen of the apocalypse. Note that they are Horsemen of the Apocalypse, not Pedestrians of the Apocalypse or Roller Bladers of the Apocalypse: we do love our horsey metaphors, which have been with us for a long time. I frowningly note the omission of pastoralism from Morris's three stages, for, if military historian John Keegan is correct, organized, large-scale war emerged from the horse-riding pastoralists of the steppes, and has been a very large transformer of human values indeed. Which should at least rate a footnote.

Here are Morris's five horsemen: uncontrollable migration; state failure—that is, the collapse of direction and infrastructure; food shortages; epidemic disease; and climate change (which, as other writers on the subject have pointed out, influences food supply and the spread of diseases, as it is already doing).

I'd like to add a sixth Horseperson of the Apocalypse: the collapse of the oceans. Never in human history have we come within a fingernail of deadening the oceans, but we're doing it now. Our efficient fishing technology is about to exterminate the reason for its own existence. We've scraped the bottom, ruining breeding grounds; we've dumped megatoxins, as in the recent Gulf of Mexico spill; we've made war on the alpha predator sharks, thus causing an explosion of their ray prey, which are now strip-mining midsize fish.

There's worse. Several billion years ago, marine algae produced the atmosphere that allows us to breathe, and these algae continue to produce from 60 to 80 percent of our oxygen. Without marine algae, we ourselves cannot survive. During the Vietnam War, huge vats of Agent Orange were being shipped across the Pacific. Should they have sunk and leaked, we would not be having this conversation today. Note: attention must be paid to the basic physical/chemical ground of our existence.

There is a seventh Horsecreature of the Apocalypse: bioengineering. We can now change species not only through selective breeding, as we've been doing for millennia, but by altering their DNA. The potential for tinkering with our own bodies and brains is vast: we won't be able to resist the morph-your-DNA temptation. We're also fooling around with animals, plants, and microorganisms—all with the noblest of goals, naturally, one of which seems to be the cornering of the world seed market by a few giant corporations. (Brief note: Nature hates monocultures.)

As with all of our tools, bioengineering can be used for ends we define as "good," and also for ends we define as "bad." Are the tools we make therefore neutral? And is the operative element that defines good and bad our common human nature with its values—those values we've been in the habit of regarding as constants?

Not so, would be Morris's implication. We make our tools, but our tools also make us. And energy-capture tools are feedback loops—if you switch to agriculture, you'll make tools to help with the farming, and those tools will in turn determine how you think about who does what. Gender roles and status diverged widely under agriculture partly because a lot of upper-body strength was needed to wield the farming tools.

In the age of fossil fuels, things went the other way—towards greater equality—because different strengths and skills were needed. Reading, writing, and typing are—from a strength-per-tool perspective—gender neutral, and it's thus become increasingly hard to justify divergent salaries based on gender.

But what will come—and what will we ourselves become—after the age of fossil fuels, supposing there is an after? New forms of cheap energy capture have to enter the picture if we are to maintain any semblance of our present complex social structure, for if we keep burning fossil fuels at the rate assumed on Morris's scale-big charts, we're scheduled to boil or bake, let alone the floods and famines that will ensue.

Many bright minds are at work on these crucial problems. Meanwhile, Professor Morris has rightly pointed out that we have ways to fail that no other society has ever had. He focuses on nuclear weapons, which are indeed a worry. However, as Chernobyl has demonstrated, Nature exposed to medium high levels of radiation carries on, albeit with more mutations, though we ourselves fare less well. We tend to get lumpy and fall apart.

But whichever way things go—upward hockey stick on the graph, and/or faceplant and wipeout—huge changes are in store for our society, our species, and our planet, including some changes in what sorts of behavior we deem to be "good." I agree that no one knows how these scenarios will play out; there are too many variables. As a fiction writer, I'm happy about that—it's open season on the future, so I can make stuff up. Which is a ray of hope, at least for me.

But we do love to speculate about the future, and for a reason. The exciting news, just in from *New Scientist Magazine* via Envil Tulving, is that the episodic memory systems in our great big brains didn't evolve to help us remember the past, which is why we're so fuzzy about where we put the car keys. On the contrary, these systems evolved to help us predict the future, in order help us navigate coming events. And that is what we've been doing with our great big brains in this meeting room today.

The human race has been through some bottlenecks before, and we're still here, thanks to our great big brains. O, Great Big Brains! Now that coming events are casting their shadows before and scaring the pants off us, we're calling on you! We need you! You'd better do some megathinking.

Thank you again to Professor Morris for sounding the wakeup call to our collective Great Big Brain.

CHAPTER 10

MY CORRECT VIEWS

ON EVERYTHING

Ian Morris

In academia, criticism is the sincerest form of flattery. I therefore owe major thanks to Phil Kleinheinz, Josh Ober, Kathy St. John, Walter Scheidel, Paul Seabright, Ken Wardle, the Princeton University Press's two anonymous reviewers, and my tireless and patient editors Steve Macedo and Rob Tempio, all of whom read and commented on earlier versions of this book.[1] But I owe even more thanks to Margaret Atwood, Christine Korsgaard, Richard Seaford, and Jonathan Spence, who not only took the trouble to travel to Princeton in October 2012 to respond to my original lectures but also took still more trouble to revise their comments in the light of the expanded text printed here as chapters 1 to 5.

I like responses. When I pick up a copy of a journal that uses them—say, *Current Anthropology* or the *Cambridge Archaeological Journal*—I usually head straight for the debates and only then decide whether to read the actual papers. This, I think, is not a bad strategy; respondents regularly raise all kinds of questions that I would not have thought of by myself, and it makes a big difference to have these in mind as I read the paper.

Despite reading so many responses, though, I don't remember a single case of an author actually recanting in the face of withering criticism; nor, I must confess, do I plan to be the first. But that is probably fine, since I doubt that extracting confessions from Tanner Lecturers is why the Center for Human Values has chosen this format. For me, the fascination of this set of responses is that its

authors—a novelist, a philosopher, a classicist, and a historian—
take such different perspectives on the evolution of human values
and range so widely around the topic, making me think about my
arguments in entirely new ways. But when it comes to responding
to the responses, that is also the problem. Even if I had the skills
to address all the issues the respondents raise, doing so would take
another five chapters (and, as one of the press's anonymous reviewers
observed, another twenty years). I doubt that anyone wants that,
although reading the responses did make me eager to think about
these questions more deeply. I have already written a book on the
long-term history of violence,[2] but now I am feeling the urge to try
my hand at another book (or three) on the long-term histories of
wealth, gender, and politics.

That will have to wait for another occasion; right now, I will limit
myself to a more manageable reaction. Although the responses have
not made me repent of my errors, they have made me see weaknesses
in my arguments and other, and perhaps better, ways that I might
have organized my case. After thinking about the responses for a
while, I now feel that my case really boils down to two assumptions, which led me to make two claims, which raised two implications. By "assumptions," I mean premises that I do not attempt to
demonstrate (not least because I lack the necessary knowledge of
biology and psychology) but take as starting points; by "claims," I
mean the points that I do try to demonstrate in chapters 2 to 5;
and by "implications," I mean points that I cannot really prove, but
that seem to follow logically if my claims are true. My plan for this
closing chapter is simply to work through these assumptions, claims,
and implications, considering in each case how the responses have
(or have not) made me see things differently.

Two Assumptions

I will not spend much time on my assumptions, because none of the
respondents directly challenges either of them. However, I do want
to say just a few words, because Christine Korsgaard offers some
significant qualifications to my second assumption, and because both

assumptions are important for the arguments I will get into with Professors Korsgaard and Seaford later in this chapter.

My two assumptions are:

1. There are several core values that nearly all humans care about deeply. There is room for debate over what belongs on the list, but fairness, justice, love, hate, respect, loyalty, preventing harm, and a sense that some things are sacred seem to be strong candidates.[3]
2. These core values are biologically evolved adaptations.

Other assumptions are certainly possible. Instead of assuming that all humans share some basic values, I could have assumed that human minds are blank slates, capable of embracing any imaginable set of values; and instead of assuming that human values are biologically evolved adaptations, I could have assumed that they came about through some other mechanism, such as the actions of an intelligent designer or sheer accident. All of these alternative assumptions seem to be reasonably compatible with my functionalist argument that different levels of energy capture push people toward different interpretations of the core human values. Even if biological evolution is in fact a fantasy, or played only a trivial part in the emergence of humanity's shared values, processes exactly the same as those I labeled "cultural evolution" could still be responsible for the differences between foragers', farmers', and fossil-fuel users' attitudes. The reason I made my two assumptions is not that they are absolutely necessary for the rest of my argument to stand, but that they appear to be true, while the blank slate, intelligent design, and accident theories all appear to be false.[4]

Although, as I said, none of the respondents really took issue with my assumptions, Christine Korsgaard did return to a point she raised in her response to Frans de Waal's Tanner Lectures. Qualifying my second assumption, she suggests that I should really be trying to explain not just the content of shared human values but also our shared ability to value things in the first place. What she means by this, she says, is that valuing a good thing is different from merely liking it. Valuing, she suggests, involves thinking badly of anyone who does not value the same thing. "I cannot value truthfulness," she says, "without thinking that I would be a deplorable human being if I became an unscrupulous liar, and without hoping very much that I will go on valuing truthfulness and actually being a person who tells the truth." Valuing is a fundamental part of each person's "evaluative or normative self-conception," and anyone (again, ourselves included) who fails to live up to this conception forfeits respect.

This all seems very sensible, which perhaps means that Professor Korsgaard and I do not disagree much on the role of biology in the evolution of valuing. Biological evolution put 2.7 pounds of magic into the skull of every modern human, and it is these 22 billion neurons, flashing 10,000 trillion electrical signals back and forth every second, that give us the consciousness we need to dream up our complicated systems of values.[5] However, much as I agree with some of Korsgaard's previously published conclusions about the relationships between humans and other animals,[6] I part company with her when she says that "I do not believe that the other animals *are* capable of normative self-conception" (emphasis hers). "Human beings," she explains, "are reflective in a particular way: we have evaluative attitudes not only about things in the world, but also about our own inner states and attitudes themselves ... [which] is a feature of human life that makes it very different from the lives of the other animals."

There is a long philosophical tradition, going back at least to third-century BC China, of trying to imagine how other animals think, feel, and value.[7] I have no plans to join it, but I have spent a lot of time around animals, and my half-century of observations makes me doubt Korsgaard's assertion. Possibly I am guilty here of yet another -ism, this time the one that behaviorists call anthropomorphism (by which they usually mean something along the lines of "the ascription of human mental experiences to animals").[8] This -ism is clearly a bad one, because an anthropomorphic response to Korsgaard's point would produce a circular argument, projecting onto other animals just those human kinds of valuing that are under debate. However, I suspect that there is in fact a lot less anthropomorphism around than behaviorists seem to believe. Rather, as de Waal has observed of primatologists, "One factor which seems to have some effect on a scientist's attitude about the controversial issue of animal mentality is the amount of experience he or she has had with the behavior of nonhuman primates . . . absolute 'nonbelievers' [in nonhuman evaluative or normative self-conception] are rare among people familiar with these species."[9]

As my own small contribution to the arguments over anthropomorphism, I would like to offer the example of one of my dogs, Milo. Milo seems, in his own way, to have as exquisitely developed a sense of hierarchy as any of the farming folk whom we met in chapter 3. It is not just that Milo wants to defend his own place in the pecking order; rather, he appears to feel obliged to punish any other animal—regardless of whether the offender is the smallest of our cats or our two enormous horses, Ray and Smarty—that fails to recognize that my wife and I are the top dogs (as it were). Milo gives every impression of valuing hierarchy as a good in itself, and of thinking badly of any animal that does not feel the same way.[10]

I cannot prove that my impression of Milo's valuing process is correct; de Waal is surely right that recognizing evaluative or normative self-conception in other species "is based mainly on human intuition."[11] However, the notion that modern humans represent one end of a spectrum, rather than being qualitatively different from all other animals, seems to be gaining ground. In the 1990s, paleoanthropologists regularly spoke of "a great leap forward" or "big bang of human consciousness" around fifty thousand years ago, making modern human cognition utterly different from that of all our precursors; nowadays, most prefer to speak of a series of "baby steps" across the last hundred thousand years, gradually separating *Homo sapiens* from other kinds of humans.[12] As so often, Darwin seems to have got the point just right when he suggested that "the mental faculties of man and the lower animals do not differ in kind, although immensely in degree."[13]

Claim 1

My first claim has two parts: that there have been three broad stages during the last twenty thousand years in how people have interpreted these biologically evolved core values, and that these claims largely correlate with the three major methods—foraging, farming, and fossil fuels—that people have found for capturing energy from the environment.

To various degrees, all four respondents touch on this claim, but before turning to their comments I should begin with a *mea culpa*. Margaret Atwood, quite rightly, "frowningly note[s] the omission of pastoralism from Morris's three stages." While I would quibble with her suggestion that "organized, large-scale war emerged from the horse-riding pastoralists of the steppes," I would not disagree for a moment with her conclusion that steppe nomadism "has been a very large transformer of human values indeed."[14] I touched much too briefly on steppe pastoralism in chapter 1; my only reason for then ignoring it (apart from the fact that pastoralism does not begin with "F," and would have spoiled my title's alliteration) is that I judged that the subject would take me too far away from my main theme without adding enough to pay for the extra length of the book. But quite possibly, as Atwood says, this was an error.

Moving on as quickly as possible from this confession, I will concentrate on two lines of questioning among the many themes raised in the responses. The first, brought up chiefly by Jonathan Spence, concerns my efforts to measure energy capture across time and space. "When we are seeking to fit past modes into modern frames," Professor Spence observes, "we encounter a . . . set of challenges, which are linked to the descriptive use of terms. Briefly put, the problem is one of detailing, of calculating whether one set of terms for the realities of everyday life do in fact fit with another." In the end, he suggests, the key question is: "how constant are his categories?"

I would like to start with the example Spence mentions, of Chinese settlements. These, I learned when working on the index of social development from which I draw my calculations for energy capture,[15] pose a very real category problem. One of the traits I used to calculate social development scores was the size of the largest settlement within a society. For some periods and places, it was relatively simple to say what counted as a settlement. Neolithic Chinese villages, for example, were regularly surrounded by a ditch and a palisade, with houses inside the enclosure and no houses outside them. As a result, archaeologists rarely argue about where a village began and ended (although they frequently argue about how to calculate the number of people who lived in the village).[16] In other periods, though, things are different. The extreme case is perhaps the Early Bronze Age city of Anyang (figure 10.1), which sprawled over something like fifteen square miles, roughly one-third the area of Manhattan. Most of the "city," however, consisted of open space, dotted with little knots of huts. Archaeologists debate whether to count Anyang as a single settlement, and if not, where to draw lines within it.[17]

Nor are archaeologists alone in being confused. When I showed up in Kenya in 1986, fresh from the Mediterranean world of sharp boundaries between town and country, I found the Luhya "village" of Shikokho baffling. There was no there there: just an apparently endless scatter of huts, gardens, and open spaces, stretching out toward the horizon in every direction. Even the locals seemed a little unsure about where Shikokho ended and the next village began.

The Shikokho problem, however, is not so much an insuperable obstacle as a variable of interest in its own right, and in this, it is entirely typical of the kind of issues that arise when measuring social development. Since the 1970s, archaeological surface surveys have revealed that many parts of the world have gone through broad swings between nucleated and dispersed settlement patterns, the former producing easily definable villages like those of the Chinese Neolithic (or Mr. George's Assiros) and the latter loose accumulations of homes such as Anyang (or Shikokho). The reasons for the swings are highly interesting in themselves,[18] and debates over the details have provided some rough-and-ready but workable methods for defining premodern settlements.[19]

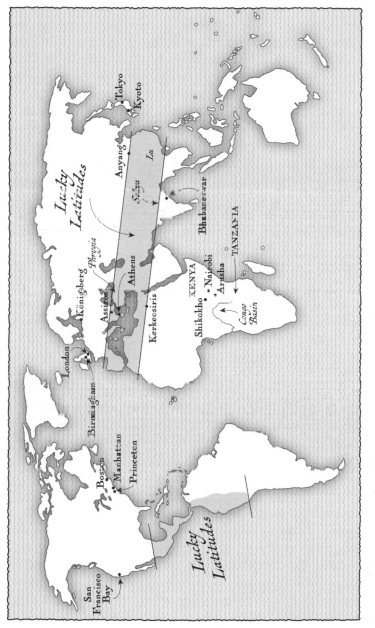

FIGURE 10.1. Locations and social groups mentioned in chapter 10.

For the arguments in this book, the most important part of the social development index is of course energy capture, and here the good news is that the definitional challenges are less acute than those involved in studying settlements. My unit of analysis is kilocalories of energy consumed per person per day. Anthropologists, historians, and philosophers have shown that the concept of the person can vary greatly through time and space,[20] but while this certainly affects how people think about themselves, it does not affect the individual body's primacy as a unit of consumption. Similarly, while it is important to distinguish between cheap and expensive calories and between food and nonfood consumption, the kilocalorie remains a valid unit of measurement across all categories.[21]

Whether we are talking about settlement size, energy capture, or my other traits of information technology and war-making capacity, the social development index operates by abstracting from the details to identify units that can be compared across cultural contexts. Historians and social scientists have long debated whether the gains in comparability that this produces compensate for the losses in specificity.[22] I believe that, when it is done right, the answer is yes, but Spence has doubts. My abstractions, he suggests, produce "a certain blandness in [my] picture of the world," and "a reduction in scope that could perhaps be called a 'gentrification of data.'" We might do better, he concludes, to prefer "a more conventional view that the demands and perils of warfare, property accumulation, child rearing and sickness, remained as they had usually been—a grim reality for hundreds of thousands, perhaps millions, of humans."

No one, I hope, would deny this grim reality, and I imagine that most people, even accused gentrifiers such as me, would agree with Spence that ignoring the nitty-gritty makes for very unsatisfactory history-writing.[23] Spence's comment, however, just brings us back to the contrast I raised at the beginning of this book between understanding and explaining other cultures. I suggested there that to understand what it felt like to live in the past, we need thick descriptions along exactly the lines of what Spence calls the "conventional view," describing the realities—grim or otherwise—of life in other times and places. (Professor Spence's own books on late imperial

China are models of the type.) To explain these realities, though, we have to go beyond the impressionistic essay to comparison and quantification. I make no apologies for that, even if Professor Spence finds the results bland and gentrified.

The second line of questioning that I want to respond to is developed most fully by Richard Seaford. As I mentioned in chapter 1, one of the most difficult parts of thinking about ideal types is knowing when you are wrong. By definition, no specific case ever matches the model exactly, but at what point does the fit with reality become so loose that we must reject the ideal type as useless? Focusing on the case of classical Athens, Professor Seaford suggests that I have misjudged this point, with the consequence that "What Ian calls 'exceptions' are more damaging to his overall theory than he is prepared to acknowledge."

To put our disagreement in context, let me quickly recap what I said on this point in chapter 3. My category of "farming society" included pretty much everyone who lived in the ten thousand years before AD 1800, so we should not be surprised that it subsumes a lot of variety. I suggested that we could represent the diversity in a diagram shaped like a three-pointed star (figure 3.1, earlier), with the classic peasant societies of the type described by Redfield and Wolf at its center, forming a kind of ideal type within the farming ideal type. Simpler horticultural societies such as the Machiguenga, which have low levels of energy capture (typically between 5,000 and 8,000 kilocalories per person per day) and organizations and values that overlap with those of foragers, form one point of the star. More complex protoindustrial nations (such as those of early-modern Eurasia) and commercial city-states (such as those of the ancient and medieval Mediterranean) form the second and third points; these kinds of farming societies have high levels of energy capture (typically above 20,000 kilocalories per person per day, sometimes above 25,000) and share many organizational and cultural features with fossil-fuel societies.

Horticultural societies provide the historical link between foraging and peasant societies, and because of this they are full of exceptions to the farming model. Similarly, protoindustrial nations provide the historical link between peasant and fossil-fuel societies, and again include many exceptions to the farming model. But what of city-states, which, despite looking in many ways as if they should have provided an alternative path to modernity, never generated an industrial revolution? I suggested in chapter 3 that what makes commercial city-states so interesting is that the energy they harvested through maritime trade eased but did not break the constraints of agriculture, qualifying but not falsifying the farming model. Professor Seaford disagrees, suggesting that the case of classical Athens does disprove the energy-values correlation. To make my case, he argues, I was forced "to downplay both the disjunction between economic and political equality (many of the politically excluded could be wealthy: women, resident foreigners, freed slaves) and the profound difference between a state ruled by the democratic assembly of all its numerous male citizens and a state ruled by a king who is (or has a special relationship with) the supreme god." Responding requires me to plunge deeper into minutiae than some readers might wish, but since my claim that energy capture correlates with human values depends on its goodness of fit with the data, I see no way to avoid this.

Historians are notoriously short of statistics for classical Athens, but even so, saying that "many of the politically excluded could be wealthy: women, resident foreigners, freed slaves" is a gross exaggeration. Very few of the politically excluded were wealthy. Athenian law allowed free women belonging to citizen families to own property (except for landed property),[24] but a woman's property was actually controlled of her *kyrios*,[25] or "master"—her father or brother until she married, her husband after she married, or her son if she was a widow. A woman's *kyrios* could not simply do what he liked with her property (and particularly not with her dowry), but neither could the woman herself. According to the orator Isaeus, speaking in a lawsuit in the 370s BC, "the law explicitly forbids a child from transacting business, or a woman from transactions for more than the value of a *medimnos* of barley"[26] (roughly enough to feed a family of four for six days, which would cost a skilled laborer two to three days' wages).[27] This law would have made it very difficult for free women to become wealthy, but, as often happens in Greek history, there is room to argue over exactly what it meant. We know of three cases of Athenian women making gifts or loans hundreds of times larger than Isaeus's limit.[28] Each story has its own interpretive problems, but these texts do suggest that some women had access to a lot of money (in one case, at least, this money clearly came from the woman's dowry). In another case, a woman selling reeds for construction work earned twenty times Isaeus's limit in what seems to have been a single transaction.[29]

Classicists have argued long and hard about these apparent contradictions between law and practice, generally concluding that Isaeus tendentiously misquoted a law that allowed a woman to make transactions above the value of one *medimnos* only if she had the approval of her *kyrios*.[30] But whatever the details (and the legal situation may in fact have been ambiguous), the consequence is clear: while free Athenian women were common in petty retail trade, they rarely controlled large sums. The few free Athenian women who got rich did so by being born to rich fathers and/or marrying rich husbands.[31]

This was not entirely true, though, of legally unfree women. Athens definitely did have some rich slaves,[32] some of whom were female. However, their numbers were tiny, and although slaves could be found in almost every walk of life in ancient Athens,[33] the rich ones seem to have been concentrated almost entirely in the financial professions.[34] One of the things that Professor Seaford and I do agree on is that Athenians insisted strongly that it was morally wrong for one citizen to exploit another financially. Because of this, few rich Athenians (especially those whose ambitions took them into democratic politics) wanted to be seen to be involved in high finance, even though such activities provided extremely lucrative outlets for their capital.[35] Their ingenious solution was to buy highly educated slaves and leave them to run what Athenians called the *aphanês ousia*, or "invisible economy," which operated behind the scenes to mobilize enormous sums for interest-bearing loans. The biggest bank in Athens was run by four successive sets of slave managers across half a century. These managers were given financial incentives to encourage them to apply their considerable talents, and one slave banker, Pasion, grew so rich that he bought first his own freedom and then the bank itself, before making such large loans to Athens that the assembly voted to grant him citizenship. Pasion's wife Archippe[36] was active in the bank, as were slave wives and daughters in several other banks, and after Pasion died in 369 BC, his former slave Phormion (who had managed the bank for some years and bought his own freedom from Pasion with his profits) married Archippe and took over the enterprise, handing over its management to slaves of his own when he too was awarded Athenian citizenship.[37]

These are extraordinary stories, but such wealthy slaves, freedmen, and freedwomen were also extraordinarily rare. So too were rich resident foreigners; although some very rich men moved to Athens to enjoy its amenities, the vast majority of free foreigners in the city were poor men and women who hoped to do better trading in Athens's large markets than in the small ones in their native cities (foreigners were barred from owning land).[38] In Athens as in every agrarian society, political and economic barriers followed each other closely. Roughly one-third of the population was enslaved, and slaves had low rates of manumission and almost no chance to gain citizenship unless they happened to belong to the charmed circle of people like Pasion and Archippe. Slaves and freedmen and -women had very little opportunity to get rich. The odds must have been better for resident foreigners, but again only a lucky few struck gold,[39] and while a few freeborn Athenian women were close to wealth, their *kyrioi* controlled their use of it.

Table 10.1, a clever comparison of ancient and modern Athenian women put together by the historian Yuval Noah Harari, nicely sums up the distance that separates classical Greece from the fossil-fuel world. Athens, as I argued in chapter 3, does not falsify the relationship between value systems and energy capture; for all its commercial success and cultural accomplishments, it remained a farming society. A minority of the population—the adult male citizens—ruled over the majority. However, Seaford is quite right to point out that this minority was a very large one, comprising perhaps one-third of the community,[40] and that there is a "profound difference between a state ruled by the democratic assembly of all its numerous male citizens and a state ruled by a king who is (or has a special relationship with) the supreme god."

Table 10.1. Yuval Noah Harari's comparison of ancient and modern Athenian women

A Female = A Biological Category		*A Woman = A Cultural Category*	
Ancient Athens	Modern Athens	Ancient Athens	Modern Athens
XX chromosomes	XX chromosomes	Can't vote	Can vote
Womb	Womb	Can't be a judge	Can be a judge
Ovaries	Ovaries	Can't hold government office	Can hold government office
Little testosterone	Little testosterone	Can't decide for herself whom to marry	Can decide for herself whom to marry
Much estrogen	Much estrogen	Typically illiterate	Typically literate
Can produce milk	Can produce milk	Legally owned by father or husband	Legally independent
Exactly the same thing		Very different things	

Source: Harari 2014, p. 149.

As I see it, some Greeks began turning away from religious legitimation of political power in the eighth century BC as their commercial networks expanded. By the fifth century, city-states that distributed authority and freedom evenly within a male citizen community were outperforming those that did not.[41] This, however, posed a problem that most ancient societies did not have to confront: how do we live good lives if the gods are not telling us what to do? In another book, I described this as "the Greek Problem," and argued that many of the Greeks' achievements, from their extraordinary art and literature to their mass male democracies, can be seen as attempts to solve it.[42] In some ways, this Greek experiment was just the local version of a larger retreat from divine authority operating all the way from the Mediterranean to China in the first millennium BC, as the climate changed, population grew, and governments centralized power,[43] but the Greek version not only produced outcomes different from those in most ancient societies but also generated debates that remain highly relevant to modern concerns about democracy, freedom, and equality. Hence my conclusion in chapter 3 that while ancient Greece does not falsify the correlation between energy capture and values, it does qualify it in important ways.

There are plenty of other points in Professor Seaford's chapter that I would enjoy following up, but I will limit myself to just one more. He suggests that "however marginal and exceptional Ian considers the Greek polis to be, it is an exception that has in the long term—along with that other marginal 'exception' Israel—had vastly more influence than the mainstream god-kings of Egypt and Mesopotamia." In one sense, this is obviously correct, but in another, framing the question in this either/or fashion strikes me as rather unhelpful. Neither Greece nor Israel existed in a vacuum, and Hellenism and Judaism both took shape as parts of larger struggles against imperialism.[44] Without Assyria and Persia, the Jewish and Greek contributions to world history would have been very different and much smaller; and without the Roman Empire, the Jews and Greeks might have made no contribution at all. Right across Eurasia, the most enduring ideas of the first millennium BC took shape in small states on the edge of expansionist empires—Confucius's homeland of Lu in China, the Buddha's of Sakya, and of course Judah and Greece—but only became genuine mass movements when they were coopted and promoted by elites in the Han, Mauryan, Tang, and Roman Empires.[45] Conventional Agrarias and radical Axial intellectuals needed each other.

Much more could be said, but for the time being I remain reasonably confident that my first claim—that there have been three main stages in human values across the last twenty thousand years, and that these correlate with the three broad stages of energy capture—is broadly correct.

Claim 2

My second claim builds on the first to suggest that the relationship between energy capture and human values is in fact causal, and that changes in energy capture drive changes in human values. This causal claim is the core of the book, but professors Korsgaard and Seaford and several friends whose opinions I sought independently have challenged it. To respond adequately I have had to make this the longest section in the chapter.

Richard Seaford suggests that the real reason that foraging societies are egalitarian is not because of energy, but "because of their small *scale*." Farming societies tend to be more hierarchical because "farming has frequently *allowed* large-scale societies, in which typically the control both of wealth-distribution and of violence is lost by the majority to a small group at the center," but even so, "Farming is perfectly consistent with egalitarian values." "Even in our society," he explains, "small active autonomous groups are likely to be more egalitarian than larger ones, and certainly more egalitarian than society as a whole. Consider a camping expedition: the group is on its own in the wild, and there is much for everyone to do: hierarchy of command and control may be acceptable, but inequality in the distribution of food or of canvas chairs will create tensions." Similarly, in "a rural village of the same size as a large foraging band, of say fifty people . . . the villagers may well maintain egalitarian values within the village." Christine Korsgaard expresses similar sentiments, suggesting that that "we might accept that authoritative structures are necessary for farming societies in a way that they are not for foraging societies, if only because of the larger populations. But that does not show why egalitarian structures are necessary or even good for foraging societies: perhaps, for whatever reason, equality is just the default when hierarchy is not necessary."

Korsgaard and Seaford propose an alternative theory of the evolution of human values: that humans naturally value shallow hierarchies, but the bigger scale of farming societies relative to foraging groups allowed narrow elites to quash this glorious idea (Korsgaard's words), distorting people's values in the process. "The horizontally

interconnected elite," says Seaford, "through the military, administrative, and ideological control provided by the state—may *impose*
what others resent as unjust, *transform* values by persuading them
that it is just, or *deter* them from egalitarianism." "Traditionally,"
Korsgaard observes, "this view has been associated with the claim
that our values are subject to distortion by what is called, in the
pejorative sense, 'ideology.'"

Korsgaard and Seaford are right that I did not pay enough attention to this alternative explanation in chapters 1 to 5, other than in
my brief comments on Jared Diamond's and Yuval Noah Harari's
respective descriptions of the coming of farming as "the worst mistake in the history of the human race" and "history's biggest fraud."
The best way to correct this omission, I think, will be to split my
remarks into two parts, focusing on the relationships between energy,
scale, and hierarchy in this section, and coming back to ideology
in the next.

The respondents are definitely right to see a causal relationship
between scale and hierarchy. As long ago as the 1950s, the anthropologist Raoul Naroll showed that groups with fewer than 100 to
150 members rarely have much permanent structural differentiation
and inequality, while those bigger than 150 to 350 quickly fission
into multiple smaller communities unless they create subgroups and
permanent ranking. More recent research has shown that the pattern
is remarkably consistent all around the world.[46] However, it is also
clear that the relationship between scale and hierarchy is nonlinear.
Since AD 1700, the world's population has increased tenfold and
the size of its largest cities thirtyfold, but, as we saw in chapter 4,
political, economic, and gender hierarchies have all weakened. The
sociologist Charles Tilly even spoke of the "dedifferentiation" of
social structures in modern times as scale increased.[47]

The reason for this pattern, however, is that while scale can be one
of several *proximate* causes of changes in hierarchy, energy capture is
the *ultimate* cause. Societies increase in scale because the amount of
energy available to them grows, although the relationship between
energy and scale is far from straightforward. As a group captures
more food calories, its members normally convert them to more

people. If the supply of energy stops growing, scale might continue increasing for a while if people reduce their living standards, but that will eventually lead to disaster. People will emigrate or starve, and the group will either shrink until the number of empty stomachs comes back into line with the energy supply or, as the economist Esther Boserup showed fifty years ago, people will ratchet up their search for energy, intensifying their subsistence strategies and driving scale back up again.[48]

Korsgaard's and Seaford's comments in this volume and the feedback from several other readers have made me see that I did not do a very good job in chapters 1 to 5 of developing a clear causal account of the relationships between energy, scale, and hierarchy, so I will have another try here. As I see it, historical change is largely a matter of what biologists call multilevel selection. This process of selection goes on simultaneously at the genetic, individual, kin, and group levels. Descent with modification operates through genes at all four levels, but it also operates though culture at the higher levels, and the cultural processes are primarily ones that work in ways very like biological natural selection.[49]

I said very little in chapters 1 to 5 about the distinction between micro- and macro-level processes. At the micro level, changes in energy capture do not force anyone to do or think anything in particular. When the world warmed up and food calories became more abundant at the end of the Ice Age, for instance, there was no physical law that required people to convert the extra energy to more people. People had free will: when they found that a day spent hunting or gathering yielded more calories than it used to, they had a choice between taking more days off or consuming more (either personally or by feeding their children better). Given that these choices came up millions of times in the centuries after the Ice Age ended, it is probably safe to assume that both options—sloth and greed/familial love—had their adherents. At the personal level, the abundance of energy determined nothing.

At the macro level, however, energy capture drove almost everything. Greedy people who worked hard to capture more energy and eat more would, on average, be bigger and healthier than their lazy neighbors who chose not to. They would—again, on average—produce bigger, healthier babies, and if they were loving as well as greedy (or, as many biologists would rephrase it, greedy for their kin as well as for themselves), their well-fed offspring would on average be likelier to survive than the scions of parents who took a lot of days off. Played out millions of times across thousands of years, the consequence of all these choices was that the greedy largely outbred, outcompeted, and replaced the lazy—or, since sloth and stupidity are very different things, the lazy learned the error of their ways, turned industrious, and joined the ranks of the greedy. Either way, the macro-level outcome was much the same: the greedy gradually took over.

"Greed, for lack of a better word, is good," says the fictional character Gordon Gekko in Oliver Stone's 1987 film *Wall Street*. "Greed is right. Greed works. Greed clarifies, cuts through, and captures the essence of the evolutionary spirit. Greed, in all its forms—greed for life, for money, for love, knowledge—has marked the upward surge of mankind."[50] Gekko, of course, gets his comeuppance in the end, but what brings him down is not the fact that he was greedy: it is that he was *too* greedy. Greed is a fact of life for everything from single-celled organisms to ourselves, but each species has evolved toward an optimum balance between selfishness and cooperation. Animals that are either too greedy or not greedy enough are less likely to pass on their genes and see their offspring flourish than those who are just greedy enough. Humans, of course, differ from other animals in being capable of cultural evolution, and because of that, our optimum level of greed shifts in parallel with our ability to capture energy. I suggested in chapter 4 that in fossil-fuel societies, the right amount of greed produces a post-tax and -transfer Gini coefficient between 0.25 and 0.35. When foragers are being just greedy enough, Gini scores settle below 0.25; when farmers are being just greedy enough, the score is above (often well above) 0.35. Gordon Gekko's problem was that his heart, like the Grinch's, was too small. He acted in ways that would have driven the coefficient up toward 1.0, and no society can tolerate that. No wonder he went to jail.

Competing against people who are just greedy enough rarely goes well. Imagine, for instance, that all the foragers in a particular valley or hunting range unanimously sign up to a religion or cultural code that forbids them from eating a lot or feeding their children well. This will avail them little unless everyone in the neighboring valley or hunting range—and the one beyond that, and the one beyond that, and so on—feels the same way. But because people have free will, that has never been a very likely outcome. Self-denial can pay off, but only if it delivers benefits of other kinds that outweigh its costs (say by increasing group solidarity with positive effects in times of war, or by training people to survive on short rations with positive effects in times of famine). Consequently, the overall pattern has been that the greedy have largely, but not completely, inherited the earth, nudging humanity toward the optimal level of selfishness.

Just like Gordon Gekko, foragers who took greed too far ultimately paid a price. The more energy they extracted from their environments and the more their numbers grew, the faster they ran into diminishing returns and the harder it became for them to continue extracting the energy they needed to fuel their lives. Sooner or later, greedy foragers ran up against Malthusian limits, although—for the reasons spelled out in chapters 3 and 5—a fortunate few in the Lucky Latitudes learned to squeeze more from the land by moving slowly toward farming, and as they became farmers, they learned to squeeze more from agriculture by moving toward hierarchy.

Once again, people were perfectly free to reject farming and hierarchy, and because we are dealing with millions of separate decisions made across many centuries, we should probably assume that plenty of people did just that. But we should probably also assume that the hunting, gathering, and freedom lobby then relearned the old lesson that it is hard to compete against greed. Farming populations grew faster than foraging ones, and hierarchical societies were better able to organize for war and other collective activities than egalitarian ones. It took millennia, but Agrarias spread across every part of the planet where geography allowed them to work.

Let me repeat that at no point in this long, hard history did energy capture *make* anyone adopt hierarchy. Rather, in situations where steep hierarchies worked well to produce large populations and efficient organizations (which means through most of the twelve millennia since the end of the Ice Age), societies that moved in that direction reaped rewards. As we saw in chapter 3, the rewards were distributed unevenly, and the millions of serfs and slaves laboring in fields, mines, and mills might not have been greatly consoled by this story. But people whose societies did not move in that direction were punished even more than the lower ranks of the hierarchical groups, often in ways that drove them to extinction. On the other hand, in situations where shallow hierarchies worked well to produce large populations and efficient organizations (which means through most of the two centuries since the industrial revolution), it was societies that moved toward egalitarianism that were rewarded, while those that clung to Agraria suffered. Despite the widening income gaps in advanced fossil-fuel societies, being at the bottom in the European Union has many advantages over being at almost any level in Afghanistan.

The macro-level shifts toward and away from hierarchy were unintended consequences of vast numbers of micro-level decisions. This is perhaps the best way to think about Richard Seaford's camping holiday. Organizing such a trip along the lines of Louis XIV's France (*la vacance, c'est moi*) is just not a very effective way to achieve the goals most people have when they head off for a weekend in the woods. No doubt there are people who enjoy authoritarian outings (my main memory of time under canvas as a Boy Scout is of constantly being ordered about), but I have been assured that even quite hierarchical organizations tend to relax the rules when they head off on teambuilding retreats in the countryside. So it was that when the very egalitarian Shoshone went on hunting expeditions in the 1930s, they had no hesitation in selecting rabbit bosses to tell them what to do, but once the camping is over, bankers and Native Americans alike go back to what works best in their everyday lives. It is not scale that makes camping egalitarian; it is our human flexibility, which allows us to select the organizations and values that work best to accomplish the tasks at hand.

As part of his argument that scale rather than energy determines hierarchy, Seaford suggests that an ancient village "of the same size as a large foraging band, of say fifty people . . . may well maintain egalitarian values within the village," despite having "vertical lines of connection in the form of patrons in the nearest town." This, I think, romanticizes village life. What little we know about village life in antiquity suggests that the countryside was indeed less hierarchical than the great cities, but the relatively well-documented case of Kerkeosiris in Egypt was nevertheless rigidly stratified by sex, age, and wealth.[51]

In more recent Agrarias with better evidence, rural hierarchy is even clearer. Let me take the example of Russia, because I happen to have been reading about it lately. In the 1860s, the bourgeois activists who called themselves Populists often shared Seaford's image of village life. "Central to their philosophy," says the historian Orlando Figes, "was the idea that the egalitarian customs of the peasant commune could serve as a model for the socialist reorganization of society." But when the "Go to the People" movement brought Populists face-to-face with actual peasants, they found that "The *mir* [village] was governed by an assembly of peasant elders which, alongside the land commune (*obshchina*), regulated virtually every aspect of village life." Many Populists were appalled; as the young Maxim Gorky remembered it, "Some dog-like desire to please the strong ones in the village took possession of [poor peasants], and then it disgusted me to look at them." The Populists' general conclusion, Figes writes, was that "The village was a hotbed of intrigue, vendettas, greed, dishonesty, meanness, and sometimes gruesome acts of violence by one peasant neighbour against another; it was not the haven of communal harmony that intellectuals from the city imagined it to be."[52]

My argument with Seaford over the organization of peasant villages is actually, I think, just one part of a bigger argument about another -ism: essentialism. In this case, however, instead of pleading guilty to the -ism myself, I want to accuse Seaford and Korsgaard of it in their claim that shallow hierarchies are the "default" setting, or essence, of humanity.

When academics call each other essentialists, we are usually claiming that our rivals have assumed that objects of analysis—which can be anything from molecules through human values to entire species—have fixed, unchanging essences. In reality, anti-essentialists assert, this is never true, because even when our categories seem to correspond quite well to external realities, they are nevertheless socially constructed, because no two members of a category are ever the same (indeed, no one member of them stays the same for very long).[53]

In practice, however, we are all at least essentialists for the working day, because it is very difficult to think about anything at all without at least a dash of essentialism. What the psychologist Steven Pinker says of the natural sciences—that "Essentialism is behind the success of chemistry, physiology, and genetics, and even today biologists routinely embrace the heresy when they work on the Human Genome Project (but everyone has a different genome!) or open up *Gray's Anatomy* (but bodies vary!)"[54]—can be extended to every field of study. This means that accusations of essentialism are in truth arguments over how much essentialism is enough.

My argument that all modern humans share an evolved essence that includes a core set of values[55] is an essentialist claim. However, it is only a qualified kind of essentialism, partly because I take it for granted that as we go on evolving biologically, our essence will change, and partly because I insist that part of our biological essence is our cultural flexibility, which includes an ability to reinterpret our core values so that we can carry on maximizing our utility[56] as the world around us changes. That, I think, is as far as we should go with essentialism. When people went from gathering nuts to plowing fields, they remained committed to fairness but started thinking that fairness meant rendering unto Caesar what was Caesar's rather than giving everyone the same share; if they go camping with Richard Seaford, their sense of fairness moves in the opposite direction. In arguing that shallow hierarchies are always our default setting, and that farmers simply got things wrong for ten thousand years, Korsgaard and Seaford seem to me to take essentialism too far.

The best way to show this is to plunge back about fifteen million years, to a time before there were any humans to have values. As well as lacking humans, that world also lacked the other great apes—chimpanzees, bonobos, and gorillas—that are today our closest genetic kin, but what it did have, swinging through the branches of the Central African rainforest, was the last common ancestor of all these modern species, a vanished creature that biologists call proto-Pan.

Just why proto-Pan evolved into animals as varied as humans and our ape cousins remains controversial, although the most popular explanation among biologists focuses on quite small differences between one part of the Congo Basin and another in the supply of wild foods from which apes could capture energy.[57] There is less debate, though, over the fact that from their shared genetic materials, the various genera have evolved very different forms of hierarchy and uses of violence. Gorillas, for instance, are profoundly hierarchical: individual alpha males each dominate a small harem of females, while non-alpha males compete violently to take over these harems. A successful alpha male will monopolize sexual access to his harem and defend it and his offspring against assault. Chimpanzees are also very hierarchical, but in a different way. Multiple males (usually genetically related) cohabit in bands, constantly struggling for dominance. These competitions can be very violent, but success depends primarily on forming coalitions of supporters. Females, which cooperate a lot less, couple promiscuously. Dominant males have more sex than beta males, but a band's males will act collectively to protect the females and young, perhaps because there is so much uncertainty over paternity. Among bonobos, sex is also promiscuous, but females cooperate much more successfully than males, hierarchies are shallow, and there is very little violence. The males that have the most sex tend to be ones that work well with females (or ones whose mothers have high status among the females).[58]

Gorillas and chimpanzees, we might say, are essentially hierarchical and violent (albeit in different ways); bonobos are essentially egalitarian and peaceful; but humans are essentially none of these things. We have evolved to be able to pick and choose how much hierarchy and violence to use, depending on the problems we face. When hierarchies work best, we are hierarchical; when hierarchies are ineffective, we do without them. We experiment constantly, and those individuals and groups that make the right choices flourish, while those that do not perish. In the foraging world, nonhierarchical collective action normally works best (although not on Shoshone rabbit hunts or among the affluent foragers of the Pacific Northwest), but this is not because humans are essentially egalitarian. Forager equality, after all, is not simply a matter of the absence of hierarchy; upstarts are constantly trying to get ahead, but are held back by what the anthropologist Christopher Boehm has called "reverse dominance hierarchies"[59]—or, to put it more bluntly, coalitions of losers.

Consequently, I think that Korsgaard and Seaford take essentialism too far in claiming that egalitarianism and pacifism are humanity's default settings. Foraging presented humans with problems that were best solved through shallow hierarchies and abundant violence, which shifted power toward coalitions of losers. Farming created a whole new set of problems, to which hierarchy provided the winning solutions, undermining coalitions of losers. Most of the time, groups that built hierarchical organizations and interpreted justice and fairness to mean that some people (such as men and godlike monarchs) deserved more than others (such as women and peasants) overwhelmed those that did not. Under exceptional circumstances, such as those prevailing in parts of the ancient and medieval Mediterranean and on the shores of the early-modern North Atlantic, this was only partly true, and in these niches somewhat shallower hierarchies flourished. In the last two hundred years, fossil fuels have created yet more new problems; less hierarchical organizations provided winning solutions to these, and the idea that justice and fairness meant treating everyone more or less the same has largely (but not entirely) swept the field. This is why I think Richard Seaford is mistaken when he says "our hardwired sense of justice is on the camping expedition generally allowed to prevail, just as it was in the foraging band." What prevails among foragers, on campsites, and in large parts of liberal fossil-fuel societies is not our hardwired sense of justice but the one out of many possible interpretations of our hardwired sense of justice that happens to work best.

Christine Korsgaard offers further criticisms of my second claim, but these too, I believe, take essentialism too far. She suggests that in chapters 1 to 5 I did not actually show that energy capture pushes people toward specific interpretations of human values. Rather, she says, "all he shows, or all he obviously shows, is that the *opposite* value is *not* especially needed to uphold the social forms in question." What this means, she says, is that "Morris points out that foraging societies do not encourage wealth inequalities, without those there is not much to inherit, and so issues about the legitimacy of children matter less. But," she adds, "that only shows that there is no special reason, based in its method of energy capture, for foraging societies to enforce marital fidelity. It does not show why marriages in such societies do take the loose form that they do." Similarly, in the case of farmers' steep gender hierarchies, my emphasis on "a strict gender-based division of labor . . . does not explain male hegemony. One can imagine a world in which women dominate men from a basis in the home, ordering them out to work in order to earn money since that is the only thing they are good for, and taking control of the money as soon as the men bring it home." My thinking on violence is also open to this objection, she argues, because even if I am right that "violence poses a bigger problem for societies organized for farming than for ones organized for foraging, and a bigger problem still for industrial societies . . . that does not explain why it is tolerated in foraging societies."

Korsgaard concludes that rather than reinterpreting our core biologically evolved values in the light of energy capture, we humans are essentially egalitarian and peaceful, and act accordingly so long as we are doing our valuing correctly. Hence her conclusion (which I quoted earlier) that foragers and fossil-fuel users are more egalitarian than farmers because "equality is just the default when hierarchy is not necessary," and her subsequent argument that the reason that foragers "fail[ed] to notice that people should not go around killing each other, while we ourselves can see that plainly . . . was the way that people thought of themselves." Premodern people, she suggests, "seem to feel that their inner identities could be damaged or destroyed by what people thought about them." Consequently, "killing someone in defense of your honor may once have seemed much more like the one form of violence that many of us even now find perfectly acceptable—namely, self-defense."

These points are well made, but I think I am guilty more of overcondensing the argument than of getting things back to front. The heart of the problem, I would say, is Professor Korsgaard's framing of the questions as either/or alternatives about the human essence (Are we egalitarian or hierarchical? Are we peaceful or violent?), because the answer is always "both." The best way to explain foragers' (and, increasingly, fossil-fuel users') rather casual attitudes about female sexuality and farmers' much harsher ones is by comparing the evolutionary payoffs available to men and women (which have remained fairly constant across the last fifty thousand years) with the strategies available for pursuing them (which have changed dramatically, in step with energy capture) and identifying the shifting balances they have produced. Doing this, however, calls for another digression into human evolution.

Individual animals succeed in evolutionary terms by transmitting genes to the next generation: the more copies of themselves they produce, the likelier their genes are to become immortal.[60] In species that reproduce sexually, though, males and females have very different ways of doing this.[61] For males, passing on genetic material is cheap and easy: they ejaculate into females. Consequently, males who have sex with a lot of females leave a bigger imprint on the genome than males who do not, and males have therefore evolved to want to have sex with lots of partners. For females, however, passing on genetic material is expensive and difficult, because they must carry their babies to term. A female who chooses her partners carefully, accepting sperm only from a male whom she expects to give her strong, smart, and healthy children, will typically leave a bigger imprint on the genome than a female who does not choose so wisely. Females have therefore evolved to be picky.

All this seems to be broadly true across much of the animal kingdom, but the evolutionary branching of different species has introduced all kinds of complexities.[62] The first involves childrearing. In some species, females give birth to babies that are basically ready to go, needing little or no parental care. In most species, however, babies need to be fed, protected, and educated, and modern humans are an extreme case of this. Because we have such big brains, we need big skulls, but if we stayed in our mothers' wombs until we were as ready to face the world as the babies of most other species of mammals, our heads would be too big to get down the maternal birth canal. Human mothers have dealt with this by in effect evolving to give birth prematurely, at the cost of greatly increasing the parental care that we need as babies.

Childrearing opens up a new front in the war of the sexes.[63] The more care that children need, the greater the incentive for each sex to try to dump the work onto the other, and the greater the payoffs for being deadbeat dads and moms; but if mother and father both follow this strategy, their child will die, taking its lazy parents' genes with it. Each species therefore evolves toward its own unique gendered division of labor, with forms of energy capture playing a major role in the outcomes. Humans differ from other animals only in the fact that they can evolve toward new equilibria culturally as well as biologically.

Gorillas evolved toward families organized around polygynous alpha males, chimpanzees and bonobos toward different kinds of promiscuous bands, and humans toward pairbonding.[64] Although the details are obscure, *Homo ergaster/erectus*[65] was probably moving in this direction by 1.8 million years ago, developing a distinctive sexual division of energy capture and social life, based on male hunting, female gathering, and some collaboration (but with women doing most of the work) in cooking and childrearing.[66]

The new sexual battlefield of pairbonding called for equally new tactics. On the one hand, we humans evolved our own unique version of love, tying us emotionally to our partners and making it easier for us to cooperate and trust one another, but on the other hand, we also found new ways to game the system. A woman could now try to maximize her genetic success by bonding with a good provider, even if she had doubts about his genetic fitness, and then going outside the relationship for sperm, bringing a genetically superior cuckoo home to the nest. A man, of course, had the opposite option, of planting cuckoos in other nests and leaving those men to pay the costs of raising them. Husbands and wives each have strong incentives to prevent their spouses from maximizing their reproductive potential in these ways, because such activity might reduce the resources available for their own offspring as well as shattering the trust between spouses. Jealousy is an evolved adaptation.

This, in a nutshell, explains not only the millions of love triangles and billions of tears shed over them throughout human history but also much of the world's literature. Despite Tolstoy's insistence that every unhappy family is unhappy in its own way, it seems to me that there are actually just three kinds of weapons available in these battles. The first is shame (or, to put it more coldly, reputational costs): Look, the betrayed partner says to the world, at what the bastard/bitch[67] did after everything I've done for him/her! A second tool is violence, which husbands are normally better equipped to deliver than wives, although a woman scorned may be able to call on her male kin to thrash her scoundrel of a husband within an inch of his life, or a wronged husband might assault the adulterer. And finally we have economics: if one partner controls vital resources, he/she is in a strong position to bargain over sex.

Each of these weapons can be effective, but its potency will depend on strings of largely unconscious cost/benefit analyses that people carry out in the face of temptation. On one side of the scale is the pain a spouse will suffer by forgoing extramarital sex (that is, the chance to maximize his/her reproductive potential) or by being betrayed (that is, allowing his/her partner to maximize her/his reproductive potential); on the other, the pain he/she will suffer from being shamed, beaten, and/or cast out penniless. To complicate calculations further, no two people have the same personalities, and the interests and advice of kin, friends, and neighbors influence everyone's thinking. Everyone's utility function is unique—*chacun à son goût*—but since psychologists suggest that the first side of the scale has roughly the same weight across cultures,[68] it is to the second side that we must look to explain the variations.

The formula is simple. The greater the pain that men can inflict through shame, violence, and economics, the more likely wives are to be faithful and husbands to stray, and the greater the pain that women can inflict through these means, the more likely husbands are to be faithful and wives to stray. The reason foragers (and to a lesser degree fossil-fuelers) accept female pre- and extramarital sex while farmers do not is not because farmers distorted humanity's egalitarian essence. It is because the amount of pain husbands and wives can inflict depends on the organization of society, which in turn depends proximately on scale but ultimately on energy capture.

Farming drew much sharper lines between male and female labor than foraging had done, requiring women to concentrate on organization within the household (food storage and preparation, weaving textiles, childrearing, and the like) and men to concentrate on energy capture outside the household (working the fields, improving the land, hunting, trading, fighting, arguing, and the like).[69] As Korsgaard says, if we sit theorizing in our fossil-fuel studies we can easily imagine a world where the organizers have the upper hand, sending otherwise-useless men out to labor for them in the fields, but in reality, the organizational needs of farming societies gave men the means to inflict devastating economic pain on faithless wives while also raising the costs for men of failing to deter women from bringing cuckoos back to the nest. Much of the time, the best that a woman exposed as unfaithful could hope for was to end up like Anna Karenina, while the worst a wandering husband had to fear was the need to remarry (or perhaps, like Prince Oblonsky in the first chapter of Tolstoy's novel, to spend three nights on the couch while his wife's rage melted away).[70] The shame suffered by sinners and the tolerance for violence directed against them, I suspect, were functions of the perceived economic costs of infidelity and the strength of the economic weapons in the wronged partner's hands. It would be interesting, though, to examine the historical and ethnographic evidence for this in more detail.

Korsgaard and Seaford concentrate on the foraging-to-farming transition rather than the farming-to-fossil fuels one, but an adequate theory must be able to explain both. As I see it, the key fact is that the explosion in energy capture since 1800 (and especially since 1900) has dramatically increased women's employment opportunities and economic power relative to men's. Because of this, the pain husbands can inflict through economic weapons has fallen sharply, and because of that, so too has the shame attached to female sexuality outside wedlock and the tolerance of violence against its practitioners. Consequently, fossil-fuelers increasingly value (or condemn) male and female sexual freedom roughly equally.

One more detail: the ancient historian Walter Scheidel and the economist Paul Seabright, who read chapters 1 to 5 in manuscript, both pointed out to me that a theory of sexual values must explain the truly surprising fact that in many fossil-fuel societies, total fertility rates have now declined below replacement levels. This question comes close to home. "Consider," say the evolutionists Peter Richerson and Robert Boyd, "one of the most bizarre traditions in the whole ethnographic record: the existence of a subculture of people who devote more time to, and are prouder of, the length of their publication list than the number of their children."[71] As a typical, WEIRD, childless-by-choice member of this exotic subculture, how do I account for myself?[72]

Richerson and Boyd provide a sophisticated explanation for this apparently maladaptive trait,[73] but I suspect that—as Zhou Enlai reportedly said of the French Revolution—it is actually too soon to tell what its consequences will be. Those fossil-fuel societies that saw their birth rates decline in the twentieth century also saw their wealth and power increase, but there is no guarantee that that correlation will continue to hold across the next hundred years. Europe, East Asia, and (to a lesser extent) North America might pay a terrible price for their top-heavy age pyramids as the planet's demographic center of gravity shifts toward Africa,[74] but then again, if any of the bolder predictions that I discussed in chapter 5 turn out to be even partly true, twenty-first-century posthumans might live largely online and reproduce asexually (if they need to reproduce at all). In that case, tumbling fertility rates will simply be irrelevant, and we childless academics will be remembered as pioneers who boldly went where no man and woman had gone before.

But enough about sex. Korsgaard also challenges my account of violence. In fact, she says, my failure to explain why foragers were so tolerant of force is "the most obvious problem" with my whole argument. Here too, though, I think my main failing was trying to set out the argument too briefly and neglecting to go into its evolutionary background, while I think Profeessor Korsgaard's main failing is taking essentialism too far.

Biology is a contentious field, but one of the few things that nearly everyone seems to agree on is that violence, like jealousy, is an evolved adaptation. Nearly every species of animal uses it in some way to settle disputes. Within each species, no two animals use violence in exactly the same ways—some are hotheads, others pacifists—but overall each species evolves through natural and sexual selection toward an equilibrium in the amount and kind of violence it uses. That equilibrium is determined by the species' physical endowments, environment, prey, predators, and competitors, and a host of other factors.[75] As animals' environments change, so do their patterns of violence, with the result that across the last 1.3 million years, bonobos and chimpanzees have diverged so far from their last common ancestor that while the former hardly ever kill each other, roughly 10 to 15 percent of the latter die from intraspecies violence.[76] The figure is very similar among human foragers.[77]

Humans, then, are just like other animals, in that we evolved biologically to be able to use force to settle disputes, and yet we are also completely unlike other animals, because we can evolve culturally as well as biologically. As our energy capture has increased, so too has the scale of our societies and the complexity of our division of labor. One of the most important kinds of specialists that farming societies spawned was specialists in violence, who constituted the first governments, and across the last five-thousand-plus years these specialists have progressively reduced the scope for other people to use force to get what they want. As I mentioned in chapter 3, my calculations suggest that by the first century AD governments in the Roman Empire and Han China had driven rates of violent death down below 5 percent. This happened not because farmers slowly got better at valuing, but because the state's increasing monopoly on violence raised the costs for individuals considering taking the law into their own hands. When Eurasian states began falling apart after

AD 200, rates of violent death in Eurasia spiked back up toward 10 percent—not because people now forgot how to value properly, but because governments were no longer strong enough to raise the costs of violence to unattractive levels. When much stronger governments returned after 1400, rates of violent death fell again. In the twentieth century, the global average was below 2 percent, and in the twenty-first below 1 percent.[78]

Finally, I want to respond to a challenge to my claim that energy capture drives our interpretations of core human values that the respondents did not raise. While the commentators focused in chapters 6 to 9 on the logic of my case, several other readers made what I would call a more historical objection, questioning the chronological relationship between my supposed cause and effect. Many of the values that I associate with fossil fuels, they observe, were already taking shape in eighteenth- and even seventeenth-century Western Europe. However, the industrial revolution only began in the 1770s, and even in England was not fully established until the 1830s; so how can what I call "fossil-fuel values" be a product of fossil fuels?

I did say a little about this earlier in the book, but because of the way I organized my argument, my comments were spread across chapters 2 to 5, and some pulling together is clearly in order. I argued that as people learn to capture more energy, their values shift. Both energy and values can be infinitely subdivided, but to make sense of the vast, confusing mass of historical and anthropological material, I clustered both energy capture and values into three ideal types. In chapter 1, I quoted Weber's comment that "In its conceptual purity, [the ideal type] can never be found empirically in reality. It is a *utopia*." But Weber went on to explain that what ideal types lose in reality, they make up for in clarity. Described at the level of ideal types, history seems to show that as people move from foraging through farming to fossil fuels, they also move through systems of values, but described at the level of individual societies and lives, things are messier.

I noted in chapter 2 that foraging societies in resource-rich maritime niches such as Japan, the shores of the Baltic, and the Pacific Coast of North America were able to capture much more energy than landlocked foraging societies. Although none of these "affluent foragers" were in the process of turning into farmers, their unusual circumstances allowed them to capture just as much energy as some farming societies did, and because of that, the scale, wealth, hierarchy, and values of affluent foragers all began moving away from those of the ideal-typical foraging society toward forms that we normally find in Agraria. There were limits on how far they could move in that direction, and no archaeologist would confuse a Jomon site with one from the Aztec Empire; indeed, because the environmental conditions that allowed some people to be affluent foragers were different from those that allowed others to become farmers, there was very little chance of an affluent foraging society independently inventing agriculture. Consequently, every affluent forager society was eventually overwhelmed and destroyed by farmers from other regions.

In chapter 3, I suggested that commercial city-states and proto-industrial nations had a certain amount in common with affluent foragers. Access to the sea seems to have been the secret of most of these unusual societies, which exploited their maritime niches to drive energy capture much higher than ideal-typical farming societies. In a rerun of the affluent-forager experience, their scale, overall wealth, and openness all increased, and their values moved away from those of Agraria, although—as I argued for Athens earlier in this chapter—no city-state truly escaped its farming roots. Similarly, no city-state ever came near having an industrial revolution, because the conditions that favored city-state development did not favor breakthroughs to fossil fuels. Consequently, agrarian empires eventually swallowed up most city-state systems.

Early-modern protoindustrial nations are rather different, because one of them—Britain—did have an industrial revolution. I suggested earlier that this was because it was able to exploit a maritime, commercial network that generated truly unparalleled amounts of organic energy, which had the unintended consequence of incentivizing British entrepreneurs to work out how to use fossil fuels to drive machinery. Northwest European energy capture soared after 1600 as the Atlantic economy took off, and by 1700 it had already passed the highest levels attained under the Roman Empire.

As the scale and wealth of their societies grew, Northwest Europeans experimented with new forms of organization, and, like the residents of certain ancient and medieval city-states, moved—haltingly and violently—toward more open orders. In the 1640s, well before industrialization began, some Englishmen risked everything to tear down hierarchy and divine right, and while Boulton and Watt were still barely known outside Birmingham, some Americans and Frenchmen went even further. If these things had happened five hundred years earlier, during the centuries of very slow growth in energy capture that characterized Europe's High Middle Ages, they would indeed falsify my claim that energy capture drove values. But because they happened in the seventeenth and eighteenth centuries, at the very moment that European energy capture was rising faster than ever before, the Enlightenment strikes me as strong evidence for my thesis.

It is not obvious how I could test the counterfactuals implied by my causal claim, but my hunch is that if Northwest European energy capture had stagnated around 35,000 kilocalories per person per day (roughly its level in 1776), the Enlightenment alone would not have led to the worldwide spread of liberal democracy. Instead, Northwest Europe and its American colonies would probably have experienced a conservative reaction against the new ideas, much as the rest of eighteenth-century Eurasia did.[79] What really mattered was the explosion of energy after 1800, which first made Enlightenment ideals viable all across the West, and then pushed them in radical new directions. (Other counterfactuals abound—if the American Revolution had failed, would rising energy capture have pushed British America to develop along much the same lines as the historical world's United States? And would British America ultimately have replaced the British Isles as the core of the global network of free trade, as the real-world United States did after 1945? Then again, if Britain had not had an industrial revolution, would the United States have turned into something like Latin America, slowly spreading slavery across the continent?[80] Or, alternatively, would the United States have had its own industrial revolution?)

The appeal to "transitional" cases is often the last refuge of the academic scoundrel, desperate to insulate some theory of historical stages against the risk of empirical falsification. No doubt some readers will judge my arguments to be just one more sorry example of the genre. It seems to me, though, that the affluent foragers, ancient and medieval city-states, and early-modern protoindustrial nations really are exceptions that prove the rule, and I therefore stick to my second claim that changes in energy capture have determined changes in how we interpret human values.

Implication 1

In 1984, Ernest Gellner (honored in chapter 3 as the discoverer of Agraria) gave up the chair in philosophy at the London School of Economics to become the professor of social anthropology at Cambridge. I was a Cambridge graduate student in those days, and when Gellner arrived, my colleagues and I discovered that he had a most disconcerting habit. He would plant himself front and center at seminars, fall asleep the moment the speaker started talking, wake up with a start during the applause, and then ask a question that laid bare the presenter's fatally flawed assumptions. One of the first times I saw him perform this trick was at a talk on social theory and archaeology given by Christopher Tilley (now one of the world's leading archaeological theorists, but then still a recently minted PhD). "They tell me you're a good archaeologist," Gellner said. "So why are you trying to be a bad philosopher?"

I thought Gellner had a pretty good point, and for nearly thirty years worked on the assumption that we archaeologists should leave philosophy to the philosophers. The Center for Human Values' invitation to give the Tanner Lectures lured me some way out of this comfort zone, but it was one of Christine Korsgaard's comments that finally made me see that Tilley had a pretty good point too. Archaeology has unavoidable philosophical implications, and until such time as good philosophers take archaeology more seriously, archaeologists have little choice but to become bad philosophers.

Professor Korsgaard suggests that the most important distinction when studying human values is not the one I made, between biologically evolved core values and the ways real people interpret these values, but one between "positive values," by which she means "the values that people actually hold" and "real moral values," meaning "the values that we ought to hold." Tracing this terminology back to early modern European roots, she says that "Philosophers do not go in for that way of talking much any more, but if we did, then we might see the difference between real moral values and positive values as the difference between eternal values and values that are in fact endorsed only in certain times and places."

If we look at things Korsgaard's way, the challenge of explaining Mr. George's values is really a matter of explaining why farmers get their values so badly wrong. However, I do not think we should look at things Korsgaard's way, because the first implication of my claims in this book is that her distinction between real moral values and positive values is meaningless. Korsgaard says at one point that "It is unclear whether Morris believes there are any real moral values," so I will clarify: I do not believe there are any real moral values in the sense that Korsgaard uses the expression.

I say this because human values can only be held by humans, and humans cannot hold any values at all unless they capture energy from their environments (grub first, then ethics, said the poet Auden).[81] This must mean that the values of real humans are by definition positive values, shaped by the ways we capture energy from the world; and that is why I say that Korsgaard's distinction between real moral values and positive values is meaningless. It is positive values all the way down.

The real/positive distinction remains meaningless even if we equate real moral values with what I have been calling biologically evolved core values. Biologically evolved core values never existed in a vacuum: they evolved among actual humans who survived by foraging, and therefore interpreted justice, love, and so on, in the ways that worked best when capturing energy from wild plants and animals and competing with other humans who were doing the same thing. Trying to imagine people who are somehow divorced from the demands of capturing energy and then speculating about what their moral values would be is an odd activity. In fact, it reminds me of nothing so much as a story told by the Greek historian Herodotus. Once upon a time, he says, the Egyptian pharaoh Psammetichus became obsessed with knowing who had been the earth's original inhabitants, and he decided to try an experiment. He ordered two newborn babes to be raised in isolation, where they never heard another human voice. After two years, the experiment paid off: the children suddenly charged at their minder with outstretched hands, shouting "*bekos!*"—the Phrygian word for bread. "The Egyptians accepted this evidence," Herodotus tells us, "and concluded that the Phrygians are older than themselves."[82]

It is a silly story, but asking what language people would speak if they were not part of a community of language speakers is really no sillier than asking what values humans would hold if they were not really humans who lived by capturing energy. Even the most sophisticated attempts to reason toward contextless, one-size-fits-all real moral values have to assume energy capture of some kind. Not surprisingly, theorists tend to take for granted the energy-capture conditions that they themselves live in, and, equally unsurprisingly, tend to conclude that the values of that world are those of the best of all possible worlds.

The obvious example of this is John Rawls's famous thought experiment in which we are asked to imagine what sort of society we would want to live in if we began behind a "veil of ignorance," not knowing whether we would be born male or female, rich or poor, greedy or lazy, healthy or frail, and so on. Rawls concluded that people would eventually agree on two principles of justice: equal liberties for all, and rules to restrict all forms of inequality except for those that benefit the worst-off members of the group.[83]

Rawls famously suggested that the society we should want is one that would require us "to share one another's fate" and to "undertake to avail [our]selves of the accidents of nature and social circumstance only when doing so is for the common benefit." As he saw it, this meant rejecting hierarchy out of hand; "Aristocratic and feudal societies," he reasoned, "are unjust because they make

... contingencies the ascriptive basis for belonging to more or less enclosed and privileged social classes."[84]

Like Rawls, I grew up in a liberal, fossil-fuel society, and I too find this an attractive idea—so long as I can assume that the world on the other side of the veil is also powered by fossil fuels. But what if domesticated plants and animals are pretty much the only sources of energy? After all, the whole point of the veil of ignorance is that we cannot assume anything. For all we know, the world we enter will be one of farmers, confronting the key agrarian conundrum that although large-scale coordination of work is necessary if we are to be able to eat, the marginal returns to labor are usually so low that the crucial tasks can be accomplished only through forced labor. Again like Rawls, I have not bothered to do any actual research to test my preconceptions,[85] but I suspect that when faced with the possibility of being born into a farming world rather than a fossil-fuel one, most people would not opt for Rawls's carefully prescribed egalitarianism. The best option *ex ante* might be a more modest commitment, to a rougher-and-readier set of biologically evolved core values of fairness, love, compassion, and the like, leaving it to the people who actually live on the other side of the veil to work which interpretations of these values will be best for keeping starvation and violence at bay.

Perhaps Gellner would have dismissed all this as bad philosophy, but it seems to me that while Rawls brilliantly elucidated one vision of liberal fossil-fuel values, he did not reason his way to what Korsgaard calls real moral values, because such eternal values do not exist. If the material conditions on the other side of the veil turn out to be medieval, people with feudal views will flourish and egalitarians will not. If I am right about that, the distinction I have drawn between biologically evolved core values and the interpretations people put on them is valid and important, while Korsgaard's between real moral values and positive values is not.

I do not, then, agree with Korsgaard when she reformulates my question about Mr. George into one about why farmers get things so badly wrong; and since I do not agree that farmers are doing their valuing badly, I can have no truck with the explanations she offers for their failures either. She suggests three possible theories about what's wrong with farmers. In the first, which she calls sociological positivism, "what people actually value can be wholly explained by sociological forces, which may in turn be driven by evolutionary forces"; in the second, the enlightenment view, "human beings have a capacity for valuing, and that capacity has some natural tendency to attach itself to real moral values. But like our capacity for scientific knowledge, it . . . only manages to bring its proper object, real moral values, slowly into view"; and in the third, the distortion view, "human beings have a capacity for valuing, and that capacity has some natural tendency to attach itself to real moral values, but its tendency to do that is vulnerable to . . . distortion by what is called, in the pejorative sense, 'ideology.'"

Although she is not very explicit, I think Korsgaard is saying that my arguments are sociologically positivist, even though her criticism of this kind of thinking does not sound much like the book I thought I had written. Korsgaard says that sociological positivism's main weakness is that "If values were just a way of maintaining the social forms called for by a certain form of energy capture, and people knew that, it is hard to see how they would work. People must believe they are living up to real moral values before values can do that job." I could not agree more, and I am therefore confident that I am not a sociological positivist (functionalist, yes; sociological positivist, no).

My reason for agreeing with Korsgaard that values are not values unless people believe in them is that the findings of history and anthropology seem clear: people normally *do* believe in their values, for the very good reason that all the evidence available to them points to that conclusion. Take the case of godlike kings. Plutarch tells a fine story that when Alexander the Great arrived on the borders of India in 324 BC after overthrowing the entire Persian Empire in ten years, he asked a local sage: "How can a man become a god?" The clever Brahmin told him: "By doing something a man cannot do."[86] I always imagine Alexander scratching his head and wondering *Who do I know who's done something that a man cannot do?* and quickly coming up with the answer:

I know. Me. I just conquered Persia. No mere mortal could do that. I am a god and I should not feel bad about killing my friends if they contradict me.

We cannot know whether Alexander really believed that he was the son of Zeus, although he certainly acted like he did, and had been propagating stories to that effect since at least 332 BC. Nor can we know whether ancient Greeks believed him. Most seem to have just laughed when, soon after the incident with the sage, Alexander ordered them to worship him. By 307 BC, however, Athenians were ready to build altars and offer sacrifices to Alexander's former generals.[87] A century later, it was entirely normal for Greeks to worship their kings as gods. Again, we will never know whether people really believed that their deeply flawed rulers were divine,[88] but believing that these men were in fact "savior gods" would have explained two obvious facts—that these men had done things that seemed beyond the abilities of mortals and wielded superhuman power—in the most economical way possible.[89]

Our knowledge of what ancient farmers were thinking is meager, but it nevertheless makes me suspect that the members of Agrarias did believe that they were interpreting their biologically evolved core values correctly when they gave men authority over women, rich over poor, and so on—just as fossil-fuel philosophers tend to think they are valuing correctly when they insist on the need for equality. But since Professor Korsgaard and I seem to agree that sociological positivism is a terrible theory, I will not labor the point.[90]

Instead, I will move on to her comment that "I think there is something to be said for the enlightenment view, but even more to be said for the distortion view." To some extent, I share her opinion on the enlightenment view, but only because (as I explained in chapters 4 and 5) I think the Enlightenment was itself a product of rising energy capture. The distortion view, however, is another matter altogether. Korsgaard and Seaford both give great weight to ideology in Agraria, the former saying that it distorts people's ability to value correctly and the latter that "the control both of wealth-distribution and of violence is lost by the majority to a small group at the center who also exercise some ideological control."

Neither Korsgaard nor Seaford defines "ideology" very closely. It is, admittedly, one of the least definable words in the social-scientific lexicon,[91] but at the risk of seeming polemical, I would lump their uses of the term into what the anthropologist Talal Asad once called "the vulgar-Marxist view of ideology as a coherent system of false beliefs which maintains a total structure of exploitation and domination." I quote Asad here because of the gloss he puts on this vision of ideology, which, he says, "might be called the Wizard of Oz theory of ideology. Like Dorothy, the anthropologist [or philosopher, or classicist] tears aside the veil of a seeming discourse to disclose the essential reality—an ordinary-looking old man busily working a hand-machine."[92]

"You may fool all the people some of the time; you can even fool some of the people all the time; but you can't fool all the people all the time," Abraham Lincoln is supposed to have said (unless it was P. T. Barnum).[93] But Korsgaard and Seaford apparently think that Lincoln/Barnum was wrong, and that for ten thousand years everyone in Agraria was led by the nose—women by men, poor by rich, everyone by priests—and robbed blind. This I just cannot credit. Humans are the cleverest animals on the planet (for all we know, the cleverest in the whole universe). We have worked out the answers to almost every problem we have ever encountered. So how, if farming values were really just a trick perpetrated by wicked elites, did they survive for ten millennia? Most of the farmers I have met have been canny folk; so why could farmers in the past not figure out what was going on behind the wizard's veil?

The answer, in my opinion, is that there was no veil. The veil is a figment of modern academics' imaginations, made necessary by the assumption that only a tiny elite could possibly have thought that hierarchy was a good thing. In reality, farmers had farming values not because they fell for a trick but because they had common sense. Common sense—by which I mean humanity's biologically evolved ability to learn from experience and adapt behavior to the circumstances of the world—told people that in any society where energy capture averaged between 8,000 and 35,000 kilocalories per person per day, farming values were what worked to keep most of them fed and safe; and when energy capture rose above 35,000 kilocalories per person per day, common sense told people that it was time to reinterpret their values.

I stress common sense because of Seaford's suggestion that "'common sense' is—paradoxically—usually *ideological.*" It is not. Far from being ideological, common sense is what ideology must struggle to overcome. Common sense is not always a very good tool for apprehending reality—after all, it tells us the sun goes round the earth, the world is flat, and air is not a substance—but it is an extremely good tool for figuring out what is going to work and the likely consequences of our actions.[94] Neither godlike kings, nor male superiority, nor natural slaves are real, but in farming societies all three ideas worked, so common sense told people to believe in them and adjust their values accordingly. Persuading people to ignore common sense is very difficult, which is why no one can fool all the people all the time (or even for ten thousand years). Common sense is corrosive, eating away at ideologies like an acid.

Seaford makes his claim about common sense being ideological in a comment on my experience among the Luhya of Kenya, and I think this actually illustrates my point rather well. I arrived in Kenya in 1986 carrying a set of firmly held fossil-fuel assumptions about the wickedness of colonialist mindsets, but quickly yielded to common sense and hired local women to bring me water. "But Ian was in Kenya as a temporary individual observer," Professor Seaford says. "For the villagers it would be better *not* to adapt to the circumstances but to *transform* them, by working for the improvement of the water-supply."

Here I think he misunderstands what was going on. Locals pointed out to my wife and me the overgrown ruins of several abandoned water pumping and purification stations, explaining that western Kenya was so poor that even if aid organizations built facilities, there were not enough wage earners to pay to keep them going, and not enough tax- or bribe-payers to make governments in distant Nairobi care. But by hauling water up from the stream in return for cash, the Luhya women *were* transforming their circumstances. They were applying their common sense and shifting from domestic work toward wage labor, just as American and European women had been doing since the 1940s. The Luhya who talked with us seemed to understand very well that the faster they moved from farming values about women's labor toward fossil-fuel ones, the faster they would bring money into western Kenya and transform their circumstances.

The contrast between Kenya and neighboring Tanzania is informative. Tanzania—then Tanganyika—achieved independence from Britain in 1961, and Kenya in 1963. Both countries were very poor, and at that point it was far from clear whether a market-based or a socialist path toward Industria would work best for them in the brave new world of independence.[95] Kenya's rulers broadly chose the former, leaving Kenyans free to follow their common sense (unless this led them to criticize the rulers), while Tanzania's chose the latter, requiring their citizens to subordinate common sense to *ujamaa*, a Swahili word meaning something like "uniting as a family." This ideology (also known as African socialism) vigorously denied many of the realities of the fossil-fuel world, and the Party of the Revolution forcibly relocated six million town and city dwellers to villages, with disastrous results.[96] In 1961, Tanganyikans were already poorer than Kenyans, earning on average just 64 cents to every dollar that a Kenyan made, but by 1986, *ujamaa* had driven that Tanzanian wage down to 51 cents. When my wife and I arrived that autumn in Arusha—coincidentally, the very place where the *ujamaa* doctrine was originally announced—we were shocked by how little food there was, compared to Kenya. One night, the only dinner we could find was "goat soup"—a bone and some fat in a bowl of warm salty water, eaten in the dark because the electricity was out. Since 2001, however, *ujamaa* has yielded to common sense. Tanzanians have embraced markets and wage labor, and by 2013 were earning 94 cents for every Kenyan's dollar.[97]

Richard Seaford and I disagree on how human values relate to material well-being, but whatever we think about that question, the Kenya-Tanzania comparison shows that even with Julius Nyerere's authority and the power of the state behind it, *ujamaa* survived only a little over a generation, because common sense told Tanzanians that it did not fit the facts. Soviet communism lasted longer, and well into the 1950s it still seemed a good description of reality to many millions of its subjects.[98] That argument became harder to sustain as the economy slowed in the 1970s, and by the 1980s common sense had made most Soviet subjects see that communism was a lie ("we pretend to work, and they pretend to pay us," went one famous joke).[99] By the end of the decade, communism was gone.

Korsgaard's distinction between real moral values and positive values requires her to see ideology as a sociological distortion that prevents people from valuing correctly—in the case of farming, for ten thousand years at a stretch. My distinction between biologically evolved core values and the interpretations people put on them, with the interpretations driven primarily by energy capture, requires me to see ideology as a pack of lies from which someone benefits[100]—but rarely for long, because common sense is such a powerful tool for revealing what will work best in the material conditions in which we find ourselves. I emphasize this definitional difference because I think it helps to explain one final disagreement between Professor Korsgaard and me, over the Taliban attack on the future Nobel laureate Malala Yousafzai in 2012.

That Korsgaard and I recall the discussion at Princeton about the shooting in such different ways is perhaps not surprising. "Different eyewitnesses give different accounts of the same events, speaking out of partiality for one side or the other or out of imperfect memories,"[101] Thucydides observed 2,400 years ago, and not much has changed since then. Korsgaard's recollection is that when asked whether the Taliban's action was wrong, I tried to sidestep making any moral claims of my own. I had not intended to do that, but perhaps I can be clearer in print than I was after a fine but boozy dinner.

Of course Yousafzai's attackers—finally arrested in September 2014, as I was writing this chapter[102]—were wrong. But if I am right that the important distinction in moral reasoning is between biologically evolved core values and the interpretations people put on them rather than between real moral values and positive values, we have to ask what "wrong" means. Extrapolating from her comments, I would guess that for Korsgaard, wrong behavior is something that violates real moral values that are independent of humanity. For me, wrong behavior is something that violates my strongly held, fossil-fuel interpretations of biologically evolved human values. I was confident in 1982 that Mr. George should not have made his wife carry the sack while he rode the donkey, and I was even more confident in 2012 that the Taliban should not have shot Malala Yousafzai. Because I realize that my own values are just a commonsense interpretation of the world that fossil fuels made, I have no problem recognizing that people with deeply held farming values might disagree with me. But on the other hand, I also have no problem in saying that I am right and they are wrong—not because I do my valuing better than them, but because the farming age is over. This is why I suggested in chapter 4 that the Taliban are guilty first and foremost of backwardness.

As I understand it, the Islamist argument[103] is that by noisily demanding education for women, Yousafzai threatened the safety and salvation of the world, and because lethal violence is an appropriate response to such an extreme threat, it is right to kill her. Some of the opinion polls that I mentioned in chapter 4 suggest that many fossil-fuelers agree that lethal violence is appropriate when the world's safety is threatened,[104] which means that the point of contention is a factual one, of what counts as such a threat. Some Islamists think that fifteen-year-old feminists meet the criteria; I (along with almost everyone else in the world) do not. This, as I say, is a factual question, and in the real world of the early twenty-first century, the Taliban are wrong on the facts. Malala Yousafzai is not a threat to world peace. She is just a threat to Islamist ideology, a pack of lies that insists that violence can force a fossil-fuel world awash with energy to return to farming values.

Professor Korsgaard does not like this argument. "Morris's text sometimes reads as if he is not one of the human beings he is theorizing about," she says, to which I can only reply that if she thinks I come from another planet, I think she needs to get out more. And not just her—like Kant in Königsberg, moral philosophers often seem happy to stay home, where they only have to argue with other WEIRD people and not make sense of men like Mr. George.

This, I think, is a mistake. Compare, for instance, the experience of the psychologist Jonathan Haidt, who, upon completing his PhD, decamped from American academia to Bhubaneswar in India. "My first few weeks," he recalls, were

> filled with feelings of shock and dissonance. I dined with men whose wives silently served us and then retreated into the kitchen, not speaking to me the entire evening. I was told to be stricter with my servants, and to stop thanking them for serving me. . . . I was immersed in a sex-segregated, hierarchically stratified, devoutly religious society.

And yet after a few more weeks, he found that

> I *liked* these people who were hosting me, helping me, and teaching me. Wherever I went, people were kind to me. . . . Rather than automatically rejecting the men as sexist oppressors and pitying the women, children, and servants as helpless victims, I began to see a moral world in which families, not individuals, are the basic unit of society, and the members of each extended family (including its servants) are intensely interdependent. In this world, equality and personal autonomy were not sacred values. Honoring elders, gods, and guests, protecting subordinates, and fulfilling one's role-related duties were more important.[105]

Welcome to Agraria.

Getting out more, I would say, makes us (whoever we happen to be) ask why perfectly reasonable people can hold views so very different from our own. Speaking for myself, it was getting out more that led me to make the two claims described earlier in this chapter and to draw the implication that Korsgaard's distinction between real moral values and positive values is meaningless. Mr. and Mrs. George's values were not distorted versions of eternal values; they were the kind of commonsense interpretations of our biologically evolved core values that billions of farmers reached when their energy capture fell between 8,000 and 35,000 kilocalories per day—and which billions of farmers abandoned once their energy capture rose much above 35,000 kilocalories.

Seeing things this way does not mean that I am an alien from another world, any more than believing in hierarchy meant that 1980s Assirotes or Bhubaneswaris were tyrants or victims. Nor does seeing things this way mean I am a moral skeptic. We live in a fossil-fuel world; therefore, fossil-fuel values are the right interpretations of our biologically evolved core values and farming and forager values are wrong—and this will remain true until Industria too passes into history.

Implication 2

Which brings me to the second implication of my claims: that interpretations of our biologically evolved core values will evolve faster than ever before across the twenty-first century, because energy capture is changing faster than ever before.

Richard Seaford does not directly say that I am wrong about this, but that does seem to be the implication of the claims he makes in chapter 6. I have suggested that the competitive process of cultural evolution that has driven history will continue working, with three big consequences—first, energy capture will increase faster than ever; second, revolutions in genetics, nanotechnology, and robotics will feed back into biological evolution, transforming what it means to be a human being; and third, the risk of nuclear war will increase as these changes play out. Seaford, however, considers this analysis "learned, stimulating, persuasive, and misleading in a way that I consider politically disastrous." While he does not spell out exactly what the politics are that this book threatens, he has no doubts about my own politics, which are "much closer to the ideas of our ruling class than to the thought that our age needs." Like all the other dummies in Oz, I have been taken in by a capitalist wizard who, pulling levers behind the veil, has tricked me into "unconsciously internaliz[ing] . . . the capitalist outlook."

Having been assured by reviewers of my last few books that I am not only "a Party intellectual who knows in which direction the evidence must be altered to fit with the multicultural line" but also "a typical modern academic: a materialist, but not a Marxist," and even someone who "peddles subjective neoconservative belief in the guise of objective scholarly theory,"[106] I have learned not to worry too much about political denunciations. But that said, Professor Seaford's effort to cure me of my right deviationism does involve some concrete historical disagreements that I would like to address.

Seaford accuses me of mistaking the logic of capitalism for the logic of history as a whole. "Capitalism's dynamic of necessary self-expansion, and the values it produces," he says, "are different in kind from what precedes it." If I have understood his argument correctly, his point is that people's propensity to try to maximize energy captured from the environment relative to energy expended on this activity is not—as I had concluded—a function of the fact that we are animals. Rather, it is a very recent phenomenon, spawned by capitalism.[107] Just look, he says, at Greece and Rome, which show that "the constant search for efficiency, familiar to us from capitalist economies, is simply not a feature of ancient economies."

I have to disagree. I have learned a lot from Seaford's writings on ancient Greek economic thought,[108] but here I think he is simply wrong. The idea that Greeks and Romans put other social considerations ahead of efficiency and profit goes back to Weber in the 1890s, and between the 1950s and 1980s Karl Polanyi and Moses Finley developed sophisticated versions of it.[109] But as Keith Hopkins noted a generation ago, the problem with this theory is that it cannot account for the very obvious intensive (that is, per capita) economic growth that took place under the Roman Empire.[110] More recent research has identified comparable growth in archaic and classical Greece,[111] and it is now clear not only that the first-millennium BC Mediterranean saw one of the strongest episodes of economic growth anywhere in the world before AD 1800[112] but also that the tireless search for economic efficiency was one of its central features.[113]

Figure 10.2 summarizes a second source of evidence, which I have mentioned repeatedly in this book: the exponential growth in energy capture since the end of the Ice Age. Far from being unique to capitalism, per capita economic growth is simply what we get when we put together modern humans and the post–Ice Age "long summer." Exponential growth has been the norm; what has changed over time is that the exponent has increased, speeding up the expansion. Across the two centuries since the industrial revolution began and capitalism took off, the world's population has grown 7-fold, its biggest city 25-fold, its stock of knowledge (by my calculation) 860-fold, and its energy capture more than 40-fold. These are extraordinary statistics, but they represent an acceleration of an older pattern, not an entirely new one. In the two thousand years before AD 1800, the size of the planet's population had quadrupled, its biggest cities almost tripled, the stock of knowledge (again, by my calculation) had grown 10-fold, and the energy under human control had increased 8-fold. Across the millennium before that, population had doubled, cities had grown 20-fold, the stock of knowledge had quadrupled, and energy capture had more than tripled.[114] The further we go back, the slower the acceleration, but economies have been growing exponentially since 10,000 BC. The size of the exponent has been a function of the scale of the system, the intensity of communication, and the size of the existing stock of knowledge, themselves ultimately driven by the amount of energy captured.

Professor Seaford is right that I do not use the word "capitalism" much in this book, but that, I hope, is not because the wizard has fooled me. Rather, as I argued in chapter 4, it is because the important thing in modern economic growth is fossil fuels, not capitalist mentalities.[115] I suggested there that when fossil fuels began flooding the world with energy, people found two main ways to organize the new abundance. I called these liberal and illiberal, but to some extent we could substitute the word "capitalist" for liberal[116] and "socialist" or "fascist" for illiberal. In the long run, liberal/capitalist methods—free markets, free trade, free speech—proved extremely effective at expanding the economy, but before concluding that capitalism has a unique dynamic of expansion, we should bear in mind that almost all postindustrial political systems, including socialism and fascism, sought and delivered more economic growth than any preindustrial political systems.

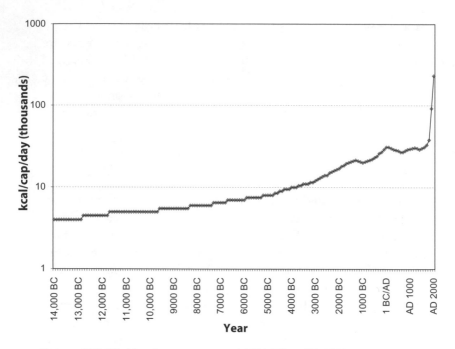

FIGURE 10.2. World peak energy capture, 14,000 BC to AD 2000.

Between 1930 and 1941, for instance, fascist Japan's economy grew by 4.1 percent per annum; between 1933 and 1939, Nazi Germany's grew by 7.2 percent per annum; between 1928 (the first year with reliable data) and 1989, Soviet economic growth averaged 3.65 percent per annum; while in the same 61-year period, American economic growth averaged 3.25 percent per annum.[117] Choosing different dates of course changes the numbers, but every choice nevertheless produces a similar result.[118] Twentieth-century illiberal economies grew faster growth than any economies before 1900 (even Mao's China, surely the poster child for economic mismanagement, saw an average of 2.5 percent per annum growth between 1950 and 1976, in spite of the Great Leap Forward and Cultural Revolution), and regularly outperformed twentieth-century capitalism. We should certainly bear in mind that these comparisons are in some ways misleading; the United States, for instance, was already largely industrialized in the 1920s, whereas Russia and China were barely beginning their industrial revolutions, as well as bouncing back from terrible wars (meaning that the Soviet and Maoist economies could pluck a lot of low-hanging fruit as they played catchup). Communists and fascists also relied heavily on forced labor, and cared even less than nineteenth-century liberal societies about devastating the environment.[119] It seems overwhelmingly likely that had Russia and China had liberal rather than communist regimes, their economies would have grown faster still, but even so, there seems to be no way to escape the conclusion that the most important force in modern economic growth has been fossil fuels, not capitalism.

Capitalism took off in early-modern Western Europe because practical people figured out that this was the most effective way to get things done in an increasingly energy-rich world. Other people disagreed, and did things differently. Conflicts and compromises ensued as the competitive logic of cultural evolution went to work and drove the less effective ways extinct. I think this is how things will work in the twenty-first century too, and I am guardedly optimistic that cultural evolution will yield the best (or perhaps least bad) outcome. Seaford disagrees, however, and seems to think that my argument is not so much glass-half-full as pure Pollyanna. "People will never accept the limitations needed to save our environment in a society of glaring inequalities," he says. "Why should I cut down on flights when the sky is full of private jets?"

The sky is indeed full of private jets (as of 2013, some 19,258 of them),[120] but I am not convinced that that is really why I, Professor Seaford, and other members of the chattering classes carry on cramming ourselves into economy seats on commercial airlines to go to places like Princeton, and I am less convinced still that these decisions are the real threat to the world's climate. By guzzling fossil fuels, Westerners drove the air's carbon content up close to 400 parts per million during the twentieth century, but for a decade now the real running has been made by East and South Asia's industrial revolutions. Hundreds of millions of people still lack reliable electricity, but these industrial revolutions are changing that. If another billion people each buy a single 60-watt lightbulb and turn it on for four hours each day—surely not much to ask—the world will need to add another 10 gigawatts of generating capacity. In 2007, the International Energy Agency predicted that global oil demand would rise from 86 million barrels per day to 116 million in 2030, while still leaving 1.4 billion people without electricity.[121] There is nothing to gain from blaming capitalism for this. The big question is not how to overthrow the wizard behind the veil but how to satisfy the very reasonable demands that newly enfranchised fossil-fuelers are making for the same good things that Richard Seaford and I already enjoy.

The answer, Seaford suggests, lies in "values sustained by emotion." Again I would have appreciated a fuller explanation of what that means, but I will proceed based on the context in which Seaford uses the term. Common sense tells most people that if almost all scientists say that the climate is changing, that fossil fuels are largely responsible, and that action is needed, it is probably true. Ideologues of many political persuasions do deny this, but the influence of their ignorance and/or lies seems to be waning. The best barometer is the same capitalist markets that Seaford warns against: coal shares are down (for Peabody Energy, the world's largest private-sector coal company, by 80 percent between 2008 and 2014), renewables are up, and even the arch-capitalists at Morgan Stanley recommend shifting investment from fossil fuels to alternative energy.[122] At a meeting of investors in Boston in 2014, Michael Liebreich, CEO of Bloomberg New Energy Finance, explained that "increasingly investors are understanding fossil fuel industry as being a low-performing and increasingly unpopular industry. People are understanding that [the] cost of solar has come way down and the cost of wind is coming way down. If we get to where people see all of this as a business opportunity we have a chance."[123]

Markets cannot solve all the world's woes, but they might help with this one. The great discovery of twentieth-century new liberalism was that government intervention was not necessarily the enemy of free markets; it could, in fact, improve markets by setting rules that reduced distortions.[124] Currently, neither sellers nor buyers normally pay the full costs of fossil fuels, because markets do not put a price on the carbon being pumped into the atmosphere. Correcting this market failure is not rocket science: economists have floated plenty of schemes for carbon taxes and cap-and-trade schemes that would reduce market imperfections and make alternative energy sources more competitive, generating faster economic growth as well as lowering emissions.[125] The big obstacle is not values or emotions but our inability to agree on who should bear the costs. That is a political question, but there has been little progress on it since the Kyoto Protocol because there is a mismatch between climate threats that operate at a global scale and political institutions that operate on a national scale. We are trying to solve a twenty-first-century problem with what are effectively nineteenth-century organizations, and consequently local interests regularly override planetary imperatives.[126]

That, for what it is worth, is what I think. I readily concede, though, that no one can foresee how—or whether—we will break through the hard ceiling that limits what is possible for a fossil-fuel economy, just as no one in the past could foresee how or whether foragers would break through the hard ceiling over their economy or farmers that over theirs. In many ways, these three great energy transitions are very similar, and yet—as Margaret Atwood observes in her sparkling commentary—this time really is different. Ten thousand years ago, hundreds of separate societies were experimenting with farming. Most failed to shatter the hard ceiling, bringing on Malthusian tragedies for the people involved, but a few succeeded. Over the last two thousand years, at least five societies have pressed against the upper limits of farming economics; four failed to break through, but the experiments kept going, until in the late eighteenth century Northwest Europeans unleashed a fossil-fuel economy. Today, however, we have a single global experiment, and failure threatens everyone with disaster.

If we fail, it will not be the first time in evolutionary history that the success of one life form has had the paradoxical effect of changing the global environment in ways that subsequently cause the successful life form to go extinct. At the end of the Permian Period, roughly 252 million years ago, a genus of microbes called

Methanosarcina evolved a new way to capture energy (in the form of organic carbon) from the oceans. This proved a huge success, and *Methanosarcina* multiplied madly. In the process, though, the tiny organisms belched out so much methane that they changed the chemistry of the seas and skies.[127] Over the next few million years, 96 percent of marine species and 70 percent of terrestrial vertebrates went extinct, and the oceans' surface temperature may have reached 104°F.[128] For the following ten million years, there was precious little life anywhere on earth (hence the decision of paleontologist Michael Benton to call his book about this episode *When Life Nearly Died*), and when plants and animals once again multiplied, entirely new species—including the ancestors of the dinosaurs—dominated the world.[129]

It remains to be seen whether we humans are simply following a script written by *Methanosarcina*, but the similarities are certainly hard to ignore. Like the Permian microbes, we have spread all over the planet and released a flood of carbon that has begun a mass extinction (this is not scare-mongering; one species of plant or land animal currently goes extinct every twenty minutes, and biologists regularly call our own age the "sixth mass extinction").[130] Our cultural evolution seems to have set in train a forcing event that is speeding up the process of biological evolution—which is why the second implication of my argument is that the twenty-first century might see the replacement of human values with something entirely different. If microbes inherit the earth or if the selective pressures of the forcing event reward our mutation into technologically enhanced posthumans, the extremely human arguments that the respondents and I had in Princeton will all be moot. Consequently, I think Seaford is missing the point when he says that we can choose to preserve a particular strand of fossil-fuel values because "it is much harder to find a value (gross domestic product?) that is so much more valuable than the moral values with which we are hardwired that it would be generally agreed to justify the extremely complex task of deactivating that hardwiring (however successful may have been the constant unacknowledged attempts to manipulate or neutralize those values)." What we agree to might not matter very much. We certainly have choices,[131] just as foragers had choices when farmers showed up and farmers had choices when fossil-fuel users arrived, but, as the foragers and farmers learned, having choices is not the same thing as controlling outcomes.

Margaret Atwood takes a very different approach. She has already spent much of her career exploring the unintended consequences of our choices in what she calls "fun-filled, joke-packed romps in which most of the human race has been obliterated." Her novel *The Handmaid's Tale*, for instance, has America turning back into something like Agraria after an anti-Islamist coup, while *Oryx and Crake* gives us a post-plague world peopled mostly by genetically modified transhumans.[132] Taking off from this work, her chapter in this book asks directly what collapse or transformation might mean for human values.

"You might think," she suggests, that if the twenty-first century sees collapse, "those of us who are left would go back one step—from fossil-fuel values to agricultural ones—but in conditions of widespread societal breakdown, we'd more likely switch to early foraging values almost immediately." After all, she observes, "nobody knows how to fix stuff any more. Your car, your computer, your outboard motor: it's all digital. If our society crashes it's unlikely to be reconstructed, because the specialized expertise needed to work the machinery of resource extraction and manufacturing will be gone with the cloud." And in that case, "urban dwellers minus their usual occupations are nomads, dependent not on what they can grow—that's a long seed-to-harvest cycle anyway—but on what they can scrounge, filch, or kill." No country for Rawlsians.

These comments led me (via a rather roundabout thought process) to ponder more carefully than I had done before just how much difference the initial conditions of collapse might make. A nuclear war in the 1980s, for instance, might have killed almost everyone in just a few weeks; and while a similar war in the 2010s might eventually have the same result, it will take several years, because there are no longer enough warheads to wipe us all out in first and second strikes. Similarly, a sufficiently nasty biological weapon might spread worldwide and abruptly end almost all life, while a more conventional pandemic (such as Ebola, much in the news as I write) might return in waves, like all the great plagues of the past, driving down population levels across decades. Climate change could perhaps collapse things in even slower motion, gradually lowering agricultural yields and flooding coastal plains.

Collapse can be fast or slow. But either way, we have to ask the question: then what? I live just a few miles from the San Francisco Bay, crowded with nearly seven million souls. Two or three missiles, each carrying a megaton's worth of destruction on multiple warheads, could kill most of us, and the unhappy few who remained might well—much as Atwood suggests—shoot each other or scatter and starve in an irradiated wasteland. Alternatively, incoming tides of germs might wash over the suburbs, or rising temperatures might gradually dry up shipments of food to Safeway and Trader Joe's. When the ancient equivalent of this happened in Italy between AD 439 and 600, the city of Rome shrank from about 800,000 people to fewer than 40,000.[133] Perhaps Palo Alto, San Jose, and Oakland will be no bigger in 2049 than they were in 1849.

The more I think about it, though, the more I suspect that collapse—especially the slow kinds—will not turn the clock back to the age of foragers.[134] The world still has plenty of people who do know how to do things, and even places right outside the San Francisco Bay, such as the Santa Cruz Mountains (where I live), have no shortage of them.[135] Plenty of these people farm, know how to generate electricity with bicycles and build shortwave radios, and can make beat-up old trucks run on biofuels. No few of them have guns and have been preparing for the end days for some time now. And for all the things they do not know how to do, there will still be books. Many of these will surely be lost, and we might need characters like the hero of Walter Miller's science fiction classic *A Canticle for Leibowitz*, working secretly to preserve the world's stock of knowledge;[136] but we will not regress to a preliterate, prescientific, foraging world.

Perhaps the most likely outcome is a hybrid economy, combining farming with fossil-fuel patches. In some ways, it could look rather like the early twentieth century AD, before the computer age began;

in others, more like the twentieth century BC. I imagine the overall effect as something like the chaotic, semi-industrialized landscape of failed states in sub-Saharan Africa. When the Western Roman Empire fell apart between the fifth and seventh centuries AD, skills that remained useful survived, those that did not disappeared, and people applied common sense and adjusted their values to the messy new realities. Much the same, I would guess, awaits the survivors of a twenty-first-century catastrophe. If I had Margaret Atwood's literary gifts, it might make for a fine novel.

A more Singularitarian world, however, racing up toward five thousand points on my social development index, might not make for much of a novel at all. It might have flashes of humor, if, as Atwood suggests, the first fruit of bioengineering—her "Horse-creature of the Apocalypse"—is "geeky-looking biologists [who] will design beautiful females with an inborn lust for geeky-looking biologists." It might also have flashes of horror, if sexual selection then pushes other males toward evolving culturally to mimic geeky-looking biologists. But maybe it would have no flashes of anything that we could even begin to relate to.

Atwood observes that when she writes her novels, she assumes that even after the apocalypse, "some [of us] have survived, because otherwise there wouldn't be any plot, would there?" Here, I think, she makes a very serious point. Atwood opens her comments with a fine defense of storytelling as an analytical tool, but the Horse-creature of the Apocalypse threatens to overturn the *sine qua non* of storytelling—humans who structure experience through narrative. If this is really where cultural evolution is taking us, I suspect that the thinking and values (if those are the right words) of a twenty-second-century posthuman superorganism will be even more profoundly alien to us and even harder for us to understand than debates at Princeton's Center for Human Values would have been for Neanderthals.

The historian Yuval Noah Harari, who, like Atwood, sees storytelling as the key to the human condition, ends his fine book *Sapiens* by asking "Since we might soon be able to engineer our desires, perhaps the real question facing us is not 'What do we want to become?,' but 'What do we want to want?' "[137] Thinking about Atwood's comments, I have to wonder whether we should not go even further. Perhaps the real question is not "What do we want to want?," but "What are we going to want, whether we want to want it or not?"

I would like to close by thanking once again the respondents and other readers of my manuscript. Even after twenty thousand words of my correct views on everything, I doubt that I have convinced them that I am right, any more than they have convinced me that I am wrong. However, they have certainly made me think harder and in new ways about my ideas, and have filled my head with more ideas and more books I'd like to write. For an academic, that's about as good as it gets.

NOTES

Note: All URLs checked on October 10, 2014.

INTRODUCTION

1. *Primates and Philosophers: How Morality Evolved*, edited by Stephen Macedo and Josiah Ober (Princeton, NJ: Princeton University Press, 2009).

CHAPTER 1: EACH AGE GETS
THE THOUGHT IT NEEDS

1. I would like to thank Professor Ken Wardle once again for finding a place for me on his Assiros project in 1982, and also to thank Professor Richard Tomlinson for inviting me on his Perachora excavation right after I was in Assiros. Professor Tomlinson drove me back and forth across Europe in the Birmingham University Field Archaeology Unit's Land Rover, which broke down only once (in the middle of what was then Yugoslavia, where Professor Tomlinson replaced a broken fan belt with a team member's nylon stocking).

2. Mr. George's wife was not Mrs. George. It was the custom in the Greek countryside to call people by their first (Christian) name, with Mr. or Mrs. added as a sign of respect (Mr. George was *Kyrios Yiorgos*). I was never told Mr. George's wife's name, and I have to confess that it never occurred to me to ask.

3. I would like to thank the Tanner Committee, the University Center for Human Values, and President Shirley Tilghman for inviting me to deliver the 2012 lectures.

4. Other writers sometimes deploy different labels. Anthropologists and archaeologists often use "hunter-gatherers" as a synonym for "foragers" (although some distinguish between the two expressions); historians, archaeologists, anthropologists, rural sociologists, and development economists sometimes use "agriculturalists" and sometimes "peasants" as alternatives to "farmers" (although they more often treat "agriculturalists" and "peasants" as distinct subcategories within the larger category of "farmers"); and scholars from all kinds of disciplines sometimes prefer to speak of an "industrial," "capitalist," or "modern" age rather than a "fossil fuel" age.

5. Weber 1968 [1922], pp. 4–22.

6. Droysen 1868, p. 11, §14. Philosophers and theologians, Droysen added, should aim for a third kind of knowledge, which he called "recognizing."

7. Weber 1968 [1922], p. 12.

8. Particularly Parsons 1937.

9. Geertz 1973, p. 5.

10. Ibid., p. 23.

11. Ibid., pp. 25, 16.

12. Darnton 1984, pp. 4–5.

13. To some extent, this is what Anastasia Karakasidou does in her book *Fields of Wheat, Hills of Blood* (1997), drawing chiefly on fieldwork conducted in Assiros in 1989.

14. Trigger 1998 gives a good brief history of the trends, and I describe my own views in more detail in Morris 2013, pp. 6–17.

15. Bagehot, quoted from Höpfl 1978, p. 19; Gatterer, quoted from Force 2009, p. 458.

16. I have found Nadel 1964, Höpfl 1978, O'Brien 2005, and Olson 2013 particularly useful. (I would like to thank Giovanna Ceserani for discussing philosophical history with me and guiding me to this reading.)

17. Spencer 1857 remains the strongest statement of classical evolutionism, and Francis 2007 puts Spencer in context.

18. Trigger 1998 and Carneiro 2003 are good participant-observer accounts of the debates, both with a preference for explaining over understanding. I got to experience the arguments from close up at Stanford, where acrimony over the issue was largely responsible for splitting the Anthropology Department in two in 1998. I was not a member of the department, but I believe I was the only member of the university to have the pleasure of serving on search committees in both of its successor departments (one of Anthropological Sciences, the other of Cultural and Social Anthropology).

19. My thinking about this has been shaped very much by Popper 1963, although Popper would probably have thought my argument historicist (Popper 1957).

20. Weber 1949, p. 90.

21. Gilbert 1966–88. The first two volumes were written by Randolph Churchill.

22. There is a vast literature on steppe societies. Khazanov 1984 is a fine introduction to the anthropology and Beckwith 2009 to the history.

23. On functionalism, see Radcliffe-Brown 1936; Parsons 1937, 1951.

24. Landgraber et al. 2012 set the date of the last common ancestor at 7–8 million years ago, roughly 2 million years earlier than was previously thought.

25. E. O. Wilson 1975, p. 562. Since the 1970s, the biological evolution of ethics has received intense study (for example, Boehm 2012; de Waal et al. 2014), and was the topic of Frans de Waal's Tanner Lectures at Princeton nine years before my own (published as de Waal et al. 2006).

26. Segerstråle 2000 discusses the debates over sociobiology, and E. O. Wilson 1994, pp. 330–53, describes some of the more extreme criticisms of his arguments. There are, of course, exceptions, such as Slingerland 2008 and Herman 2014.

27. On the exceptions, see Wrangham 2006; Whiten 2011.

28. Cultural evolution has produced a huge literature. In many ways, L. White 1949 and Steward 1955 are the starting points for most modern discussions. Richerson and Boyd 2005 is a particularly good presentation of contemporary ideas, and I have also learned enormous amounts from Wright 2000; Boyer 2001; D. S. Wilson 2003; Bellah 2011; and Whiten et al. 2011.

29. See discussions in Dawkins 1976; Cavalli-Sforza and Feldman 1981; and Durham 1991.

30. Memes: Dawkins 1976; Dennett 1995; Blackmore 1999. Attractors: Sperber 1996.

31. Genes: Dawkins 1982. Multilevel selection: Hamilton 1964; Alexander 1974; and Bowles and Gintis 2011.

32. Richerson and Boyd 2005, pp. 80, 81.

33. Ibid., p. 6.

34. L. White 1949, pp. 390–91.

35. L. White 1943, p. 338 (emphasis in original).

36. Haidt 2012, p. 31.

37. My thanks to Jesus College, Cambridge, for funding this anthropological excursion.

38. According to http://quoteinvestigator.com/2011/07/22/keynes-change-mind/, the line is a misattribution of a misquotation of a comment actually made by the economist Paul Samuelson in a 1970 interview.

39. Published as Renfrew 1994.

40. Turchin 2003, p. 1.

41. See www.yale.edu/hraf/.

42. I am thinking particularly of the Evolution Institute's Historical Database of Sociocultural Evolution (Turchin et al. 2012).

43. I describe my social development index in Morris 2010 and 2013. On general methodological criteria, I have found Gerring 2001 particularly helpful.

44. See http://www.worldvaluessurvey.org/wvs.jsp.

45. For discussions of the WVS's methods, see Macintosh 1998; Silver and Dowley 2000; Hofstede 2001; and Minkov 2012.

46. Inglehart and Welzel 2005, p. 5.

47. I take these figures from https://www.cia.gov/library/publications/the-world-factbook/fields/2012.html#lo.

48. R^2 scores range from 0 (the distribution of data points is completely random, and a linear regression does not correlate with the observations at all) to 1.0 (the data points fall in a perfectly straight line, and the linear regression runs through every one).

49. Inglehart and Welzel 2005, p. 5.

50. Figures 1.3 and 1.4 include only 72 societies, because my data source (the *CIA World Factbook* for 2012—see n. 52, later) did not contain usable information for two of the WVS's cases (Northern Ireland is not an independent country, and so has no entry, and the figures for the three sectors of the Slovak economy add up only to 80 percent, not 100 percent).

51. See http://www.worldvaluessurvey.org/WVSContents.jsp. The website's authors add that this is "a somewhat simplified analysis."

52. This was of course the *yeografika diamerisma* (geographical district) of Makedonia in northern Greece, not to be confused with the Former Yugoslav Republic of Macedonia, created in 1991, which is the "Macedonia" marked by Inglehart and Welsel in figure 1.5.

53. Data from https://www.cia.gov/library/publications/the-world-factbook/fields/2012.html#lo. (The tiny Falkland Islands, where sheep outnumber humans, have the highest contribution from farming, at 95 per cent of GDP; among larger countries, Liberia is the highest, at 76.9 percent.)

Chapter 2: Foragers

1. Lee and Daly 1999b, p. 3.

2. Panter-Brick et al. 2001, p. 2 (emphasis in original).

3. See particularly Kelly 2013.

4. Earle and Johnson 1987, pp. 65–83 and 172–86, have a good discussion.

5. The dating depends on whether we give priority to genetic and skeletal evidence, which suggest that "anatomically modern humans"—people who looked like us—appeared near the beginning of this long period, or archaeological evidence, which suggests that "behaviorally modern humans"—people who acted and thought like us—evolved only toward its end. Renfrew 2008 refers to the time lag between modern bodies and modern behavior as the "sapient paradox." Klein 2009 reviews the evidence, although advances in this field come so quickly that Klein's account is already out of date in several respects.

6. Kuhn and Stiner 2001.

7. Lee and Daly 1999a; Panter-Brick et al. 2001b; and Kelly 2013 are excellent overviews of foraging societies.

8. Rowley-Conwy 2001 is particularly good on this issue.

9. Herodotus 4.13, 18, 23, 25. Mayor 2000, pp. 29–53, shows convincingly that Herodotus had access to accounts by travelers (including the seventh-century poet Aristeas) who had journeyed far beyond the steppes.

10. Hartog 1988 is the classic analysis, although he labors the point somewhat; Thomas 2002 is more concise.

11. Barnard 2004 gives a concise account of intellectual traditions.

12. Particularly Binford 1980; Woodburn 1980.

13. Schrire 1984 is the classic exposition; the papers in Sassaman and Holly 2011 show what this approach means for North American prehistory.

14. Especially Fabian 1983.

15. Lee and Daly 2004 give a brief overview, with much bibliography.

16. Binford 2001.

17. Childe 1936, 1942; Morgan 1877.

18. Kent 1996; Kelly 2013.

19. Compare, for instance, Marlowe 2010 on the Hadza of Tanzania and Binford 1978 on the Nunamiut of Alaska.

20. On tradition and belief, Cannon 2011 and Cummings 2013; on rational choice, Winterhalder and Smith 1981.

21. Bettinger 2009.

22. Barker 2006, pp. 47–54.

23. Lee and DeVore 1968, p. 11.

24. Service 1971, pp. 46–48; Johnson and Earle 1987, pp. 30–31, 34–37; Ingold 1999, p. 401.

25. The calculation of group size comes from Wobst (1974).

26. Johnson and Earle 1987, pp. 27–61, 132–38, and 161–72 provide a good overview of community sizes, and Heizer 1978 and Suttles 1990 go into detail about the Pacific Coast examples.

27. Mithen 2003 has an evocative account of these processes.

28. Lee and Daly 1999a, Panter-Brick 2001, and Kelly 2013 contain much information, and Johnson and Earle 1987, pp. 27–61 draw out the general pattern.

29. Lee 1979, pp. 116–332, on the !Kung San of the Kalahari, remains the classic study.

30. Torrence 2001; Kelly 2013, pp. 114–36.

31. Sahlins 1972.

32. Ibid. 1972, p. 37.

33. Wilmsen 1989, also focusing on the !Kung San, puts the case most forcefully.

34. On the Jomon, see Habu 2004; on the Pacific Northwest, sources in n. 26, earlier.

35. I expand on this point in Morris 2013, pp. 60–141.

36. See especially Binford 1980; Woodburn 1982.

37. Gurven and Kaplan 2007.

38. Panter-Brick 2001b, pp. 170–266; Boone 2002. Diamond 2012, pp. 173–240, has a good overview of forager demography.

39. There are many excellent studies; I have found Cashdan 1980; Gardner 1991; and Boehm 1993 particularly helpful.

40. Lee and Daly 1999a.

41. Flannery and Marcus 2012, pp. 66–87, describe the rise of political hierarchy and inequality along North America's Pacific Coast between AD 800 and 1200.

42. Angelbeck and Grier 2012 make this claim for the Coast Salish of the Pacific Northwest, although I do not find the argument entirely convincing.

43. Lee 1979, p. 348.

44. Quoted from Boehm 1999, p. 62.

45. Silberbauer 1982. The method is strikingly like that followed in many academic settings.

46. Steward 1938, pp. 106–107.

47. Lee 1979, p. 246. Upstartism: Boehm 1999, p. 44.

48. Examples taken from Boehm 1999, p. 75.

49. Myers 1986, p. 224.

50. Johnson and Earle 1987, p. 81.

51. Engels 1972 [1884].

52. Johnson and Earle 1987, p. 96. Johnson and Earle use the term "family-level organization" to cover most foragers and some of the simplest farming societies.

53. The Gini coefficient, developed by Corrado Gini in 1909, is the most commonly used measure of inequality. However, it has its critics. To some economists (for example, Bellù and Liberati 2006), the fact that very different patterns of income inequality can produce the same score limits its value, while others insist that "it is impossible to summarize a multidimensional reality with a unidimensional index without unduly simplifying matters and mixing up things that should not be treated together" (Piketty 2014, p. 266). Breaking down income inequality in different ways, as Piketty 2014 shows, can reveal different patterns. However, I use Gini scores here because historians have calculated them (however approximately) all the way back to antiquity and because the data collected by Smith et al. 2010 also give us some sense of Gini scores for wealth inequality in foraging and small-scale farming societies. By contrast, although the decile-level income graphs that Piketty presents (which divide the population into ten income groups and compare the share of wealth going to each group in each period) have numerous advantages, decile-by-decile wealth/inheritance distributions can be calculated only back to the early eighteenth century (and even then only for Europe and its overseas colonies), and decile-by-decile income patterns only to the beginning of Western income-tax records in the 1910s.

54. Smith et al. 2010. Economists always distinguish strongly between wealth inequality (that is, variations between the assets held by different individuals or groups) and income inequality (that is, variations between the earnings of different individuals or groups). I follow their lead in this book, but the short-comings of the evidence available for premodern societies mean that it is not always possible to calculate Gini scores for both types of inequality in every

context. Where possible, I provide scores for income inequality, but Smith et al.'s 2010 calculations of wealth inequality are the only Gini scores available for foragers. Every time I present Gini scores in the text, I say explicitly whether they are for wealth or income. On the whole, wealth inequality tends to be greater than income inequality, because setting aside earnings to accumulate capital is easier for high-income individuals or groups than for those on low income, who are forced to spend a higher proportion of their income on the necessities of food, shelter, clothing, and fuel.

55. Tron 2013, pp. 25–29; Trinkaus et al. 2014.

56. See Flannery and Marcus 2012 (n. 41, earlier).

57. Marx and Engels's writings on this topic are widely scattered and sometimes contradictory, but Bloch 1983, pp. 91–94, has a good summary.

58. Steward 1977, pp. 375–78.

59. Arnold 1995, 2007.

60. Wenzel et al. 2000; Henrich 2012; Kelly 2013, pp. 137–65.

61. Kamei 2005, p. 354.

62. Peterson 1993; Wilson 1998; Marlowe 2010, pp. 225–54.

63. *Matatus* were (in the 1980s) ancient vans, which, for a price, would take you almost anywhere, whether there was a road or not. They were notorious for fatal collisions.

64. Shostak 1981, p. 139.

65. There is a large literature on all these matters, but the economist Paul Seabright provides an excellent overview (2013b, pp. 12–15, 67–82).

66. Shostak 1981, p. 243.

67. Endicott 1999.

68. See, among others, Johnson and Earle 1987; LeBlanc and Register 2003; Otterbein 2004.

69. Chagnon 1988; Beckerman et al. 2009.

70. See, for example, the figures in Keeley 1996; Gat 2006; and Pinker 2011. For arguments that these data misrepresent a much more peaceful reality, see the papers in Fry 2013; and for powerful rebuttals of the "peaceful prehistory" argument, LeBlanc 2013, 2014.

71. See Chagnon 1988 and Beckerman et al. 2009 (n. 68, earlier).

72. Milner 2005 discusses some of the main problems of interpretation. On Neanderthal and early-modern human traumas, see Trinkaus 2012.

73. Thomas 1959. Comparison of rate of violent death with Detroit: Knauft 1985, p. 375, table E.

74. I elaborate my views on this in Morris 2014, pp. 288–319.

75. I say "him" rather than "him or her" because in every society for which we have documentation, whether it consists of foragers, farmers, or fossil-fuel users, men commit more than 90 percent of the violent crime (Ghiglieri 1999 explains why).

76. Axelrod 1984 and Bowles and Gintis 2011 explain the logic behind this outcome.

77. Agatha Christie's famous 1934 novel in which twelve travelers on a train to Istanbul jointly kill the despicable thirteenth passenger, who—a classic upstart—has earlier committed a murder that affected all of them. Hercule Poirot solves the case, but, fully in sympathy with forager values, declines to present the facts to the authorities.

78. Ethnographers have recorded many examples; see, for example, Hoebl 1954, pp. 88–92; Lee 1982, p. 47; Woodburn 1982, p. 436; Knauft 1987, pp. 475–76.

CHAPTER 3: FARMERS

1. Panter-Brick et al. 2001a, p. 2; Lee and DeVore 1968, p. 11.

2. See http://www.ars.usda.gov/Services/docs.htm?docid=8964.

3. Of the many descriptions of domestication, Zohary et al. 2013 is particularly good.

4. Some scholars prefer the term "swidden" or "slash-and-burn" farming to "horticulture," referring to the way that some groups operate by burning a patch of forest to clear it and put carbon into the soil. They then work the clearing until its nutrients (and yields) decline, before moving on to the next patch of forest.

5. Wolf 1966, p. 11.

6. Out of the enormous literature, I have found Moore 1967; E. Weber 1976; Gellner 1983; and Hall 1985 particularly illuminating.

7. Ober 2015 addresses some of the differences in the case of ancient Greece.

8. Redfield 1956, p. 62.

9. I use the population estimates in Christian 2004, table 6.2. All estimates involve wide margins of error, but I am not aware of any estimates that depart so far from Christian's as to cancel out this pattern.

10. There are far fewer general surveys of farming societies than of foraging societies, and of these few, most are by anthropologists (for example, Potter et al. 1967; Shanin 1971; and Johnson and Earle 1987, pp. 207–312) rather than historians (for example, Crone 1989; Christian 2004, pp. 206–332). Cipolla 1980 has a fine account of Europe between AD 1000 and 1700, and Braudel 1981 of Europe between AD 1400 and 1800.

11. One of the most important distinctions in historical scholarship is between primary sources, texts written by people living through the events and processes being studied, and secondary sources, texts written by people who lived later than the events and processes in question or in a different place. Secondary sources are worthless unless they can be traced back to primary sources.

12. Harris 1989; for second-millennium AD England, Stone 1964, 1969. I make a rough comparison of Eastern and Western literacy rates in Morris 2013, pp. 218–37.

13. Le Roy Ladurie 1978.

14. Botanists usually set the cutoff point for "large" grains at 10 milligrams, and zoologists set that for "large" mammals at 40 kilograms (100 pounds). I will return to the Hilly Flanks in chapter 5.

15. Smart and Simmonds 1995; Hancock 2012; Zohary et al. 2013.

16. On most of these expansions, see Mithen 2003; on Oceania, Kirch 2000. Colledge and Connolly 2007 document the transport of domesticated plants and animals from the Hilly Flanks across Europe.

17. East Asia did, of course, have its own Mediterranean-like body of water in the South China Sea, but this (and similar inland seas such as the Baltic and Caribbean Seas) was neither unified by a single empire nor bounded by so many potential trading partners.

18. I tell this story, as I see it, in Morris 2010, pp. 81–342.

19. Morris 2013, pp. 66–109. This long process was explored particularly well by Andrew Sherratt (1997, pp. 155–248), who called it the "secondary products revolution." On the brutality of the process, see Harari 2014, pp. 93–97.

20. As a standard rule of thumb, the conversion ratio from cereals to meat (via animals eating grain and then being eaten by people) is roughly 10:1. See Morris 2013, pp. 53–58 and 102–6 on methods of calculation.

21. Malthus had already recognized the importance of the distinction between food and nonfood calories in the 1790s. "It should be remembered always," he wrote, "that there is an essential difference between food and those wrought commodities, the raw materials of which are in great plenty. A demand for these last will not fail to create them in as great quantity as they are wanted. The demand for food has by no means the same creative power" (Malthus 1970 [1798], pp. 99–100).

22. Morris 2013, pp. 66–80, 98–102. On organic economies, Wrigley 2000.

23. Literary sources preserve some statistics about fifth-century BC Athenian naval expeditions lasting multiple days. At least 10 percent of the population must have taken part in them, and the true figure may be 15 or even 20 percent.

24. Vagnari DNA: http://www.independent.co.uk/news/science/archaeology/news/ambassador-or-slave-east-asian-skeleton-discovered-in-vagnari-roman-cemetery-1879551.html. Roman ambassadors: Leslie and Gardner 1996.

25. Brook 1998, p. 19.

26. Johnson and Earle 1987, p. 324. Prehistoric foragers presumably occupied resource-rich environments such as southern Japan and the Baltic coasts in higher densities.

27. Hansen 1985, 2006. By my rough calculation (2006), Greeks occupied about 60,000 square miles in the fourth century BC. The total number of Greeks

was somewhere around six million, pointing to an average population density of about 100 people per square mile.

28. I collect some relevant data in Morris 2013, pp. 146–65.

29. The classic study of peasant labor is Chayanov 1986 [1925], to be read with the essays on economics in Potter et al. 1967 and Shanin 1971.

30. Hesiod, *Works and Days* 382. Classicists have long argued over the authorship and composition of this text, with some suggesting that "Hesiod" was in fact a poetic persona rather than a real person (see Lamberton 1988; Rosen 1997), but these arguments probably do not affect the ways I use the *Works and Days* here. E. Francis 1945 and Millett 1984 analyze the peasant features of Hesiod's world.

31. Vincenzo Padula, cited in Friedmann 1967, p. 325.

32. Skeletons: Armelagos and Harper 2005; C. Larsen 1995, 2006. Kopke and Baten 2005 survey skeletal evidence for stature, concluding that there were no great changes under the Roman Empire.

33. Shennan et al. 2013.

34. Medieval Warm Period: Fagan 2008 gives an entertaining account. Mortality in the Black Death: Benedictow 2004. Wages: Allen 2001 (Pamuk and Shatzmiller 2014 compare European Black Death mortality and wages with those in the Middle East and the consequences of the Justinianic plague that began in the sixth century AD). Le Roy Ladurie 1976 is a fine account of how the fourteenth- through sixteenth-century cycle played out in southern France.

35. John Quincy Adams, U.S. Minister to Prussia, letters written from Silesia in 1800 (cited from Blum 1976, pp. 181, 183).

36. Anton Chekhov, "Peasants" (1897), section IV, cited from http://www.online-literature.com/o_henry/1285/. (My thanks to Rob Tempio for drawing my attention to this story.)

37. Maddison 2010. His figures are expressed in 1990 International Geary-Khamis dollars, a unit designed to bypass the problem of establishing nominal vs. purchasing power parity rates.

38. Morris 2013. I suggest there (pp. 77–80) that the ways economists calculate GDP/capita and real wages may understate the wealth of premodern societies.

39. Figes 2006, pp. 84–121, has a good brief overview of the state of actual Russian peasants in the late nineteenth century, and Vucinich 1968 provides more detail (including a chapter on peasants in Russian literature).

40. Pliny the Elder, *Natural History* 33.135 and 18.7 (discussed in Garnsey and Saller 1987, pp. 67–68).

41. Wickham 2009, p. 29.

42. Data and calculations from Scheidel and Friesen 2009.

43. Milanovic et al. 2007; cf. Milanovic 2006.

44. As noted in chapter 2, Gini scores for wealth inequality tend to be higher than those for income inequality.

45. Smith et al. 2010.

46. I base these arguments on Goody 1976.

47. Bocquet-Appel and Bar-Yosef 2008.

48. Livi-Bacci 2001, pp. 9–28.

49. See the data collected in the Human Relations Area Files (www.yale.edu/hraf/).

50. Moore et al. 2000.

51. Morris 2010, pp. 481–83. A flood of recent books has greatly clarified our understanding of the Roman economy (for example, Harris 2010; Bowman and Wilson 2012, 2013a, 2013b; Scheidel 2012; Temin 2012; Flohr 2013; Kay 2014; Russell 2014).

52. Pliny, *Natural History* 18.107. Pliny was writing in the 70s AD.

53. Saller 2007, table 4.1.

54. Treggiari 1979, p. 78.

55. Goody 1976; Smith et al. 2010.

56. Friedmann 1967 [1953], p. 328.

57. Hodder 2006 describes developments at Çatalhöyük.

58. I develop these points in more detail in Morris 2010, pp. 97–112. Jack Goody's classic West African ethnography *Death, Property and the Ancestors* (1962) remains well worth reading.

59. Out of a huge literature, I have benefited particularly from Sahlins 1972, pp. 101–48; Costin 1991, 1996; Earle 2002, pp. 127–61; and Trigger 2003, pp. 338–74.

60. Hesiod, *Works and Days* 407–8.

61. Ibid., 414–57. Barber 1994 is an excellent cross-cultural survey of premodern weaving.

62. *Works and Days* 493–94.

63. Ibid., 25–26.

64. See, for example, Bradley and Edmonds's 1993 study of stone axes in Neolithic Europe.

65. Grosman et al. 2008.

66. Larsen 1967, 1977; Stolper 1985; Abraham 2004.

67. Goitein 1967–88; Greif 2006; Kuhn 2009, pp. 205–9. Family firms of course remain important even in the most sophisticated economies (Colli 2003).

68. As just one example of the vast amounts of labor mobilized by farming societies, one Roman source (Frontinus, *On Aqueducts* 7.4–5) tells us that in the late 140s BC, the Senate set aside 180 million sesterces—enough to pay for 30–45 million days of labor—for repairs and new construction of sewers and aqueducts. Dan-el Padilla Peralta (2014, pp. 63–64) calculates that the project

probably employed somewhere between 100,000 and 150,000 men across four years, each working on average for 75 days per year.

69. Carballo 2013 is an excellent set of papers discussing the archaeological evidence for how—and why—prehistoric people solved collective action problems.

70. Earle 1997, 2002.

71. Parker Pearson 2012.

72. *Works and Days* 602, with West 1978, pp. 309–10.

73. Postgate 1992, pp. 234–40; M. A. Powell 1987.

74. Garnsey 1980.

75. See, for example, Braudel 1982, pp. 52–54; Pamuk and Shatzmiller 2014; Chaudhuri 1990, pp. 297–337; Broadberry and Gupta 2006; Parthasarathi 2011, pp. 37–46; Brook 1998, pp. 114, 256; Pomeranz 2000, pp. 91–106.

76. G. Wright 1978, p. 47.

77. Scheidel 2010 is a pioneering attempt to calculate ancient real wages.

78. I present this argument in more detail in Morris 2002.

79. Watson 1980; O. Patterson 1982.

80. Finley 1959.

81. Finley 1980 and O. Patterson 1982 have outstanding discussions.

82. Akkermans and Schwartz 2003, p. 88; Schmandt-Besserat 1992; Demattè 2010.

83. del Carmen Rodríguez Martínez et al. 2005; Saturno et al. 2006.

84. Jack Goody (1977, 1986, 1987) has been the main champion of this view, and the classicist Barry Powell (2012) has developed it in new directions. There have been frequent announcements of the "implosion" of Goody's theory (for example, Halverson 1992), but so far, all have been premature.

85. There is a huge scholarly literature on state formation. Trigger 2003 and Flannery and Marcus 2012 have good bibliographies.

86. Of the many excellent accounts of the political sociology of agrarian states, I have found Eisenstadt 1963; Mann 1986; Tilly 1992; and Bang and Scheidel 2013 particularly useful.

87. Gellner 1988, p. 17.

88. Ibid., pp. 9–10.

89. Prince G. E. Lvov, quoted from Figes 2006, p. 46.

90. Hall 1985.

91. Gellner 1988, p. 22.

92. Gellner also counted "Small communities of producers, often pastoralists or mountain peasants, whose environment makes it possible for them to resist domination" as major exceptions to his generalizations (1988, p. 22). Anthropologists normally treat pastoralists as a very different category from farmers, and many scholars, following definitions like Wolf's, would also say that mountain cultivators who remain beyond the reach of state governments are by definition not really peasants.

93. Hansen 2000 is an excellent overview of city-states.

94. Food imports: Garnsey 1988. Economic growth: Morris 2004; Ober 2010. Real wages: Scheidel 2010. Literacy: Harris 1989. Cultural explosion: Ober 2008; Morris 2009, pp. 151–53. (Many of these developments are paralleled in other ancient Greek city-states, but Athens was the extreme case and is by far the best documented.) Starr 2013 gives a superb account of the cultural efflorescence of central Asian city-states in the early second millennium AD, which also merits the label "classical."

95. Ober (2015) is particularly strong on this point in the case of classical Greece.

96. Originally presented, with more discussion, in Morris 1997.

97. On the Athenian elite, Davies 1971 and 1981 and Ober 1989 remain classics.

98. On Athenian democracy, see Ober 1989 and Hansen 1991. Hansen and Nielsen 2004 give an encyclopedic overview of the practices in other Greek cities.

99. Morris 2000, pp. 140–41. Geof Kron (forthcoming) calculates an overall Gini score for wealth inequality of 0.71 from data in Athens' 322 BC census; Ober 2015.

100. Wages: Scheidel 2010. Houses: Morris 2004. Discussion: Ober 2010, 2015.

101. Greek slavery: Bradley and Cartledge 2009, pp. 22–213. Greek gender systems: Foxhall 2013.

102. Ober 2008, pp. 254–55.

103. I make this argument in detail in Morris 2009.

104. Jakob Gujer to Prince Ludwig Eugen of Württemberg (1765), cited from Blum 1976, p. 295.

105. *Classic of Rites* 7, translated in Kim and Kim 2014, p. ix.

106. Hesiod *Words and Days* 225–35; *Theogony* 79–93. I translate the Greek word *basileis* as "lords." Some classicists prefer "chiefs" and a few opt for "kings," but the word clearly means the holders of political power (Drews 1983 remains a good discussion).

107. Translated in Cooper 1986, n. 9.

108. Oakley 2006 pursues this idea vigorously.

109. Hesiod, *Works and Days* 313, 319.

110. Augustine, *Sermon* 345.1, cited from P. Brown 2012, p. 345.

111. Blum 1976, p. 114.

112. Gellner 1983, p. 10.

113. Both examples cited from Crone 1989, p. 105.

114. D. Brown 1991, p. 1.

115. Wiser and Wiser 1963, pp. 124, 127.

116. Kroeber 1948, p. 248.

117. Redfield 1956, pp. 31, 68, 70.

118. Freedman 1999, p. 3.
119. Scott 1990, p. 95.
120. Figes 2014, p. 194; more generally, Field 1976.
121. Hobsbawm 1959 has a highly readable account.
122. Court records of Ely, July 20, 1381, cited from Kirshner and Morrison 1986, pp. 461–63.
123. Russian peasant in conversation with Bernard Pares, 1907, cited from Figes 2006, p. 203.
124. Bagley 1999, pp. 230–31; Shaughnessy 1999, pp. 313–17.
125. 1 Samuel 16:1 (King James translation, 1604–11).
126. Micah 3:11–12 (King James translation). The Books of the Prophets in the Hebrew Bible pose even thornier interpretive problems than Hesiod. At one extreme of the scholarly range are scholars who conclude that, with due allowance for later editing and obvious interpolations, we can take the authorial personas in the texts more or less at face value (for example, Dever 2001; Provan et al. 2003); at the other are scholars who conclude that the texts were mostly composed in Hellenistic times and that the authors under whose names the various books have been preserved were in fact largely fictional (for example, P. Davies 1996). In the middle are scholars who conclude that the texts were mostly written in the generation or two either side of the Babylonian sack of Jerusalem in 586 BC, as part of a large-scale reimagining of early Israelite history (for example, Liverani 2005).
127. Hesiod, *Works and Days* 38–39, 240–47.
128. II Kings 16:2.
129. Sallust, *Conspiracy of Catiline* (written 43–40 BC) 10.
130. Gunesekara 1994, p. 83.
131. Chekhov, "Peasants" (1897), section VI.
132. Augustine, *Sermon* 37.4, cited from P. Brown 2012, p. 349.
133. Brisch 2012 surveys early divine kingship around the world.
134. The discussions in Postgate 1994 and Kemp 2005 are excellent.
135. Jaspers 1953 [1949], p. 1.
136. Of the large literature on the Axial Age, Eisenstadt 1986; Arnason et al. 2005; Armstrong 2006; and Bellah 2011 are particularly valuable.
137. Momigliano 1975, p. 9.
138. In this and what follows, I draw on the fuller discussions in Morris 2010, pp. 245–63, 320–30.
139. Ashoka, Major Rock Edict V, and Kandahar Bilingual Rock Inscription (Aramaic text), translated in Thapar 1973, pp. 252, 260. On Ashoka and *dhamma*, see also Seneviratna 1994.
140. Generally, see Balazs 1964; and on the Song dynasty (AD 960–1279), probably the high point of state Confucianism, Kuhn 2009.
141. Shaw 1985; Rowe and Schofield 2000, part II; Barnes 2011; P. Brown 1995, 2012.

142. Matthew 19:24.

143. P. Brown 2012, p. xxiv.

144. Blum 1976, pp. 47–48.

145. Elkins 1959. Lane 1971 summarizes the "Sambo thesis" controversy.

146. Ober 1989 is outstanding on Athenian views of political and economic inequality. On lavish houses and tombs, see Morris 1992, pp. 103–55. Invisible economy: Cohen 1992.

147. Richard Rumbold (1685), cited from Hill 1984, p. 37; Abiezer Cooper, *A Fiery Flying Roll* I (1649), cited from Hill 1984, p. 43.

148. Cited from Elvin 1973, p. 246.

149. The most famous exception is probably Plato (*Republic* 449a–466d), but he also had Socrates insist strongly that the arrangements discussed in the *Republic* were just theoretical speculations, that could never exist in the real world (471c–473e).

150. Cited from Ebrey 1993, p. 152.

151. Cicero, *Republic* 1.67 (paraphrasing Plato, *Republic* 562c–563e).

152. Aristophanes, *Thesmophoriazousai* (ca. 411 BC) and *Ekklesiazousai* (ca. 392 BC).

153. Donker van Heel 2014.

154. Cox 1990, p. 15. Bornstein 1979 reproduces some of the most important texts. Warner 2011 discusses the French tradition, and Apetrei 2010 follows the story into early eighteenth-century England.

155. Discussed in Kelly 1984, p. 74 (which challenges this notion).

156. There are many surveys of misogynistic literature; Wilson and Makowski 1990, covering Europe between the first and fourteenth centuries AD, is particularly striking.

157. Thomas and Znaniecki 1971 [1918], p. 24.

158. Ibid., p. 24.

159. Mitterauer and Sieder 1982 [1977], p. 104.

160. Thompson 1993, pp. 467–538, has vivid examples from eighteenth-century England.

161. Shakespeare, *Henry VI Part 3* (ca. 1591), act I, scene iv, lines 140, 144–45; Paston Letters (January 1454), cited from Weir 1995, p. 183. There are surprisingly few academic studies of Margaret; Erlanger 1970 is perhaps still the best.

162. Egan 2013 discusses Li's biography and the interpretive debates over her poetry.

163. The oration does not actually name the husband or the wife, but there are good reasons to think that she was the Turia and he the Quintus Lucretius Vespillo mentioned by the Roman writer Valerius Maximus (*Memorable Deeds and Sayings* 6.7). A translation of the eulogy is available at www.stoa.org /diotima/anthology/wlgr/wlgr-publiclife168.shtml.

164. Described in Treggiari 1991, pp. 183–228.

165. William Shakespeare, *Troilus and Cressida* (ca. 1602), act 1, scene 3, lines 101–24.

166. Hobbes actually uses the famous phrase *bellum omnium contra omnes* in the preface to *De Cive* (1642), but uses very similar expressions in *Leviathan* (1651), chapter 14.

167. See sources mentioned in n. 66 to chapter 2, earlier, and Morris 2014, pp. 109–11, 145–47.

168. Hobbes, *Leviathan* (1651), chapter 17.

169. Gellner 1983, p. 10.

170. I document this process in Morris 2014, pp. 27–215.

171. Weber 1968, p. 904.

172. Harris 2004; Elias 1982 [1939]; Spierenburg 2008, pp. 1–164; Pinker 2011, pp. 59–188.

173. Aulus Gellius, *Attic Nights* 1.26 (ca. AD 175). The story must be set somewhere around AD 100. Saller 1994, pp. 133–53, is excellent on the symbolism of the whip in Greco-Roman domestic hierarchy.

CHAPTER 4: FOSSIL FUELS

1. Crosby 2006 is an excellent nontechnical introduction; Smil 1991 and 1994 provide more detail.

2. A.H.V. Smith 1997; Mokyr 1990, pp. 21–22.

3. On the details of the English industrial revolution, Landes 1969 remains a classic, to be updated with Floud and McCloskey 1994; Wrigley 2000; Allen 2009; and Mokyr 2010.

4. Calculations from Morris 2013, pp. 63–65.

5. Frieden 2006 is particularly good on this.

6. Morris 2013, pp. 218–37, and especially figures 6.5 and 6.6.

7. Marx and Engels 1977 [1848], p. 224.

8. Ferguson 2003, p. 59. Belich 2009 gives a fine account of what he calls "the rise of the Anglo-World."

9. Calculated from Christian 2004, table 11.1.

10. Data from ibid., table 6.2; *Economist Pocket World in Figures 2013 Edition* (London: Profile, 2013), p. 19; Morris 2013, tables 4.1, 4.2.

11. Malthus 1970 [1798], now to be read with Mayhew 2014.

12. Deaton 2013 has an excellent account of the "great escape" from poverty.

13. Adam Smith, *An Inquiry into the Nature and Causes of the Wealth of Nations* (1776), book 1, chapter 1.

14. Ibid., book 4, chapter 2.

15. Thompson 1963 and 1993, pp. 352–403, are particularly good on this.

16. When Britons did starve by their millions, in the horrific 1840s Irish potato famine, the disaster came in the part of the kingdom that had the fewest factory jobs.

17. See the works listed under n. 3, earlier.

18. Allen 2007.

19. In his bestselling book *Capital in the Twenty-First Century*, the economist Thomas Piketty (2014) argues that because the Gini scores conflate the shares of income due to capital and labor, they obscure a more important pattern, which saw the returns to capital growing faster than the economy as a whole until the exogenous shock of the World Wars forced political changes that derailed this trend. The aftereffects of this shock, he suggests, lasted into the 1970s, at which point inequality began rising again. To some extent, Piketty's empirical claims rest on his choice of decile-by-decile measures of inequality over Gini coefficients, and I return to the issue in n. 46, later.

20. By Piketty's calculations (2014), the pre-tax share of Britain's wealth held by the top 10 percent and top 1 percent continued rising until shortly after 1900, then fell sharply.

21. Kuznets 1955; Lindert and Williamson 1983, p. 102; Morrisson and Snyder 2000, p. 76; Lindert and Williamson 2012.

22. In one more irony, the Middle Eastern countries that extracted and exported—so much of the world's fossil fuel in the twentieth century were among the slowest to industrialize and move toward the social structures and values (including rejection of slavery) that characterize fossil fuel societies.

23. See http://data.un.org/Data.aspx?d=PopDiv&f=variableID%3A77; MacDorman and Matthews 2009; https://www.cia.gov/library/publications /the world factbook/rankorder/2091rank.html.

24. Ray 1998, pp. 302–26, has an excellent summary, and Becker 1991, pp. 135–78, has a more theoretical analysis.

25. Livi-Bacci 2000, pp. 126–89; Caldwell 2006.

26. Goldin and Katz 2002 is particularly good on the impact of the pill on women's career options.

27. EU rate: http://epp.eurostat.ec.europa.eu/statistics_explained /index.php/Fertility_statistics. Global rate: http://data.un.org/Data. aspx?d=PopDiv&f=variableID:54.

28. Greenwood et al. 2005.

29. J. Patterson 1996, pp. 32–34; 2005, pp. 54–55. Seabright 2013b has an excellent analysis of male-female income differences.

30. Pfeffer 2013 has some interesting observations on persistent barriers.

31. Like most historians and political scientists who look at these trends, I use "liberal" and "illiberal" in their nineteenth-century senses, the former referring to policies that made individual liberty the highest priority, and the latter to policies that put individual liberty second (sometimes a very

distant second) to group concerns. The labels can cause confusion, however, largely because twenty-first-century Americans tend to use "liberal" to describe ideas that in the nineteenth century would have been called "socialist," and "conservative" to refer to the kind of business-friendly, small-government, individualist values that in the nineteenth century would have been called "liberal." To muddy the waters further, nineteenth-century "conservatives"— who tended to be defenders of royal and aristocratic privileges, established churches, racial hierarchy, and gender inequality—would probably now be labeled "reactionaries." Some analysts try to sidestep this terminological quagmire by speaking of "egocentric" and "sociocentric" paths rather than "liberal" and "illiberal" ones.

32. Wawro 2014, p. 4. Emphasis in original.

33. *Die Zeit*, February 6, 1913, cited from Wawro 2014, p. 15.

34. Bruce 2013, p. 1.

35. Chadwick 1990; Taylor 2007.

36. Cited from Horne 1965, p. 337.

37. Bruce 2002, pp. 63–64 and 205–8, discusses the statistics.

38. Thomas Rainsborough, speeches at the Putney Debates, October 29, 1647, cited from Cochrane et al. 1987, pp. 353, 351.

39. Pincus 2009; G. Wood 1993; Israel 2011, 2014.

40. Acemoglu and Robinson 2012 develop this thesis.

41. Dunn 2006; on the current distribution of democracy, http://pages.eiu .com/rs/eiu2/images/Democracy-Index-2012.pdf; http://www.freedomhouse. org.

42. A Health and Morals of Apprentices Act was actually passed in 1802 and the Cotton Mills, etc., Act in 1819, but the main series of Factory Acts began in 1833.

43. Ryan 2012.

44. Brauer 1979.

45. Britain: Driver 1993 (few inmates but the elderly and sick remained in workhouses by the 1870s, but the program was not abolished until 1930, and in fact continued under a different name until 1948). United States: Banner 2005. Quotation from Howe 2007, p. 422.

46. Snyder 2010 describes the extreme case, in 1930s–1940s Eastern Europe, in disturbing detail.

47. Figes 2014, p. 4.

48. Beardson 2013 is excellent on China's problems.

49. See http://www.freedomhouse.org/.

50. There are many excellent accounts of this twentieth-century "War of the World." Ferguson (who coined this expression) 2006 is particularly readable, and I give my own interpretation in Morris 2014, pp. 235–87. On the Soviet collapse, see now Plokhy 2014.

51. OECD: Chu et al. 2000, table 2; OECD 2011. United States: Atkinson 2010; Kenworthy and Smeeding 2013, figure 2.1.1. Piketty and Saez 2003; Atkinson et al. 2011; Alvaredo et al. 2013; and Piketty 2014 all avoid Gini scores, providing instead more detailed decile-by-decile data, with charts showing very clearly a great compression of American inequality in the 1940s and its expansion since the 1980s. Researchers at the *Financial Times* have identified errors in Piketty's data and raised questions about his methods (http://www.ft.com/intl/cms/s/0/c9ce1a54-e281–11e3–89fd-00144feabdc0. html#axzz32awKrUCI), but as I write (in late 2014), it is not clear how seriously these affect the broader argument (http://www.economist.com/blogs /freeexchange/2014/05/thomas-pikettys-capital). Solt 2009 provides pre- and post-transfer scores for every country in the world since 1960, updated online to 2013 (http://myweb.uiowa.edu/fsolt/swiid/swiid.html). 2012 Gini scores, http://www.stats.oecd.org.

52. Most economists emphasize technology and globalization (for example, Frieden 2006), but Piketty 2014 suggests that we should see the 1940s to 1970s as a temporary aberration, caused by the policies required to win World War II, of the long-term trend for returns to capital to outrun overall economic growth. Ferguson et al. 2010 discuss the 1970s watershed, and Yergin and Stanislaw 2002 give a vivid narrative of the changes of the 1980s to 1990s.

53. Piketty 2014, p. 1.

54. Maddison 2010.

55. Milanovic 2011, 2012a, 2012b.

56. Iriye et al. 2012 document the international human rights revolution.

57. Belkin et al. 2013.

58. See http://www.gallup.com/poll/163730 /back-law-legalize-gay-marriage-states.aspx.

59. Examples from Pinker 2011, pp. 148, 473. Singer 1975 remains required reading, to be updated with Sunstein and Nussbaum 2005.

60. I. B. Singer 1982 [1968], p. 269. C. Patterson 2002 develops Singer's theme in a powerful analysis.

61. George H. W. Bush, "Address Accepting the Presidential Nomination at the Republican National Convention in New Orleans," August 18, 1988, available at http://www.presidency.ucsb.edu/ws/?pid=25955.

62. Statistics from Spierenburg 2008; Roth 2009.

63. I try to document these claims in Morris 2014.

64. See http://www.who.int/violence_injury_prevention/violence/en.

65. See http://www.cnn.com/2012/11/28/justice/new-york-murder-free-day /index.html.

66. Gilens and Page 2014; Clark 2014.

67. Goldstone 2009.

68. Morris 2010, pp. 459–89.

69. I have found Shapin 1994 and 1996 particularly informative.

70. John Locke, *Second Treatise of Government* (1690), chapter 8, section 95.

71. Pincus 2009.

72. Denis Diderot, "Encyclopedia [Philosophy]" (1751), translated at www. hti.umich.edu/d/did.

73. Voltaire and China: Spence 1990, pp. 133–34.

74. Frederick II, letter to Christian Wolff (1740), cited from Upton 2001, p. 307. Frederick is also supposed to have said that "my people and I have come to an agreement that satisfies us both. They are to say what they please, and I am to do what I please," although no one has yet traced this *bon mot* back to a primary source.

75. Famously, Rousseau had rather little to say about the general will in *The Social Contract*, mentioning it only briefly at 4.5 and 4.7 (see Riley 2001). "We the People" comes from the preamble to the U.S. Constitution (1787), and the general will from article 6 of the *Declaration of the Rights of Man* (1789).

76. G. Wood 1992 is excellent on this.

77. There are many accounts of the nineteenth-century transformation of political values; Hobsbawm 1975 remains my favorite.

78. Sen 1999a.

79. See, for example, poll data at http://www.pewglobal.org/files/2009/02 /Global-middle-class-FINAL.pdf; http://www.latinobarometro.org/latOnline .jsp; and in Bratton and Houssou 2014.

80. Data from de Vasconcelos 2012, p. 40.

81. Alexander Hamilton, "Views on the French Revolution" (1794), cited in G. Wood 2009, p. 302.

82. Engels 1878, part III, chapter 2.

83. Apor et al. 2004; Zimmerman 2014.

84. Orwell 1949. On Mao, see Spence 1990, pp. 596–601; the Kims, Martin 2004; Hitler, Kershaw 1998.

85. Soviet Union: Nikita Khrushchev, "On the Cult of Personality and Its Consequences" (February 1956), available at https://archive.org /stream/TheCrimesOfTheStalinEraSpecialReportToThe20thCongressOfThe /stalin2#page/n0/mode/2up; "Program of the Communist Party of the Soviet Union" (October 1961), available at https://www2.stetson.edu/secure/history /hy308C01/cpsuprogram.html, where the Russian is translated as "state of the entire people." China: Spence 1990, pp. 645–67, 690–96. North Korea: Lankov 2014.

86. Nozick 1974, p. ix.

87. Particularly Mosca 1939 [1896]; Michels 1962 [1915]; and Pareto 1935 [1916].

88. And, for that matter, ancient democracy: Josiah Ober's classic book *Mass and Elite in Democratic Athens* (1989) describes a very similar struggle in fourth-century BC Greece.

89. Cited from G. Wood 2009, pp. 17, 34. Hamilton was speaking of Abraham Yates, a shoemaker, part-time lawyer, and populist politician from Albany, NY.

90. Schwartz 1987.

91. Quotations from G. Wood 2009, pp. 75, 25–26. The second quotation is from James Wilson, during the debate in the New York Ratifying Convention (June–July 1788).

92. This strategy too is closely paralleled in classical Athens. Ober 1989 describes how the immensely rich Athenian politicians Apollodorus and Demosthenes humbled themselves by claiming to be exactly the same as any other "middling" (in Greek, *metrios*) citizen.

93. See http://www.jpost.com/Jewish-World/Jewish-Features /Worlds-50-most-influential-Jews.

94. United States: Shaw and Gaffey 2012; http://www.gallup.com/poll/161927 /majority-wealth-evenly-distributed.aspx. Minimum wage: http:// www .washingtonpost.com/politics /split-appears-in-gop-as-more-call-for-raising-federal-minimum-wage/2014/05 /09/fce84490-d7ab-11e3-aae8-c2d44bd79778_story.html. China: http://www .pewglobal.org/2013/09/19 /environmental-concerns on the rise in china/#china inequality. Europe: http:// www.pewglobal.org/2013/05/13 /chapter-1-dispirited-over-national-conditions/. India: http://www.pewglobal .org/2014/03/31/chapter-1-indians-in-a-sour-mood/.

95. This is an old definitional debate, disputed vigorously by ancient Greeks (Harvey 1965).

96. There are immense and polemical literatures on the issue. Stiglitz 2013 and Piketty 2014 present the new liberal/socialist view; for the classical liberal /libertarian, Hayek 1944 and Friedman 1962 remain fundamental.

97. Evans 2005, pp. 460–62.

98. Quotations from Figes 2006, pp. 769–70.

99. Goldman 1924, p. 79.

100. Fitzpatrick et al. 1991; Zubok 2007.

101. Deng Xiaoping, speech of September 2, 1986 (cited from Gittings 2005, p. 103). Gittings 2005 is particularly good on China's post-Mao economic growth. Gini scores: Solt 2009.

102. John Stuart Mill, *On Liberty* (1859), chapter 1.

103. Nozick 1974, p. 172.

104. Rousseau, *The Social Contract* (1762), book III, chapter 15.

105. William Beveridge, address at Oxford University, December 6, 1942 (cited from Boyer and Goldstein 1987, pp. 503–15; quotations from pp. 506, 514).

106. Scores from Solt 2009.

107. Coontz 2005 provides a very readable overview of the history of fossil-fuel families and family values, focusing on the United States.

108. John Stuart Mill, *The Subjection of Women* (1869), chapter 1.

109. See http://www.bbc.com/news/world-middle-east-27726849?utm_.

110. See http://www.worldpublicopinion.org/pipa/pdf/mar08 /WPO_Women_Mar09_rpt.pdf.

111. Cited from Suny 2010, p. 278.

112. Nikita Khrushchev, Moscow, July 24, 1959, available at http:// teachingamericanhistory.org/library/index.asp?document=176.

113. Stites 1978 and Fitzpatrick 1999, pp. 139–63, have good accounts. Engel and Posadskaya-Vanderbeck 1997 provide fascinating eyewitness stories.

114. Koonz 1987; Stephenson 2000.

115. Poll data at www.ropercenter.uconn.edu/data_access/ipoll /power-of-ipoll/changing-role-of-women.html, with analysis of the slow changes up to the 1970s in Spitze and Huber 1980.

116. See https://web.archive.org/web/20080130023006/http://www .president.harvard.edu/speeches/2005/nber.html.

117. See http://www.nytimes.com/2006/02/22/education/22harvard. html?pagewanted=all&_r=0; http://www.washingtonpost.com/business /economy/larry-summers-withdraws-name-from-fed-consideration/2013/09/1 5/7565c888-1e44-11e3-94a2-6c66b668ea55_story.html.

118. Ghiglieri 1999.

119. Using "innate" here in the sense defined by psychologist Jonathan Haidt (2012, p. 153), meaning a mind "organized in advance of experience."

120. Discussed at length in Wrangham and Peterson 1996 and Ghiglieri 1999, and contested in Fry 2013.

121. Pinker 2011, pp. 684–89.

122. Ceadel 1996, pp. 141–65.

123. Bell 2009, pp. 1–119.

124. Ceadel 1996, pp. 166–221.

125. Generally, see Ceadel 1996, 2001; Cortright 2008.

126. Ceadel 1996, p. 2, discussed more fully in Ceadel 1987, pp. 4–5, and Walzer 1977.

127. See http://www.gallup.com/poll/157067/views-violence.aspx. The polls revealed interesting regional variations, with North Americans having particularly strong feelings on both sides of the interpersonal violence question (77 percent never justified, 21 percent sometimes justified) but being unusually tolerant of interstate violence (50 percent never justified, 47 percent sometimes justified), while the Middle East–North Africa region was the most strongly opposed to violence in any form (interpersonal, 85 percent never justified, 9 percent sometimes; interstate, 79 percent never, 13 percent sometimes).

128. See http://www.pewglobal.org/2011/11/17
/the-american-western-european-values-gap/. Separate polls conducted in 2012
produced similar results, finding that 69 percent of Britons and 50 percent of
Americans thought that their governments should use force only if they first
obtained United Nations approval, available at http://www.angusreidglobal
.com/wp-content/uploads/2012/02/2012.02.01_ForPol_USA.pdf
; http://www.angusreidglobal.com/polls/44489
/britons-want-un-mandate-before-using-force-against-another-nation/.

129. "Postheroic" is the term used by Edward Luttwak 2001, pp. 68–80.

130. See http://www.angusreidglobal.com/polls/27829/
global_poll_finds_varied_views_on_nuclear_weapons/.

131. I say this because whereas table treats value systems as nominal data,
figure 4.12 effectively converts them to interval data, adding an extra (and, I
admit, arbitrary) level of abstraction by assuming that the distance separating
"bad" from "middling" is the same as that separating "middling" from "good."
Consequently, the vertical axis functions as a numerical scale, implying that if
we give the value 0 to "middling," "good" scores +1 and "bad" scores −1. This
then yields a "values score" for each level of energy capture, with foragers scoring
−0.5 points, farmers +0.875 (counting the "sometimes middling" entry in the
violence cell for the farmers as ±0.5 [midway between "bad" and "middling"],
for a total of +3.5/4 = +0.875), and fossil-fuel users −0.75.

132. Henrich et al. 2010.

133. This is even more true if we shorten the acronym to EIRD: I teach
plenty of students who grew up in India, Singapore, Hong Kong, coastal China,
Japan, and South Korea; EEIRD (the first "E" standing, of course, for Eastern)
and WEIRD seem to be pretty much indistinguishable subsets of EIRD.

134. This is the excellent expression that the psychologist Steven Pinker uses
in his book *The Better Angels of Our Nature* (2011, p. 658). I have no idea how
I phrased it back in 1996.

135. See http://www.theguardian.com/world/2012/oct/09
/taliban-pakistan-shoot-girl-malala-yousafzai; http://www.telegraph.co.uk/news
/worldnews/asia/pakistan/10375633
/Malala-Yousafzai-recounts-moment-she-was-shot-in-the-head-by-Taliban.html.

136. See http://www.newyorker.com/online/blogs/newsdesk/2012/10
/the-girl-who-wanted-to-go-to-school.html. The prime minister, Yousaf Raza
Gilani, had himself survived an assassination attempt in 2008 and was fired
from his position by Pakistan's Supreme Court six months before the attack on
Yousafzai; see http://www.theguardian.com/world/2012/jun/19
/pakistan-yousuf-raza-gilani.

137. See http://www.nobelprize.org/nobel_prizes/peace/laureates/2014
/press.html.

138. On Taliban values, I rely particularly on Bergen and Tiedemann 2013.

139. See http://www.bbc.com/news/world-africa-27998502.

140. See http://news.bbc.co.uk/1/hi/8172270.stm.

141. See http://www.bbc.com/news/world-africa-27373287. The two episodes came together in July 2014, when Malala Yousafzai met with Nigerian president Goodluck Jonathan to urge him to take stronger measures to free the girls kidnapped by Boko Haram; see http://www.bbc.co.uk/news/world-africa-28292480.

142. Plato, *Apology* 24b.

CHAPTER 5: THE EVOLUTION OF VALUES: BIOLOGY, CULTURE, AND THE SHAPE OF THINGS TO COME

1. E. O. Wilson 1975, p. 562.

2. E. O. Wilson 1975, p. 547.

3. I develop this theme more explicitly in Morris 2015.

4. Charles Darwin, *On the Origin of the Species by Means of Natural Selection* (London: John Murray, 1859), chapter 4.

5. There are many excellent accounts of how biological evolution works. I particularly recommend Dawkins 1976; Coyne 2009; Dennett 1995; and Vermeij 2010.

6. van Valen 1973; popularized by Ridley 1993.

7. Lewis Carroll, *Through the Looking-Glass, and What Alice Found There* (1871), chapter 2.

8. I develop this idea more fully in my book *War! What Is It Good For?* (Morris 2014, pp. 84–87). Prehistoric war seems to have been dominated by small-scale raids, but starting around 5000 BC, people in the Middle East began building walls around their villages to keep raiders out. Raiders responded by making battering rams, heaping up mounds of dirt against the walls, and even by digging tunnels and building siege towers. Both sides ran faster and faster, expending huge amounts of energy, but apparently getting nowhere; by 3000 BC, attackers sometimes managed to sack enemy settlements and sometimes did not, just as had been the case before 5000 BC. However, contrary to what the Red Queen theory says, the Middle East was not in the same place as it had been before 5000 BC, because the military race had transformed society. In order to build fortifications (by 3100 BC, Uruk in what is now southern Iraq had a wall six miles long) and to sustain armies that could mount lengthy sieges, societies had to develop more complex internal structures. Those that mutated in this direction created genuine governments, raised taxes, and mobilized vast numbers of people; those that did not went extinct.

9. Diamond 1987; Harari 2014, p. 79.

10. Boyd et al. 2001.

11. I borrow the idea of vanishingly small probabilities from Dennett 1995, pp. 107–13.

12. Roberts 2014 is an excellent overview of post–Ice Age climate history.

13. There is some debate over the period's exact dating (Muscheler 2008) and its causes (Eisenman et al. 2009; Laviolette 2011; Bunch et al. 2012; Meltzer et al. 2014), but the shutdown of the Gulf Stream following North American deglaciation still seems the most likely explanation (Broecker 2006).

14. Fagan 2004.

15. Another technical detail is vitally important to this story, but is probably best discussed in a note rather than interrupting the main narrative. Unless we go back more than 600,000 years, all the earlier interstadials differed from the long summer in being much shorter, and had the post–9600 BC warmup followed the normal pattern, the world would have moved into a new ice age before 5000 BC, cutting off any possibility that humans would create Agraria and Industria. Just why this did not happen remains controversial, but the geologist William Ruddiman has suggested that cause and effect were completely intermingled. Global warming plus modern humans, he suggests, generated the first farming systems between 9600 and 6000 BC; and early farmers pumped so much carbon back into the atmosphere (by burning forests to clear fields and rearing domestic animals that generated methane) that they created a greenhouse effect, which kept temperatures high enough to block the otherwise-inevitable slide back into ice age conditions. Ruddiman's thesis, if correct, underlines the way that global warming and modern humans operated together as necessary causes for the coming of farming (Ruddiman 2005).

16. Mithen 2003. Population estimates based on Christian 2004, table 6.2.

17. Morris 2010, p. 85.

18. Archaeologists have told the story many times. Barker 2006 is a particularly thorough account. The discussion in the next few paragraphs summarizes the argument I make in Morris 2010, pp. 81–134.

19. Diamond 1997, pp. 131–56.

20. In technical terms, cultivated species are those with characteristics that would not have evolved without humans intervening in the process of natural selection, while domesticated species are those that could not exist without humans continuously intervening in their reproduction.

21. On the cultivation/domestication distinction, see particularly Fuller 2007. One unnaturally large rye seed dating around 11,000 BC was also found at Abu Hureyra in Syria (Willcox et al. 2008), which might mean that cultivation was also under way during the warm period before the Younger Dryas, but if so, the mini–ice age seems to have stopped the process in its tracks.

22. Barker 2006, pp. 200–204 and 364–70, has good brief accounts of prehistoric Japan and the Baltic.

23. I explain my own views on this in Morris 2010, pp. 94–97, 102–3, and 177–90. The role of religion in early civilization is among the most hotly contested issues in prehistory: for other ideas, see Bellah 2011; Hodder 2010, 2014.

24. I summarize my views on the first-millennium BC transformations in Morris 2010, pp. 227–79; and 2014, pp. 66–75 and 100–111, and plan to develop them further in a new book.

25. *Mahabharata*, Shanti Parvan 67.16.

26. Morris 2013, pp. 66–84, 123–26, and 137–39.

27. Spence 1974 and 1980 and Brockey 2007 have excellent accounts; I lay out my own views in Morris 2010, pp. 468–81.

28. Among many books on this question, I have found Jones 1987; Landes 1998; Frank 1998; Pomeranz 2000; Allen 2009; Goldstone 2009; Parthasarathi 2011; Ferguson 2011; and Acemoglu and Robinson 2012 particularly interesting.

29. Morris 2010, pp. 399–468.

30. Morris 2013, pp. 87–88.

31. Pamuk 2007 presents the European wage data, and Pamuk and Shatzmiller 2014 suggest that the same patterns apply to the Middle East too. I am not aware of any comparable Chinese wage series for this period, although literary sources suggest that the fifteenth century was a golden age for peasants in China too (Morris 2010, pp. 435–43).

32. Morris 2010, pp. 490–507.

33. I discuss the probabilities and alternatives in Morris 2010, pp. 571–77.

34. Not my actual great-great-grandparents, I hasten to add. On one side of the family, the men of that generation were mostly skilled manual workers in Holland; on the other, most were coalminers in Staffordshire. The women, so far as I can tell from the documents available, were kept hard at work in the home.

35. Morris 2010, pp. 582–90. These predictions all measure GDP at nominal currency exchange rates; measuring at purchasing power parity (PPP), the International Monetary Fund concluded in October 2014 that China's GDP had already overtaken America's (http://www.imf.org/external/pubs/ft/weo/2014/02/).

36. This argument can take very different forms; compare, for example, Rostow 1960, Sen 1999b, and Acemoglu and Robinson 2012.

37. J. Mann 2008, p. 1.

38. Francis Fukuyama's 1992 thesis of "the end of history," predicting the global triumph of liberal capitalism, is the best-known presentation of this case.

39. World Bank 1993; Campos and Root 1996; Schuman 2010. Lee Kuan Yew's memoirs (Lee 1998, 2000) are fascinating on this topic.

40. Kaplan 2014 is a good example.

41. This is the main thesis of Jacques 2009.

42. Root 2013, p. 1.

43. Qing 2012; Kim and Kim 2014.

44. This calculation of course depends on a string of further assumptions, and different assumptions of course produce different results. If we assume that energy capture (as distinct from the social development score as a whole)

continues rising in the twenty-first century at the same speed that it did in the twentieth, it will reach "only" 575,000 kcal/cap/day in the West and 221,000 in the East. If we instead assume that the rate at which energy capture increases in the twenty-first century will accelerate over the twentieth-century rate of growth by the same amount that the twentieth-century rate accelerated over that of the nineteenth, the West scores 594,000 kcal/cap/day and the East 344,000. Any set of linear assumptions, however, seems to lead to the same conclusion: energy capture increases a lot.

45. Morris 2010, pp. 590–98.

46. Kurzweil 2005, 2013.

47. See www.humanbrainproject.eu; www.wired.com/wiredscience/2013/05/neurologist-markram-human-brain-all/.

48. See http://www.nature.com/news/computer-modelling-brain-in-a-box-1.10066.

49. Miguel Nicolelis, February 18, 2013, available at www.technologyreview.com/view/511421/the-brain-is-not-computable/. Rat experiment: www.nature.com/srep/2013/130228/srep/01319/full/srep01319.html.

50. See www.dailymail.co.uk/sciencetech/article-2095214/As-scientists-discover-translate-brainwaves-words-Could-machine-read-innermost-thoughts.html.

51. See http://www.hpcwire.com/2014/01/15/supercomputer-models-human-brain-activity/.

52. On Neanderthal values, see now Wynn and Coolidge 2012.

53. Carbon dioxide levels: http://co2now.org. Possible consequences: http://www.sciencemag.org/site/special/climate2013/. Stable temperatures, 2002–12: www.nhuoaa.gov/pdf/719139main_2012_GISTEMP_summary.pdf. Scientific consensus: http://www.ipcc-wg2.gov/AR5/.

54. Historians nowadays tend to be uncomfortable with the expression "dark age" (back in 1981, when I began my PhD on Greece between 1200 and 700 BC, almost everyone called this period the Greek Dark Age; a generation later, almost everyone calls it the Early Iron Age), but it strikes me as a pretty good name for any era that sees massive declines in population, living standards, nutrition, health, literacy, the stock of knowledge, and technical skills, combined with state failures and rising levels of violence.

55. Kristensen and Norris 2013, 2014.

56. I spelled out my ideas on the looming threats in Morris 2010, pp. 598–622; 2014, pp. 332–93. Among the most recent discussions, I have found National Intelligence Council 2012; Guillén and Ontiveros 2012; Brynjolfsson and McAfee 2014; and Burrows 2014 particularly helpful. Bracken 2012 is excellent on what he calls "the second nuclear age."

57. Einstein, interview with Alfred Werner, published in *Liberal Judaism* (April–May 1949), cited from Isaacson 2007, p. 494.

58. I borrow this term from Dawkins 1976, pp. 19, 24, who suggests that focusing on the gene as the basic unit of evolution requires us to see animals' bodies as survival machines, chosen by natural selection to maximize the likelihood of genes passing their DNA on to the next generation. Human societies function in much the same way.

59. I sometimes suspect that I am just about as WEIRD and fossil-fuely as it is possible to get, having grown up in the English Midlands—the cradle of the industrial revolution—and living now on the edge of Silicon Valley, which promises (or threatens) to be the cradle of the post-industrial revolution.

60. Sandel 2009 provides a highly entertaining survey of some of the main principles that have been suggested.

Chapter 6: On the Ideology of Imagining That "Each Age Gets the Thought It Needs"

1. Solon fragment 17.31–3; Aristotle *Politics* 1.9.
2. See *Oxford Classical Dictionary*, 4th ed. (2012), s. liturgy.
3. Ps. Xen., *The Constitution of the Athenians* (the "Old Oligarch"), 1.13.
4. Thucydides 6.39.
5. W. Burkert, *Homo Necans* (Berkeley: University of California Press, 1983).
6. See my *Money and the Early Greek Mind* (Cambridge, UK: Cambridge University Press, 2004).

Chapter 8: Eternal Values, Evolving Values, and the Value of the Self

1. Originally quoted by Richard Lee in *The !Kung San: Men, Women, and Work in a Foraging Society* (Cambridge, UK: Cambridge University Press, 1979), p. 348. Quoted by Morris in chapter 1 in this volume.
2. The translation is that of the King James Bible.
3. Immanuel Kant in *The Groundwork of the Metaphysics of Morals*, translated by Mary Gregor (Cambridge, UK: Cambridge University Press, 1998), 4:432 and 4:436. The numbers are those of the volume and page number of *The Prussian Academy Edition of the Works of Kant*, found in the margins of most translations.
4. Morris, chapter 1 in this volume.
5. *Nicomachean Ethics* 5.7 1134b18. I am quoting from the translation by W. D. Ross revised by J. O. Urmson in *The Complete Works of Aristotle* (Princeton, NJ: Princeton University Press, 1984), p. 1790.
6. Morris, chapter 1 in this volume. The reference is to Frans De Waal, *Primates and Philosophers: How Morality Evolved*, edited by Stephen Macedo and Josiah Ober (Princeton, NJ: Princeton University Press, 2006).

7. Christine M. Korsgaard, "Morality and the Distinctiveness of Human Action," in Frans De Waal, *Primates and Philosophers: How Morality Evolved*, pp. 98–119. For a fuller version of the argument, see my "Reflections on the Evolution of Morality," available at http://www.amherstlecture.org/korsgaard2010/index.html.

8. Morris, chapter 1 in this volume.

9. De Waal's target was people who think that animals are not "moral" because they are savage and ruthless. My point now and in my response to De Waal is that animals lack the capacity for action that is either morally good or evil.

10. Gilbert Harman. *The Nature of Morality: An Introduction to Ethics* (New York: Oxford University Press, 1977), chapter 1.

11. See Bernard Mandeville, *The Fable of the Bees: or, Private Vices, Public Benefits*, edited by F. B. Kaye (Indianapolis: Liberty Classics, 1988), especially the section "An Enquiry into the Origin of Moral Virtue," pp. 41–57. Mandeville himself denied that he meant either that virtue is unreal or that it is not worth having.

12. For Hume's discussion, see the *Enquiry Concerning the Principles of Morals* (in David Hume: *Enquiries Concerning Human Understanding and Concerning the Principles of Morals*, 3rd ed., edited by L. A. Selby-Bigge and P. H. Nidditch (Oxford, UK: Clarendon Press, 1975), p. 214. For Hutcheson's, see the selections from *Inquiry Concerning the Original of Our Ideas of Beauty and Virtue*, in D. D. Raphael's *British Moralists 1650–1800* (Indianapolis: Hackett Publishing Company, 1991), volume I, p. 291.

13. The view described in the text is the meta-ethical or metaphysical theory these days known as "constructivism." To make it a little less abstract, consider Kant's idea that the values relevant to the guidance of action—the values of rightness, obligation, and permissibility—emerge when we see whether we can impose the form of rightness—the form of universal law—on a maxim of action. Of course, a further story has to be told about why this counts as a correct exercise of the power of valuing, and it is the work of Kant's moral philosophy to tell it. Once the story is told, however, it is a story about how values find their way into the world, not a story about how preexisting values are apprehended. Values enter the world when valuers endorse certain maxims as laws.

14. See for example Simon Blackburn, *Ruling Passions: A Theory of Practical Reason* (Oxford, UK: Clarendon Press, 1998), pp. 8–14. "Expressivism" is the metaethical view that normative language is not descriptive but rather expressive of certain evaluative states of mind.

15. Harry Frankfurt, *Taking Ourselves Seriously and Getting It Right*, edited by Debra Satz (Stanford, CA: Stanford University Press, 2006), pp. 18–19.

16. Hobbes, in the *Leviathan*, edited by Edwin Curley (Indianapolis: Hackett Publishing Company, 1994); Rousseau, in the *Discourse on the Origin of Inequality*, in *The Basic Political Writings of Jean-Jacques Rousseau*, trans-

lated by D. A. Cress (Indianapolis: Hackett Publishing Company, 1987); and Adam Smith, in *Theory of the Moral Sentiments*, edited by D. D. Raphael and A. L. Macfie (Indianapolis: Liberty Classics 1982), all try to give psychological, developmental accounts of how this feature of the human condition arose.

17. See Christine M. Korsgaard, *Self-Constitution: Agency, Identity, and Integrity* (Oxford, UK: Oxford University Press, 2009).

18. In making these remarks, I am not ignoring the difference between respecting yourself, in the sense of demanding recognition for your standing as a creature with rights and interests of your own, and esteeming yourself, in the sense of thinking that you are superior to others in virtue of your social class, gender, race, or in terms of certain abilities, accomplishments, or other attributes, and that that superiority carries with it an entitlement to be treated in certain ways. But the story I have in mind relies on the familiar idea that there is a complex developmental connection between these two ideas of roughly the sort described by Rousseau and Hobbes. Both concepts involve thoughts about "worthiness-for" that connect the value of the self to the value of its interests and projects. People who esteem themselves think themselves entitled to be treated in certain ways because they are superior to others; we begin to learn respect when we learn that we should extend esteem of the relevant kind to all people equally. As Kant pointed out all too vividly, a comparative element remains, for at this stage of moral evolution, people learn to respect each other by deciding that they occupy some sort of rank that places them higher than the other animals. (See "Conjectures on the Beginning of Human History," in *Kant: Political Writings*, 2nd ed., trans. H. B. Nisbet, ed. Hans Reiss [Cambridge, UK: Cambridge University Press, 1991], pp. 225–26, 8:114 in the Prussian Academy edition pages found in most translations.) That is why people protesting against those who fail to treat them with respect so often say things like: "You are treating me like an animal!" It is also why people are frightened by the idea that nonhuman animals are worthy of anything but the most meager moral consideration: they think that if they grant this, they will lose their own entitlement to respect. In my own view, the opposite is true: respect will retain a taint of comparative thinking until we have learned to extend the kind of consideration it calls for to the other animals.

19. John Rawls, *Political Liberalism* (New York: Columbia University Press, 1993), p. 32.

20. Morris, chapter 1 in this volume.

21. This is closely related to a point that has been made effectively by Sharon Street in several of her papers—that the explanation of how we come to value certain things should not make it seem accidental that we sometimes manage to value the right things. See, for instance, "A Darwinian Dilemma for Realist Theories of Value," *Philosophical Studies* 127, no. 1 (January 2006), pp. 109–66.

22. Later (in n. 26), I will mention some reasons for thinking that this name for the view I might have in mind might not be exactly right.

23. See Friedrich Nietzsche, *On the Genealogy of Morals* (in *On the Geneaology of Morals and Ecce Homo*, trans. Walter Kaufmann and R. J. Hollingdale [New York: Random House, 1967]); and Sigmund Freud, *Civilization and Its Discontents*, trans. James Strachey (New York: W. W. Norton and Company, 1961).

24. Morris, chapter 2 in this volume.

25. Hume tells a similar story to explain why chastity is considered important in women but not in men. See David Hume, *A Treatise of Human Nature*, book 3, part 2, section 12.

26. If we think of the older, more public, and the modern, more inward ways of individuating the self merely as different, rather than thinking of one of them as a distortion, then "distortion view" is a little too crude for the form of explanation I have in mind. Some differences in value would be distortions, like the ones dependent on silly gender ideals, while others would simply be different forms the same values take when refracted, as it were, through different lenses. Notice that this is still different from a more familiar kind of case, where the same values point us toward different actions in light of different views of the facts. A familiar example from ethics textbooks is of a tribe that killed people at a certain age, because they believed that you are preserved for all eternity in the form you are in when you die. The case I discuss in the text has some affinities with that—we find the value intelligible once we understand the view, but in the case in the text, it does not follow that we approve of the value once we understand the view.

27. Richard Lee, *The !Kung San*; Frank Marlowe, *The Hadza: Hunter-Gatherers of Tanzania* (Berkeley and Los Angeles: University of California Press: 2010).

28. As Morris himself notes in chapter 2 in this volume.

29. Morris, chapter 4 in this volume.

30. Ibid.

31. Morris, chapter 5 in this volume.

32. Morris, chapter 4 in this volume.

CHAPTER 10: MY CORRECT VIEWS ON EVERYTHING

1. I also owe thanks to the historian Peter Novick, from whom I stole this chapter's title. I first saw the title when Novick used it for a response to reviews of his book *That Noble Dream* (Novick 1988, 1991), and I have waited more than twenty years for an opportunity to steal it. Having committed the theft, however, I learned from Rob Tempio that Novick had himself stolen the title, from Leszek Kolakowski's open letter to E. P. Thompson in *The Socialist Register* (Kolakowski 1974). All things considered, a title that goes back to a

fight between a philosopher and a historian over the possibility of a socialist paradise seems particularly appropriate here.

2. Morris 2014.

3. D. Brown 1986, pp. 39–87, reviews anthropologists' attempts to define (or deny) human universals; and Haidt 2012 has much to say from a psychological perspective.

4. For the sorts of reasons spelled out by Pinker 2002; de Waal 2009; Boehm 2012; and Haidt 2012, among others.

5. My thinking on this has been much influenced by Dennett 1992.

6. Korsgaard 2005, 2013.

7. Waley 1937, pp. 7, 32. The most famous modern example is the philosopher Thomas Nagel's (1974) reflection on what it is like to be a bat.

8. Asquith 1984, p. 138. Kennedy 1992 provides a sustained critique of anthropomorphism.

9. de Waal 1986, p. 221.

10. Milo's views on violence, however, seem to fall closer to the foraging end of the human spectrum (Morris 2014, p. 296).

11. de Waal 1986, p. 221.

12. The change in thinking is often traced back to McBrearty and Brooks 2000. The discovery of what may be 40,000-year-old Neanderthal art at Gorham Cave, Gibraltar, in July 2012 and of a 500,000-year-old engraving on a shell from Java are the most spectacular examples (Rodríguez-Vidal et al. 2014; Joordens et al. 2014).

13. Darwin 1871, p. 255.

14. I give my views on pastoral nomadism at great length in Morris 2014, pp. 94–164; see also Turchin et al. 2013.

15. Morris 2013.

16. Liu 2004, pp. 73–116.

17. Thorp 2006, pp. 125–71, and Li 2013, pp. 66–89, have detailed descriptions of the remains at Anyang, and Liu 2006 discusses some of the methodological issues.

18. Davis 1991.

19. I discuss the Chinese cases at Morris 2013, pp. 160–64.

20. Carrithers et al. 1985; B. Morris 1994; Sorabji 2006.

21. Morris 2013, pp. 53–59; Malanima 2014.

22. See the classic debate in Fogel and Elton 1983.

23. I like to think that in some of my books (Morris 2010, 2014) I balanced abstraction and the nitty-gritty by moving back and forth between vast impersonal forces and the stories of individuals, but I suppose that no two historians ever agree on where the perfect balance lies.

24. The exception that proves the rule was when a landowning Athenian male citizen died leaving no male heirs. In that case, his nearest female relative would

become an *epiklêros*. As such, she did not own the land, but instead served as the channel through which the land would pass to the deceased's nearest male relative, thereby keeping the real estate within the patriline. If the *epiklêros* or the deceased's nearest male relative were already married, they were legally required to divorce their current spouses and marry one another (C. Patterson 1998, pp. 91–106).

25. The same word as in *Kyrios Yiorgos*, the Mr. George with whom I opened the book.

26. Isaeus 10.10.

27. Schaps 1979, p. 61.

28. Lysias 31.21; Demosthenes 36.14, 41.8–9.

29. *IG* II² 1672.64.

30. See Schaps 1979, pp. 52–58, although Schaps himself modifies this interpretation.

31. Schaps 1979 remains the best discussion.

32. Some slaves even owned slaves of their own (for example, *IG* II² 1570.78–79).

33. Garlan 1982, pp. 60–69.

34. For some wealthy slaves, such as the Pittalakos mentioned in Aeschines 1 (delivered in 345 BC), we cannot be sure. Pittalakos was described as being a public slave (although even that fact was disputed), but we do not know whether he worked in the financial sector or not.

35. Finance is as controversial as any other area in Athenian history. On the scale and profitability of banking, I generally side with Edward Cohen (1992), albeit with some reservations (Morris 1994).

36. Archippe was one of the three women mentioned earlier who are known to have had access to large amounts of money (Demosthenes 36.14).

37. Cohen 1992; Trevett 1992.

38. Whitehead 1977 remains the classic treatment.

39. "Struck silver" might actually be a more appropriate metaphor, since plenty of resident aliens bought leases to work the Athenian silver mines, either with their own hands or with slave labor (M. Crosby 1950; Hopper 1953, 1968), and some must have been successful.

40. At the height of Athens's population, in the 430s BC, about 350,000 people lived in the territory of Attica. Only about 60,000 of them were adult male citizens (Hansen 1986), but I describe the ruling elite as containing one-third of the population because it seems sensible to me to include the citizens' sons, who were basically apprentice rulers.

41. This is the central argument of Ober 2008.

42. Morris and Powell 2009.

43. Morris 2010, pp. 245–63.

44. See, for example, Liverani 2005, E. Hall 1989, and Momigliano 1975.

45. I develop my thoughts on this topic in Morris 2010, pp. 262–63, 320–30.

46. Naroll 1956, p. 693; Carneiro 1967. More recent analyses, Bandy 2004; consistency, Bintliff 1999, p. 528

47. Tilly 1984, pp. 46–50.

48. Boserup 1965. The demographer James Wood (1998) has shown how the various processes fit together to form what he calls the "Malthus-Boserup ratchet"; and the geographer Ruth DeFries (2014) has described a rather similar idea as the "big ratchet."

49. On multilevel selection, I have learned a great deal from Richerson and Boyd 2005; Wilson and Wilson 2007; Okasha 2007; Turchin and Gavrilets 2009; and Bowles and Gintis 2011.

50. See http://www.americanrhetoric.com/MovieSpeeches/moviespeechwallstreet.html.

51. The best evidence comes from the archive of Menches, a scribe in the Egyptian village of Kerkeosiris in the 110s BC (Crawford 1971; Verhoogt 1997; http://tebtunis.berkeley.edu). MacMullen 1974, pp. 1–27, has a fine overview of rural life in the Roman Empire.

52. Figes 1996, pp. 89, 90; Maxim Gorky, *My Universities* (1923), cited from Figes 1996, p. 86.

53. I found Cartwright 1968 very helpful on this issue.

54. Pinker 1997, p. 326.

55. Between them, Betzig 1997 and Ehrlich 2000 provide a good overview of ideas about human nature.

56. I slip into the jargon of economists here because it captures the central point so well. Economists make no assumptions about personal preferences; everyone is different from everyone else. I like watching television, but you might like going camping, and someone else might like drinking rare wines. An economist would say that each of us has our own utility function. All utility functions are equally valid, and, once we recognize that, we must also see that the actual content of utility functions is unimportant for economics. Utility is basically just personal satisfaction. In the words of the most widely read economics textbook, saying that people maximize utility simply "means that they choose the bundle of consumption goods that they most prefer" (Samuelson and Nordhaus 2009, p. 107).

57. Wrangham and Peterson 1996, pp. 220–30; Potts 2004; Furuichi 2009; Hohmann et al. 2010.

58. Primatologists have done an excellent job of communicating their research to nonspecialists. I particularly recommend Harcourt and Stewart 2007; de Waal 1982; Wrangham and Peterson 1996; and Boesch 2009.

59. Boehm 1993, 1999.

60. Dawkins 1976.

61. Darwin (1871) identified the basic principles, and suggested that sexual selection was just as important in evolution as natural selection. Until about 1.5 billion years ago, all reproduction was asexual, through cloning.

62. E. O. Wilson 1975.

63. Seabright 2013a is very good on this.

64. People have of course invented countless variations on pairbonding. Most societies have allowed rich men some form of *de iure* or *de facto* polygyny, and just what a male-female pair means varies greatly from culture to culture (Fox 1984; Betzig 1986; Scheidel 2009).

65. I use this compound name because there is some debate over whether the African members of this class of *Homo* should be called *ergaster* or *erectus*.

66. Wrangham 2009.

67. The image of shameless women as bitches is very old, going back at least as far as the poet Semonides (fragment 7 West) in seventh-century BC Greece (discussed at length in Franco 2014).

68. Hupka and Ryan 1990; DeSteno et al. 2006.

69. As in so many other ways, horticulturalists relying on hoe rather than plow agriculture seem to lie midway between foragers and peasants (Goody 1976).

70. In practice, of course, the size of the wife's dowry, the power of her family, the personalities of the people involved, and the society's religious and legal systems would all affect the outcome.

71. Richerson and Boyd 2005, p. 77.

72. My wife is not an academic, but—to our mutual relief—we discovered after we got married that neither of us had much interest in raising a family.

73. Richerson and Boyd 2005, pp. 169–87.

74. There have been many analyses: see, for instance, http://www.cconomist .com/news/21589074-boomers-need-think-harder-about-their-retirement-income-says-larry-fink-chairman-and-chief; http://www.reuters.com /article/2013/05/15/us lifeexpectancy idUSBRE94E16620130515; http:// www.gapminder.org/videos/dont-panic-the-facts-about-population/# .VBsb90s718M; www.stimson.org/spotlight/whither-the-demographic-arc-of-instability-/; P. Taylor 2014.

75. I explain my views more fully in Morris 2014, pp. 288–312.

76. Hill et al. 2001; M. Wilson 2013.

77. Human forager and chimpanzee violence compared: Wrangham and Glowacki 2012.

78. Pinker 2011; Morris 2014, pp. 112–287, 319–25, 332–40.

79. On the reaction, Goldstone 2009.

80. The historian Niall Ferguson has a fascinating discussion in his book *Civilization* (2011, pp. 96–140).

81. His pithy translation (Auden 1965) of Bertold Brecht's "Erst kommt das Fressen, dann kommt die Morale," in his *Threepenny Opera* (1928).

82. Herodotus 2.2. Psammetichus I reigned 664–610 BC. King James IV of Scotland is supposed to have run a similar experiment in 1493, leaving two children with a mute woman on the otherwise unoccupied island of Inchkeith.

"When they cam to the aige of perfyte speech," said the sixteenth-century chronicler Robert Lindsay (in Dalyell 1814, pp. 249–50), "Some sayes they spak guid Hebrew, but I knaw not by authoris rehearse."

83. Rawls 1971, pp. 11–22, 136–42.

84. Rawls 1971, p. 102.

85. Experiments have in fact shown that plenty of fossil-fuel folk do their valuing differently from the way that Rawls said we should (Frohlich et al. 1976). Some critics even "wonder whether Rawls's enterprise is merely an attempt to find arguments in support of the political opinions of professors of his social class" (Gordon 2008).

86. Plutarch, *Life of Alexander* 64. Plutarch lived four centuries after these events, and there is a very good chance that the story is fictional; however, Plutarch had access to primary sources that did not survive for us to read, and it is very likely that if the story is a fabrication, it is one that goes back to the late fourth century BC, and was part of the campaign to promote Alexander to the status of a godlike king. See the discussion in Hamilton 1969, *ad loc.*

87. Plutarch, *Life of Demetrius* 9–13.

88. Price 1984 offers fascinating reflections on whether Greeks of the first few centuries AD really believed that Roman emperors were gods.

89. I muse further on these developments in Morris and Powell 2009, pp. 443, 477–79.

90. Korsgaard seems to suggest that Sociological Positivism is actually just a subset of the Distortion View when she says Distortionists believe that the "capacity for valuing . . . is vulnerable to distortion by sociological forces." As I understand it, Distortionism holds that ideology is very powerful, duping the masses into believing what elites tell them, while Sociological Positivism holds that ideology is very weak, and does not trick anyone into believing anything. Distortionism assumes that most people are stupid, and Sociological Positivism that they are spineless.

91. Gerring 2001, pp. 71–86, has an excellent summary.

92. Asad 1979, pp. 621–22.

93. Normally attributed to Lincoln in his speeches at Clinton, Illinois, on September 2, 1858, but no one has found the words in Lincoln's papers (http://www.bartleby.com/73/609.html).

94. This, of course, is why common sense evolved. People who could judge what would work and what the results of different strategies might be were more likely to pass on their genes than people who could not, and societies that showed equally sound collective judgment were more likely to grow and expand than societies that did not.

95. Frieden 2006, pp. 435–52, has a good account of African development in these years.

96. For the official interpretation of *ujamaa*, Nyerere 1968; for analyses, Coulson 1982 and McHenry 1979. On the Kenyan economy, Bates 1989.

97. Kenyan and Tanzanian incomes: for 1961–86, Maddison 2010; for 2013, https://www.cia.gov/library/publications/the-world-factbook/fields/2012.html#lo.

98. Spufford 2010 has an extraordinary account.

99. The most moving denunciation of its lies, in my opinion, is the playwright and politician Vaclav Havel's essay "The Power of the Powerless" (1978), while the sharpest is Ben Lewis's *Hammer and Tickle* (2008), a collection of Soviet jokes.

100. This interpretation of ideology does not require us to assume that the liars know they are lying; the most convincing ideologues, I suspect, are people who sincerely believe their own falsehoods.

101. Thucydides 1.22.

102. See http://www.bbc.com/news/world-asia-29177946.

103. As I mentioned in chapter 4, I rely here heavily on Bergen and Tiedemann 2013.

104. I am among them, for reasons I explain in my book *War! What Is It Good For?* (2014). I realize that plenty of other fossil-fuelers, including many moral philosophers, disagree.

105. Haidt 2012, p. 119.

106. See http://www.history.ac.uk/reviews/review/1091; http://www.theguardian.com/books/2014/apr/20/war-what-is-it-good-for-ian-morris, http://www.thetimes.co.uk/tto/arts/books/non-fiction/article4046770.ece.

107. Seaford does not define "capitalism"; to keep things simple, I will assume that he means something along the lines of Milton Friedman's widely used definition of "the organization of the bulk of economic activity through private enterprise operating in a free market" (M. Friedman 2002 [1962], p. 4).

108. Particularly Seaford 2004.

109. Weber's remarks are scattered through his many publications (for example, Weber 1968, pp. 305–6, 927–37, 1354–59); Polanyi et al. 1957; Finley 1973.

110. Hopkins 1980, 1983.

111. Morris 2004; Scheidel 2010; Ober 2015.

112. Saller 2005; Morris et al. 2007.

113. Peter Acton's recent study (2014) of the size and structure of firms in classical Athens illustrates this nicely, neatly explaining the features that Finley (1973) interpreted as "economically irrational."

114. Data from Morris 2013.

115. A point also made in Malanima 2014.

116. As, in fact, Milton Friedman did (2002 [1962], p. 5).

117. These and all other figures in this paragraph are calculated from Maddison 2010. Fascist Italy is an outlier, seeing just 1.4 percent per annum growth between 1922 and 1939; but then again, in a period of the same length between 1991 and 2008 (the most recent year in Maddison's database), Italian growth averaged just 1.1 percent.

118. Even in the heady years 1958–68, the Soviet and American economies grew at roughly the same pace (slightly above 4.75 percent in the United States; slightly below in the Soviet Union). Only in the 1980s did the U.S. economy decisively outperform the Soviet (3.1 to 1.6 percent), whereupon Soviet subjects promptly withdrew what little remained of their support.

119. Shapiro 2001 has a harrowing account of the Chinese experience.

120. See http://www.forbes.com/sites/davidewalt/2013/02/13 /thirty-amazing-facts-about-private-jets/. This is the total number of planes registered for use.

121. T. Friedman 2008, pp. 31, 73.

122. See http://www.economist.com/news/united-states /21603492-american-investors-are-taking-climate-change-more-seriously-nob odys-fuels.

123. See http://www.bostonglobe.com/opinion/editorials/2014/01/24 /investors-see-green-clean-energy/F7sxg6y3Ljfsp2WwARNGZN/story.html.

124. North 1990 is particularly good on the logic of this, and Frieden 2006 on the history.

125. For example, http://www.cnn.com/2014/10/03/opinion /mcgahey-climate-change/; http://newclimateeconomy.report. Rose and Tepperman 2014 discuss some of the options.

126. I make these points at more length in Morris 2010, pp. 608–13; 2014, pp. 367–69.

127. Rothman et al. 2014.

128. Sun et al. 2012.

129. Benton 2005 (Rothman et al.'s 2014 research supersedes Benton's explanation of the end-Permian extinction).

130. Kolbert 2014 has an accessible account.

131. See http://www.economist.com/news/special-report /21599522-robots-offer-unique-insight-what-people-want-technology-makes- their for a fascinating discussion of what people currently want from robots.

132. Atwood 1985, 2003.

133. Wickham 2005, pp. 33, 653. AD 439 was when the Vandals cut off the city's grain trade with North Africa.

134. Here I am revising the arguments I made in Morris 2010, pp. 92–94, 580, and 598–619, where I suggested that after tens of thousands of years in which "Nightfall" scenarios were in fact unimaginable, the coming of nuclear weapons had made them very possible.

135. Sadly, I am not myself one of these people who knows how to do things; I pin my post-apocalyptic hopes on having friends who are competent and on being a quick learner.

136. W. Miller 1960.

137. Harari 2014, p. 414.

REFERENCES

Note: All URLs checked on October 10, 2014.

Abraham, Kathleen. 2004. *Business and Politics under the Persian Empire: The Financial Dealings of Marduk-nasir-apli of the House of Egibi*. Bethesda, MD: CDL Press.

Acemoglu, Daron, and James Robinson. 2012. *Why Nations Fail: The Origins of Power, Prosperity, and Poverty*. New York: Crown.

Acton, Peter. 2014. Poiesis: *Manufacturing in Classical Athens*. New York: Oxford University Press.

Akkermans, Peter, and Glenn Schwartz. 2003. *The Archaeology of Syria*. Cambridge, UK: Cambridge University Press.

Alexander, Richard. 1974. "The Evolution of Social Behavior." *Annual Review of Ecology and Systematics* 5, pp. 325–83.

———. 1987. *The Biology of Moral Systems*. Hawthorn, NY: de Gruyter.

Allen, Robert. 2001. "The Great Divergence in European Wages and Prices from the Middle Ages to the First World War." *Explorations in Economic History* 38, pp. 411–48.

———. 2007. "Engels' Pause: A Pessimist's Guide to the British Industrial Revolution." Oxford University Department of Economics Working Paper 315. Available at http://www.economics.ox.ac.uk/Department-of-Economics-Discussion-Paper-Series/engel-s-pause-a-pessimist-s-guide-to-the-british-industrial-revolution.

———. 2009. *The British Industrial Revolution in Global Perspective*. Cambridge, UK: Cambridge University Press.

Allen, Robert, et al. 2011. "Wages, Prices and Living Standards in China, 1738–1925: A Comparison with Europe, Japan and India." *Economic History Review* 64 (supplement), pp. 8–38.

Alvaredo, Facundo, et al. 2013. "The Top 1 Percent in International and Historical Perspective." *Journal of Economic Perspectives* 27, pp. 3–20.

Angelbeck, Bill, and Colin Greer. 2012. "Anarchism and the Archaeology of Anarchic Societies: Resistance to Centralization in the Coast Salish Region of the Pacific Northwest Coast." *Current Anthropology* 53, pp. 547–87.

Apetrei, Sarah. 2010. *Women, Feminism and Religion in Early Enlightenment England*. Cambridge, UK: Cambridge University Press.

Apor, Balász, et al., eds. 2004. *The Leader Cult in Communist Dictatorship: Stalin and the Eastern Bloc*. New York: Palgrave Macmillan.

Armelagos, George, and Kristin Harper. 2005. "Genomics at the Origins of Agriculture." *Evolutionary Anthropology* 14, pp. 68–77, 109–21.

Armstrong, Karen. 2006. *The Great Transformation: The Beginning of Our Religious Traditions*. New York: Knopf.

Arnason, Johann, et al., eds. 2005. *Axial Civilizations and World History*. Leiden: Brill.

Arnold, Jeanne. 1995. "Transportation Innovation and Social Complexity among Maritime Hunter-Gatherer Societies." *American Anthropologist* 97, pp. 733–47.

———. 2007. "Credit Where Credit Is Due: The History of the Chumash Oceangoing Plank Canoe." *American Antiquity* 72, pp. 196–209.

Asad, Talal. 1979. "Anthropology and the Analysis of Ideology." *Man* n.s. 14, pp. 607–27.

Asquith, P. 1984. "The Inevitability and Utility of Anthropomorphism in Description of Primate Behavior." In Rom Harré and Vernon Reynolds, eds., *The Meaning of Primate Signals*, pp. 138–76. Cambridge, UK: Cambridge University Press.

Atkinson, Anthony. 2010. "Income Inequality in Historical and Comparative Perspective." Available at www.gini-research.org/system/uploads/19/original/Atkinson_GINI_Mar2010_.pdf?1269619027.

Atkinson, Anthony, et al. 2011. "Top Incomes in the Long Run of History." *Journal of Economic Literature* 49, pp. 3–71.

Atwood, Margaret. 1985. *The Handmaid's Tale*. Toronto: McClelland and Stewart.

———. 2003. *Oryx and Crake*. Toronto: McClelland and Stewart.

Auden, W. H. 1965. "Grub First, Then Ethics." In W. H. Auden, *About the House*, p. 33. London: Faber and Faber.

Axelrod, Robert. 1984. *The Evolution of Cooperation*. New York: Basic Books.

Bagley, Robert. 1999. "Shang Archaeology." In Loewe and Shaughnessy 1999, pp. 124–231.

Balazs, Etienne. 1964. *Chinese Civilization and Bureaucracy*. New Haven, CT: Yale University Press.

Bandy, Matthew. 2004. "Fissioning, Scalar Stress, and Social Evolution in Early Village Societies." *American Anthropologist* 106, pp. 322–33.

Bang, Peter, and Walter Scheidel, eds. 2013. *The Oxford Handbook of the State in the Ancient Near East and Mediterranean*. Oxford, UK: Oxford University Press.

Banner, Stuart. 2005. *How the Indians Lost Their Land: Law and Power on the Frontier*. Cambridge, MA: Belknap Press.

Barber, Elizabeth. 1994. *Women's Work: The First 20,000 Years—Women, Cloth, and Society in Early Times*. New York: Norton.

Barker, Graeme. 2006. *The Agricultural Revolution in Prehistory: Why Did Foragers Become Farmers?* Oxford, UK: Oxford University Press.

Barnard, Alan, ed. 2004. *Hunter-Gatherers in History, Archaeology and Anthropology*. Oxford, UK: Berg.

Barnes, Timothy. 2011. *Constantine: Dynasty, Religion and Power in the Later Roman Empire*. Oxford, UK: Wiley-Blackwell.

Bates, Robert. 1989. *Beyond the Miracle of the Market: The Political Economy of Agrarian Development in Kenya*. Cambridge, UK: Cambridge University Press.

Beardson, Timothy. 2013. *Stumbling Giant: The Threats to China's Future*. New Haven, CT: Yale University Press.

Becker, Gary. 1991. *A Treatise on the Family*. Enlarged edition. Cambridge, MA: Harvard University Press.

Beckerman, Stephen, et al. 2009. "Life Histories, Blood Revenge, and Reproductive Success among the Waorani of Ecuador." *Proceedings of the National Academy of Sciences* 106, pp. 8134 39.

Beckwith, Christopher. 2009. *Empires of the Silk Road: A History of Central Eurasia from the Bronze Age to the Present*. Princeton, NJ: Princeton University Press.

Belich, James. 2009. *Replenishing the Earth: The Settler Revolution and the Rise of the Anglo-World, 1783–1939*. Oxford, UK: Oxford University Press.

Belkin, Aaron, et al. 2013. "Readiness and the DADT Repeal: Has the New Policy of Open Service Undermined the Military?" *Armed Forces & Society* 39, pp. 587–601.

Bell, David. 2009. *The First Total War: Napoleon's Europe and the Birth of Warfare as We Know It*. Boston: Houghton Mifflin.

Bellah, Robert. 2011. *Religion in Human Evolution from the Palaeolithic to the Axial Age*. Cambridge, MA: Harvard University Press.

Bellù, Lorenzo Giovanni, and Paolo Liberati. 2006. "Inequality Analysis. The Gini Index." Rome: United Nations Food and Agriculture Organisation, EASYPol 40. Available at http://www.fao.org/docs/up/easypol/329/gini_index_040EN.pdf.

Benedictow, Ole. 2004. *The Black Death 1346–1353: The Complete History*. Rochester, NY: Boydell Press.

Benton, Michael. 2005. *When Life Nearly Died: The Greatest Mass Extinction of All Time*. London: Thames & Hudson.

Bergen, Peter, and Katherine Tiedemann, eds. 2013. *Talibanistan: Negotiating the Borders between Terror, Politics, and Religion*. New York: Oxford University Press.

Bettinger, Robert. 2009. *Hunter-Gatherer Foraging: Five Simple Models*. New York: Eliot Werner Publications.

Betzig, Laura. 1986. *Despotism and Differential Reproduction: A Darwinian View of History*. Chicago: Aldine.

———, ed. 1997. *Human Nature: A Critical Reader*. New York: Oxford University Press.

Binford, Lewis. 1978. *Nunamiut Ethnoarchaeology*. New York: Academic Press.
——. 1980. "Willow Smoke and Dogs' Tails: Hunter-Gatherer Settlement Systems and Archaeological Site Formation." *American Antiquity* 45, pp. 4–20.
——. 2001. *Constructing Frames of Reference: An Analytical Method for Archaeological Theory Building Using Ethnographic and Environmental Data Sets*. Berkeley: University of California Press.
Bintliff, John. 1999. "Settlement and Territory." In Graeme Barker, ed., *Companion Encyclopedia of Archaeology* I, pp. 505–44. London: Routledge.
Blackmore, Susan. 1999. *The Meme Machine*. Oxford, UK: Oxford University Press.
Bloch, Maurice. 1983. *Marxism and Anthropology*. Oxford, UK: Oxford University Press.
Blum, Jerome. 1976. *The End of the Old Order in Rural Europe*. Princeton, NJ: Princeton University Press.
Blumenthal, Ute-Renate. 1988. *The Investiture Controversy: Church and Monarchy from the Ninth to the Twelfth Century*. Philadelphia: University of Pennsylvania Press.
Bocquet-Appel, Jean-Pierre, and Ofer Bar-Yosef, eds. 2008. *The Neolithic Demographic Transition and Its Consequences*. Amsterdam: Springer.
Boehm, Christopher. 1993. "Egalitarian Society and Reverse Dominance Hierarchy." *Current Anthropology* 34, pp. 227–54.
——. 1999. *Hierarchy in the Forest: The Evolution of Egalitarian Behavior*. Cambridge, MA: Harvard University Press.
——. 2012. *Moral Origins: The Evolution of Virtue, Altruism, and Shame*. New York: Basic Books.
Boone, J. 2002. "Subsistence Strategies and Early Human Population History: An Evolutionary Ecological Perspective." *World Archaeology* 34, pp. 6–25.
Borgerhoff Mulder, Monique, et al. 2009. "Intergenerational Wealth Transmission and the Dynamics of Inequality in Small-Scale Societies." *Science* 326, pp. 682–88. Online supporting materials available at https://scholarblogs.emory.edu/phooper/files/2014/08/BorgerhoffMulder2009Suppl.pdf.
Bornstein, Diane, ed. 1979. *The Feminist Controversy of the Renaissance*. New York: Scholars' Facsimiles and Reprints.
Boserup, Esther. 1965. *Conditions of Agricultural Growth*. Chicago: Aldine.
Bowles, Samuel, and Herbert Gintis. 2011. *A Cooperative Species: Human Reciprocity and Its Evolution*. Cambridge, UK: Cambridge University Press.
Bowman, Alan, and Andrew Wilson, eds. 2012. *Settlement, Urbanization, and Population*. Oxford, UK: Oxford University Press.
——. 2013a. *Quantifying the Roman Economy: Methods and Evidence*. Oxford, UK: Oxford University Press.
——. 2013b. *The Roman Agricultural Economy: Organization, Investment, and Production*. Oxford. UK: Oxford University Press.

Boyd, Peter, et al. 2001. "Was Agriculture Impossible during the Pleistocene but Mandatory during the Holocene?" *American Antiquity* 66, pp. 387–411.

Boyer, John, and Jan Goldstein, eds. 1987. *University of Chicago Readings in Western Civilization* IX: *Twentieth-Century Europe*. Chicago: University of Chicago Press.

Boyer, Pascal. 2001. *Religion Explained: The Evolutionary Origins of Religious Thought*. New York: Basic Books.

Bracken, Paul. 2012. *The Second Nuclear Age: Strategy, Danger, and the New Power Politics*. New York: Times Books.

Bradley, Keith, and Paul Cartledge, eds. 2009. *The Cambridge World History of Slavery* I: *The Ancient Mediterranean World*. Cambridge, UK: Cambridge University Press.

Bradley, Richard, and Mark Edmonds. 1993. *Interpreting the Axe Trade: Production and Exchange in Neolithic Britain*. Cambridge, UK: Cambridge University Press.

Bratton, Michael, and Richard Houessou. 2014. "Demand for Democracy Is Rising in Africa, but Most Political Leaders Fail to Deliver." Afrobarometer Research Paper 11. Available at http://www.afrobarometer.org/files/documents/policy_brief/ab_r5_policypaperno11.pdf.

Braudel, Fernand. 1981. *Civilization and Capitalism, 15th–18th Century* I: *The Structures of Everyday Life*. Trans. Siân Reynolds. New York: Harper & Row
———. 1982. *Civilization and Capitalism, 15th–18th Century* II: *The Wheels of Commerce*. Trans. Siân Reynolds. New York: Harper & Row.

Brauer, Carl. 1979. *John F. Kennedy and the Second Reconstruction*. New York: Columbia University Press.

Briant, Pierre. 2002. *From Cyrus to Alexander: A History of the Persian Empire*. Winona Lake, IN: Eisenbrauns.

Brisch, Nicole, ed. 2012. *Religion and Power: Divine Kingship in the Ancient World and Beyond*. Chicago: Oriental Institute Seminar Series 4.

Broadberry, Stephen, and Bishnupriya Gupta. 2006. "The Early Modern Great Divergence: Wages, Prices, and Economic Development in Europe and Asia, 1500–1800." *Economic History Review* n.s. 59, pp. 2–31.

Brockey, Liam. 2007. *Journey to the East: The Jesuit Mission to China, 1579–1724*. Cambridge, MA: Harvard University Press.

Broecker, Wallace. 2006. "Was the Younger Dryas Triggered by a Flood?" *Science* 312, pp. 1146–48.

Brook, Timothy. 1998. *The Confusions of Pleasure: Commerce and Culture in Ming China*. Berkeley: University of California Press.

Brown, Donald. 1991. *Human Universals*. Philadelphia: Temple University Press.

Brown, Peter. 1995. *Authority and the Sacred: Aspects of the Christianisation of the Roman World*. Cambridge, UK: Cambridge University Press.

Brown, Peter. 2012. *Through the Eye of a Needle: Wealth, the Fall of Rome, and the Making of Christianity in the West, 350–550 AD*. Princeton, NJ: Princeton University Press.

Bruce, Steve. 2002. *God Is Dead: Secularization in the West*. Oxford, UK: Wiley-Blackwell.

———. 2013. *Secularization: In Defense of an Unfashionable Theory*. New York: Oxford University Press.

Brynjolfsson, Erik, and Andrew McAfee. 2014. *The Second Machine Age: Work, Progress, and Prosperity in a Time of Brilliant Technologies*. New York: Norton.

Bunch, T., et al. 2012. "Very High-Temperature Impact Melt Products as Evidence for Cosmic Impacts and Airbursts 12,900 Years Ago." *Proceedings of the National Academy of Sciences* 109, pp. 1903–12.

Burrows, Mathew. 2014. *The Future, Declassified: Megatrends That Will Undo the World Unless We Take Action*. New York: Palgrave Macmillan.

Caldwell, John. 2006. *Demographic Transition Theory*. Amsterdam: Springer.

Campos, Jose Egardo, and Hilton Root. 1996. *The Key to the Asian Miracle: Making Shared Growth Credible*. Washington, DC: Brookings Institution Press.

Cannon, Aubrey. 2011. *Structured Worlds: The Archaeology of Hunter-Gatherer Thought and Action*. London: Equinox.

Carballo, David, ed. 2013. *Cooperation and Collective Action: Archaeological Perspectives*. Boulder: University of Colorado Press.

Carneiro, Robert. 1967. "On the Relationship between Size of Population and Complexity of Social Organization." *Southwestern Journal of Anthropology* 23, pp. 234–41.

———. 2003. *Evolutionism in Cultural Anthropology*. Boulder, CO: Westview Press.

Carrithers, Michael, et al. 1985. *The Category of the Person: Anthropology, Philosophy, History*. Cambridge, UK: Cambridge University Press.

Cartwright, R. L. 1968. "Some Remarks on Essentialism." *Journal of Philosophy* 65, pp. 615–26.

Cashdan, Elizabeth. 1980. "Egalitarianism among Hunters and Gatherers." *American Anthropologist* 82, pp. 116–20.

Cavalli-Sforza, Luigi, and Marcus Feldman. 1981. *Cultural Transmission and Evolution: A Quantitative Approach*. Princeton, NJ: Princeton University Press.

Ceadel, Martin. 1987. *Thinking about Peace and War*. Oxford, UK: Oxford University Press.

———. 1996. *The Origins of War Prevention: The British Peace Movement and International Relations, 1730–1854*. Oxford, UK: Oxford University Press.

———. 2001. *Semi-Detached Idealists: The British Peace Movement and International Relations, 1854–1945*. Oxford, UK: Oxford University Press.

Chadwick, Owen. 1990. *The Secularization of the European Mind in the Nineteenth Century*. Cambridge, UK: Cambridge University Press.

Chagnon, Napoleon. 1988. "Life Histories, Blood Revenge, and Warfare in a Tribal Society." *Science* 239, pp. 985–92.

Chaudhuri, K. N. 1990. *Asia before Europe: Economy and Civilisation of the Indian Ocean from the Rise of Islam to c. 1750.* Cambridge, UK: Cambridge University Press.

Chayanov, A. V. 1986 [1925]. *Theory of the Peasant Economy.* Trans. Daniel Thorner et al. Madison: University of Wisconsin Press.

Chekhov, Anton. 1897. "Peasants." Cited from http://www.online-literature. com/o_henry/1285/.

Childe, V. Gordon. 1936. *Man Makes Himself.* London: Watts and Co.

——. 1942. *What Happened in History.* London: Penguin.

Christian, David. 2004. *Maps of Time: An Introduction to Big History.* Berkeley: University of California Press.

Chu, Ke-young, et al. 2000. "Income Distribution and Tax and Government Spending in Developing Countries." IMF Working Paper WP/00/62. Available at http://www.imf.org/external/pubs/ft/wp/2000/wp0062.pdf.

Cipolla, Carlo. 1980. *Before the Industrial Revolution: European Society and Economy, 1000–1700.* 2nd ed. New York: Norton.

Clark, Gregory. 2007. *A Farewell to Alms: A Brief Economic History of the World.* Princeton, NJ: Princeton University Press.

——. 2014. *The Son Also Rises: Surnames and the History of Social Mobility.* Princeton, NJ: Princeton University Press.

Cochrane, Eric, et al., eds. 1987. *University of Chicago Readings in Western Civilization VI: Early Modern Europe: Crisis of Authority.* Chicago: University of Chicago Press.

Cohen, Edward. 1992. *Athenian Economy and Society: A Banking Perspective.* Princeton, NJ: Princeton University Press.

——. 2000. *The Athenian Nation.* Princeton, NJ: Princeton University Press.

Colledge, Susan, and James Connolly, eds. 2007. *The Origins and Spread of Domestic Plants in Southwest Asia and Europe.* Walnut Creek, CA: AltaMira.

Colli, Andrea. 2003. *The History of Family Business, 1850–2000.* Cambridge, UK: Cambridge University Press.

Coontz, Stephanie. 2005. *Marriage, a History: How Love Conquered Marriage.* New York: Penguin.

Cooper, Jerrold. 1986. *Sumerian and Akkadian Royal Inscriptions: Pre-Sargonic Inscriptions.* Winona Lake, IN: Eisenbrauns.

Cooperson, Michael. 2005. *Al-Ma'mun.* Oxford, UK: Oneworld.

Cortright, David. 2008. *Peace: A History of Movements and Ideas.* Cambridge, UK: Cambridge University Press.

Costin, Cathy. 1991. "Craft Specialization: Issues in Defining, Documenting, and Explaining the Organization of Production." *Advances in Archaeological Method and Theory* 3, pp. 1–56.

Costin, Cathy. 1996. "Exploring the Relationship between Gender and Craft in Complex Societies." In Rita Wright, ed., *Gender and Archaeology*, pp. 111–40. Philadelphia: University of Pennsylvania Press.

Coulson, Andrew. 1982. *Tanzania: A Political Economy*. Oxford, UK: Clarendon Press.

Cox, Virginia. 1990. *Moderata Fonte (Modesta Pozzo): The Worth of Women, Wherein Is Clearly Revealed Their Nobility and Their Superiority to Men*. Chicago: University of Chicago Press.

Coyne, Jerry. 2009. *Why Evolution Is True*. New York: Viking.

Crawford, Dorothy. 1971. *Kerkeosiris: An Egyptian Village in the Ptolemaic Period*. Cambridge, UK: Cambridge University Press.

Crone, Patricia. 1989. *Pre-Industrial Societies*. Oxford, UK: Blackwell.

Crosby, Alfred. 2006. *Children of the Sun: A History of Humanity's Unappeasable Appetite for Energy*. New York: Norton.

Crosby, Margaret. 1950. "The Leases of the Laurion Mines." *Hesperia* 19, pp. 189–312.

Cummings, Vicki. 2013. *The Anthropology of Hunter-Gatherers: Key Themes for Archaeologists*. London: Bloomsbury.

Dalton, George. 1971. *Economic Anthropology and Development*. New York: Basic Books.

Dalyell, John, ed. 1814. *The Cronicles of Scotland, by Robert Lindsay of Pitscottie, Published from Several Old Manuscripts* I. Edinburgh: George Ramsay.

Darnton, Robert. 1984. *The Great Cat Massacre and Other Episodes in French Cultural History*. New York: Basic Books.

Darwin, Charles. 1871. *The Descent of Man and Selection in Relation to Sex*. Vol. 1. London: John Murray. Available at http://www.gutenberg.org.

Davies, John K. 1971. *Athenian Propertied Families, 600–300 BC*. Oxford, UK: Clarendon Press.

———. 1981. *Wealth and the Power of Wealth in Classical Athens*. New York: Arno Press.

Davies, Philip, ed. 1996. *The Prophets: A Sheffield Reader*. Sheffield, UK: Sheffield Academic Press.

Davis, Jack. 1991. "Contributions to a Mediterranean Rural Archaeology: Historical Case Studies from the Ottoman Cyclades." *Journal of Mediterranean Archaeology* 4, pp. 131–216.

Dawkins, Richard. 1976. *The Selfish Gene*. Oxford, UK: Oxford University Press.

———. 1982. *The Extended Phenotype: The Gene as the Unit of Selection*. San Francisco: Freeman.

Dawson, Raymond, trans. 1993. *Confucius: The Analects*. Harmondsworth, UK: Penguin.

Deaton, Angus. 2013. *The Great Escape: Health, Wealth, and the Origins of Inequality*. Princeton, NJ: Princeton University Press.

de Bary, Theodore, and Irene Bloom, eds. 1999. *The Sources of Chinese Tradition* I. 2nd ed. New York: Columbia University Press.

DeFries, Ruth. 2014. *The Big Ratchet: How Humanity Thrives in the Face of Natural Crisis.* New York: Basic Books.

del Carmen Rodríguez Martínez, Maria, et al. 2005. "Oldest Writing in the New World." *Science* 313, pp. 1610–14.

Demattè, Paola. 2010. "The Origins of Chinese Writing: The Neolithic Evidence." *Cambridge Archaeological Journal* 20, pp. 211–28.

Dennett, Daniel. 1992. *Consciousness Explained.* New York: Back Bay Books.

———. 1995. *Darwin's Dangerous Idea.* New York: Simon & Schuster.

DeSteno, David, et al. 2006. "Jealousy and the Threatened Self: Getting to the Heart of the Green-Eyed Monster." *Journal of Personality and Social Psychology* 91, pp. 626–41.

de Vasconcelos, Álvaro, ed. 2012. *Global Trends 2030—Citizens in an Interconnected and Polycentric World.* Paris: European Union Institute for Security Studies. Available at http://www.iss.europa.eu/uploads/media/ESPAS_report_01.pdf.

de Waal, Frans. 1982. *Chimpanzee Politics: Power and Sex among Apes.* Baltimore: Johns Hopkins University.

———. 1986. "Deception in the Natural Communication of Chimpanzees." In Robert Mitchell and Nicholas Thompson, eds., *Deception: Perspectives on Human and Nonhuman Deceit*, pp. 221–44. Buffalo: State University of New York Press.

de Waal, Frans, et al. 2006. *Primates and Philosophers: How Morality Evolved.* Princeton, NJ: Princeton University Press.

———, eds. 2014. *Evolved Morality: The Biology and Philosophy of Human Consciousness.* Leiden: Brill.

Dever, William. 2001. *What Did the Biblical Writers Know and When Did They Know It? What Archaeology Can Tell Us about the Reality of Ancient Israel.* Grand Rapids, MI: Eerdmans.

Diamond, Jared. 1987. "The Worst Mistake in the History of the Human Race." *Discover Magazine* (May), pp. 64–66. Available at http://discovermagazine.com/1987/may/02-the-worst-mistake-in-the-history-of-the-human-race.

———. 1997. *Guns, Germs, and Steel: The Fates of Human Societies.* New York: Norton.

———. 2012. *The World before Yesterday: What Can We Learn from Traditional Societies?* New York: Viking.

Donker van Heel, Koenraad. 2014. *Mrs. Tsenhor: A Female Entrepreneur in Ancient Egypt.* Cairo: American University in Cairo Press.

Drews, Robert. 1983. *Basileus.* New Haven, CT: Yale University Press.

Driver, Felix. 1993. *Power and Pauperism: The Workhouse System, 1834–1884.* Cambridge, UK: Cambridge University Press.

Droysen, Johann Gustav. 1897 [1868]. *Outline of the Principles of History (Grundriss der Historik)*. Trans. E. Benjamin Andrews. Boston: Ginn & Company.

Dunn, John. 2006. *Democracy: A History*. Washington, DC: Atlantic Monthly Press.

Durham, William. 1991. *Coevolution: Genes, Culture, and Human Diversity*. Stanford, CA: Stanford University Press.

Earle, Timothy. 1997. *How Chiefs Come to Power: The Political Economy in Prehistory*. Stanford, CA: Stanford University Press.

———. 2002. *Bronze Age Economics*. Boulder, CO: Westview.

Ebrey, Patricia Buckley. 1993. *The Inner Quarters: Marriage and the Lives of Chinese Women in the Sung Period*. Berkeley: University of California Press.

Edwards, Anthony. 2004. *Hesiod's Ascra*. Berkeley: University of California Press.

Egan, Ronald. 2013. *The Burden of Female Talent: The Poet Li Qingzhao and Her History in China*. Cambridge, MA: Harvard University Press.

Ehrlich, Paul. 2000. *Human Natures: Genes, Cultures, and the Human Prospect*. Washington, DC: Island Press.

Eisenman, Ian, et al. 2009. "Rain Driven by Receding Ice Sheets as a Cause of Past Climate Change." *Paleoceanography* 24. Available at http://onlinelibrary. wiley.com/doi/10.1029/2009PA001778/full.

Eisenstadt, Shmuel. 1963. *The Political System of Empires*. Glencoe, IL: Free Press.

———, ed. 1986. *The Origins and Diversity of the Axial Age*. Albany: State University of New York Press.

Elias, Norbert. 1982 [1939]. *The Civilizing Process*. Trans. Edmund Jephcott. Oxford, UK: Blackwell.

Elkins, Stanley. 1959. *Slavery: A Problem in American Institutional and Intellectual Life*. New York: Universal Press.

Elvin, Mark. 1973. *The Pattern of the Chinese Past*. Stanford, CA: Stanford University Press.

Endicott, Karen. 1999. "Gender Relations in Hunter-Gatherer Societies." In Lee and Daly 1999a, pp. 411–18.

Engel, Barbara, and Anastasia Posadskaya-Vanderbeck, eds. 1997. *A Revolution of Their Own: Voices of Women in Soviet History*. Boulder, CO: Westview Press.

Engels, Friedrich. 1946 [1878]. *Anti-Dühring: Herr Eugen Dühring's Revolution in Science*. London: Progress Publishers. Available at http://www.marxists .org/archive/marx/works/1877/anti-duhring/index.htm.

———. 1972 [1884]. *The Origin of the Family, Private Property and the State*. London: Lawrence & Wishart.

Erlanger, Philippe. 1970. *Margaret of Anjou: Queen of England*. London: Elek.

Evans, Richard. 2005. *The Third Reich in Power*. London: Allen Lane.

Fabian, Johannes. 1983. *Time and the Other: How Anthropology Constructs Its Object*. New York: Columbia University Press.

Fagan. Brian. 2004. *The Long Summer: How Climate Changed Civilization*. New York: Basic Books.

———. 2008. *The Great Warming: Climate Change and the Rise and Fall of Civilizations*. New York: Bloomsbury Press.

Ferguson, Niall. 1997. "Introduction." In Niall Ferguson, ed., *Virtual History: Alternatives and Counterfactuals*, pp. 1–90. New York: Basic Books.

———. 2003. *Empire*. New York: Basic Books.

———. 2006. *The War of the World: Twentieth-Century Conflict and the Decline of the West*. London: Penguin Press.

———. 2011. *Civilization: The West and the Rest*. London: Allen Lane.

Ferguson, Niall, et al., eds. 2010. *The Shock of the Global: The 1970s in Perspective*. Cambridge, MA: Harvard University Press.

Fernández-Armesto, Felipe. 2006. *Pathfinders: A Global History of Exploration*. New York: Norton.

Field, Daniel. 1976. *Rebels in the Name of the Tsar*. Boston: Houghton Mifflin.

Figes, Orlando. 2006. *A People's Tragedy: A History of the Russian Revolution*. London: Jonathan Cape.

———. 2014. *Revolutionary Russia, 1891–1991: A History*. New York: Metropolitan Books.

Finley, Moses. 1959. "Was Greek Civilization Based on Slave Labour?" *Historia* 8, pp. 145–64.

———. 1973. *The Ancient Economy*. 1st ed. Berkeley: University of California Press.

———. 1980. *Ancient Slavery and Modern Ideology*. London: Chatto & Windus.

Fitzpatrick, Sheila. 1999. *Everyday Stalinism. Ordinary Life in Extraordinary Times: Soviet Russia in the 1930s*. New York: Oxford University Press.

Fitzpatrick, Sheila, et al., eds. 1991. *Russia in the Era of the NEP*. Bloomington: Indiana University Press.

Flannery, Kent, and Joyce Marcus. 2012. *The Creation of Inequality: How Our Prehistoric Ancestors Set the Stage for Monarchy, Slavery, and Empire*. Cambridge, MA: Harvard University Press.

Flohr, Miko. 2013. *The World of the Roman Fullo: Work, Economy, and Society in Roman Italy*. Oxford, UK: Oxford University Press.

Floud, Roderick, and Donald McCloskey, eds. 1994. *The Economic History of Britain since 1700*. 2 vols. Cambridge, UK: Cambridge University Press.

Fochesato, Mattia, and Samuel Bowles. 2014. "Nordic Exceptionalism? Social Democratic Egalitarianism in World-Historic Perspective." *Journal of Public Economics* 117.

Fogel, Robert, and Geoffrey Elton. 1983. *Which Path to the Past?* New Haven, CT: Yale University Press.

Force, Pierre. 2009. "Voltaire and the Necessity of Modern History." *Modern Intellectual History* 6, pp. 457–84.

Fox, Robin. 1984. *Kinship and Marriage: An Anthropological Perspective*. Cambridge, UK: Cambridge University Press.

Foxhall, Lin. 2013. *Studying Gender in Classical Antiquity*. Cambridge, UK: Cambridge University Press.

Francis, E.K.L. 1945. "The Personality Type of the Peasant According to Hesiod's Works and Days: A Culture Case Study." *Rural Sociology* 10, pp. 275–95.

Francis, Mark. 2007. *Herbert Spencer and the Invention of Modern Life*. Ithaca, NY: Cornell University Press.

Franco, Cristiana. 2014. *Shameless: The Canine and the Feminine in Ancient Greece*. Berkeley: University of California Press.

Frank, Andre Gunder. 1998. *ReOrient: Global Economy in the Asian Age*. Berkeley: University of California Press.

Freedman, Paul. 1999. *Images of the Medieval Peasant*. Stanford, CA: Stanford University Press.

Fried, Morton. 1967. *The Evolution of Political Society*. New York: Random House.

Frieden, Jeffry. 2006. *Global Capitalism: Its Fall and Rise in the Twentieth Century*. New York: Norton.

Friedman, Milton. 2002 [1962]. *Capitalism and Freedom*. Chicago: University of Chicago Press.

Friedman, Thomas. 2008. *Hot, Flat, and Crowded: Why We Need a Green Revolution*. New York: Farrar, Straus & Giroux.

Friedmann, F. G. 1967 [1953]. "The World of 'La Miseria.'" In Jack Potter et al., eds., *Peasant Society: A Reader*, pp. 324–36. Boston: Little, Brown.

Frohlich, Norman, et al. 1976. "Choices of Principles of Distributive Justice in Experimental Groups." *American Journal of Political Science* 31, pp. 606–36.

Fry, Douglas, ed. 2013. *War, Peace and Human Nature: The Convergence of Evolutionary and Cultural Views*. Oxford, UK: Oxford University Press.

Fukuyama, Francis. 1992. *The End of History and the Last Man*. New York: Free Press.

Fuller, Dorian. 2007. "Contrasting Patterns in Crop Domestication and Domestication Rates." *Annals of Botany* 2007, pp. 1–22.

Furuichi, Takeshi. 2009. "Factors Underlying Party Size Differences between Chimpanzees and Bonobos." *Primates* 50, pp. 197–209.

Galinsky, Karl. 2012. *Augustus: Introduction to the Life of an Emperor*. Cambridge, UK: Cambridge University Press.

Gardner, Peter. 1991. "Foragers' Pursuit of Individual Autonomy." *Current Anthropology* 32, pp. 543–58.

Garlan, Yvon. 1982. *Slavery in Ancient Greece*. Trans. Janet Lloyd. Ithaca, NY: Cornell University Press.

Garnsey, Peter, ed. 1980. *Non-Slave Labour in the Greco-Roman World*. In *Proceedings of the Cambridge Philological Society*, supp. vol. 6. Cambridge, UK: Cambridge University Press.

———. 1988. *Famine and Food Supply in the Graeco-Roman World*. Cambridge, UK: Cambridge University Press.

Garnsey, Peter, and Richard Saller. 1987. *The Roman Empire: Economy, Society and Culture*. London: Duckworth.

Gat, Azar. 2006. *War in Human Civilization*. Oxford, UK: Oxford University Press.

Geertz, Clifford. 1973. *The Interpretation of Cultures*. New York: HarperCollins.

Gellner, Ernest. 1983. *Nations and Nationalism*. Oxford, UK: Blackwell.

———. 1988. *Plough, Sword and Book: The Structure of Human History*. Oxford, UK: Blackwell.

Gerring, John. 2001. *Social Science Methodology: A Criterial Framework*. Cambridge, UK: Cambridge University Press.

Ghiglieri, Michael. 1999. *The Dark Side of Man: Tracing the Origins of Male Violence*. New York: Basic Books.

Gilbert, Martin. 1966–88. *Winston S. Churchill*. 8 vols. in 13 parts. London: Heinemann.

Gilens, Martin, and Benjamin Page. 2014. "Testing Theories of American Politics: Elites, Interest Groups, and Average Citizens." *Perspectives on Politics* 12, pp. 564–81.

Gittings, John. 2005. *The Changing Face of China: From Mao to Market*. Oxford, UK: Oxford University Press.

Goitein, Shlomo. 1967–88. *A Mediterranean Society: The Jewish Communities of the Arab World as Portrayed in the Documents of the Cairo Geniza*. 5 vols. Berkeley: University of California Press.

Goldin, Claudia, and Lawrence Katz. 2002. "The Power of the Pill: Oral Contraceptives and Women's Career and Marriage Choices." *Journal of Political Economy* 110, pp. 730–70.

Goldman, Emma. 1924. *My Further Disillusionment in Russia*. Garden City, NY: Doubleday, Page & Co.

Goldstone, Jack. 2002. "Efflorescences and Economic Growth in World History." *Journal of World History* 13, pp. 323–89.

———. 2009. *Why Europe? The Rise of the West in World History, 1500–1850*. Boston: McGraw-Hill.

Goody, Jack. 1962. *Death, Property and the Ancestors: A Study of the Mortuary Customs of the Lo Dagaa of West Africa*. Stanford, CA: Stanford University Press.

———. 1973. "Bridewealth and Dowry in Africa and Eurasia." In Jack Goody and S. J. Tambiah, *Bridewealth and Dowry*, pp. 1–58. Cambridge, UK: Cambridge University Press.

Goody, Jack. 1976. *Production and Reproduction: A Comparative Study of the Domestic Domain*. Cambridge, UK: Cambridge University Press.

———. 1977. *The Domestication of the Savage Mind*. Cambridge, UK: Cambridge University Press.

———. 1986. *The Logic of Writing and the Organization of Society*. Cambridge, UK: Cambridge University Press.

———. 1987. *The Interface between the Written and the Oral*. Cambridge, UK: Cambridge University Press.

Gordon, David. 2008. "Going Off the Rawls." *The American Conservative*, July 28. Available at http://www.theamericanconservative.com/articles /going-off-the-rawls/.

Greenwood, Jeremy, et al. 2005. "Engines of Liberation." *Review of Economic Studies* 72, pp. 109–33.

Greif, Avner. 2006. *Institutions and the Path to the Modern Economy: Lessons from Medieval Trade*. Cambridge, UK: Cambridge University Press.

Grosman, Leore, et al. 2008. "A 12,000-Year-Old Shaman Burial from the Southern Levant (Israel)." *Proceedings of the National Academy of Sciences* 105, pp. 17665–69.

Guillén, Mauro, and Emilio Ontiveros. 2012. *Global Turning Points: Understanding the Challenges for Business in the 21st Century*. Cambridge, UK: Cambridge University Press.

Gunesekara, Tamara. 1994. *Hierarchy and Egalitarianism: Caste, Class and Power in Sinhalese Peasant Society*. London: Athlone.

Gurven, Michael, and Hillard Kaplan. 2007. "Longevity among Hunter-Gatherers: A Cross-Cultural Examination." *Population and Development Review* 33, pp. 321–65.

Habu, Junko. 2004. *Ancient Jomon of Japan*. Cambridge, UK: Cambridge University Press.

Haidt, Jonathan. 2012. *The Righteous Mind: Why Good People Are Divided by Politics and Religion*. New York: Random House.

Hall, Edith. 1989. *Inventing the Barbarian*. Oxford, UK: Oxford University Press.

Hall, John. 1985. *Powers and Liberties: The Causes and Consequences of the Rise of the West*. Oxford: Blackwell.

Halverson, John. 1992. "Goody and the Implosion of the Literacy Thesis." *Man* 27, pp. 301–17.

Hamilton, J. R. 1969. *Plutarch's "Alexander": A Commentary*. Oxford, UK: Clarendon Press.

Hamilton, William. 1964. "Genetic Evolution of Social Behavior." *Journal of Theoretical Biology* 7, pp. 1–52.

Hancock, James. 2012. *Plant Evolution and the Origin of Crop Species*. 3rd ed. Wallingford, UK: CABI.

Hansen, Mogens. 1986. *Demography and Democracy*. Copenhagen: Systime.

———. 1991. *The Athenian Democracy in the Age of Demosthenes*. Oxford, UK: Blackwell.

———, ed. 2000. *A Comparative Study of Thirty City-State Cultures*. Copenhagen: Kongelike Danske Videnskabernes Selskab, Historisk-filosofiske Skrifter 21.

Hansen, Mogens, and Thomas Nielsen. 2004. *An Inventory of Archaic and Classical Poleis*. Oxford, UK: Oxford University Press.

Harari, Yuval Noah. 2014. *Sapiens: A Brief History of Humankind*. London: Harvill Secker.

Harcourt, Alexander, and Kelly Stewart. 2007. *Gorilla Society: Conflict, Compromise, and Cooperation between the Sexes*. Chicago: University of Chicago Press.

Harris, William. 1989. *Ancient Literacy*. Cambridge, MA: Harvard University Press.

———. 2008. *Restraining Rage: The Ideology of Anger Control in Classical Antiquity*. Cambridge, MA: Harvard University Press.

———. 2010. *The Monetary Systems of the Greeks and Romans*. Oxford, UK: Oxford University Press.

Hartog, François. 1988. *The Mirror of Herodotus: The Representation of the Other in the Writing of History*. Trans. Janet Lloyd. Berkeley: University of California Press.

Harvey, F. David. 1965. "Two Kinds of Equality." *Classica et Medievalia* 26, pp. 101–46.

Havel, Vaclav. 1978. "The Power of the Powerless." Originally published in samizdat form and circulated secretly in Czechoslovakia. Available at http://vaclavhavel.cz/showtrans.php?cat=eseje&val=2_aj_eseje.html&typ=HTML.

Hayden, Brian. 1995. "Pathways to Power: Principles for Creating Socioeconomic Inequities." In T. D. Price and Gary Feinman, eds., *Foundations of Social Inequality*, pp. 15–85. New York: Plenum.

Hayek, Friedrich. 1944. *The Road to Serfdom*. Chicago: University of Chicago Press.

Heizer, Frank, ed. 1978. *Handbook of North American Indians* VIII: *California*. Washington, DC: Smithsonian Institution Press.

Henrich, Joseph. 2012. "Hunter-Gatherer Cooperation." *Nature* 481, pp. 449–50.

Henrich, Joseph, et al. 2010. "The Weirdest People in the World?" *Behavioral and Brain Sciences* 33, pp. 61–135.

Herman, Gabriel. 2014. "Towards a Biological Re-Interpretation of Culture." *GSTF International Journal of Law and Social Sciences* 3, pp. 52–66.

Hill, Christopher. 1984. *The Experience of Defeat: Milton and Some Contemporaries*. New York: Penguin.

Hill, Kim, et al. 2001. "Mortality Rates among Wild Chimpanzees." *Journal of Human Evolution* 40, pp. 437–50.

Hobsbawm, Eric. 1959. *Primitive Rebels*. New York: Norton.

Hobsbawm, Eric. 1962. *The Age of Revolution, 1789–1848*. New York: Vintage.

———. 1975. *The Age of Capital, 1848–1875*. New York: Vintage.

Hodder, Ian. 2006. *The Leopard's Tale: Revealing the Mysteries of Çatalhöyük*. London: Thames and Hudson.

———, ed. 2010. *Religion in the Emergence of Civilization: Çatalhöyük as a Case Study*. Cambridge, UK: Cambridge University Press.

———, ed. 2014. *Religion at Work in a Neolithic Society: Vital Matters*. Cambridge, UK: Cambridge University Press.

Hoebel, E. Adamson. 1954. *The Law of Primitive Man: A Study in Comparative Legal Dynamics*. Cambridge, MA: Harvard University Press.

Hofstede, Geert. 2001. *Culture's Consequences*. 2nd ed. Thousand Oaks, CA: Sage Publications.

Hohmann, Gottfried, et al. 2010. "Plant Foods Consumed by *Pan*: Exploring the Variation of Nutritional Energy across Africa." *American Journal of Physical Anthropology* 141, pp. 476–85.

Höpfl, H. M. 1978. "From Savage to Scotsman: Conjectural History in the Scottish Enlightenment." *Journal of British Studies* 17, pp. 19–48.

Hopkins, Keith. 1978. "Economic Growth and Towns in Classical Antiquity." In P. Abrams and E. A, Wrigley, eds., *Towns in History*, pp. 35–79. Cambridge, UK: Cambridge University Press.

———. 1980. "Taxes and Trade in the Roman Empire." *Journal of Roman Studies* 70, pp. 101–25.

———. 1983. "Introduction." In Peter Garnsey et al., eds., *Trade in the Ancient Economy*, pp. ix–xxv. Cambridge, UK: Cambridge University Press.

Hopper, R. J. 1953. "The Attic Silver Mines in the Fourth Century BC." *Annual of the British School at Athens* 48, pp. 200–254.

———. 1968. "The Laurion Mines: A Reconsideration." *Annual of the British School at Athens* 63, pp. 293–326.

Horne, Alistair. 1965. *The Fall of Paris: The Siege and the Commune 1870–71*. New York: Penguin.

Howe, Daniel Walker. 2007. *What Hath God Wrought: The Transformation of America, 1815–1848*. New York: Oxford University Press.

Hupka, R. B., and J. M. Ryan. 1990. "The Cultural Contribution to Jealousy: Cross-Cultural Aggression in Sexual Jealousy Situations." *Behavior Science Research* 24, pp. 51–71.

Inglehart, Ronald, and Christian Welzel. 2005. *Modernization, Cultural Change, and Democracy: The Human Development Sequence*. Cambridge, UK: Cambridge University Press.

Ingold, Timothy. 1999. "On the Social Relations of the Hunter-Gatherer Band." In Lee and Daly 1999a, pp. 399–410.

Iriye, Akira, et al., eds. 2012. *The Human Rights Revolution: An International History*. New York: Oxford University Press.

Isaacson, Walter. 2007. *Einstein: His Life and Universe*. New York: Simon and Schuster.

Israel, Jonathan. 2011. *A Revolution of the Mind: Radical Enlightenment and the Intellectual Origins of Modern Democracy*. Princeton, NJ: Princeton University Press.

———. 2014. *Revolutionary Ideas: An Intellectual History of the French Revolution from The Rights of Man to Robespierre*. Princeton, NJ: Princeton University Press.

Jacques, Martin. 2009. *When China Rules the World: The Rise of the Middle Kingdom and the End of the Western World*. London: Allen Lane.

Janko, Richard. 1982. *Homer, Hesiod and the Hymns*. Cambridge, UK: Cambridge University Press.

Jaspers, Karl. 1953 [1949]. *The Origin and Goal of History*. New Haven, CT: Yale University Press.

Johnson, Allen, and Timothy Earle. 1987. *The Evolution of Human Societies: From Foraging Group to Agrarian State*. Stanford, CA: Stanford University Press.

Jones, Eric. 1987. *The European Miracle: Environments, Ecologies and Geopolitics in the History of Europe and Asia*. 2nd ed. Cambridge, UK: Cambridge University Press.

Joordens, Josephine, et al. 2014. "Homo Erectus at Trinil on Java Used Shells for Tool Production and Engraving." *Nature* (2014). doi. 10.1038/nature13962.

Kamei, Nobutaka. 2005. "Play among Baka Children in Cameroon." In Barry Hewlett and Michael Lamb, eds., *Hunter-Gatherer Childhoods: Evolutionary, Developmental & Cultural Perspectives*, pp. 343–64. New Brunswick, NJ: Transaction Publishers.

Kaplan, Robert. 2014. *Asia's Cauldron: The South China Sea and the End of a Stable Pacific*. New York. Random House.

Karakasıdou, Anastasia. 1997. *Fields of Wheat, Hills of Blood: Passages to Nationhood in Greek Macedonia, 1870–1990*. Chicago: University of Chicago Press.

Kay, Philip. 2014. *Rome's Economic Revolution*. Cambridge, UK: Cambridge University Press.

Keeley, Lawrence. 1996. *War before Civilization: The Myth of the Peaceful Savage*. New York: Oxford University Press.

Kelly, Joan. 1984. *Women, History, and Theory: The Essays of Joan Kelly*. Chicago: University of Chicago Press.

Kelly, Robert. 2013. *The Lifeways of Hunter-Gatherers: The Foraging Spectrum*. 2nd ed. Cambridge, UK: Cambridge University Press.

Kemp, Barry. 2005. *Ancient Egypt: Anatomy of a Civilization*. 2nd ed. Cambridge, UK: Cambridge University Press.

Kennedy, John S. 1992. *The New Anthropomorphism*. Cambridge, UK: Cambridge University Press.

Kent, Susan. 1996. *Cultural Diversity amongst Twentieth-Century Foragers: An African Perspective*. Cambridge, UK: Cambridge University Press.

Kenworthy, Lane, and Timothy Smeeding. 2013. "Growing Inequalities and Their Impact in the United States." GINI Country Report. Available at http://gini-research.org/system/uploads/443/original/US.pdf?1370077377.

Kershaw, Ian. 1998. *Hitler, 1889–1936: Hubris*. New York: Norton.

Khazanov, Anatoly. 1984. *Nomads and the Outside World*. Cambridge, UK: Cambridge University Press.

Kim, Young-oak, and Jung-kyu Kim. 2014. *The Great Equal Society: Confucianism, China and the 21st Century*. Singapore: World Scientific Publishing.

Kirch, Patrick. 2000. *On the Road of the Winds: An Archaeological History of the Pacific Islands before European Contact*. Berkeley: University of California Press.

Kirshner, Julius, and Karl Morrison, eds. 1986. *University of Chicago Readings in Western Civilization* IV: *Medieval Europe*. Chicago: University of Chicago Press.

Klein, Richard. 2009. *The Human Career*. 3rd ed. Chicago: University of Chicago Press.

Knauft, Bruce. 1985. *Good Company and Violence: Sorcery and Social Action in a Lowland New Guinea Community*. Berkeley: University of California Press.

———. 1987. "Reconsidering Violence in Simple Human Societies: Homicide among the Gebusi of New Guinea." *Current Anthropology* 28, pp. 487–500.

Kolakowski, Leszek. 1974. "My Correct Views on Everything." *The Socialist Register* 11, pp. 1–20. Available at http://socialistregister.com/index.php/srv/article/view/5323#.VDR8sN4718M.

Kolbert, Elizabeth. 2014. *The Sixth Extinction: An Unnatural History*. New York: Henry Holt.

Koonz, Claudia. 1987. *Mothers in the Fatherland: Women, the Family and Nazi Politics*. New York: St Martin's Press.

Korsgaard, Christine. 2005. "Fellow Creatures: Kantian Ethics and Our Duties to Animals." In Grethe Peterson, ed., *The Tanner Lectures on Human Values* XXV, pp. 79–110. Salt Lake City: University of Utah Press. Available at http://tannerlectures.utah.edu/_documents/a-to-z/k/korsgaard_2005.pdf.

———. 2013. "Kantian Ethics, Animals, and the Law." *Oxford Journal of Legal Studies* 33, pp. 1–20.

Kristensen, Hans, and Robert Norris. 2012. "Russian Nuclear Forces, 2012." *Bulletin of the Atomic Scientists* 68, pp. 87–98.

———. 2013. "US Nuclear Forces, 2013." *Bulletin of the Atomic Scientists* 69, pp. 77–86.

Kroeber, A. L. 1948. *Anthropology*. New York: Harcourt, Brace and Co.

Kron, Geof. Forthcoming. "Growth and Decline; Forms of Growth; Estimating Growth in the Greek World." In Elio Lo Cascio et al., eds., *The Oxford Handbook of Economies in the Classical World*. Oxford, UK: Oxford University Press.

Kuhn, Dieter. 2009. *The Age of Confucian Rule: The Song Transformation of China*. Cambridge, MA: Harvard University Press.

Kuhn, Steven, and Mary Stiner. 2001. "The Antiquity of Hunter-Gatherers." In Panter-Brick et al. 2001, pp. 99–142.

Kurzweil, Ray. 2005. *The Singularity Is Near: When Humans Transcend Biology.* New York: Viking.

———. 2013. *How to Create a Mind: The Secret of Human Thought Revealed.* New York: Viking.

Kuznets, Simon. 1955. "Economic Growth and Income Inequality." *American Economic Review* 45, pp. 1–28.

Lamberton, Robert. 1988. *Hesiod.* New Haven, CT: Yale University Press.

Landes, David. 1969. *The Unbound Prometheus: Technological Change 1750 to the Present.* Cambridge, MA: Harvard University Press.

———. 1998. *The Wealth and Poverty of Nations: Why Some Are So Rich and Some Are So Poor.* New York: Norton.

Landgraber, Kevin, et al. 2012. "Generation Times in Wild Chimpanzees and Gorillas Suggest Earlier Divergence Times in Great Ape and Human Evolution." *Proceedings of the National Academy of Sciences* 109, pp. 15716–21.

Lane, Ann, ed. 1971. *The Debate over Slavery: Stanley Elkins and His Critics.* Urbana: University of Illinois Press.

Lankov, Andrei. 2014. *The Real North Korea: Life and Politics in the Failed Stalinist Utopia.* New York: Oxford University Press.

Larsen, Clark. 1995. "Biological Changes in Human Populations with Agriculture." *Annual Review of Anthropology* 24, pp. 185–213.

———. 2006. "The Agricultural Revolution as Environmental Catastrophe." *Quaternary International* 150, pp. 12–20.

Larsen, Mogens Trolle. 1967. *Old Assyrian Caravan Procedures.* Istanbul: Nederlands historisch archaeologisch Instituut in het Nabiye Oosten.

———. 1977. "Partnerships in the Old Assyrian Trade." *Iraq* 39, pp. 119–45.

Laviolette, P. 2011. "Evidence for a Solar Flare Cause of the Pleistocene Mass Extinctions." *Radiocarbon* 53, pp. 303–23.

LeBlanc, Steve. 2013. "Warfare and Human Nature." In T. K. Hansen and R. D. Shackleton, eds., *The Evolution of Violence*, pp. 73–97.

———. 2014. "Forager Warfare and Our Evolutionary Past." In M. W. Allen and T. L. Jones, eds., *Re-Examining a Pacified Past: Violence and Warfare among Hunter-Gatherers*, pp. 26–46. Walnut Creek, CA: Left Coast Press.

LeBlanc, Steve, and Katherine Register. 2003. *Constant Battles: Why We Fight.* New York: St. Martin's Press.

Lee Kuan Yew. 1998. *The Singapore Story: Memoirs of Lee Kuan Yew.* Upper Saddle River, NJ: Prentice-Hall.

———. 2000. *From Third World to First: The Singapore Story, 1965–2000.* New York: Harper.

Lee, Richard. 1979. *The !Kung San: Men, Women and Work in a Foraging Society.* Cambridge, UK: Cambridge University Press.

Lee, Richard. 1982. "Politics, Sexual and Non-Sexual, in an Egalitarian Society." In Eleanor Leacock and Richard Lee, eds., *Politics and History in Band Societies*, pp. 37–59. Cambridge, UK: Cambridge University Press.

Lee, Richard, and Richard Daly, eds. 1999a. *The Cambridge Encyclopedia of Hunters and Gatherers*. Cambridge, UK: Cambridge University Press.

———, eds. 1999b. "Introduction: Foragers and Others." In Lee and Daly 1999a, pp. 1–19.

———. 2004. "Preface to the Paperback Edition." In Richard Lee and Richard Daly, eds., *The Cambridge Encyclopedia of Hunters and Gatherers*, pp. xiii–xvi. Cambridge, UK: Cambridge University Press.

Lee, Richard, and Irven DeVore. 1968. "Problems in the Study of Hunters and Gatherers." In Richard Lee and Irven DeVore, eds., *Man the Hunter*, pp. 3–12. Chicago: Aldine.

Lerner, Gerda. 1986. *The Creation of Patriarchy*. New York: Oxford University Press.

Le Roy Ladurie, Emmanuel. 1976. *The Peasants of Languedoc*. Trans. John Day. Urbana: University of Illinois Press.

———. 1978. *Montaillou: The Promised Land of Error*. Trans. Barbara Bray. New York: Braziller.

Leslie, D. D., and K.J.H. Gardiner. 1996. *The Roman Empire in Chinese Sources*. Rome: Bardi.

Lewis, Ben. 2008. *Hammer and Tickle*. London: Orion.

Lewis, David. 1973. *Counterfactuals*. Oxford, UK: Oxford University Press.

Lewis, Mark. 2007. *The Early Chinese Empires: Qin and Han*. Cambridge, MA: Harvard University Press.

Lewis-Williams, David, and David Pearce. 2005. *Inside the Neolithic Mind: Consciousness, Cosmos and the Realm of the Gods*. London: Thames and Hudson.

Li, Feng. 2013. *Early China: A Social and Cultural History*. Cambridge, UK: Cambridge University Press.

Lindert, Peter, and Jeffrey Williamson. 1983. "Reinterpreting Britain's Social Tables, 1688–1913." *Explorations in Economic History* 20, pp. 94–109.

———. 2012. "American Incomes 1774–1860." Cambridge, MA: National Bureau of Economic Research Working Paper 18396. Available at http://www.nber.org/papers/w18396.

Liu, Li. 2004. *The Chinese Neolithic*. Cambridge, UK: Cambridge University Press.

———. 2006. "Urbanization in Early China: Erlitou and Its Hinterland." In Glenn Storey, ed., *Urbanism in the Preindustrial World*, pp. 161–89. Tuscaloosa: University of Alabama Press.

Liverani, Mario. 2005. *Israel's History and the History of Israel*. London: Equinox.

Livi-Bacci, Massimo. 2001. *A Concise History of World Population*. 3rd ed. Trans. Carl Ipsen. Oxford, UK: Blackwell.

Loewe, Michael, and Edward Shaughnessy, eds. 1999. *The Cambridge History of Ancient China*. Cambridge, UK: Cambridge University Press.

Luttwak, Edward. 2001. *Strategy: The Logic of War and Peace*. Rev. ed. Cambridge, MA: Belknap Press.

MacDorman, Marian, and T. J. Mathews. 2009. "The Challenge of Infant Mortality: Have We Reached a Plateau?" *Public Health Reports* 124, pp. 670–81. Available at http://www.ncbi.nlm.nih.gov/pmc/articles/PMC2728659/.

Macintosh, Randall. 1998. "Global Attitude Measurement: An Assessment of the World Values Survey's Postmaterialist Scale." *American Sociological Review* 63, pp. 452–64.

MacMullen, Ramsay. 1974. *Roman Social Relations 50 BC to AD 284*. New Haven, CT: Yale University Press.

Maddison, Angus. 2010. *Statistics on World Population, GDP, and Per Capita GDP, 1–2008 AD*. Available at www.ggdc.net/maddison/Maddison.htm.

Malanima, Paolo. 2014. "Energy in History." In Mauro Agnoletti and Simone Neri Serneri, eds., *The Basic Environmental History*, pp. 1–29. Amsterdam: Springer.

Malthus, Thomas. 1970 [1798]. *An Essay on the Principle of Population*. Ed. Anthony Flew. Harmondsworth, UK: Penguin.

Mann, James. 2008. *The China Fantasy*. New York: Penguin.

Mann, Michael. 1986. *The Sources of Social Power I: From the Beginning to A.D. 1760*. Cambridge, UK: Cambridge University Press.

Marlowe, Frank. 2010. *The Hadza: Hunter-Gatherers of Tanzania*. Berkeley: University of California Press.

Martin, Bradley. 2004. *Under the Loving Care of the Fatherly Leader: North Korea and the Kim Dynasty*. New York: Thomas Dunne.

Mayhew, Robert. 2014. *Malthus: The Life and Legacies of an Untimely Prophet*. Cambridge, MA: Belknap Press.

Maynard Smith, John, and Eors Szathmáry. 1998. *The Major Transitions in Evolution*. Oxford, UK: Oxford University Press.

Mayor, Adrienne. 2000. *The First Fossil Hunters: Paleontology in Greek and Roman Times*. Princeton: Princeton University Press.

Mayr, Ernst. 1982. *The Growth of Biological Thought: Diversity, Evolution, and Inheritance*. Cambridge, MA: Harvard University Press.

———. 1989. *Toward a New Philosophy of Biology*. Cambridge, MA: Harvard University Press.

McBrearty, Sally, and Alison Brooks. 2000. "The Revolution That Wasn't: New Interpretations of the Origin of Modern Human Behavior." *Journal of Human Evolution* 39, pp. 453–563.

McHenry, Dean. 1979. *Tanzania's Ujamaa Villages: The Implementation of a Rural Development Strategy*. Berkeley: University of California Press.

McLellan, David, ed. 1977. *Karl Marx: Selected Writings*. Oxford, UK: Oxford University Press.

Meltzer, D., et al. 2014. "Chronological Evidence Fails to Support Claim of an Isochronous Widespread Layer of Cosmic Impact Indicators Dated to 12,800 Years Ago." *Proceedings of the National Academy of Sciences* 111, pp. E2162–71.

Michels, Robert. 1962 [1915]. *Political Parties: A Sociological Study of the Oligarchical Tendencies of Modern Democracy*. Glencoe, IL: Free Press.

Milanovic, Branko. 2006. "An Estimate of Average Income and Inequality in Byzantium around Year 1000." *Review of Income and Wealth* 52, pp. 449–70.

———. 2011. "A Short History of Global Inequality: The Past Two Centuries." *Explorations in Economic History* 48, pp. 494–506.

———. 2012a. "Global Income Inequality by the Numbers: In History and Now." Washington, DC: World Bank Policy Research Paper 6259. Available at http://elibrary.worldbank.org/doi/pdf/10.1596/1813–9450–6259.

———. 2012b. *The Haves and the Have-Nots: A Brief and Idiosyncratic History of Global Inequality*. New York: Basic Books.

Milanovic, Branko, et al. 2007. *Measuring Ancient Inequality*. Working Paper 13550. Cambridge, MA: National Bureau of Economic Research.

Miller, Maureen, ed. 2005. *Power and the Holy in the Age of the Investiture Conflict*. New York: Bedford/St. Martin's.

Miller, Walter, Jr. 1960. *A Canticle for Leibowitz*. New York: J. B. Lippincott & Co.

Millett, Paul. 1984. "Hesiod and His World." *Proceedings of the Cambridge Philological Society* 210, pp. 84–115.

Milner, G. R. 2005. "Nineteenth-Century Arrow Wounds and Perceptions of Prehistoric Warfare." *American Antiquity* 70, pp. 144–56.

Minkov, Michael. 2012. *Cross-Cultural Analysis: The Science and Art of Comparing World's Modern Societies and Their Cultures*. Thousand Oaks, CA: Sage Publications.

Mithen, Steven. 2003. *After the Ice: A Global Human History 20,000–5000 BC*. Cambridge, MA: Harvard University Press.

Mitterauer, Michael, and Reinhard Sieder. 1982 [1977]. *The European Family*. Trans. Karla Oosterveen and Manfred Hörzinger. Oxford, UK: Blackwell.

Mokyr, Joel. 2010. *The Enlightened Economy: An Economic History of Britain*. New Haven, CT: Yale University Press.

Momigliano, Arnaldo. 1975. *Alien Wisdom: The Limits of Hellenization*. Cambridge, UK: Cambridge University Press.

Moore, Andrew, et al. 2000. *Village on the Euphrates: From Foraging to Farming at Abu Hureyra*. New York: Oxford University Press.

Moore, Barrington. 1967. *Social Origins of Dictatorship and Democracy: Lord and Peasant in the Making of the Modern World*. 1st ed. Boston: Beacon Press.

Morgan, Lewis Henry. 1877. *Ancient Society*. New York: Henry Holt.

Morris, Brian. 1994. *Anthropology of the Self: The Individual in Cultural Perspective*. Boulder, CO: Pluto Press.

Morris, Ian. 1992. *Death-Ritual and Social Structure in Classical Antiquity.* Cambridge, UK: Cambridge University Press.

———. 1994. "The Athenian Economy Twenty Years after *The Ancient Economy.*" *Classical Philology* 89, pp. 351–66.

———. 1997. "An Archaeology of Equalities? The Greek City-States." In Deborah Nichols and Thomas Charlton, eds., *The Archaeology of City-States: Cross-Cultural Approaches*, pp. 91–105. Washington, DC: Smithsonian Institution.

———. 2000. *Archaeology as Cultural History: Words and Things in Iron Age Greece.* Oxford, UK: Blackwell.

———. 2002. "Hard Surfaces." In Paul Cartledge et al., eds., *Money, Labour and Land: Approaches to the Economics of Ancient Greece*, pp. 8–43. London: Routledge.

———. 2004. "Economic Growth in Ancient Greece." *Journal of Institutional and Theoretical Economics* 160, pp. 709–742.

———. 2005. "The Athenian Empire (478–404 BC)." Princeton-Stanford Working Papers in Classics, no. 120508. Available at http://www.princeton.edu/~pswpc/papers/authorMZ/morris/morris.html.

———. 2006. "The Collapse and Regeneration of Complex Society in Greece, 1500–500 BC." In Glenn Schwartz and J. J. Nichols, eds., *After Collapse: The Regeneration of Complex Societies*, pp. 72–84. Tucson: University of Arizona Press.

———. 2009. "The Greater Athenian State." In Ian Morris and Walter Scheidel, eds., *The Dynamics of Ancient Empires*, pp. 99–177. New York: Oxford University Press.

———. 2010. *Why the West Rules—For Now: The Patterns of History, and What They Reveal about the Future.* New York: Farrar, Straus & Giroux.

———. 2013. *The Measure of Civilization: How Social Development Decides the Fate of Nations.* Princeton, NJ: Princeton University Press.

———. 2014. *War! What Is It Good For? Violence and the Progress of Civilization, from Primates to Robots.* New York: Farrar, Straus & Giroux.

———. 2015. "The Hundred-Thousand-Year Question: History as a Subfield of Biology." *Journal of World History* 26.

Morris, Ian, et al. 2007. "Introduction." In Walter Scheidel et al., eds., *The Cambridge Economic History of Greco-Roman Antiquity*, pp. 1–12. Cambridge, UK: Cambridge University Press.

Morris, Ian, and Barry Powell. 2009. *The Greeks: History, Culture, and Society.* Upper Saddle River, NJ: Pearson.

Morris, Ian, and Walter Scheidel, eds. 2009. *The Dynamics of Ancient Empires.* New York: Oxford University Press.

Morrisson, Christian, and Wayne Snyder. 2000. "The Income Inequality of France in Historical Perspective." *European Review of Economic History* 4, pp. 59–83.

Mosca, Gaetano. 1939 [1896]. *The Ruling Class.* Trans. Hannah Kahn. New York: McGraw-Hill..

Muscheler, Raimund. 2008. "Tree Rings and Ice Cores Reveal ^{14}C Calibration Uncertainties during the Younger Dryas." *Nature Geoscience* 1, pp. 263–67.

Myers, Fred. 1986. *Pintupi Country, Pintupi Self.* Washington, DC: Smithsonian Institution Press.

Nadel, George. 1964. "Philosophy of History before Historicism." *History and Theory* 3, pp. 291–315.

Nagel, Thomas. 1974. "What Is It Like to Be a Bat?" *Philosophical Review* 83, pp. 435–50.

Naroll, Raoul. 1956. "A Preliminary Index of Social Development." *American Anthropologist* 58, pp. 687–715.

National Intelligence Council. 2012. *Global Trends 2030: Alternative Worlds.* Washington, DC: Office of the Director of National Intelligence. Available at http://www.dni.gov/index.php/about/organization/global-trends-2030.

North, Douglass. 1990. *Institutions, Institutional Change and Economic Performance.* Cambridge, UK: Cambridge University Press.

Novick, Peter. 1988. *That Noble Dream: The "Objectivity Question" and the American Historical Profession.* Cambridge, UK: Cambridge University Press.

———. 1991. "My Correct Views on Everything." *American Historical Review* 96, pp. 699–703.

Nozick, Robert. 1974. *Anarchy, State, and Utopia.* New York: Basic Books.

Nyerere, Julius. 1968. *Ujamaa: Essays on Socialism.* Oxford, UK: Oxford University Press.

Oakley, Francis. 2006. *Kingship.* Oxford, UK: Blackwell.

Ober, Josiah. 1989. *Mass and Elite in Democratic Athens: Rhetoric, Ideology, and the Power of the People.* Princeton, NJ: Princeton University Press.

———. 2008. *Democracy and Knowledge: Innovation and Learning in Classical Athens.* Princeton, NJ: Princeton University Press.

———. 2010. "Wealthy Hellas." *Transactions of the American Philological Association* 140, pp. 241–86.

———. 2012. "Democracy's Dignity." *American Political Science Review* 106, pp. 827–46.

———. 2013. "Democracy's Wisdom." *American Political Science Review* 107, pp. 104–22.

———. 2015. *The Rise and Fall of Classical Greece.* Princeton, NJ: Princeton University Press.

O'Brien, Karen. 2005. *Narratives of Enlightenment: Cosmopolitan History from Voltaire to Gibbon.* Cambridge, UK: Cambridge University Press.

Okasha, Samir. 2007. *Evolution and the Levels of Selection.* New York: Oxford University Press.

Olson, Richard. 2013. "The Human Sciences." In Roy Porter, ed., *The Cambridge History of Science* IV: *The Eighteenth Century*, pp. 436–62. Cambridge, UK: Cambridge University Press.

Organisation for Economic Cooperation and Development (OECD). 2011. "An Overview of Growing Income Inequalities in OECD Countries: Main Findings." Available at http://www.oecd.org/els/soc/49499779.pdf.

Orwell, George. 1949. *Nineteen Eighty-Four*. London: Secker & Warburg.

Otterbein, Keith. 2004. *How War Began*. College Station: Texas A&M University Press.

Padilla Peralta, Dan-el. 2014. "Divine Institutions: Religious Practice, Economic Development, and Social Transformation in Mid-Republican Rome." Unpublished PhD dissertation, Stanford University.

Pamuk, Sevket. 2007. "The Black Death and the Origins of the 'Great Divergence' across Europe, 1300–1600." *European Review of Economic History* 11, pp. 289–317.

Pamuk, Sevket, and Maureen Shatzmiller. 2014. "Plagues, Wages, and Economic Change in the Islamic Middle East, 700–1500." *Journal of Economic History* 74, pp. 196–229.

Panter-Brick, Catherine, et al. 2001a. "Lines of Enquiry." In Panter-Brick et al. 2001b, pp. 1–11.

———, eds. 2001b. *Hunter-Gatherers: An Interdisciplinary Perspective*. Cambridge, UK: Cambridge University Press.

Pareto, Vilfredo. 1935 [1916]. *The Mind and Society* 4 vols. New York: Dover.

Parker Pearson, Michael. 2012. *Stonehenge—A New Understanding: Solving the Mysteries of Prehistory's Greatest Monument*. New York: Simon & Schuster.

Parsons, Talcott. 1937. *The Structure of Social Action*. New York: McGraw-Hill.

———. 1951. *The Social System*. Glencoe, IL: The Free Press.

Parthasarathi, Prasannan. 2011. *Why Europe Grew Rich and Asia Did Not: Global Economic Divergence, 1600–1850*. Cambridge, UK: Cambridge University Press.

Patterson, Charles. 2002. *Eternal Treblinka: Our Treatment of Animals and the Holocaust*. New York: Lantern Books.

Patterson, Cynthia. 1998. *The Family in Greek History*. Cambridge, MA: Harvard University Press.

Patterson, James. 1996. *Grand Expectations: The United States, 1945–1974*. New York: Oxford University Press.

———. 2005. *Restless Giant: The United States from Watergate to Bush v. Gore*. New York: Oxford University Press.

Patterson, Orlando. 1982. *Slavery and Social Death*. Cambridge, MA: Harvard University Press.

Peterson, Nicholas. 1993. "Demand Sharing: Reciprocity and the Pressure for Generosity among Foragers." *American Anthropologist* 95, pp. 860–74.

Pfeffer, Jeffrey. 2013. "You're Still the Same: Why Theories of Power Hold over Time and across Contexts." *Academy of Management Perspectives* 27, pp. 269–80.

Piketty, Thomas. 2014. *Capital in the Twenty-First Century*. Trans. Arthur Goldhammer. Cambridge, MA: Harvard University Press.

Piketty, Thomas, and Emmanuel Saez. 2003. "Income Inequality in the United States, 1913–1998." *Quarterly Journal of Economics* 118, pp. 1–39.

Pincus, Steve. 2009. *1688: The First Modern Revolution*. New Haven, CT: Yale University Press.

Pinker, Steven. 1997. *How the Mind Works*. New York: Norton.

———. 2002. *The Blank Slate: The Modern Denial of Human Nature*. New York: Viking.

———. 2011. *The Better Angels of Our Nature: Why Violence Has Declined*. New York: Viking.

Plokhy, Serhii. 2014. *The Last Empire: The Final Days of the Soviet Union*. London: Oneworld.

Polanyi, Karl. 1944. *The Great Transformation*. Boston: Beacon.

Polanyi, Karl, et al., eds. 1957. *Trade and Market in the Early Empires*. Glencoe, IL: Free Press.

Pomeranz, Kenneth. 2000. *The Great Divergence: China, Europe, and the Making of the Modern World Economy*. Princeton, NJ: Princeton University Press.

Popper, Karl. 1957. *The Poverty of Historicism*. London: Routledge and Kegan Paul.

———. 1963. *Conjectures and Refutations*. London: Routledge and Kegan Paul.

Postgate, Nicholas. 1992. *Early Mesopotamia: Society and Economy at the Dawn of History*. London: Routledge.

Potter, Jack, et al., eds. 1967. *Peasant Society: A Reader*. Boston: Little, Brown.

Potts, R. 2004. "Paleoenvironmental Basis of Cognitive Evolution in Great Apes." *American Journal of Primatology* 62, pp. 209–28.

Powell, Barry. 2012. *Writing: Theory and History of the Technology of Civilization*. Oxford, UK: Wiley-Blackwell.

Powell, M. A., ed. 1987. *Labor in the Ancient Near East*. New Haven, CT: American Oriental Society Series 68.

Price, Simon. 1984. *Rituals and Power: The Roman Imperial Cult in Asia Minor*. Cambridge, UK: Cambridge University Press.

Provan, Iain, et al. 2003. *A Biblical History of Israel*. Louisville, KY: Westminster John Knox Press.

Puett, Michael. 2002. *To Become a God: Cosmology, Sacrifice, and Self-Divinization in Early China*. Cambridge, MA: Harvard University Press.

Qing, Jiang. 2012. *A Confucian Constitutional Order: How China's Ancient Past Can Shape Its Political Future*. Princeton, NJ: Princeton University Press.

Radcliffe-Brown, Arthur. 1936. *A Natural Science of Society*. Glencoe, IL: The Free Press.

Rashid, Ahmed. 2010. *Taliban: Militant Islam, Oil, and Fundamentalism in Central Asia*. 2nd ed. New Haven, CT: Yale University Press.

Rawls, John. 1971. *A Theory of Justice*. 1st ed. Cambridge, MA: Belknap Press.

Ray, Debraj. 1998. *Development Economics*. Princeton, NJ: Princeton University Press.

Redfield, Robert. 1956. *Peasant Society and Culture*. Chicago: University of Chicago Press.

Renfrew, Colin. 1994. "The Archaeology of Identity." In G. B. Peterson, ed., *The Tanner Lectures on Human Values* XV, pp. 283–348. Salt Lake City: University of Utah Press.

———. 2008. "Neuroscience, Evolution, and the Sapient Paradox: The Factuality of Value and of the Sacred." *Transactions of the Royal Society B* 363, pp. 2041–47.

Richerson, Peter, et al. 2001. "Was Agriculture Impossible during the Pleistocene but Mandatory during the Holocene?" *American Antiquity* 66, pp. 387–411.

Richerson, Peter, and Robert Boyd. 2005. *Not by Genes Alone: How Culture Transformed Human Evolution*. Chicago: University of Chicago Press.

Ridley, Matthew. 1993. *The Red Queen: Sex and the Evolution of Human Nature*. New York: Penguin.

Riehl, Simone, et al. 2013. "Emergence of Agriculture in the Foothills of the Zagros Mountains of Iran." *Science* 341, pp. 65–67.

Riley, Patrick. 2001. "Rousseau's General Will." In Patrick Riley, ed., *The Cambridge Companion to Rousseau*, pp. 124–53. Cambridge, UK: Cambridge University Press.

Roberts, Neil. 2014. *The Holocene: An Environmental History*. 3rd ed. Oxford, UK: Wiley-Blackwell.

Rodriguez-Vidal, Joaquín, et al. 2014. "A Rock Engraving Made by Neanderthals in Gibraltar." *Proceedings of the National Academy of Sciences* 112, pp. 13301–6. Available at http://www.pnas.org/content/111/37/13301.full.

Root, Hilton. 2013. *Dynamics among Nations: The Evolution of Legitimacy and Development in Modern States*. Cambridge, MA: MIT Press.

Rose, Gideon, and Jonathan Tepperman, eds. 2014. "Power to the People: What Will Fuel the Future?" *Foreign Affairs* 93, no. 3, pp. 2–37.

Rosen, Ralph. 1997. "Homer and Hesiod." In Ian Morris and Barry Powell, eds., *A New Companion to Homer*, pp. 463–88. Leiden: Brill.

Rostow, Walt. 1960. *The Stages of Economic Growth: A Non-Communist Manifesto*. 1st ed. Cambridge, UK: Cambridge University Press.

Roth, Randolph. 2009. *American Homicide*. Cambridge, MA: Harvard University Press.

Rothman, Daniel, et al. 2014. "Methanogenic Burst in the End-Permian Carbon Cycle." *Proceedings of the National Academy of Sciences* 111, pp. 5462–67.

Rowe, Christopher, and Malcolm Schofield, eds. 2000. *The Cambridge History of Greek and Roman Political Thought*. Cambridge, UK: Cambridge University Press.

Rowley-Conwy, Peter. 2001. "Time, Change and the Archaeology of Hunter-Gatherers." In Panter-Brick et al. 2001b, pp. 39–71.

Ruddiman, William. 2005. *Plows, Plagues, and Petroleum: How Humans Took Control of Climate.* Princeton, NJ: Princeton University Press.

Russell, Ben. 2014. *The Economics of the Roman Stone Trade.* Oxford, UK: Oxford University Press.

Ryan, Alan. 2012. *The Making of Modern Liberalism.* Princeton, NJ: Princeton University Press.

Sahlins, Marshall. 1972. *Stone Age Economics.* Chicago: Aldine.

Saller, Richard. 1994. *Patriarchy, Property and Death in the Roman Family.* Cambridge, UK: Cambridge University Press.

———. 2005. "Framing the Debate over Growth in the Ancient Economy." In J. G. Manning and Ian Morris, eds., *The Ancient Economy: Evidence and Models*, pp. 223–38. Stanford, CA: Stanford University Press.

———. 2007. "Household and Gender." In Walter Scheidel et al., eds., *The Cambridge Economic History of the Greco-Roman World*, pp. 87–112. Cambridge, UK: Cambridge University Press.

Samuelson, Paul, and William Nordhaus. 2009. *Economics.* 19th ed. New York: McGraw-Hill.

Sandel, Michael. 2009. *Justice: What's the Right Thing to Do?* New York: Farrar, Straus & Giroux.

Sassaman, Kenneth, and Donald Hardy, eds. 2011. *Hunter-Gatherer Archaeology as Historical Process.* Tucson: University of Arizona Press.

Saturno, William, et al. 2006. "Early Maya Writing at San Bartolo, Guatemala." *Science* 311, pp. 1281–83.

Schaps, David. 1979. *The Economic Rights of Women in Ancient Greece.* Edinburgh: Edinburgh University Press.

Scheidel, Walter. 2009. "Sex and Empire: A Darwinian Perspective." In Morris and Scheidel 2009, pp. 255–324.

———. 2010. "Real Wages in Early Economies: Evidence for Living Standards from 1800 BCE to 1300 CE." *Journal of the Economic and Social History of the Orient* 53, pp. 425–62.

———, ed. 2012. *The Cambridge Companion to the Roman Economy.* Cambridge, UK: Cambridge University Press.

Scheidel, Walter, and Steven Friesen. 2009. "The Size of the Economy and the Distribution of Income in the Roman Empire." *Journal of Roman Studies* 99, pp. 61–91.

Schmandt-Besserat, Denise. 1992. *Before Writing.* Austin: University of Texas Press.

Schrire, Carmel, ed. 1984. *Past and Present in Hunter-Gatherer Societies.* San Francisco: Academic Press.

Schuman, Michael. 2010. *The Miracle: The Epic Story of East Asia's Quest for Wealth.* New York: Harper Business.

Schwartz, Barry. 1987. *George Washington: The Making of an American Symbol.* New York: Free Press.

Scott, James. 1990. *Domination and the Arts of Resistance: Hidden Transcripts.* New Haven, CT: Yale University Press.

Seabright, Paul. 2010. *The Company of Strangers: A Natural History of Economic Life.* Rev. ed. Princeton, NJ: Princeton University Press.

———. 2013a. "The Birth of Hierarchy." In Sterelny et al. 2013, pp. 109–16.

———. 2013b. *The War of the Sexes: How Conflict and Cooperation Have Shaped Men and Women from Prehistory to the Present.* Princeton, NJ: Princeton University Press.

Seaford, Richard. 2004. *Money and the Early Greek Mind: Homer, Philosophy, Tragedy.* Cambridge, UK: Cambridge University Press.

Segerstråle, Ullica. 2000. *Defenders of the Truth: The Sociobiology Debate.* Oxford, UK: Oxford University Press.

Sen, Amartya. 1999a. "Democracy as a Universal Value." *Journal of Democracy* 10, pp. 3–16. Available at http://www.journalofdemocracy.org/article/democracy-universal-value.

———. 1999b. *Development as Freedom.* Oxford, UK: Oxford University Press.

Seneviratna, Anuradha, ed. 1994. *King Ashoka and Buddhism.* Kandy, Sri Lanka: Buddhist Publication Society.

Service, Elman. 1971. *Primitive Social Organization: An Evolutionary Perspective.* 2nd ed. New York: Random House.

———. 1975. *Origins of the State and Civilization.* New York: Norton.

Shanin, Teodor, ed. 1971. *Peasants and Peasant Societies.* Harmondsworth, UK: Penguin.

Shapin, Steve. 1994. *A Social History of Truth: Credibility and Science in Seventeenth-Century England.* Chicago: University of Chicago Press.

———. 1996. *The Scientific Revolution.* Chicago: University of Chicago Press.

Shapiro, Judith. 2001. *Mao's War against Nature: Politics and the Environment in Revolutionary China.* Cambridge, UK: Cambridge University Press.

Shaughnessy, Edward. 1999. "Western Zhou History." In Loewe and Shaughnessy 1999, pp. 292–351.

Shaw, Brent. 1985. "The Divine Economy: Stoicism as Ideology." *Latomus* 44, pp. 16–54.

Shaw, Greg, and Laura Gaffey. 2012. "American Public Opinion on Economic Inequality, Taxes, and Mobility: 1990–2011." *Public Opinion Quarterly* 76, pp. 576–96.

Shennan, Stephen, et al. 2013. "Regional Population Collapse Followed Initial Agriculture Booms in Mid-Holocene Europe." *Nature Communications* 4, article no. 3486, doi:10.1038/ncomms3486. Available at http://www.nature.com/ncomms/2013/131001/ncomms3486/full/ncomms3486.html.

Sherratt, Andrew. 1997. *Economy and Society in Prehistoric Europe*. Edinburgh: Edinburgh University Press.

Shostak, Marjorie. 1981. *Nisa: The Life and Words of a !Kung Woman*. New York: Random House.

Silberbauer, George. 1982. "Political Process in G/Wi Bands." In Eleanor Leacock and Richard Lee, eds., *Politics and History in Band Societies*, pp. 23–35. Cambridge, UK: Cambridge University Press.

Silver, Brian, and Kathleen Dowley. 2000. "Measuring Political Culture in Multi-Ethnic Societies: Reaggregating the World Values Survey." *Comparative Political Studies* 31, pp. 517–50.

Singer, Isaac Bashevis. 1982. "The Letter Writer." In Isaac Bashevis Singer, *The Collected Stories*, pp. 250–76. New York: Farrar, Straus & Giroux. First published in *The New Yorker*, January 31, 1968.

Singer, Peter. 1975. *Animal Liberation*. New York: HarperCollins.

Slingerland, Edward. 2008. *What Science Offers the Humanities: Integrating Body and Culture*. Cambridge, UK: Cambridge University Press.

Smartt, Joseph, and Norman Simmonds. 1995. *Evolution of Crop Plants*. 2nd ed. Oxford, UK: Wiley-Blackwell.

Smil, Vaclav. 1991. *General Energetics: Energy in the Biosphere and Civilization*. New York: Wiley.

———. 1994. *Energy in World History*. Boulder, CO: Westview Press.

Smith, A.H.V. 1997. "Provenance of Coals from Roman Sites in England and Wales." *Britannia* 28, pp. 297–324.

Smith, Eric Alden, et al. 2010. "Intergenerational Wealth Transmission and Inequality in Premodern Societies." *Current Anthropology* 51, pp. 1–126.

Snyder, Timothy. 2010. *Bloodlands: Europe between Hitler and Stalin*. New York: Basic Books.

Solt, Frederick. 2009. "Standardizing the World Income Inequality Database." *Social Science Quarterly* 90, pp. 231–42.

Sorabji, Richard. 2006. *Self: Ancient and Modern Insights about Individuality, Life, and Death*. Chicago: University of Chicago Press.

Spence, Jonathan. 1974. *Emperor of China: Self-Portrait of K'ang-hsi*. New York: Vintage.

———. 1980. *To Change China: Western Advisers in China*. New York: Penguin.

———. 1990. *The Search for Modern China*. New York: Norton.

Spencer, Herbert. 1857. "Progress: Its Law and Cause." *Westminster Review* 67, pp. 445–85.

Sperber, Daniel. 1996. *Explaining Culture: A Naturalistic Approach*. Oxford, UK: Blackwell.

Spierenburg, Pieter. 2008. *A History of Murder: Personal Violence in Europe from the Middle Ages to the Present*. Cambridge, UK: Polity.

Spitze, Glenna, and Joan Huber. 1980. "Changing Attitudes toward Women's Non-family Roles 1938 to 1978." *Work and Occupations* 7, pp. 317–35.

Spufford, Francis. 2010. *Red Plenty! Industry! Progress! Abundance! Inside the Soviet Fifties' Dream.* London: Faber and Faber.

Starr, S. Frederick. 2013. *Lost Enlightenment: Central Asia's Golden Age from the Arab Conquest to Tamerlane.* Princeton, NJ: Princeton University Press.

Stephenson, Jill. 2000. *Women in Nazi Germany.* London: Routledge.

Sterelny, Kim. 2013. "Life in Interesting Times: Cooperation and Collective Action in the Holocene." In Sterelny et al. 2013, pp. 89–107.

Sterelny, Kim, et al., eds. 2013. *Cooperation and Its Evolution.* Cambridge, MA: MIT Press.

Steward, Julian. 1938. *Basin-Plateau Aboriginal Sociopolitical Groups.* Washington, DC: Bureau of American Ethnology.

———. 1955. *Theory of Culture Change: The Methodology of Multilinear Evolution.* Urbana: University of Illinois Press.

———. 1977. "The Foundations of Basin-Plateau Shoshonean Society." In Julian Steward and Robert Murphy, eds., *Evolution and Ecology*, pp. 366–406. Urbana: University of Illinois Press.

Stiglitz, Joseph. 2013. *The Price of Inequality: How Today's Divided Society Endangers Our Future.* New York: Norton.

Stites, Richard. 1978. *The Women's Liberation Movement in Russia: Feminism, Nihilism, and Bolshevism, 1860–1930.* Princeton, NJ: Princeton University Press.

Stolper, Matthew. 1985. *Entrepreneurs and Empire: The Murashû Archive, the Murashû Firm, and Persian Rule in Babylonia.* Leiden: E. J. Brill.

Stone, Lawrence. 1964. "The Educational Revolution in England, 1560–1640." *Past and Present* 28, pp. 41–80.

———. 1969. "Literacy and Education in England 1640–1900." *Past and Present* 42, pp. 69–139.

Sunstein, Cass, and Martha Nussbaum, eds. 2005. *Animal Rights: Current Debates and New Directions.* New York: Oxford University Press.

Sun, Yadong, et al. 2012. "Lethally Hot Temperatures during the Early Triassic Greenhouse." *Science* 338, pp. 366–70.

Suny, Ronald. 2010. *The Soviet Experiment: Russia, the USSR, and the Successor States.* 2nd ed. New York: Oxford University Press.

Suttles, Wayne, ed. 1990. *Handbook of North American Indians VII: Northwest Coast.* Washington, DC: Smithsonian Institution Press.

Taagepera, Rein. 1978. "Size and Duration of Empires: Growth-Decline Curve, 3000–600 BC." *Social Science Research* 7, pp. 180–96.

———. 1979. "Size and Duration of Empires: Growth-Decline Curve, 600 BC–600 AD." *Social Science Research* 8, pp. 115–38.

Taylor, Charles. 2007. *A Secular Age.* Cambridge, MA: Harvard University Press.

Taylor, Paul. 2014. *The Next America.* New York: Pew Research Center.

Temin, Peter. 2012. *The Roman Market Economy*. New York: Oxford University Press.

Thapar, Romila. 1973. *Asoka and the Decline of the Mauryas*. 2nd ed. Delhi: Oxford University Press.

Thomas, Rosalind. 2002. *Herodotus in Context: Ethnography, Science and the Art of Persuasion*. Cambridge, UK: Cambridge University Press.

Thomas, William, and Florian Znaniecki. 1971 [1918]. "A Polish Peasant Family." In Shanin 1971, pp. 23–29.

Thompson, E. P. 1963. *The Making of the English Working Class*. London: Gollancz.

———. 1993. *Customs in Common: Studies in Traditional Popular Culture*. New York: Free Press.

Thorp, Robert. 2006. *China in the Early Bronze Age*. Philadelphia: University of Pennsylvania Press.

———. 1984. *Big Structures, Large Processes, Huge Comparisons*. New York: Sage-Russell.

Tilly, Charles. 1992. *Coercion, Capital and European States: AD 990–1990*. Oxford, UK: Blackwell.

Torrence, Robin. 2001. "Hunter-Gatherer Technology." In Panter-Brick 2001, pp. 73–98.

Treggiari, Susan. 1979. "Lower Class Women in the Roman Economy." *Florilegium* 1, pp. 65–86.

———. 1991. *Roman Marriage: Iusti Coniuges from the Time of Cicero to the Time of Ulpian*. Oxford, UK: Oxford University Press.

Trevett, Jeremy. 1992. *Apollodorus Son of Pasion*. Oxford, UK: Oxford University Press.

Trigger, Bruce. 1998. *Sociocultural Evolution*. Oxford, UK: Blackwell.

———. 2003. *Understanding Early Civilizations*. Cambridge, UK: Cambridge University Press.

Trinkaus, Eric. 2012. "Neandertals, Early Modern Humans, and Rodeo Riders." *Journal of Archaeological Science* 39, pp. 3691–93.

Trinkaus, Eric, et al. 2014. *The People of Sunghir: Burials, Bodies, and Behavior in the Earlier Upper Paleolithic*. Oxford, UK: Oxford University Press.

Tron, Heinz. 2013. *Bestattungen des frühen und mittleren Jungpaläolithikums*. Berlin: GRIN Verlag.

Turchin, Peter. 2003. *Historical Dynamics: Why States Rise and Fall*. Princeton, NJ: Princeton University Press.

Turchin, Peter, and Sergei Gavrilets. 2009. "Evolution of Complex Hierarchical Societies." *Social History and Evolution* 8, pp. 167–98.

Turchin, Peter, et al. 2012. "A Historical Database of Sociocultural Evolution." *Cliodynamics* 3, pp. 271–93. Available at http://escholarship.org/uc/item/2v8119hf#page-1.

———. 2013. "War, Space, and the Evolution of Old World Complex Societies." *Proceedings of the National Academy of Sciences* 110, pp. 16384–89.

Twitchett, Denis, and Michael Loewe, eds. 1986. *The Cambridge History of China* I: *The Ch'in and Han Empires, 221 B.C.–A.D. 220*. Cambridge, UK: Cambridge University Press.

Upton, Anthony. 2001. *Europe, 1600–1789*. London: Arnold.

van Valen, Leigh. 1973. "A New Evolutionary Law." *Evolutionary Theory* 1, pp. 1–30.

Verhoogt, Arthur. 1997. *Menches, Komogrammateus of Kerkeosiris: The Doings of a Village Scribe in the Late Ptolemaic Period (120–110 BC)*. Leiden: E. J. Brill.

Vermeij, Geerat. 2010. *The Evolutionary World: How Adaptation Explains Everything from Seashells to Civilization*. New York: Thomas Dunne Books.

Vucinich, Wayne, ed. 1968. *The Peasant in Nineteenth-Century Russia*. Stanford, CA: Stanford University Press.

Waley, Arthur. 1937. *Three Ways of Thought in Ancient China*. Stanford, CA: Stanford University Press.

Walzer, Michael. 1977. *Just and Unjust Wars: A Moral Argument with Historical Illustrations*. New York: Basic Books.

Warner, Lyndan. 2011. *The Ideas of Man and Woman in Renaissance France: Print, Rhetoric, and Law*. Farnham, UK: Ashgate.

Watson, James, ed. 1980. *African and Asian Systems of Slavery*. Oxford, UK: Blackwell.

Wawro, Geoffrey. 2014. *A Mad Catastrophe: The Outbreak of World War I and the Collapse of the Habsburg Empire*. New York: Basic Books.

Weber, Eugen. 1976. *Peasants into Frenchmen: The Modernization of Rural France, 1870–1914*. Stanford, CA: Stanford University Press.

Weber, Max. 1949. *The Theory of Economic and Social Organization*. Glencoe, IL: Free Press.

———. 1968 [1922]. *Economy and Society*. 2 vols. Ed. Guenther Roth and Claus Wittich. Berkeley: University of California Press.

Weir, Alison. 1995. *Lancaster and York: The Wars of the Roses*. London: Jonathan Cape.

Wenzel, George, et al., eds. 2000. *The Social Economy of Sharing: Resource Allocation and Modern Hunter-Gatherers*. Osaka: National Museum of Ethnology.

West, Martin. 1978. *Hesiod's Works and Days*. Oxford, UK: Clarendon Press.

White, Leslie. 1943. "Energy and the Evolution of Culture." *American Anthropologist* 45, pp. 335–56.

———. 1949. *The Science of Culture*. New York: Grove Press.

White, Matthew. 2011. *The Great Big Book of Horrible Things: The Definitive Chronicle of History's 100 Worst Atrocities*. New York: Norton.

Whitehead, David. 1977. *The Ideology of the Athenian Metic*. Supp. vol. 4. Cambridge, UK: Cambridge Philological Society.

Whiten, Andrew. 2011. "The Scope of Culture in Chimpanzees, Humans, and Ancestral Apes." *Philosophical Transactions of the Royal Society B* 366, pp. 997–1007.

Whiten, Andrew, et al. 2011. "Culture Evolves." *Philosophical Transactions of the Royal Society B* 366, pp. 938–48.

Wickham, Chris. 2005. *Framing the Early Middle Ages: Europe and the Mediterranean 400–800*. Oxford, UK: Oxford University Press.

———. 2009. *The Inheritance of Rome: Illuminating the Dark Ages, 400–1000*. New York: Penguin.

Wilkinson, Richard, and Kate Pickett. 2010. *The Spirit Level: Why Greater Equality Makes Societies Stronger*. London: Bloomsbury Press.

Willcox, George. 2013. "The Roots of Cultivation in Southwestern Asia." *Science* 341, pp. 39–40.

Willcox, George, et al. 2008. "Early Holocene Cultivation before Domestication in Northern Syria." *Vegetation History and Archaeobotany* 17, pp. 313–25.

Wilmsen, Edwin. 1989. *Land Filled with Flies: A Political Economy of the Kalahari*. Chicago: University of Chicago Press.

Wilson, David Sloan. 1998. "Hunting, Sharing, and Multilevel Selection: The Tolerated-Theft Model Revisited." *Current Anthropology* 39, pp. 73–97.

———. 2003. *Darwin's Cathedral: Evolution, Religion, and the Nature of Society*. Chicago: University of Chicago Press.

Wilson, David Sloan, and Edward O. Wilson. 2007. "Rethinking the Theoretical Foundations of Sociobiology." *Quarterly Review of Biology* 82, pp. 327–48.

Wilson, Edward O. 1975. *Sociobiology: The New Synthesis*. Cambridge, MA: Harvard University Press.

———. 1994. *Naturalist*. Washington, DC: Island Press.

Wilson, Katharina, and Elizabeth Makowski, eds. 1990. *Wykked Wives and the Woes of Marriage: Misogamous Literature from Juvenal to Chaucer*. Albany: State University of New York Press.

Wilson, Michael. 2013. "Chimpanzees, Warfare, and the Invention of Peace." In Douglas Fry, ed., *War, Peace and Human Nature*, pp. 361–88. Oxford, UK: Oxford University Press.

Winterhalder, Bruce, and Eric Alden Smith, eds. 1981. *Hunter-Gatherer Foraging Strategies: Ethnographic and Archeological Analyses*. Chicago: University of Chicago Press.

Wiser, William, and Charlotte Viall Wiser. 1963. *Behind Mud Walls*. Berkeley: University of California Press.

Wobst, Martin. 1974. "Boundary Conditions for Palaeolithic Social Systems: A Simulation Approach." *American Antiquity* 39, pp. 147–78.

Wolf, Eric. 1966. *Peasants*. Englewood Cliffs, NJ: Prentice-Hall.

———. 1982. *Europe and the People without History*. Berkeley: University of California Press.

Wood, Gordon. 1992. *The Radicalism of the American Revolution*. New York: Vintage.

———. 2009. *Empire of Liberty: A History of the Early Republic, 1789–1815*. New York: Oxford University Press.

Wood, James. 1998. "A Theory of Preindustrial Population Dynamics." *Current Anthropology* 39, pp. 99–135.

Woodburn, James. 1980. "Hunters and Gatherers Today and Reconstruction of the Past." In Ernest Gellner, ed., *Soviet and Western Anthropology*, pp. 95–117. London: Duckworth.

———. 1982. "Egalitarian Societies." *Man* 17, pp. 31–51.

World Bank. 1993. *The East Asian Miracle: Economic Growth and Public Policy.* New York: Oxford University Press.

Wrangham, Richard. 2009. *Catching Fire: How Cooking Made Us Human.* New York: Basic Books.

Wrangham, Richard, and Luke Glowacki. 2012. "Intergroup Aggression in Chimpanzees and War in Nomadic Hunter-Gatherers." *Human Nature* 53, pp. 5–29.

Wrangham, Richard, and Dale Peterson. 1996. *Demonic Males: Apes and the Origins of Human Violence.* Boston: Houghton Mifflin.

Wright, Gavin. 1978. *The Political Economy of the Cotton South.* New York: Norton.

Wright, Robert. 2000. *Nonzero: The Logic of Human Destiny.* New York: Pantheon.

Wrigley, E. A. 2000. *Continuity, Chance and Change: The Character of the Industrial Revolution in England.* Cambridge, UK: Cambridge University Press.

Wynn, Thomas, and Frederick Coolidge. 2012. *How to Think Like a Neanderthal.* Oxford, UK: Oxford University Press.

Yergin, Daniel, and Joseph Stanislaw. 2002. *The Commanding Heights: The Battle for the World Economy.* Rev. ed. New York: Free Press.

Zimmerman, William. 2014. *Ruling Russia: Authoritarianism from the Revolution to Putin.* Princeton, NJ: Princeton University Press.

Zohary, Daniel, et al. 2013. *Domestication of Plants in the Old World.* 4th ed. New York: Oxford University Press.

Zubok, Vladislav. 2007. *A Failed Empire: The Soviet Union in the Cold War from Stalin to Gorbachev.* Chapel Hill: University of North Carolina Press.

CONTRIBUTORS

Margaret Atwood received her undergraduate degree from Victoria College at the University of Toronto and her master's degree from Radcliffe College. She is the author of more than fifty volumes of poetry, children's literature, fiction, and nonfiction and is perhaps best known for her novels, which include *The Edible Woman* (1969), *The Handmaid's Tale* (1985), *The Robber Bride* (1993), *Alias Grace* (1996), and *The Blind Assassin*, which won the prestigious Booker Prize in 2000. Atwood's dystopic novel, *Oryx and Crake*, was published in 2003. *The Tent* (mini-fictions) and *Moral Disorder* (short stories) both appeared in 2006. Her most recent volume of poetry, *The Door*, was published in 2007. Her nonfiction book, *Payback: Debt and the Shadow Side of Wealth*, part of the Massey Lecture series, appeared in 2008, and her most recent novel, *MaddAddam*, in the autumn of 2013. Her latest work is a book of short stories called *Stone Mattress: Nine Tales* (2014).

Christine M. Korsgaard is Arthur Kingsley Porter Professor of Philosophy at Harvard University, where she has taught since 1991. She works on moral philosophy and its history, practical reason, the nature of agency, personal identity, normativity, and the ethics of our treatment of animals. She is the author of four books: *Creating the Kingdom of Ends* is a collection of papers on Kant's moral philosophy; *The Sources of Normativity* (1996) is an exploration of modern views about the basis of obligation; *The Constitution of Agency* (2008), a collection of papers on practical reason and moral psychology; and *Self-Constitution: Agency, Identity, and Integrity* (2009), an account of practical reason and morality grounded in the nature of agency. She is currently at work on *Fellow Creatures*, a book about the moral and legal standing of nonhuman animals.

Stephen Macedo is the Laurance S. Rockefeller Professor of Politics and the University Center for Human Values at Princeton University, where he has also been the Founding Director of the Program on Law and Public Affairs (1999–2001), and Director of the University Center for Human Values (2001–9). He writes and teaches on political theory, ethics, American constitutionalism, and public policy. His books include *Liberal Virtues: Citizenship, Virtue, and Community in Liberal Constitutionalism* (1990); *Diversity and Distrust: Civic Education in a Multicultural Democracy* (2000); and the forthcoming *Just Married: Same-Sex Couples, Monogamy, and the Future of Marriage* (2015). He is editor or co-editor of fifteen books on topics ranging from the legacy of the 1960s to universal jurisdiction in international law. He has been Vice President of the American Political Science Association and is a member of the American Academy of Arts and Sciences.

Richard Seaford is Emeritus Professor of Ancient Greek Literature at the University of Exeter. He views the study of ancient culture as a vital form of liberation (from the triviality and increasing narrowness of our own media culture). He has published on subjects that include Homer, Greek lyric poetry, Greek religion (in particular the cult of Dionysos), the earliest philosophy, Greek tragedy, Greek satyric drama, and the New Testament. His books include *Reciprocity and Ritual: Homer and Tragedy in the Developing City-State* (1995); *Money and the Early Greek Mind: Homer, Philosophy, Tragedy* (2004); *Dionysos* (2006); and *Cosmology and the Polis: The Social Construction of Space and Time in the Tragedies of Aeschylus* (2012).

Jonathan D. Spence is the Sterling Professor of History at Yale University. He is the world's foremost authority on Chinese civilization and the role of history in shaping modern China. He was named a MacArthur Fellow and is the author of more than 15 books. Among his books are *The Gate of Heavenly Peace: The Chinese and Their Revolution, 1895–1980* (1981) and *Mao Zedong* (1999). His critically acclaimed *The Search for Modern China* (1990) has become one of the standard texts on the last several hundred years of Chinese history.

INDEX

Numbers in italics refer to figures.